TREES FOR ALL SEASONS

TREES FOR ALL SEASONS
Broadleaved Evergreens for Temperate Climates

SEAN HOGAN

TIMBER PRESS
Portland · London

Frontispiece: *Arbutus menziesii*, Rogue Valley, Oregon

All photographs not specifically credited were taken by the author.

Published in 2008 by Timber Press, Inc.

The Haseltine Building   2 The Quadrant
133 S.W. Second Avenue, Suite 450   135 Salusbury Road
Portland, Oregon 97204-3527   London NW6 6RJ
www.timberpress.com   www.timberpress.co.uk

Printed in China

Library of Congress Cataloging-in-Publication Data

Hogan, Sean.
    Trees for all seasons: broadleaved evergreens for temperate climates/Sean Hogan.
        p. cm.
    Includes bibliographical references and index.
    ISBN-13: 978-0-88192-674-3
    1. Evergreens, Broad-leaved—Encyclopedias. 2. Ornamental trees—Encyclopedias. I. Title. II. Title: Broadleaved evergreens for temperate climates.
    SB435.H65 2008
    635.9′7715—dc22   2008010053

A catalog record for this book is also available from the British Library.

To Mache Parker Sanderson,
without whose patience and partnership
this would not have been possible

Nothofagus solanderi, "autumn" color in late spring

CONTENTS

Banksia integrifolia

FOREWORD
by Roy Lancaster

I AM A PLANTSMAN with catholic tastes, a keen student of the world's native floras, and an avid traveller; it should surprise no one, then, that my suburban garden of just a third of an acre in Hampshire, England, displays an eclectic mix of woody plants and perennials. Having majored in ornamental horticulture with more than a passing interest in botany, I sought to create in my garden a workshop, trial ground, and memory bank, one that serves as an inspiration and a place of reunions and rejuvenation. Naturally, it has also provided a sanctuary for me and my family, a private space where we can play, potter, exercise, or simply chill out.

When asked by earnest journalists about my planting policies, I tell them that I will try, within reason, almost any plant I think I might get away with. I have both acid sand and heavy clay as well as full sun and shade, which allows me to enjoy and to experiment. I like my plants, especially rare ones, to thrive; if they don't, I pass them on to someone more likely to succeed, who just might be a neighbour.

So, what has this got to do with the subject of this book and, just as importantly, its author? Having met Sean Hogan on more than one occasion in the Northwest, I am aware of the passion he has for plants and the knowledge he has accumulated over many years concerning their rich variety and garden merit, not to mention their special uses and cultivation needs. Like me, he has travelled widely in search of plants both wild and cultivated and then done his damnedest to introduce them to the wider gardening public on the theory that a treasure shared is a treasure saved. Nowhere is this talent better demonstrated than in his book.

Not every gardener is aware of the importance of broadleaved evergreens, except perhaps in winter, when they stand out in the deciduous fraternity. A rough survey reveals that a good third of my garden's woody plants are evergreen, which I believe is the right balance, providing satisfying effects the year through. I am pleased to find in Hogan's recommendations a number that I grow here and which I would not be without, including *Acacia pravissima, Schefflera taiwaniana, Embothrium coccineum,* and that most wonderful snow gum, *Eucalyptus pauciflora* subsp. *debeuzevillei.* There are many others discussed here with which I have long been familiar, in others' gardens, both in North America and Europe; and his choice of candidates is both wide-ranging and adventurous. Indeed, it is the challenging, throw-down-the-gauntlet nature of this book that makes it so exciting for gardeners, wherever they may garden.

It is one thing being cautious, quite another being resistant to all but well-tried and grandpa-grew-it old-timers. Of course these have their place---always will---but such is the wealth of new plants being made available that it would surely be a backward step for gardeners to deny themselves the chance of a new and possibly enriching experience (and I haven't even mentioned the effects of climate change).

For several good reasons, there could not be a better time for the arrival of Sean Hogan's book, with its promise of a better tomorrow in a world that's ever green.

ACKNOWLEDGMENTS

WITH MUCH to be thankful for and many people to recognize, I begin with David and Dorothy Rodal, without whom the nursery, its gardens, and all the wonderful experiments and adventures that happen there would not be possible or anywhere near as much fun.

My grateful thanks to all those knowledgeable friends and colleagues who have so freely given of their time, information, and assistance. Tony Avent, Frank Calia, Frank Callahan, Mike Dirr, John Grimshaw, Dan Hinkley, Hayes Jackson, Arthur Lee Jacobson, Michael Lee, Todd Lasseigne, Neal Maillet, Pat McCracken, Rosemary Brown, Marleen Neal, Bart O'Brien, Pierre Piroche, Michael Remmick, Gary Rogowski, Bruce Rutherford, Ted Stephens, Roger Warner, and Peter Wharton. While there is always more to add, I hope I have deciphered and conveyed your information well.

My thanks and appreciation as well to the staff at Cistus (gardens and nursery) without whom I could not spend so much time looking for plants or staring at a computer screen: to Jim Mecca whose friendship and many skills are so important to every endeavor; to Deborah Chaffee for time and insights that helped move the book forward; and each valued staff member past and present—Shawna Burke, Maureen Caviness, Adam Kennedy, Josh McCullough, Kenny Kneeland, Christopher Roberts, Jessica Tenenbaum, Michelle Benoit, Ian Connor, Bob Hackney, Bob Huff, Sean McMillen, Cary Ransome, and Mandie Rose.

Quercus hypoleucoides, as a "street tree"

INTRODUCTION

WHY BROADLEAVED EVERGREENS?

Why broadleaved evergreens? The best answer is that they are end-lessly fascinating, providing wonderful textures in foliage and branch structure; surprising contrasts of leaves and bark; flowers and fruits, from the insignificant to the stunningly gorgeous; and—perhaps best of all—year-round interest. What's not to love and explore? I remem-ber a certain winter's day; I was performing an errand in a high-rise neighborhood in my home city of Portland, Oregon—a city usually painted winter-green. I saw only gray, a monotone—indeed, a mono-culture—of deciduous trees. I realized that even a few evergreen specimens, seen from a distance along our urban grid, would bring a lushness now almost entirely lacking.

More plants are available than ever before, many of them ever-green. And yet, with so much information accessible through the Internet—about what is available and, more importantly, what is pos-sible among so many new choices—it is surprising that so much of this potential remains untapped in our gardens and also that very little, if any, literature is entirely dedicated to this subject. It seems a good time for broadleaved evergreens to emerge as a worthy subject.

Many gardeners are familiar with the category of broadleaved ever-greens, especially those who garden in warm climates of U.S. Department of Agriculture (USDA) zone 9 or above (see the map on page 23), where prolonged freezes are rare and the lowest temperatures in winter average 20°F (–7°C). But many other plant lovers continue to think of evergreens as necessarily having needles or cones, in spite of the laurel hedges, camellias, myrtles, and occasional holly trees in the landscape. This book is addressed to both audiences, introducing the category to some and increasing the available options for others.

For those gardeners lucky enough to live in climates where winter temperatures remain above 0 to 10°F (–18 to –12°C)—and nearly half do in the United States alone—enormous choice exists among species and cultivated selections. Even in the warm temperate climates of zones 7 to 9—where, in North America at least, the average lowest winter temperatures remain above 0°F (–18°C) and temperatures are not mild enough for the reliable cultivation of tropical or subtropical plants—even in these "in-between zones" there are wonderful choices available. Here too we can indulge in year-round foliage interest with infinite variations in sizes and textures and combinations of green, silver, red, yellow, and white. Who would want to forego the pleasure of observing slanting winter sunlight reflecting off the silvery white leaf undersides of *Quercus hypoleucoides* (silverleaf oak) or the blue- and red-hued, gracefully weeping boughs of *Eucalyptus perriniana* (spinning gum) cooling the "feel" of the garden during the heat of summer and warming it in winter?

Once experienced, broadleaved evergreens are compelling and, yes, addictive. They will doubtless come to have a permanent role in any garden, especially in parts of the world where deciduous plants now dominate the winter scene.

WHAT ARE THEY?

Simply defined for our purposes here, broadleaved evergreens, excluding conifers or monocots (palms, yuccas, and the like), are those woody plants that retain their foliage for the vast majority of the year—enjoying nearly all the variations of form, color, and texture that exist in the larger world of plants. Some characteristics are even exaggerated because the life of each leaf is less fleeting than in deciduous counterparts. Some have rather small leaves that could hardly be called "broad"; others have phyllodes (flattened stems) masquerading as leaves; some might have a brief or partial leaf drop seasonally or under extreme conditions, and many have leaves that are not green at all, but silver, blue, red, yellow, or perhaps maroon.

While some plants are evergreen by nature, some are evergreen only by default. For instance, a plant derived from, or at least allied to, a deciduous species may exist in the wild where conditions don't cause leaf drop. Or a cold-climate plant may be planted in a warm garden that doesn't provide the cold signal to shed the season's leaves for a winter nap. A *Liquidambar styraciflua*, even one of northern provenance (they range from New England on the East Coast of North America to Guatemala), could be signaled by the lower light of autumn to begin leaf drop but, in a mild climate, might take the entire season to complete the job. The same species collected from the far south of its range might not shed at all until spring's growth pushes the still-green leaves away or might go quite deciduous in an unaccustomed, hard early frost. Few would define *Betula pendula* (European white birch) as evergreen, but in my Portland, Oregon, neighborhood, in most years, many a well-watered specimen has active green growth in January.

We are not nit-picking about this or that technicality here—there is no need to "scrounge" for evergreens—but selecting for reliability in suitable gardens. In our garden, the birch does not fit the description, while, in principle, the southern liquidambar does (although not actually included here due to the general unavailability of select clones of good provenance).

WHERE DO THEY COME FROM?

Broadleaved evergreens, those plants that don't find it necessary to shed leaves during the cool seasons, come, mostly, from areas where severe cold is not part of their ancient history, as might be expected. Indeed some groups are represented in great numbers in warm latitudes. The oaks for example, though temperate in origin, number in the hundreds of species north of the tropics but south of frequent severe cold. It is places like this, with great variations in elevation and into which flora was pushed south by ice ages, that have produced selections much more capable of tolerating cold. Whether through genetic memory or by selection on the northern frontier or the highest mountain frost pockets, these forms are cold tolerant beyond the dictates of current conditions in their native ranges and, often, more so than selections currently in gardens. In the opposite extreme, some oaks (*Quercus durifolia*, for example) have become at least partially deciduous with spring drought, growing on picturesque but drought-prone limestone pinnacles in mid- and high-elevation eastern Sonora, where winter and spring are the dry season.

In many cases, the type of climate from which a plant comes can be intuited by the growth habit or the shape and consistency of the leaf. In woody plants, spiny or tangled stems often signal a sunny, windy, or dry habitat, as well as an adaptation against rampant browsing by local wildlife. Leaves that are hairy—particularly if they are leathery, spiny, or very small as well—can dictate the same. Open crowns or layered branches usually indicate a wet or shady habitat; in such areas,

Quercus durifolia showing new growth after the onset of early summer rains

leaves are often larger and thinner and might have a long narrow drip tip to shed excess water.

Some of the adaptations that help a plant succeed in the wild are also attractive to us as horticulturists and artists as we paint our surroundings with color and texture. The blue powder covering one leaf or the golden fur coating the underside of another might help conserve water by limiting evaporation in the wild, but in our own gardens, they give us wild thoughts about color combinations. The red color (anthocyanins) often seen in new growth (or throughout the foliage, in some species) offers protection from sun and sometimes frost—or is it simply an evolutionary trait selected for its beneficial link between the plant and animal kingdom, to seduce us into planting and propagating? By such criteria, *Photinia ×fraseri* is most successful, having found a host to plant it along nearly every freeway in western North America.

By far the greatest diversity of plants comes from lower middle latitudes. South and East Asia are still barely tapped for garden trees. Mirroring the southeastern sections of North America in the generous rains of the summer monsoons, each mountain range has trapped its own group of species, each with its own set of desirable characteristics. The floras and gardens of Australia, New Zealand, and southern Chile have many possibilities for cool maritime zones to be further

Typical mixed evergreen oak woodland, Chiricahua Mountains, Arizona

exploited both at home and abroad. For increasingly water-conscious gardeners in Mediterranean climates, central Chile, the Cape of South Africa, southern Europe, and the North American West offer ever more subjects, while the arid regions of central Asia and interior North America extend choices for those perennially short of water.

CRITERIA FOR INCLUSION

For this volume, the focus is on trees—a category that itself needs some definition. Although it can seem obvious that trees and shrubs are differentiated by size, trees being the larger of the two, one has only to think of bonsai to realize that we easily recognize trees by their form rather than their height. Consider, too, the untrimmed cherry laurel hedge (*Prunus laurocerasus*), definitely a shrub no matter what the height.

Simply put, trees have a sparser branch structure, the lower branches having been trimmed or "lifted" to expose a single trunk or multiple stems. Some plants included here achieve tree form easily and naturally; others require some training and trimming here and there.

Each selection for this volume is based either on my own experience or the enthusiastic recommendation of others whose experience I greatly value, an important first criteria being that subjects not only keep their leaves year-round, or nearly so, but also remain attractive while doing so. Throughout the book, icons accompanying each main entry convey visually my best stab at the rough form and likely ultimate size of the subject tree. I hope they and the lists in the back matter help readers scanning for quick, approximate information.

Suitability for garden situations was an important factor as well as cold hardiness. Many taxa have high-elevation populations, or ranges and counterparts extending toward colder latitudes or thriving in situations otherwise thought too adverse. Some plants have long histories in cultivation, including records of individual plants that have withstood temperatures or other conditions thought too extreme for the species. I once saw a *Magnolia grandiflora* in Dearborn, Michigan, a tree of some age and, indeed, one of considerable interest to those hard at work looking for individual clones able to thrive in northern zone 6, far outside the typical *M. grandiflora* comfort zone. So it has been important to showcase individual clones or selections as well. Provenance has been an important consideration as well as choices of individual clones or selections. I have tried here to showcase possibilities from each situation as well as reintroduce garden stalwarts.

Of all the choice plants to be found, points were added for those likely to be successful in zone 7 and below. As well, with limited space, some preference has been given to trees scarce but available, even if some search is required, in hopes of encouraging their use.

A few plants warranted description just because of their frequency in temperate gardens, including *Photinia ×fraseri* and *Prunus laurocerasus*, so commonly planted as to be shunned in some regions, but so iconic as to be necessary in this book.

And yet not everything could be included. Indeed some large and important genera are not represented here, or only cursorily discussed. Some groups consisting of or including broadleaved evergreens are covered quite well elsewhere, the two most notable being the genera *Rhododendron* and *Camellia*. Palms, tree-like yuccas, and other similar creatures, though thoroughly fitting with the genre, are not covered; nor are other groups occurring in tropical or severe desert climates.

Also missing (I hope) are any possibly invasive plants: those likely to escape into natural areas. In looking for well-adapted species, it is important not to promote the too-well-adapted species, sometimes a fine line!

Clearly this small volume is but the beginning of a discussion on broadleaved evergreens. One of the greatest pleasures of interacting with the world of plants lies in knowing that our knowledge is ever less complete with ever more study. My wish is to encourage those with new or different experiences to enter this conversation so subsequent work can be more detailed and even more useful.

BROADLEAVED EVERGREEN TREES IN THE LANDSCAPE

Broadleaved evergreens are wonderful additions to the gardener's palette, providing everything from large-leaved, tropical-looking plants to tiny-leaved, fine-textured possibilities, imposing street trees to arresting garden features. Here are foliage in a variety of sizes, shapes, and colors, and flowers with exciting aromas and fruits that brighten the landscape. These plants not only provide structure and "bones" for a garden, their presence is year-round.

Where privacy is a concern, the plants in this volume offer many delicious possibilities. A common plaint heard in Portland area nurseries decries "the new infill development going up right next door." Certainly all over western North America, and in many other places for that matter, cities are becoming increasingly dense. In my own Portland, we have agreed to greater density in order to protect the farmland and natural areas so important and necessary to us. Still, accustomed to generous urban space, we resist too much direct eye contact with new neighbors. Evergreen plants provide many textures found in their deciduous counterparts, but do so throughout the year, creating effective screens.

Fine-textured, small evergreen trees and shrubs can accentuate bold textures planted in front or enhance the form, autumn color, or

Arbutus ×andrachnoides, Royal Botanic Gardens, Kew. Photo by Michael A. Dirr

flowers of deciduous specimens when used as background. Evergreens are also particularly useful for framing buildings and views and creating a visual foundation for garden- or cityscapes. Even a few individual evergreen trees can liven up an avenue of shade trees, giving a feeling of lushness, an allée of green, in an otherwise dismal scene of winter gray, while letting the sun through between.

Broadleaved evergreens can be focal points themselves. Some, the loquat (*Eriobotrya japonica*) for example, present large, interestingly textured leaves that emerge with and are often coated on the undersides with a light silky hair, making a bold statement and reflecting light toward the ground. Add winter flowers and delicious fruit, and a well-used space is created.

We have grown, trialed, experimented with, loved, and occasionally lost, many of the plants in this book in what I have referred to as "our garden"—which is, in fact, a collection of gardens. Parker Sanderson and I founded the Cistus Nursery garden in 2003, after creating the home garden, begun in 1996 (and since then, extended and spread to many places in urban northeast Portland). The nursery garden continues to serve as test plot, propagation stock, garden walk, demonstration garden, and event space. The home garden and its satellites are for the enjoyment of all, a cooperative project, always growing, maintained by the combined efforts of dedicated nursery staff, volunteers, and neighbors who allow them to thrive and progress—with an occasional snippet taken here and there for purposes of procreation.

ZONES VERSUS CLIMATE

Just as natural habitats have particular characteristics, the places where we live and garden have sets of soil, climate, and space parameters. While a few entries in this book are accepting of wide-ranging conditions, most perform better in one area over all others. Making the best plant choices requires recognizing garden conditions as well as understanding plant needs and correlating the two.

The zone maps included here are based on the average lowest temperature likely to be reached each season. The U.S. Department of Agriculture (USDA) has developed ten-degree incremental "zones" based on the lowest temperature reached each season. Maps illustrating heat accumulation have been added, but here we simply suggest which cline each plant prefers. Neither extremes of high or low temperature nor their duration are taken into account. In some places that might be a brief dip, in others a prolonged cold period, and still others might experience dips far below these averages but as a much rarer occurrence.

Though understanding zones can be helpful (as cold is indeed the factor that most influences what we grow), local growing conditions that determine what is best grown where are influenced by other factors as well, including humidity, heat accumulation, and how much moisture falls and at what time of year. For our purposes, "climate" is the overall accumulation of local weather events that in the short term decide how frequently we might dine on the patio but in the longer view determine what sort of tree provides us shade while we enjoy our meal.

Heat accumulation or lack thereof is an important condition, as broad categories of plants either like or dislike high temperatures. Southerly or summer monsoonal climates are hot over a long period of summer, allowing plants that enjoy heat accumulation to "ripen" and complete their flowering or growth cycles. Many species of evergreen magnolias are at their best here. Lack of enough heat can mean less than satisfactory performance or decreased frost hardiness.

In climates of interior regions where periodic to prolonged drought occurs, often plants are "hardened" for the impending frost by drought as much as or more than by colder autumn temperatures; examples include *Ceanothus* and *Arbutus menziesii*. In these summer-dry climates, water might be withheld in late summer; in wet areas conditions might have to be adjusted (for example, through extra drainage or overhead coverage).

Mediterranean and cool maritime climates are a third and fourth category with much in common. Proximity to cool ocean waters in both instances creates low humidity summers with high diurnal or daily temperatures ranges. Even hot weather here is most often followed by cool nighttime temperatures that allow a plant to rest. Plants requiring high heat accumulation might not thrive in such conditions, though planting against a south wall or other reflective sources helps by providing extra heating calories. On the other hand, plants adapted to cool climates, such as the many species of *Pseudopanax* or *Hoheria*, often suffer with high heat and additional summer moisture or monsoonal climates, as they are not adapted to moisture plus heat, or the ensuing root or soil fungal pathogens that occur in those circumstances. The cool maritime climates, such as New Zealand, coastal northwest Europe, and the northern Pacific Northwest of North America, often enjoy long growing seasons that can, in some cases, correct for lack of heat by simply allowing a plant a much greater time to get there (ripen); whereas Mediterranean climates (roughly five in the world) experience long periods of summer drought and can be hot in the day or coastal and cooler.

This book includes as many helpful hints as possible to those plants that are universal to all climates—and yes, they do exist. But studying what might seem like minutiae helps create an intuition for one's own gardening region and helps with the understanding that, for instance, a plant from Florida labeled zone 8 might sulk along the West Coast and a zone 8 plant from the West Coast might melt with southeastern humidity and warmth.

Studying native plants as well as established plants in local gardens can provide important information on local conditions. Native trees can be presumed hardy, and well-established exotics instill confidence of long-term success. If native plants exhibit drought resistance, similar characteristics might be sought for the garden, or for public plants not likely to receive routine care. Lush foliage might be suggested by a damp climate. Though native trees can be presumed adapted to local rigors, their usefulness in the garden is in the eye of the beholder (or pavement-repair person). Well-established exotics should be fair game. With a plant that is new on the scene, willingness to experiment might be based both on information provided and consideration of local, long-term weather history.

Understanding long-term temperatures and climate conditions can be important for investment purposes as well. Decisions can be made rather easily about perennials or small shrubs: they can be protected during a cold winter spell, or a certain amount of loss might be calculated into the greater scheme. However, trees and even large shrubs require more careful consideration. They are important furniture, and their longevity is important to quality of life, especially in large, public plantings. So when weather takes them away, they leave a much larger hole in our local environment, the loss being of greater consequence especially after an investment of many years or dollars, with the extra firewood a negligible recompense. Wisdom would suggest researching a thirty- to fifty-year weather history and choosing plants rated for the lowest temperatures. For example, if a zone 8 region experiences occasional dips into zone 7 temperatures, prudence would suggest choosing a zone 7 tree for long-term insurance. However, if a damaging weather event (mostly likely severe cold) occurs only every thirty to fifty years, certainly the chancier investment might be worth it. Although global warming is sometimes referenced with guarded optimism in the plant world, the schizophrenic weather caused by extra energy in the weather system can also cause more severe and unexpected events. My own personal philosophy is this: the greater the size and the more public the planting, the more conservative the choice.

The key to making successful choices among plants is to understand local conditions as well as the origins of desired plants. The more knowledge acquired, the more confidence can be taken in a planting choice, and the more a garden situation can be manipulated to accommodate plants with different needs. (Cheating is allowed.)

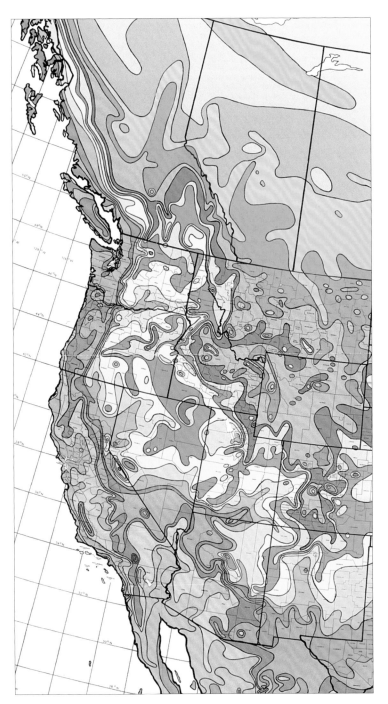

°Celsius		°Fahrenheit
−45.6 and below	Zone 1:	below −50°
−42.8° to −45.5°	Zone 2a:	−45° to −50°
−40.0° to −42.7°	Zone 2b:	−40° to −45°
−37.3° to −40.0°	Zone 3a:	−35° to −40°
−34.5° to −37.2°	Zone 3b:	−30° to −35°
−31.7° to −34.4°	Zone 4a:	−25° to −30°
−28.9° to −31.6°	Zone 4b:	−20° to −25°
−26.2° to −28.8°	Zone 5a:	−15° to −20°
−23.4° to −26.1°	Zone 5b:	−10° to −15°
−20.6° to −23.3°	Zone 6a:	−5° to −10°
−17.8° to −20.5°	Zone 6b:	0° to −5°
−15.0° to −17.7°	Zone 7a:	5° to 0°
−12.3° to −15.0°	Zone 7b:	10° to 5°
−9.5° to −12.2°	Zone 8a:	15° to 10°
−6.7° to −9.4°	Zone 8b:	20° to 15°
−3.9° to −6.6°	Zone 9a:	25° to 20°
−1.2° to −3.8°	Zone 9b:	30° to 25°
−1.6° to 1.1°	Zone 10a:	35° to 30°
4.4° to 1.7°	Zone 10b:	40° to 35°
4.5° and above	Zone 11:	40° and above

USDA hardiness zones for western North America

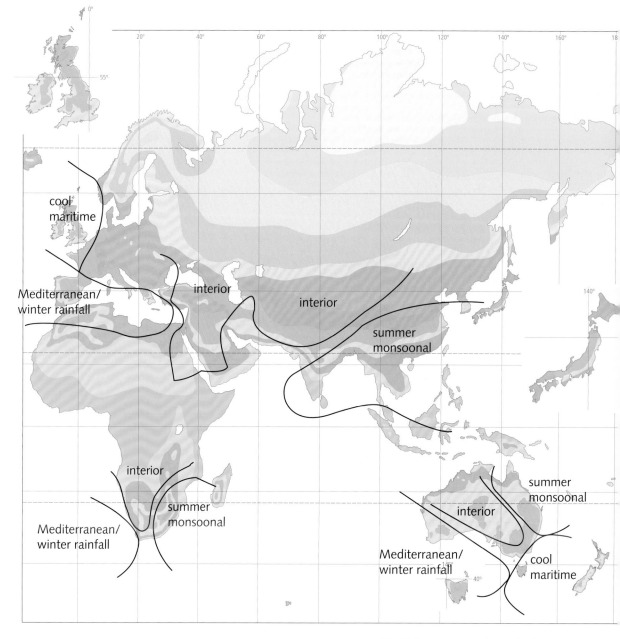

World climate regimes and USDA hardiness zones

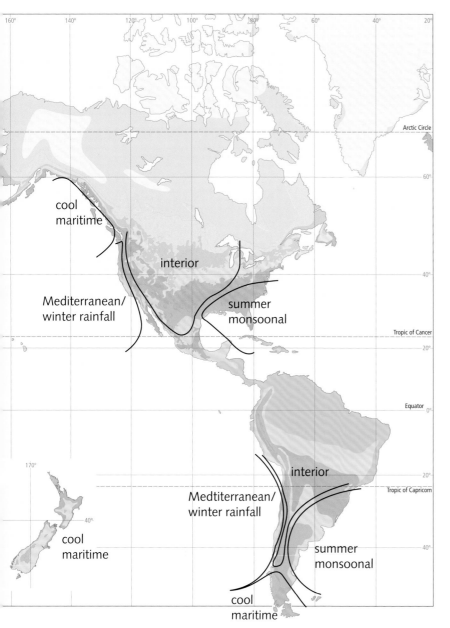

Zone	°Fahrenheit	°Celsius
12	50 to 60	10 to 16
11	40 to 50	4 to 10
10	30 to 40	-1 to 4
9	20 to 30	-7 to -1
8	10 to 20	-12 to -7
7	0 to 10	-18 to -12
6	-10 to 0	-23 to -18
5	-20 to -10	-29 to -23
4	-30 to -20	-34 to -29
3	-40 to -30	-40 to -34
2	-50 to -40	-46 to -40
1	-60 to -50	-51 to -46

cool maritime

interior

Mediterranean/ winter rainfall

summer monsoonal

interior

Medtiterranean/ winter rainfall

summer monsoonal

cool maritime

cool maritime

Arctic Circle

Tropic of Cancer

Equator

Tropic of Capricorn

A-TO-Z ENCYCLOPEDIA
of Broadleaved Evergreen Trees

Acacia   **Fabaceae**

This genus of over 1000 species is native throughout the warm parts of the world with the majority of evergreen species coming from Australia. Many residents of warm climates, especially the Mediterranean, have fond memories of the bright yellow pompoms of *Acacia dealbata* sweetening the winter air with the fragrance of baby powder. It should be noted that the flowering times given for the acacias listed here are for the northern hemisphere.

Acacias are native through much of the warm temperate to tropical world. Many desert species are shrubby and bear relatively small leaves, often contrasted with very large thorns. Others from more mesic areas can form forest trees with lush canopies. With such a big and wide-ranging genus, it would be expected that lots of forms and interesting adaptations would exist. Some species actually house ants in hollow spines, ants that reciprocate by protecting the plant, their home. Others, in what is thought to be a drought adaptation, give up what is considered a typical leaf, dissected into many leaflets, for what appears to be one single leaf held close to the stem but is actually a phyllode, a flattened petiole serving the same function as a leaf.

Though some *Acacia* species inhabit swampy places in their natural range, most exhibit amazing drought tolerance and thrive where

Quercus virginiana var. fusiformis

27

so many other garden plants suffer. Exceptions exist, but many of the most garden-worthy, including the following, are from Australia and range in their habitats from dry to swampy. There are many species from which to choose; those listed below combine the benefits of beauty, hardiness to frost, and the most widespread availability.

Acacia baileyana (cootamundra wattle, golden mimosa). From southeastern Australia, a small tree to about 30 ft. (9 m) tall, tending toward a single, upright trunk and oval form, usually found in gritty, well-drained soil (sometimes on clay) but not in standing water. It also is found in mixed company, sometimes in a near forest association and occasionally standing as a solitary tree in clearings or with shrubs and grasses. All its habitats can experience some summer drought.

Flowers appear in winter in small pompoms, creamy to "Big Bird" (deep, vibrant, primary) yellow, with a rather sweet fragrance. The twice-pinnate foliage is about 5 in. (13 cm) long, very finely cut and, most often, a very attractive steely blue. And it is dense, making *Acacia baileyana* a wonderful background tree. As well, the bark is of interest, with stems up to two years old remaining a green-tinted blue and older bark becoming silvery and smooth.

Acacia baileyana 'Purpurea' is in a category of its own, achieving virtual cult status when viewed in the cool season. The exquisite purple to almost red-tinted new growth can also be the deepest maroon, occasionally with orange overtones, and makes a striking contrast with the silvery blue older growth. This form is often grown from seed: the best should be selected from among batches of kin.

Acacia baileyana. Photo by Michael A. Dirr

Frost hardy with brief exposure to 16 to 18°F (−9 to −8°C), it is a reasonable plant for mild localities; in regions having great heat, it is extremely fast-growing and somewhat shorter lived, as well as sometimes being susceptible to chlorosis. One small drawback is its slowness or inability to resprout after a hard freeze. Where freezes are frequent, gardeners often use these as temporary fillers or fabulous container plants. Like so many other plants exhibiting drought tolerance, *Acacia baileyana* looks great in an established situation in the garden even after many weeks and sometimes months without moisture, a feat that is accomplished by roots spreading far and wide. For those grown in containers with limited root space, more attention must be paid to moisture.

Although we lost a young, unprotected plant at 16°F (−9°C), specimens have been brought through colder conditions with mulch and liberal use of that emergency insulation we all have stored in the garage (often at the expense of our vehicles). Prolonged cold (more than just a few hours), overnight frost, or cold accompanied by wind are the greatest hazards.

Propagation is most often accomplished by seed, which germinates readily, spring planting being the most desirable. A cool stratification for thirty days or so has increased germination, as has a brief hot water treatment so often used with legumes. For your favorite purple form, autumn and winter cuttings will be most successful; use somewhat hardened, current season's growth in a mineral media, allowing limited moisture on the leaves.

Acacia dealbata (silver wattle, mimosa). Native to southeastern Australia, a medium to fairly large tree that can reach over 100 ft. (30 m) after a long time in favored situations and often spreads into colonies. In cultivation the plant's growth tends to slow greatly before reaching 30 ft. (9 m). Not only larger but a more open tree than *A. baileyana*, with which it is sometimes confused, it has the silvery bark in common but a more graceful habit. And, like *A. baileyana*, the leaves are finely dissected but larger, to 6–8 in. (15–20 cm). In most forms the leaves are olive-green, though very silver forms do exist. This is the "mimosa" of many people's memories, whether in the south of France, England's Cornwall, or along the California and Oregon coasts where, in the depths of winter, the cheery yellow pompoms drip from the trees beginning as early as the end of December and lasting until early spring. The fragrance, though certainly memorable and sometimes carrying pleasant associations, resembles that of *A. baileyana*, though stronger and, to some noses, unfortunately mixed with a bit of electrical fire—an acquired taste.

Acacia dealbata resprouts vigorously after fires, so other events such as overzealous pruning or hard freezes are met with luxuriant new growth. Therefore, it's often found in colder garden locations than might be expected. Vigorous shoots can grow 10 ft. (3 m) or more in a single season, making it a good coppice plant. As with many Australian plants, a drying period in late summer and autumn can increase frost hardiness by shutting down the plants before a period of cold. Tolerant of sun and, in hotter climates, shade, *A. dealbata* prefers sun in the United Kingdom and other cool-climate regions.

Acacia dealbata subsp. *subalpina* is common on the central plateau of Tasmania. Though its differences from the species are questionable, it has been thought, in general, to be more frost hardy. So far, not true. What is important for the entire species is collection provenance. Some mainland forms—those from the highest valleys that receive abundant frost—seem the best choice for seed if one is gardening on the lower end of their tolerance. Though specimens in horticulture have withstood temperatures down to 12 to 15°F (−11 to −9.5°C) without permanent damage, top damage can occur anywhere below, roughly, 20°F (−7°C). The very suckering characteristic that

Acacia dealbata. Photo by John Grimshaw

Acacia dealbata subsp. *subalpina*.
Photo by Michael A. Dirr

can make *A. dealbata* mildly annoying is a lifesaver after a cold spell, as the tree is usually quick to resprout from the base or root suckers. Temperatures nearer 0°F (–18°C) and even below in some places in cold pockets of the Willamette Valley, though killing established specimens to the ground in 1972, saw many resprouting only a month or two afterward. It is, however, highly recommended not to have cold spells of that magnitude.

The leaves of the subspecies tend to be a bit more on the green side than the silver. As well, plants grown from seeds of the often shrubby forms found in the wild on the Tasman plateau have not necessarily maintained that silvery characteristic. Fast-growing, one plant in a Portland, Oregon, garden has attained nearly 20 ft. (6 m) in three years from seed.

Although quite drought tolerant, *Acacia dealbata* often inhabits riparian areas and sometimes quite marshy soil in its native haunts. Plants once installed as ornamentals near the Darlingtonia Wayside Preserve on the central Oregon coast have spread from dry stable sand dunes into a bog situation with saturated peaty soil and seem equally at home in both.

Acacia dealbata has escaped in a few locations, including the one just mentioned, making it a little worrisome where the plant is too happy. But, like running bamboo, it tends to spread stoloniferously from a planted specimen. Seeding into the wild seems to be rare, at least in the western United States.

Propagation from seed is easiest; about a month of cool stratification is helpful. A brief submersion in boiling water (only the seeds) also can increase germination as with so many other legumes. Cuttings in autumn and winter on ripened growth are usually successful, as is the removal of small root suckers.

Acacia pataczekii. Described only in 1978, this endemic to the perennially cool and moist Tasman plateau has only recently been introduced. A small tree slowly reaching 25–35 ft. (7.5–10.5 m) with single leaves, blue-green in color and narrow, about 2½ in. (6 cm) long by only 6 mm wide. The pale yellow flowers, though relatively small, are numerous and create a very pretty, late-winter display alongside the bluish leaves. The reddish brown seedpods, evident among the leaves later in the season, are, to my eye, even more attractive, possibly because they very well might contain seeds of this hard-to-find species.

Though it must be acknowledged that there might just be acacias more attractive than *Acacia pataczekii*, cold hardiness could be its greatest attribute, plants having withstood 0°F (–18°C) in protected locations with no evident damage. One specimen, growing behind the Alpine House at the Royal Botanic Gardens, Kew, is several years old and a very handsome, small tree.

Although *Acacia pataczekii* exhibits some drought tolerance, its native habitat is quite cool and moist year-round, and often buried in snow for long periods in winter. It also dislikes the often warm soil of containers and should be transferred from pot to ground as early as possible. In our Portland, Oregon, garden only one specimen so far has lived long enough to make this transition, but we are determined to declare it a success. Happiness seems finally to have resulted from its inclusion in a mixed New Zealand/Australian planting at the nursery with gritty but well-watered soil surrounded by ground covers and a north-facing aspect, so the ground has remained as cool as possible—a spot where such finicky treasures as *Embothrium coccineum* (Chilean flame tree), *Lomatia ferruginea*, another proteaceous plant from Chile, and even *Celmisia*, the lovely alpine daisies, have become happy campers. Luckily, this plant is relatively easy from cuttings if taken in the autumn or winter, and seed is becoming more available on lists.

Acacia pataczekii

Acacia pravissima (Ovens wattle). Looking like something from a Dr. Seuss book (perhaps entitled *The Depraved Wattle*), young plants of this southeastern Australia species exist as a series of long arching branches with triangular phyllodes, about 1½ in. (4 cm) long, held tightly against them like little shark fins, distributed in what appear to be rows up and down the stems. Some stay shrub-like for a number of years, eventually breaking away from their wacky (some say awkward) youth and becoming, in a few more years, graceful, weeping small trees, 25–35 ft. (7.5–10.5 m) tall. The adult plant has an arching appearance with upright trunks that lead to weeping branches, a little like an evergreen weeping willow with a blue cast. Small bundles of flower buds appear in autumn and open by January or February (sometimes as late as April) with no hint of electrical-fire aroma. The flowers are fairly typical of the wattles in having a sunny yellow pompom of about 6 mm or less.

One of the hardiest of the Australians, temperatures of 7 to 8°F (−14°C) have not harmed it in some locations, though, where temperatures fall below 20°F (−7°C) regularly, protected siting would be best, especially to maintain the flowers. Of similar frost hardiness is *Acacia retinodes*, which bears long, very slender phyllodes and maintains a shrubbier appearance; it too has several forms that behave as prostrate shrubs or even ground covers.

Drought tolerant and accepting of a wide range of soils, *Acacia pravissima* does respond energetically to ample moisture and deep, well-amended soil. Use fertilizers sparingly; though less susceptible to

Acacia pravissima. Photo by Michael A. Dirr

phosphorous than other Australians, too much will indeed cause yellowing. Striking when used against a simple wall or with other plants exhibiting bold architecture.

Propagation is the same as for the other acacias, though cuttings have been a bit easier, for me, possibly because I have kept taking them until I was sure to have enough.

Acacia riceana (Rice's wattle). From Tasmania, another weeper, this 15–30 ft. (4.5–9 m) small tree begins life as a somewhat confused mass of prickly, needle-like phyllodes. After but a few seasons, it finds itself, producing one to several upright shoots with both a nodding tip and drooping branches, the newest weeping almost straight down. The phyllodes indeed resemble the needles of a conifer, being very narrow (under 3 mm), very dark green, and 1–2 in. (2.5–5 cm) in length.

Although the midwinter flowers are often described as consistently yellow, forms in cultivation often vary to creamy white. Another of the more frost hardy acacias, *Acacia riceana* has survived temperatures of 10°F (–12°C) or lower. Experience in our garden took it to 16°F (–9°C) as a young plant with no visible damage and, after three years from a cutting, it was 15 ft. (4.5 m) tall. Temperatures near 20°F (–7°C) with an exceedingly dry wind took this beautiful specimen to the ground in January 2004, but it resprouted and survived. As with *A. pravissima*, *A. riceana* appears to be quite tolerant of a wide range of soils and drainage. Although its native habitat is quite wet year-round, it doesn't seem phased by periodic drought.

Its weeping form provides a striking silhouette and its texture combines well with other small-leaved plants; alternatively, plants can be used to create a fine contrast with larger foliage. Placement must be done carefully since a single plant in the wrong context can, much like the ever-popular *Sequoiadendron giganteum* 'Pendulum', look a bit like "Swamp Thing."

Propagation is similar to that of other acacias—great success with seeds, but our trials have provided only about thirty percent take from winter cuttings.

Acca	guava	Myrtaceae

A couple of evergreen species hailing from the rich lands between the tropics and temperate zones from east of the Andean cordillera in the scrublands of southwestern Brazil to northwestern Argentina. Both spend their early years as shrubs, eventually reaching tree size. The one described here, *Acca sellowiana*, is the more useful of the two and the better candidate for temperate gardens.

Acca sellowiana (syn. *Feijoa sellowiana*; pineapple guava). From the uplands of southwestern Brazil to northwestern Argentina, from the edge of the Chaco country into the more lush, nearly rainforest sections of the Andean foothills. The habitat receives plentiful summer rain in the form of showers and dry winters with surprisingly frequent frost, especially in the higher elevations. Although they can be kept as shrubs or espaliered plants, one of their best uses is as a small garden specimen with branches trimmed from the base.

Old specimens have been recorded at over 25 ft. (7.5 m), and a plant in Arthur Lee Jacobson's Seattle garden is reported to have reached 17 ft. (5 m) tall. Certainly in the garden *Acca sellowiana* can reach 12–15 ft. (3.5–4.5 m) or more in height within ten years, maturing into a beautiful dome shape with roughly 2–3 in. (5–8 cm) leaves, matte green above and reflective silver-white below, and bark that exfoliates into a deep rusty orange. Although for fruit production plants are often clipped into almost hedge-like creatures, specimens grown as small trees are much more attractive, as one can then see not only the beautiful bark but also the reflective leaf undersides. The flowers and fruit are, of course, added attractions. The typical myrtleloid flowers, up to 1–1½ in. (2.5–4 cm) with fleshy white petals surrounding a boss of deep red stamens, are pleasant enough—but wait, there's more. The petals are quite sweet and provide endless hours of snacking entertainment in the garden or make a nice addition to a salad. The flowers often occur beginning in May and June, with the ensuing guavas, usually 1 in. (2.5 cm) by 3 in. (8 cm), ripening in mid to late autumn. These have a tough exterior skin, but the innards are a gelat-

Acca sellowiana, flowers

Acca sellowiana. Photo by Michael A. Dirr

Acca sellowiana, fruits.
Photo by Michael A. Dirr

inous mass and, indeed, taste of tangy pineapple. If you can handle eating ripe figs, these are easy, too.

The attractions of *Acca sellowiana* in the garden certainly outweigh the sometimes messy production of fruit, and its usefulness as a landscape plant goes beyond the zones where fruit might always ripen. In cool coastal zones where winter frost is a factor, fruit might be only a luxury, and plants might be planted against a sunny wall for heat protection—or one might have to be satisfied with munching on the petals. By the way, if only the petals are consumed without disturbing the stamens in the center, flowers can go on to set fruit.

Numerous cultivars exist. *Acca sellowiana* 'Trask' and *A. s.* 'Unique' both have rounded, particularly silvery leaves and are known for their ability to self-pollinate, although any cultivar would benefit from having a friend of a different clone nearby for the best chance at fruit.

Again, pineapple guavas are lovers of heat and, though they seem to grow satisfactorily in any soil that isn't boggy in full sun to dappled shade, they are at their best in bright situations where heat can accumulate. In regions where frost is not a factor one need not be quite as concerned about heat accumulation as the fruit will simply ripen into the winter season. However, heat does factor in the ripening of the wood, and where severe frosts are likely to occur, plants should be placed in full sun with as much warmth as possible and given a drying period prior to any autumn frost to encourage dormancy.

As to actual cold hardiness, all cultivars seem unharmed by temperatures of 18°F (–8°C) or so but can face leaf drop or twig damage and overall loss of vigor with prolonged cold or temperatures in the range of 10 to 15°F (–12 to –9.5°C). Stories abound of plants surviving even slightly below 0°F (–18°C) and resprouting from trunks or from the ground.

We have enjoyed finding old specimens in western Oregon that have taken the harshest of winters past, including one specimen in downtown Hillsboro, with a trunk nearly 6 in. (15 cm) in diameter, which has survived temperatures below 10°F (–12°C) on occasion.

Though seed is occasionally available for propagation, it is very fine and sometimes difficult to extract. The best method is from cuttings of known clones, though, unfortunately, success does not come easily. My best luck has been with the present season's ripened wood—taken just prior to turning from green to brown, preferably in August to September or October (in the northern hemisphere, of course)—using a fairly strong hormone together with bottom heat and mist. Rooting is slow, and the percentage is not always high. My philosophy with *Acca* is possibly a lazy one—just take a lot of cuttings and at least a few will succeed.

| *Acer* | maple | Aceraceae |

The vast majority of the approximately 150 species in *Acer* are deciduous. A few, however, not only hold their leaves but remain quite attractive while doing so. Interestingly, the evergreen characteristics of maples seem to be rather randomly distributed through the genus. Most species inhabit typical maple-friendly places that have high rainfall, but those keeping their leaves inhabit more southern locales not subject to the winter cold and wind that make evergreen characteristics less feasible. A couple have gone the "Mediterranean" route, with leaves that are small and tough, withstanding long periods of drought. Light and water requirements vary but none resent deep, consistent watering. The flowers—really only significant to the maples themselves, their pollinators, and a few botanists—become samaras, winged fruit that, en masse, can provide a pleasing effect.

The following selections, though certainly able to be propagated with seeds from the samaras, have been successfully rooted from late-summer season, semi-hardwood cuttings.

Acer buergerianum, bark.
Photo by Michael A. Dirr

Acer buergerianum var. *formosanum*. An Asian taxon, worthy of seeking out for situations where adequate moisture can be provided. As this is a variety of the normally deciduous *A. buergerianum*, which is widespread from eastern China to Japan and nearby places, one would not be surprised that collections from southern provenances would be evergreen. *Acer buergerianum* var. *formosanum*, from a high-elevation collection in Taiwan, has been planted at the University of Washington Arboretum and in the last ten or so years has received no visible injury from frost at 14 to 16°F (–10 to –9°C). The leaves are three-lobed, sometimes becoming somewhat acute as the tree ages, and only about 3 in. (8 cm) in length and width. A pleasing glossy green on the surface is contrasted by a powdery blue underside. The bark has the same delicate plating as *A. buergerianum*, and the branch structure seems slight less angular. Should reach 25 ft. (7.5 m) in a reasonable time.

Acer oblongum (oblong leaf maple). From the Himalayas into western and central China, a handsome and graceful tree, fast-growing to about 30 ft. (9 m), upright when young and becoming gracefully rounded in age. In juvenile stages the leaves exhibit some lobing, tending to become entire and oval after only a few years. They are 1–2 in. (2.5–5 cm) wide and 3–4 in. (8–10 cm) long and nearly always exhibit a powdery bluish underside—this in concert with silver-hued bark that becomes flaky with age. The red new growth is also a plus.

Acer oblongum, foliage. Photo
by Michael A. Dirr

Acer oblongum

Acer oblongum var. *concolor* is more consistently blue-leaved with a more striking silvery underside.

Acer oblongum resents extended drought, losing luster, and should be provided with deep regular watering in any climate not experiencing abundant rainfall and away from cool, coastal areas. It should be sited in either a light woodland or a north aspect, giving it dappled shade or, at least, relief from the hottest of afternoon sun in climates with hot, dry summers. As might be expected, it would also love deep, fertile soil but does not demand it as long as enough moisture is present. Though said by some to be cold hardy to below 10°F (–12°C), even temperatures a few degrees above can cause leaf and sometimes twig damage, especially with wind exposure.

Increasingly available in specialty nurseries and seed lists, *Acer oblongum* might be best used where the bark and the structure of the tree can be appreciated via close inspection, or to add grace to a woodland garden. The large, teardrop-shaped leaves create bright shade, with their spring-green surfaces and blue reverse. Effective as a patio tree, it will quickly achieve its potential as well as the gardener's purpose with its rapid rate of growth.

At the University of Washington Arboretum in Seattle, a Taiwan collection as *Acer albopurpurascens*, a name sometimes synonymized with *A. oblongum*, has been successful for a number of years, though with leaf bronzing and drop after 16°F (–9°C).

Acer paxii (Pax's evergreen maple). Found in central China, another fairly small tree to an eventual 35 ft. (10.5 m) or more but with a slower rate of growth than *A. oblongum*. The 2 × 1½ in. (5 × 4 cm) leaves are somewhat fluted with three prominent and equal lobes colored a matte green on the surface with powdery blue beneath. The twigs are very dark, enhancing the contrast. The tree is often single-trunked, often a bit shrubby in youth, but eventually presents a pleasing rounded form providing bright shade. The reflective, silvery blue undersurface coupled with the trifoliate shape creates a particularly outstanding leaf that refracts light. Another potential garden centerpiece, easily enhanced by careful pruning to provide glimpses into the layered canopy, and a good candidate for garden uplighting. Even without electrical enhancement, the somewhat recurved leaves can be seen from a distance flashing their blue undersides.

Though not at its best in full sun in hot, dry climates, it is, however, quite a bit more drought tolerant than *Acer oblongum* and is successful in coastal areas or with some dappled afternoon shade where particularly hot and dry. *Acer paxii* seems also more at home than *A. oblongum* with more sterile, rocky soil conditions, again provided some moisture is present. Rated to zone 8, the tree appears fit after a fairly extended spell in the mid teens (14 to 16°F, –10 to –9°C) but as temperatures approach 10°F (–12°C) damage can occur.

Acer paxii

Acer saccharum var. *skutchii* (syn. *A. skutchii*; Skutcher's sugar maple). Northern Central America and, arguably, into the Sierra Madre Oriental of northeastern Mexico. Though taxonomically a bit confusing (except, probably, to the maples), this group seems to be a conglomerate of different southern forms of sugar maple. One thing they do have in common is the tendency to be evergreen, though less so as one moves north in Mexico. Collections from Nuevo Leon, Mexico—further north there than the subspecies is said to be found—have formed beautiful small trees to about 35 ft. (10.5 m) with several characteristics that make them valuable to horticulture. The leaves are typical sugar maple size, to about 6 in. (15 cm), with a number of sharp lobes, but they exhibit a leathery texture and a bluish underside that is a great complement to the silvery bark. As with many plants considered evergreen, they do not keep every leaf they ever produce but have a season of shedding, often just before the new leaves push out in early spring, as early as February or March—or on the day of

Acer saccharum var. *skutchii*, new leaves. Photo by Michael A. Dirr

Acer sempervirens. Photo by Michael A. Dirr

the big garden party. Forms growing in our Portland garden actually exhibit stunning "autumn" color sometime in January, color that lasts until the deep red new growth begins in earliest spring.

These trees are surprisingly drought tolerant, although some supplemental water should be given in extended summer dry spells. The soils in their habitat range from deep and humusy to limestone crags. That lack of preference seems to translate to the garden, where they have been indifferent to varying soil types. They have thriven from the Carolinas to southcentral Texas to the Mediterranean West, occasionally with minimum supplemental water. All forms have withstood to near 0°F (–18°C) but forms from Nuevo Leon have withstood –9°F (–23°C) in the Carolinas, though all traces of ever-green-osity disappeared at those temperatures. Again, at home in any but waterlogged soil in sun or shade. The leaf undersides add light to a dark garden or a dark area, but the winter coloring is less dramatic.

Acer sempervirens (Cretan maple). Native of the eastern Mediterranean and sometimes offered as *A. orientalis*, the first impression this maple gives is that of a dryland, evergreen oak. The leaves, under 2 in. (5 cm) in diameter, are leathery and sometimes spine-tipped with three lobes compressed into a rounded form. A deep dark green in color, they are very rough to the touch—both characteristics of plants in hot, dry climates. The undersides are, in some forms, somewhat powdery blue, making a nice contrast.

The plants begin life as a somewhat divaricated (browse-proof) shrub, later becoming small rounded trees, single- or multi-stemmed, to under 25 ft. (7.5 m). In the garden, where with any luck browsing is a minor problem, they achieve tree size much faster. Along with its substantial presence, one of the best attributes of this maple is drought hardiness and the ability to endure long periods without water in both its Mediterranean haunts and in the dry garden. Growing in its home on both rubbly screes and in mesic glades, it's another maple that needs no coddling with fertile soil, save for good drainage. Individuals can be dense and rounded; those in groves are more open. Although frost hardy to at least 0°F (–18°C), sustained periods of cold often induce leaf shed. (We ignore this fact, however, to keep it eligible for inclusion in this book.)

With its ability to withstand drought and thrive in harshly bright conditions, it should be one of the easiest maples for the Interior West. Experience so far has found that the brighter and drier the environment, the more compact and full the specimen becomes with the blackish green leaves simply becoming blacker and greener, rather than taking on that round-margined look so often seen in Japanese maples. A collection made in Crete by Wayne Roderick has performed admirably with no irrigation in northern California and Oregon's Willamette Valley after becoming established.

Agonis   Myrtaceae

Southwestern Australian genus of only eleven species, many of them quite tender to frost, but one, *Agonis flexuosa*, most suitable to a wider range of conditions. From shrubs to trees with solid or shredding bark, these have long, narrow, alternate leaves, aromatic when crushed and often smelling of peppermint; small clusters of white to occasionally light pink flowers; and tiny seed capsules held along the stems. They are related to and indeed resemble a very large leptospermum. Known for their tolerance of great drought, both humid and dry conditions, and poor, even poorly drained soils, their only shortcoming is that of tenderness to cold.

Agonis flexuosa (willow myrtle, peppermint tree). Included here for its striking composure, a graceful tree to over 40 ft. (12 m) with strongly pendulous branches and long, willowy leaves, blue-green to deep green in the species. Ben Gardner has a fine representative of the type in his coastal garden in Pistol River, Oregon (see photo). Growing among South African heathers and telopeas, this specimen is about 25 ft. (7.5 m) and appears from a distance to be a bluish green weeping willow.

Certainly a common plant of horticulture in Australian gardens and a denizen of old gardens in coastal California and Oregon. Quite tolerant of salt spray, plants prefer full sun to only lightly dappled shade. Inland or where temperatures fall to 20°F (–7°C), peppermint tree should be enjoyed only as a container specimen. Several cultivars are gaining popularity along the West Coast; one new introduction, *Agonis flexuosa* 'Jervis Bay After Dark', offers very dark purple leaves.

Cuttings have been difficult; those taken in mid summer to early autumn have proven most successful, though slow. The fine seed can be sown in early spring, but to maintain cultivars, clonal material must be done by cutting or graft.

Agonis flexuosa

Alnus   alder   Betulaceae

About thirty-five species, almost all northern hemisphere, but a few escaping into the Andean cordillera of South America. The overwhelming majority are deciduous, many growing in quite cool temperate climates and to high elevation and high latitudes. They can be quite fast-growing and therefore somewhat short-lived. A number of species are pioneer plants, colonizing disturbed wet soil. The rapid growth can be a key benefit where a quick fill or, at least, an instant reward is desired. As well, the genus has nitrogen-fixing roots. The few evergreen species, as one would expect, come from warm temperate subtropical climates and seem well behaved in the garden.

The flowers are tiny and of significance only to other alders but provide good texture when the catkins form in autumn and winter. The cone-like capsules, typical of any alder, can be used in dried arrangements.

Alnus jorullensis. Mexico through Central America, at high elevations near or in cloud forest situations extending into mostly winter-dry mixed forest. These small to medium trees remain under 15 ft. (4.5 m) for a time, though most eventually achieve a pyramidal 30–35 ft. (9–10.5 m) and have been reported to almost 80 ft. (25 m) in forest situations. They possess an intricately patterned bark in shades of silver and 2½–3½ in. (6–9 cm) leaves that are glossy and sharp-pointed with very small serrations along the margins. The leaves have a faint, yellowish pubescence on the underside, making a pleasing contrast.

This has been an easy tree in cultivation, withstanding some summer drought only a little worse for the wear. Plants can be grown in full sun to nearly full shade, but plants in shade tend to be quite sparse. Native to regions of sometimes shallow but often rich soil, always with plentiful moisture. It seems any soil will do even with periods of standing water.

Perhaps the species' greatest attribute is that of a solid, small tree with shiny leaves that can take a good deal more fluctuation in soil and dryness than many others and tends to be longer lived than alders are thought to be—unless backed over by the family Humvee. Plants with good provenance (i.e., from higher elevations) have survived with only leaf damage at 10 to 12°F (–12 to –11°C), but 12 to 15°F (–11 to –9.5°C) is a good assumption of their low temperature tolerance.

Seed, when available, should be sown fresh. Cuttings have been successful in late summer, and plants are increasingly available in specialty nurseries.

Alnus nitida (shiny alder). Warm temperate into subtropical, broad-leaved evergreen forests on the south sides of the Himalayas. Another alder with attractive, silvery bark breaking into a pleasing pattern of scales. As the common name implies, the leaves are extra shiny and deep green. They are toothed and fairly narrow, 3–5½ in. (8–14 cm) long, larger on young trees. A fast-growing tree to over 30 ft. (9 m), *A. nitida* is not for smaller gardens unless used as a coppice plant.

Frost hardy into the low teens (13 to 14°F, –10.5 to –10°C) and leaf hardy to about 20°F (−7°C), the deep lustrous leaves, like pools of water, form the tree's most attractive feature. The leaf gloss on a sunny day can be seen for some distance, a wonderful texture where a plant such as *Magnolia grandiflora* would take years to fill in. As with most alders, consistent moisture is a plus. The tree's fast rate of growth and size—upwards of 50 ft. (15 m) in just a few years—make careful siting a must. Quite at home in bright light, yet equally tolerant of the shade in a mixed forest situation. But, like *Alnus jorullensis*, it has a much more open form in shade. Any soil will do, provided it's damp.

Successful cuttings have been rooted from freshly ripened wood in late summer well into winter.

Alnus nepalensis is another Himalayan species, much larger, to nearly 125 ft. (38 m), with larger glossy leaves. Although an impressive tree, it has been damaged at warmer temperatures, in the mid to upper teens (14 to 18°F, −10 to −8°C), and seems to lose its shine more easily with frost.

Arbutus   Ericaceae

Fourteen species, all evergreen shrubs or trees, from the Mediterranean, western Europe, and western North America, south to Central America. Hardly a more beautiful genus of plants exists with so many good characteristics, all pleasing to the eye, from bark that flakes or peels into smooth almost skin-like texture to shiny leaves and attractive flowers. Most come with the additional benefit of enduring such tough garden conditions as drought and poor soil. The majority are native to Mediterranean climates, where summer rainfall is scarce, while others (mostly those from the southwestern United States and Mexico) accept periodic drought any time of the year.

All are tolerant of harsh light, the most shade tolerant being the shrubby *Arbutus occidentalis* of Central America. The bark ranges from attractive to exquisite; the least interesting, that of *A. unedo*, is merely shaggy, while the rest peel in patches or stripes varying in color from mahogany to russet-orange to cream and white. The flowers are small, ⅓ in. (1 cm), in that lily-of-the-valley shape (urceolate) so common in the family Ericaceae, and appear in clusters colored from white to pinkish. They are followed by orange to red, round fruit of various sizes, most under ⅓–½ in. (1–1.5 cm), their striking show perhaps best exemplified by the displays of brilliant balls (1 in., 2.5 cm) on *A. unedo*, aptly called the strawberry tree.

By examining the native haunts of any arbutus, one quickly discovers the clear need for well-drained soil—some plants even appear to be growing from piles of boulders. Those from summer-rainfall

The exquisite peeling bark of *Arbutus menziesii*

Arbutus andrachne. Photo © Global
Book Publishing Photo Library

Arbutus ×andrachnoides, bark.
Photo by Michael A. Dirr

habitats are the most accepting of, at least, some garden irrigation, but supplemental water should be carefully avoided with those from the Mediterranean or the West Coast of North America.

With the great range in size, adaptability, and cold hardiness (into zone 7), it is a wonder more have not been sought for garden use. With the exception of *Arbutus menziesii*, all can be reproduced from cuttings from mid summer through winter and are relatively easy from seed with moderate stratification.

Arbutus andrachne (Grecian strawberry tree). From the summer-dry regions of southern Europe and Asia Minor, a medium tree to 40 ft. (12 m) with bark that peels to an attractive red-brown color. The leaves are oval, sometimes having small teeth, about 4 in. (10 cm) long, and a very dark green with a somewhat paler underside. Flowers are in clusters and usually creamy white in early spring, with the fruit a granular "ball" to ½ in. (1.5 cm), similar to *A. unedo*, with which it often hybridizes. More common in cultivation in western Europe than in North America and adaptable mostly to Mediterranean or near Mediterranean climates, this species resents the combination of heat and humidity.

More common in cultivation though a bit smaller, to 35 ft. (10.5 m), is *Arbutus ×andrachnoides*, a hybrid of *A. andrachne* and *A. unedo* with attractive, deep red bark with 1¼–4 in. (3–10 cm), sharp-pointed leaves and ivory-white flowers appearing in late autumn to early spring. Personal experience has shown *A. andrachne* and its hybrids to be less sensitive to summer garden irrigation than instinct might suggest.

With its wide range, temperature tolerance varies accordingly. Depending on provenance, forms from coastal areas can be reliable into the mid teens (14 to 16°F, −0 to −9°C) while interior and mountain forms have survived close to 0°F (−18°C) with no perceivable ill effects. It is not, however, thrilled by long cold spells accompanied by winds—as who is.

Arbutus 'Marina', another hybrid, is of uncertain origin (though *A. andrachne* is probably included). Having been brought to light early in the twentieth century in the San Francisco Bay area, it makes a handsome small tree to about 25 ft. (7.5 m), with early exfoliating bark of a rich orange. Specimens can be seen in San Francisco at the Strybing Arboretum. The winter and early spring flowers are somewhat fragrant and a rich cherry-pink; and the fruit, though smaller than *A. unedo*, only to about ½ in. (1.5 cm), has the same texture and is borne in hanging clusters under the leaves. This plant too is tolerant of a little overexuberance with the garden hose. Its only real drawback is somewhat less cold hardiness, being leaf- and twig-damaged below 15°F (–9.5°C) and sometimes frozen to the ground at temperatures approaching 10°F (–12°C) if of long duration or accompanied by drying winds. Bummer.

Arbutus arizonica (Arizona madroña). Southwestern United States from southern Arizona and New Mexico south into the mountains of Mexico. A small, delicate tree, 15–20 ft. (4.5–6 m) can be expected in a reasonable amount of time with 18–24 in. (45–60 cm) of growth per year on young vigorous trees; with age, 50 ft. (15 m) is possible. Young plants can be upright and pyramidal, evolving into a picturesque form with layered branches and a flattened top and bark that peels to a gentle cream to buff, sometimes in patches. Older bark not exfoliated.

The 3 in. (8 cm) leaves, a glossy dark green with contrasting pale undersides, are narrow and nearly toothless, an unwelcome attribute in some species, but one that adds to the attractiveness of this plant.

Arbutus 'Marina'. Photo by Michael A. Dirr

Arbutus xalapensis

Arbutus arizonica

The white to pearly pink flowers, relatively small, 2–2¾ in. (5–7 cm), are held in tight panicles, pleasantly scented in early spring, and produce deep orange fruit that lasts into autumn and winter. This species and the similar *Arbutus xalapensis*, although native to dry mountains often above desert country, have the great garden advantage of being drought tolerant but gratefully accepting water whenever it's given. The one caveat is their desire for well-drained soil, like the rest of the genus. Observing *A. arizonica* at 7800 ft. (2400 m) in the Chiricahua Mountains of southeastern Arizona growing among other beauties (the evergreen *Quercus hypoleucoides* and *Q. rugosa* with an understory of *Garrya wrightii*, *Agave parryi*, and *Yucca torreyi*), in what appears to be pure limestone, the need for drainage is driven home.

The habitats of *Arbutus arizonica* are subject to periodic cold and, at higher elevations, long periods under snow. Although most forms have survived temperatures to 10°F (–12°C) with little or no damage, provenances should be sought where plants could easily endure well below 0°F (–18°C). In our Portland garden, plants are thriving under irrigated conditions and have shown no signs of disease.

Arbutus menziesii (madroña, Pacific madrone). West Coast of North America from southern California to extreme southwest British Columbia and ranging in size from a majestic tree, reaching over 115 ft. (35 m) in favored locations, down to a large shrub in the driest southern habitats. The tree can be single- or multi-stemmed, with a wide crown, if in the open, to a narrow vase shape when grown with friends. The oval leaves are about 6 in. (15 cm) long and mostly entire, some juvenile leaves having small serrations on vigorous growth. The leaves often partially shed with the first dry weather in spring. The flowers, white to a pearly pink, occur in mid spring in about 6 in. (15 cm) panicles and are substantial enough to make the madrone outstanding from some distance. The fruit, more berry-like in appearance than its European counterparts, is about ½ in. (1.5 cm) and begins to color in late summer, often presenting brilliant displays from autumn into winter.

This is an emblematic tree of the West Coast and has the furthest north distribution of the North American Pacific Coast, Mediterranean flora. It occurs from rocky soil at water's edge on Vancouver Island, British Columbia, into the Puget Sound of Washington State and becomes a savanna tree in Oregon's Willamette Valley, occasionally forming pure forests in southwest Oregon. Uplands in dry regions such as Oregon's Rogue Valley and the mountains of southern California, *Arbutus menziesii* occurs with numerous other chaparral or sclerophyllic genera, including *Ceanothus* and the related *Arctostaphylos*. Sclerophyll, by the way, defines seasonally dry shrub and

Arbutus menziesii flowering with viburnum

tree communities, the majority consisting of evergreen species, many of which drop an inordinate amount of detritus in the form of either leaves or bark. In this author's Eden, the Siskiyous of southern Oregon and northern California, examples of both extremes in habitat exist, from a mixed evergreen forest with 100 ft. (30 m) tall specimens having leaves only at the very top of the canopy and exhibiting the brilliant orange and cream bark like ghosts in the deep woods, to savanna trees, each a gumdrop in the golden meadows of the Rogue Valley, to the areas in between where, in chaparral country, the colors of the deep orange bark with the dark green glossy leaves mixed with the golden grass and the screaming silver-blue of the manzanitas define a wonderfully rich region—all within thirty miles.

Arbutus menziesii, fruit

As with other Murphy's law (or Sod's law) situations, the desire to grow a plant in one's garden is sometimes inversely proportional to one's ability to grow it. It is true that *Arbutus menziesii*, like so many other western U.S. natives requiring a strictly Mediterranean climate, is entirely unprepared for the heat of summer mixed with garden irrigation. Though some summer irrigation seems to be tolerated along the immediate coast, where temperatures remain cool throughout the summer, inland, soil fungi become active with warmth plus water, attacking roots and sometimes killing the tree quickly. It sometimes seems the species can sense the nearness of a gardener with a garden hose and simply decide to end it all quickly.

As for cold hardiness, this arbutus is one of the most resistant. The forms from near sea level might show damage at temperatures dropping below 10 to 15°F (−12 to −9.5°C), but many populations exist where temperatures are likely to fall below 0°F (−18°C) on occasion. As these creatures are best from seed anyway, while looking for such, seek high elevation provenances. Northern vs. southern collection sites might not be a useful distinction since plants around the Puget Sound are at sea level, often within salt spray.

Arbutus blackspot, possibly having arrived on imported *Arbutus unedo*, has also taken its toll on native stands, sometimes killing entire groves. That said, especially in its native and formerly native range, this species should be tried and tried and tried again. In Oregon's Willamette Valley many a gardener has succeeded by planting in unamended soil with excellent drainage and an open situation completely out of reach of that garden hose, no matter how many extensions are attached. In some neighborhoods of North Portland, ancient trees, relics of the Willamette Valley savanna, persist in garden situations, probably because of deep, very gravelly soil and a lucky streak of neglect. They are often growing alongside a wonderful form of *Cornus nuttallii*, which can have a great display of flowers in late September and October, possibly a drought adaptation.

Along with a few small difficulties in cultivation comes the near impossibility of transplanting established plants. However, seeds sprout readily in mineral soil (without addition of organic compost) and grow rapidly to about 10 ft. (3 m) in four or five years. Selections are being made from individual specimens that have withstood urban or otherwise improper conditions with no ill effects.

Arbutus unedo (strawberry tree). A large shrub to smallish tree, 6–8 ft. (2–2.5 m) in dwarf forms to over 35 ft. (10.5 m) in mature specimens and plants with the right provenance. Native to Asia Minor and southwestern Europe, centering around the Andalusian area of Portugal and Spain with, arguably, relict populations in southwest Ireland.

In the nursery trade one frequently encounters a wide-eyed look of mild panic from the plant lover who, having just chosen that perfect plant, learns it is a very large shrub, anywhere from 4 ft. (1.2 m) to 15 ft. (4.5 m), by definition. But describe that same plant as a very small, even miniature tree, the defining difference being the removal of a few lower limbs or thinning of the main stems, and mild panic quickly turns to delight. *Arbutus unedo* is one such plant. Portland exhibits too many relics of nursery excursions where the strawberry tree that looked so cute and inviting in its one-gallon container, all dressed in bright red berries or decorated with its lily-of-the-valley flowers, has become a cube under the picture window, trimmed to shape many times yearly. Though compact forms exist, even many of those eventually become small trees.

Hedge pruners aside, when treated as a small tree, *Arbutus unedo* has a petite, rounded form and displays bark that, though less glamorous than other species, is still lovely when seen standing alone. The 1½–3 in. (4–8 cm) leaves are oval, somewhat serrated, and rather shiny above. The most decorative features, however, are the abundant flowers, occurring anywhere from late autumn or winter into early spring, depending on the form, and the marble-sized red fruit that follows, maturing in late summer to mid autumn and often hanging on well into winter—unless devoured by critters or removed by inclement weather. Edible though bland, and not likely to be the next designer condiment.

Like the others—excepting *Arbutus menziesii*—*A. unedo* accepts dryness in the summer yet also handles garden water, if not inundated, perhaps being the species most tolerant of garden conditions.

The species is surely among the top ten most planted in the Mediterranean West of the United States and nearly as common in other, similar, parts of the world. Underused are some of the forms that have been selected either in habitat or during their long history in cultivation. *Arbutus unedo* f. *rubra* has flowers tinted in a deep pink rather

Arbutus unedo

than the normal white to pale pink, while *A. u.* f. *integerrima* has leaves without the typical small teeth, a dubious distinction as many older plants eventually lose their teeth anyway. *Arbutus unedo* 'Quercifolia' is a medium grower that has wonderfully lobed leaves, adding texture to the plant; a beautiful specimen can be seen growing behind the main house at Hillier Arboretum, England.

Equally at home in mixed woodland with dappled shade or out on its own in bright light, only the compactness and form varies. Though *Arbutus unedo* is tolerant of garden water, as stated earlier, good drainage is a must. Most forms are reliable to temperatures reaching 10°F (–12°C) or lower if brief. Temperatures approaching 0°F (–18°C) will burn leaves and even kill back the plant, especially if lasting longer than a day or two or accompanied by wind. If these events are infrequent, the strawberry tree is well worth including in the garden as it resprouts from the roots or from the base of the stem, quickly making up for lost time.

Propagation is easy from newly ripened wood, doubtless one of the reasons for its garden popularity. Also easy from the abundantly produced seed, although not all forms are the same, so it might be best to work with cuttings from a clone of a known form.

ANOTHER SPECIES of note, *Arbutus canariensis*, also a small shrub to small tree with some reaching 30 ft. (9 m) or more, has shiny serrate leaves and an attractive glaucesence underneath. It flowers earlier and in somewhat looser panicles than most of the other species, often in autumn, producing granular orange-red fruit in early to mid summer. Looking more similar to *A. menziesii* than other European species—and occupying a similar niche in its native habitat in the Canary Islands—it is one of the less frost hardy species but is much more tolerant of water. Although rated to zone 8, if one is hopeful of the plant reaching tree size, it should be sited out of the wind where temperatures are likely to drop below 20°F (–7°C) for any length of time. It is likely to be done in at 10°F (–12°C).

Arbutus unedo bearing "strawberries."
Photo by John Grimshaw

Arctostaphylos	manzanita, bear berry	Ericaceae

Over fifty shrubs and, yes, even small trees, almost entirely native to western North America from Mexico to British Columbia, with a couple of ground covers heading east in boreal areas, one losing its leaves altogether while doing so. Save for these and some boreal species, most of the shrubs and tree-like forms (and all that are mentioned here) are at their best in winter-rainfall climates and in full sun, with as mineral a soil as possible. Like so many other Mediterranean plants, too rich a soil or water during high summer temperatures can cause collapse or, at least, general lethargy. The leaves are simple and range from lance-shaped to round or even spatulate; they can be deep green and glossy to blue or silvery white and pubescent. The flowers are in small terminal racemes with pendulous, lantern-shaped, fused petals; the fruit is in the form of a drupe or dry berry.

The Spanish name *manzanita* ("little apple") is appropriate. The fruits have been a dietary mainstay, stored or eaten out of hand by native peoples, and an ingredient in pemmican, a medley of berries and other good stuff that is dried and saved. It is a pleasure while hiking in autumn through the hot chaparral country of the western United States to taste these and be reminded of the little straws of powdered candy we got as kids. By the time the fruit is mature, it is essentially powdery inside and tastes of sweet apple. But, for this volume, its uses in the garden are more important. Though the vast majority of species could never be considered more than ground covers or shrubs, a few can reach 15–25 ft. (4.5–7.5 m) in height and resemble none other than their close relatives in *Arbutus*.

Propagation is straightforward from seed collected in autumn, cleaned, and planted straightaway in an area that is left to chill or after having been stratified for about thirty days in the veggie-crisper. Cuttings in most species are best as the weather cools in mid to late autumn to early spring before new growth appears, using the oldest past season's wood that has not yet begun to exhibit the peeling, brown bark.

Arctostaphylos glauca (big-berried manzanita, blue manzanita). My first encounter with the species was in the Wilson Range of central California, as I struggled to find my way through the thick, shrapnel-infused chaparral to an enticing barren, undoubtedly replete with interesting species. Amid the tangle of branches I encountered a tree trunk, 18 in. (45 cm) across, the tree itself rising over 15 ft. (4.5 m)—a manzanita that, upon keying, turned out to be *A. glauca*. It was the first week of March, and even in a light rain the leaves were a glowing blue, setting off the nearly pure white flowers. I was already a fan of the genus so just the thought of a plant growing to such proportions with such a large trunk of fluted mahogany was enough to make the species an instant favorite (which it remained until I encountered the next manzanita).

In garden situations, as with the others in the genus, mineral soil is much preferred, and the brightest of sun further ensures its best performance. The winter flowers, along with rounded leaves that can exceed 2 in. (5 cm), make it a contender for a garden focal point. While not as tolerant of long winter cold spells as some others, temperatures in the low teens (13°F, −10.5°C) for several days have not affected it and, given its native geography, even colder temperatures should not injure it. Though slow to establish from cuttings, within three to five years the plant can be head height with a trunk already exhibiting the characteristic musculature and reddish brown color.

Arctostaphylos manzanita (manzanita, Parry's manzanita). Central California coast range as far north as southern Oregon. Grows in an open vase shape and, like the others, can be kept as a shrub or, with gentle encouragement, maintained as a beautiful, small tree reaching as high as 15 ft. (4.5 m) or more in time. The bark and branches are sinuous and a deep, rich mahogany, with the plant's vigorous growth easily seen between the branches. The leaves, in contrast to the following species, *A. viscida*, are more deeply colored in green, often with a bluish cast. The flowers vary somewhat in color but are most often a very pale pink or white and occur in February and March with the fruit, rather pale when young, becoming a chocolatey reddish brown. Again, they adore a Mediterranean climate and can endure long periods of summer drought and plentiful winter moisture, providing soil is well drained and preferably not too rich. Cold hardiness varies

Arctostaphylos manzanita, bark. Photo by Michael A. Dirr

Arctostaphylos manzanita, flowers. Photo by Michael A. Dirr

Arctostaphylos manzanita in winter snow

depending on provenance, but plants seem to be unharmed by temperatures of 10 to 15°F (−12 to −9.5°C) or even brief dips a bit below.

Arctostaphylos manzanita 'Dr. Hurd', introduced by the Saratoga Horticultural Research Foundation, is a particularly large and stout grower, easily reaching 6 ft. (2 m) or more in three years from a small container. *Arctostaphylos manzanita* 'St. Helena', introduced by plantsman and great arctostaphylist M. Nevin Smith, has rich blue-green leaves and white flowers.

Arctostaphylos viscida (sticky manzanita, silver manzanita). Native to the dry interior country of California and southern Oregon, this species is one of the main components of the chaparral country, where it enriches the color palette, the silver-blue of its leaves contrasting with the often mahogany-red of its stems, the acid greens of nearby broad-leaved evergreens, and the gold of the summer grass. Though the standard height of the plant is 6–8 ft. (2–2.5 m), 15 ft. (4.5 m) and even 20 ft. (6 m) plants are not uncommon in favored situations (those with a little more moisture or deeper soil). The pearly pink flowers offer wonderful accompaniment to the gray-blue leaves, and they appear later than those of some of its compatriots—very latest winter but more likely in late spring. In garden situations, this species can put forth bursts of flowers nearly any time. The fruits, which beautifully match the cinnamon-colored bark, occur from the end of summer into winter.

Arctostaphylos viscida

Both here and in the carefully tended garden, with lower branches trimmed, the canopy of silver leaves contrasting with the smooth, muscular, deep red bark is stunning. Though capable of growing in light dappled shade, in general, the brighter and more exposed the situation, the better *Arctostaphylos viscida* performs. Vigorous when young, growing 18–24 in. (45–60 cm) a year, in three to five years a plant from a small container already begins to stop garden visitors in their tracks.

Sadly, for those not living in a Mediterranean climate, it's a plant for visitation only. However, where the summer garden can be kept dry and winter temperatures never fall below −10°F (−23°C), gardeners enjoy this long-lived species.

Arctostaphylos viscida, flowers

Garden cohorts might include the native *Rhamnus californica* and its forms, Pacific Coast irises, and *Ceanothus* and *Zauschneria* species.

Propagation from seed requires a cool stratification in autumn and winter and, preferably, planting in mineral soil. Cuttings are best taken from the oldest of the past season's green wood with a high hormone and a cool situation, preferably without mist, from November and December to as late as March.

Arctostaphylos viscida, fruit

Arctostaphylos canescens, also from California and Oregon, is slightly smaller though specimens have been seen to 10 ft. (3 m) or more with the same muscular mahogany stems but with lightly hairy leaves, somewhat more turquoise in color, and rather bright pink flowers from January or February through March. Should be provided good air circulation and mineral soil with a minimum of summer water.

| *Argyrocytisus* | broom | Fabaceae |

Now widely recognized as a separate genus, *Argyrocytisus*, consisting of one species, *A. battandieri* (described here), is, for practical purposes, part of the genus *Cytisus*, to which it is closely related and which includes a large group of shrubs with some small trees, all from North Africa, west Asia, Europe, and the Canary Islands. Their characteristics range from deciduous to evergreen and from minutely leaved—contradicting somewhat the idea of "broadleaved" evergreen—to large-leaved. Many make ideal garden subjects; others, however, have given the entire group a bad name having been wildly (really!) successful colonizing foreign lands. On the West Coast of North America many people immediately make some sort of "dispel evil" sign at the mere mention of *Cytisus*, even a noninvasive species such as the very useful broom described below. The change in genus is probably as great a benefit to the politics of the plant as it is to the nomenclature.

Argyrocytisus battandieri (pineapple broom, Moroccan broom). Morocco. Several features set *A. battandieri* apart. Possibly the most important is that it bears no resemblance to a broom, instead appearing more like an evergreen golden chain (*Laburnum*). Still not common in cultivation, they can be used as large shrubs, 6–8 ft. (2–2.5 m) or more, but are most graceful if allowed to become small trees of 12–15 ft. (3.5–4.5 m). Trimmed as a tree they attain a rather wide, umbrella shape with branch ends that weep somewhat, especially when laden with flowers.

Plants possess three-parted, spring-green leaves that average 5–6 in. (13–15 cm) but can be over 20 in. (50 cm) in shade or on young vigorous growth—definitely a very un-broom-like leaf. In full sun and as the leaves mature, they tend toward an entirely silver look, having an upper leaf surface replete with a silver sheen of minute hairs and an underside that is silvery as well.

The flowers are in dense racemes, about 5 in. (13 cm) long, which contain dozens of rich yellow flowers, each under ⅓ in. (1 cm), borne at the ends of the branches. Their fragrance is that of a ripe pineapple. Thus far, at least in our part of the world, even with multiple clones growing together, they have not set abundant seed, nor have they germinated in the garden, thus appearing so far to be free of their too-prolific cousins' bad habits.

Plants are at their best in full sun but tolerant of at least dap-

Argyrocytisus battandieri

pled shade especially in hot climates, and they are adapted to summer drought, thus making them perfect for a Mediterranean garden. However, as part of that adaptation, summer drought slows growth and subjects them to at least a little leaf loss. On the other hand, though they are tolerant of average garden water if the soil is well drained, in too rich a soil and with too much summer moisture they can grow rank and need continual pruning. Overall, they are somewhat subject to collapse if treated too well—i.e., abundant compost, fertilizer, and summer water. The best plan might be to plant in lean soil and provide for them generously when young and, when desired size is reached, put them on a diet, withholding fertilizer and reducing water. At their best in cool coastal and Mediterranean-leaning climates, they do seem to suffer in areas of high summer heat and humidity. As well, where temperatures are particularly cool in the summer, growth is slow and tree height might be only a hope. For example, pineapple broom seems to have at least twice the growth rate in Portland, Oregon, with its warmer summers, in comparison to Seattle's lower summer heat accumulation. In cooler climates, the benefit of a south wall will help spur growth.

Unharmed by temperatures of 10 to 15°F (−12 to −9.5°C), bouts to near 0°F (−18°C) have certainly made them look ratty, to say the least, or become mostly deciduous—as they are described in some literature. If hammered by a particular cold spell, it might be best to allow them to resprout from the roots rather than attempt to revive sickly top growth. Either way, the plants do respond well to coppicing, with large leaves and luxuriant growth but fewer flowers. Plants in the Denver Botanic Garden have regrown each season after being "coppiced" by winter temperatures approaching −20°F (−29°C).

As is typical for pea germination, *Argyrocytisus battandieri* is enhanced by the addition of boiling water (poured over the seeds, only, please). We have found they are best sown in autumn under cool conditions, with germination taking place over the winter and spring. Cuttings have been somewhat daunting, with some luck using mature present-season's wood in late summer without soft growth. Alternatively, try very new growth in late winter to early spring while conditions are still cool, using the shoots removed with part of the prior season's bud attached, and with the addition of some mist and bottom heat. Still, the fine line between rooting and rotting is a difficult one to catch as the fleshy, fur-covered leaves are prone to insta-cooties.

Aristotelia   Elaeocarpaceae

Under a half-dozen species, all southern hemisphere natives from New Zealand to Australia to Pacific coastal South America, some as shrubs, including tightly divaricated forms from New Zealand.

Aristotelia chilensis (maquei). A rangy large shrub to small tree with pointed, ovate, toothed leaves to 3–4 in. (8–10 cm), small greenish white flowers in clusters, and edible, purple-black fruit often used for preserves in its native Chile. This is a species that took some getting used to in our garden as young plants were gawky, balking at attempts to create good structure. However, after plants had grown to 12 ft. (3.5 m) in about five years, we were won over by the greenish bark on mature trunks, the bright red petioles, the red-tinted leaves in late summer, and abundant clusters of dark fruit that taken together create a handsome component in the bright understory. Though not everyone agrees, I have come to enjoy the open, arching habit as well.

Native from creek edges to stony places, mostly in summer-dry central and southern Chile, this is clearly a species quite amenable to many garden situations though probably not thrilled with excessive heat coupled with humidity. Our plants, originally from the Biobio drainage in southcentral Chile, have withstood temperatures as low as 13°F (–10.5°C) with no damage save for some leaf drop. *Aristotelia chilensis* 'Variegata' is a rarity coveted by this author.

Summer and autumn cuttings of semi-ripened current season's growth have rooted easily, and they are easy from seed, both in the garden and in the propagation house.

Azara   Flacourtiaceae

Just under a dozen species entirely endemic to South America, mostly in Chile and adjacent Argentina, some ranging a little to the north and east into Bolivia, Uruguay, and southwestern Brazil. The majority of species lie west of the north/south Andean axis that separates maritime, winter-rainfall Chile and southernmost Argentina, with fewer species in northern Argentina and to the east, where summer rainfall rules. Species such as *Azara microphylla* inhabit areas influenced heavily by the cool Pacific Ocean which experience only moderate temperature change throughout the year. In the south, with the cool moisture-laden winds typical of the Roaring 40s (a term used by mariners describing the seemingly ever-present storms occurring in that latitude of the southern hemisphere), the Pacific windward side receives plentiful rainfall and very mild winters for latitudes exceeding 50°S. Because the Andes' low altitude here presents less of a barrier, these winds cross into Argentina, although they are drier on the east side. At lower altitudes, some species are also surprisingly less frost hardy than one might think. Thus, even with the southerly growing *A. microphylla*, provenance is important and, if frost hardiness is an issue, collection from the coldest areas is also key. In actuality, numerous species, including *A. microphylla*, have provenances with greater hardiness much further north because of higher elevations. Most Chilean species do exhibit a fair amount of cold tolerance, but they resent summer heat when coupled with moisture. Those species ranging to the north are surprisingly tolerant of the summer drought typical of the Mediterranean climate; those to the south have a distinct dislike of drought at any time. Other species inhabiting islands of mesic flora further north have quite a bit more tolerance for summer drought, notably *A. celastrina* and, to some degree, *A. petiolaris*. The jury is still out as to their ability to withstand excessive summer moisture.

East of the cordillera and to the north, a few species (arguably, only one) occur in northwest Argentina and into Uruguay and southwestern Brazil. *Azara uruguayensis*, from higher-elevation sites, might be a perfect candidate for trial in areas such as the U.S. Southeast: in its habitats, summers are hot and steamy; some winter drought can occur, and winters receive hard frosts on occasion, with temperatures as low as 10 to 15°F (–12 to –9.5°C).

Even those from the most lush situations inhabit light mineral soil, low in fertility, and resent heavy and overly fertile soil in garden situations. And, while enduring cultivation, all seem to benefit from a little afternoon shade to maintain their clean, shiny green best.

Although a few have been in cultivation for a long time, as a genus they still deserve much more use. All have attractive leaves that are, in most species, exceedingly glossy and subtended by a rounded, smaller accessory leaf, making their arrangement as a whole of particular interest when aligned along the stem and giving each leaf cluster and branch a wonderfully layered look. The leaves range from smaller than ⅓ in. (1 cm) and very shiny to gray-green and over 1½ in. (4 cm). The flowers range from tiny paintbrushes to large pompoms and from a creamy color to bright yellow in winter or early spring. Those grown in particularly warm climates are often caught having a rebloom in autumn. The fruit is a major attraction as well, often white, stained blue and violet to nearly black.

Propagation has been particularly easy with semi-ripened, present season's growth, from mid summer through winter. Best results have been with medium hormone levels after the greatest summer heat has passed. Mist is a must. Seed has been easy as well, with increased germination after some cool stratification.

Azara dentata. From Chile, where it grows in moist sites in mixed forests and occasionally into open volcanic areas. A small tree to 20–25 ft. (6–7.5 m), single- or few-trunked, sometimes suckering, with numerous ascending branches combining into a rounded form. The leaves, among the lightest green of the genus, almost appearing yellow in full sun, are 1–1½ in. (2.5–4 cm) by about 2 in. (5 cm), with, as the name would imply, relatively even dentation, more numerous toward the tip of the leaf. Both stems and leaves are often covered with a fine pubescence.

The flowers resemble those of *Acacia* with bundles of small (6 mm) pompoms held among the leaves from March through April in the northern hemisphere. They are abundant enough to make the entire tree noticeable from a great distance—out-pompoming that "Big Bird" yellow (saturated, bright yellow) acacia down the street—although that was over by now anyway. Not to be satisfied with mere color, the flowers are sweetly fragrant, the scent resembling that of *Albizia julibrissin* (silk tree). The fruit is as lovely as that of the rest of the azaras.

Appreciative of regular deep watering and some afternoon protection from blasting sun, it is otherwise a carefree plant. Opinions vary as to the actual cold hardiness: 16°F (–9°C) in Portland, Oregon, has not fazed it, but 10 to 12°F (–12 to –11°C) in places north have burned leaves and lush growth. If cut back by severe weather or any pruning tool, *Azara dentata* responds quickly with dense, new growth, though the present year's growth may not flower under such conditions.

In garden situations where *Azara dentata* is likely to experience prolonged drought and, occasionally, as the plants become older, growth can become sparse, though the handsome form remains. A careful head reduction (pruning back to shorter branches) along with deep watering and mulch can reverse the situation, encouraging more luxuriant growth.

Azara serrata is a similar species and often confused with *A. dentata* in the trade, though its foliage is more glabrous and somewhat narrower, with minutely forward-pointing teeth or serrations. Another worthy plant requiring similar conditions but a bit slower growing.

Azara integrifolia. Though described by some as a shrub, experience has dictated recognizing it as a very small tree, 10–12 ft. (3–3.5 m). Often multi-trunked if left to its own devices, with open branches, bearing leaves 1½ in. (4 cm) long and 1¼ in. (3 cm) wide, sparsely toothed when young but essentially entire with age and with small accessory leaves of under ⅓ in. (1 cm). Less shrubby and more graceful out of full sun. With good corrective pruning when young, it makes for a wonderful scale where a larger tree isn't required, with its layered branching and an exuberance of creamy yellow flowers—less intensely fragrant than those of other species—in March and April in the northern hemisphere. The fruit, ripening in autumn and often persisting through winter, begins a steely dark blue, aging to nearly black. *Azara integrifolia* often produces enough to not only share with friends but also to induce the tree's branches to weep gracefully.

Nearly on par with hardier clones of *Azara microphylla*, temperatures of 10°F (–12°C) or a little lower have, if brief, done little irrepara-

Azara dentata. Photo © Global Book Publishing Photo Library

Azara dentata, fruit

Azara integrifolia

Azara lanceolata

Azara microphylla

ble damage where some overhead protection of larger plants is available. Denser in full sun but at its most elegant with a little dappled or afternoon shade, especially away from coastal situations.

Azara integrifolia 'Variegata' has been in commerce for some years. This variegated clone is truly shrubby, reaching 5 ft. (1.5 m) in a reasonable amount of time, with a weeping form and rounded leaves, mottled a creamy yellow.

Azara lanceolata. From southern Chile and bordering Argentina, growing in cool, perennially moist forests (a necessity in garden situations) often as an understory tree but occasionally in clearings or in the open on rocky slopes. One of the most interesting leaves, to ⅓–1½ in. (1–4 cm) wide and 2½–3 in. (6–8 cm) long, with shorter, almost ruffled subtending leaves: they present an elegant picture—as of a fancy cuffed hand holding a sword—when displayed on layered branches. Usually staying under 25 ft. (7.5 m), it makes a superb understory plant with dappled shade, ideally. In March and April, yellow, pompom-like, sweetly scented flowers appear amid the branches and last for the better part of a month, followed by clusters of pearl-like fruit beginning white and aging to a deep violet-blue. Though a highly valued plant in our garden, it is one of the more frost tender, having lost buds and gained blackened leaves at 16°F (–9°C). The benefit of some overhead cover (larger broadleaved evergreen trees, for instance) would increase the cold hardiness.

Azara microphylla. Chile, in mesic forest situations of high rainfall and cool temperatures. My first in-the-garden encounter with this species was on a February day when, wafting on the breeze, there came the aroma of Ibarra, a Mexican chocolate, deliciously mixed with vanilla and, maybe, a touch of cinnamon with, possibly, a clove in the distance—in short, a fragrance requiring immediate attention. By following my nose I discovered this 20 ft. (6 m), gracefully layered tree, with small, ⅓ in. (1 cm), glossy leaves and shavingbrush-like creamy flowers of less than ⅓ in. (1 cm). I was dazzled (and immediately overcome with the need for a mocha latte). Although I thought I was familiar with the species, I had obviously not yet understood its great, garden potential. In cool maritime or Mediterranean climes, there is little else that can substitute.

The natural habitat of *Azara microphylla* is cool and moist with lean soils. Because of its range in altitude and latitude, many forms in cultivation have received only little damage in the low teens (13 to 14°F, –10.5 to –10°C) and survived 0°F (–18°C), though sometimes having to resprout from the most woody growth. They are at their most elegant in light woodland and provide an excellent backdrop for bold-leaved plants. In brighter light, or with occasional tipping back, they can be quite dense and pyramidal; in more shade, they produce soft, layered branches from a strong, upright, vase-shaped scaffold of several trunks. (Plants can easily be held to one trunk where desired.) Rich soils certainly speed growth with rates of 3 ft. (1 m) or more a year possible; but, for the health and strength of the tree, it is best to hold off a bit, especially after the first couple of years.

Because of its refined texture, ability to grow in sun or shade, and manageable size, *Azara microphylla* is a good candidate for a small garden feature or a patio tree. It is always a good habit to plant winter-flowering plants near entrances or other places one is likely to pass by in cool weather. The wonderfully fragrant flowers provide a surprise pleasure in late winter—especially for those of us who have short memories for flowering seasons. And then there's the miraculous presentation of chocolate aroma without chocolate calories. In my experience, specimens in cultivation are hesitant to set fruit, possibly because it is rare to have more than one single clone together. When it does, the small clusters can approach rose to nearly red in color.

Once relegated to collectors' gardens and seen mostly in older gardens of the U.S. West Coast and the United Kingdom, *Azara microphylla* is now increasingly available in more adventurous nurseries. The superb *A. m.* 'Variegata' is also available, though less so, with a smaller-growing, somewhat weeping habit, to about 15 ft. (4.5 m). Though the plant can appear somewhat stunted in the sun, the striking green and creamy white leaves stand out beautifully in any shady setting. To be saved for the coolest, coastal climates of the western United States, or all but the coldest areas of the United Kingdom.

Azara microphylla 'Variegata'

Azara petiolaris. South to central Chile in more mesic situations and extending into places with periodic to pronounced summer drought. Rounded tree to 25 ft. (7.5 m) with leaves on long petioles. Leaves are 2–2½ in. (5–6 cm) wide and long with a dull shine; evenly spaced, sharp dentations; and a more succulent texture than other species. Flowers are creamy yellow and held more between the leaves than in other species; the berries are particularly dark—violet to navy blue—and last through at least early winter.

Having grown *Azara petiolaris* from a number of sources and having found it a valuable garden subject, I considered myself familiar with the species—until I found myself in a canyon in southcentral Chile, where a superb high-elevation azara grows and keys nearly perfectly to *A. petiolaris*. Of course, plants in nature are variable, and the form we happened upon and now grow is, by my own definition, the best of all. Possibly the most exciting feature—other than the handsome roundness of the tree, the color of the deep violet autumnal fruit, and the fact of our having found it in nature—is its potential for great cold hardiness. Other than a stand of *Maytenus boaria* and a few

Austrocedrus chilensis, these were the alpine trees in the Biobio river area in the central Chilean Andes where 0°F (–18°C) is not unheard of, nor is wind-driven snow. In our own garden this as yet unnamed form flowered in four years and grew to about 8 ft. (2.5 m) in the same amount of time. The leaves turn an almost blue-green in the winter months, sometimes burnished red. The round shape together with the long petioles creates an appearance and movement reminiscent of a quaking aspen.

The plants in this northern habitat were growing in almost riparian fashion, though several specimens were quite at home in the grass and scrub on nearby hillsides. These canyons in central Chile, though possessing protected pockets of moisture-loving species, experience long summer drought and relatively low rainfall, often below 20 in. (50 cm). So many of these species are capable of enduring an impressive amount of dryness.

In general, *Azara petiolaris* deserves greater trial because of its overall garden-worthiness, and also its potential ability to withstand more drought than other *Azara* species.

BUT WAIT, THERE'S MORE. Other species, newer in my experience, seem worthy of growing, if for nothing more than that with such a small genus, one could have them all.

Azara alpina, which didn't impress me with its horticultural potential when viewed in the wild, has become a very graceful specimen in the garden and, though remaining shrubby through much of its life, has reached small tree status at about 10 ft. (3 m). Another west-of-the-Andes specimen that seems cold tolerant, as the name would imply, into at least the low teens (–10.5°C), *A. alpina* has exhibited drought tolerance—though with too little water it begins to resemble the wild plant of my first impressions.

As mentioned in the introduction to the genus, *Azara uruguayensis* is a plant with great potential where summers are hot and humid, though it is often found growing at some elevation, even nearing warm, cloud forest conditions, east of the Andean cordillera from northwestern Argentina and north. Gardens in areas such as the U.S. Southeast could benefit from its acceptance of cool, dry winters and plenty of heat and stickiness in the summer—the opposite of climatic regimes for most of the other species. I have made at least three attempts to collect seeds: so far none have been fruitful, either literally or figuratively, but the climbing was fun. Our examples of this impressive tree—unfortunately of unknown provenance—with large oval leaves and very small, subtending leaves, have so far been successful through at least one freeze of temperatures dropping into the upper teens (16 to 18°F, –9 to –8°C) with wind.

And finally, a brief mention of *Azara celastrina*, which is not included in the featured section only because of my own inability to definitively key it in the wild. We are now growing plants—which must be this species because they are not the others!—that have produced straight-trunked, rounded young trees with 1 in. (2.5 cm) rounded leaves tinted purple-blue and small axillary leaves. So far, in our garden, it is one of the more graceful species with flowers that appear from mid March through April. Though not as large and attractive as some of the other species, they are lightly fragrant and certainly very pretty amid the still purple-gray, winter-colored leaves. The bluish black fruit is possibly the most attractive feature, maturing in late summer through fall, hanging in large clusters that contrast nicely with the leaves. Although our plants have received plentiful garden moisture, their northern habitats indicate the possibility that this species may be among the most drought tolerant.

A few more years of observation in several gardens is needed for better evaluation of these three species—*Azara alpina*, *A. uruguayensis*, and *A. celastrina*. So try them, and let me know.

Banksia   Proteaceae

This large genus, comprising seventy-five or more proteaceous shrubs and small trees, is an important element of the Australian flora. All have upright inflorescences, somewhat resembling the bottlebrush flowers of *Callistemon*, and cone-like seed structures that make the genus easily recognizable, especially to the sunbirds that pollinate them. As with other members of the protea family, care should be taken with soils high in clay or organic matter and with phosphates used in fertilizers. And if that weren't enough, most resent high summer temperatures with humidity. Most species are too tender or otherwise fickle for inclusion here, but at least one (and a sidekick) cannot go without mention.

Banksia integrifolia (coast banksia). Variable large shrub to small tree found in southeastern Australia from coastal situations, indeed within salt spray, to high-altitude habitats. One of the more garden-tolerant species, reaching up to 50 ft. (15 m) in time with sparkly toothed leaves, deep green above and a most attractive reflective silver beneath. Particularly handsome when the plants are seen from underneath, they should be used over patios or with uplighting—any situation or device that enhances the view.

The flowers, again in cone-like structures, are set most often in autumn and winter but can be seen at any time in gardens along the immediate West Coast of North America. They are creamy yellow,

Banksia integrifolia

Banksia ericifolia

the exserted stamens looking like candles set among the branches, and fragrant with, to my nose, a hint of baking bread.

Banksia integrifolia shares a trait with many other species—that of a basal burl, a fire adaptation for plant recovery that, assuming the average garden is not prone to bush fires, serves the same purpose after a particularly hard winter. Plants that are generally frost hardy to between 16 and 18°F (–9 and –8°C) for short periods have resprouted handily after exposure to 12°F (–11°C).

Sun to very lightly dappled shade is best. Though tolerant of summer drought, regular irrigation in dry spots encourages faster growth. Easily grown in containers, plants can be pruned after heavy flowering to encourage bushy growth.

Propagation is by seeds extracted from the cone-like pods with some winter stratification helpful—slow "baking" in the oven helps open seedpods for easier extraction—or by cuttings from ripened current season's growth in autumn or winter, aided by bottom heat or mist.

The related *Banksia ericifolia*, widespread in southeastern Australia, contains several forms that can attain small tree size with proper pruning. The finely textured leaves, contrasted with the yellow-orange "cones," make you feel all tingly inside. Great fine texture for the small garden.

Brachychiton	bottletree	Sterculiaceae

Over thirty species of trees and shrubs from eastern and northern Australia to Papua New Guinea. In an exceedingly variable family (that includes the chocolate producers), this genus has the greatest sense of humor, with trunks of trees often quite succulent, sometimes creating nearly rounded spheres, and leaves that range from maple-like to lanceolate. The leaves are either evergreen or winter-deciduous and that usually because of drought rather than cold. They can be entire to palmate and are often green, infused with purple tints, appearing almost succulent. The flowers are carried in small, weeping cymes of fused petal-like structures; they are a light yellow or red that is attractive to birds—and humans. Though decidedly tender, with most species damaged below 20°F (–7°C), there is hardly a better group for planting in areas of drought or exceedingly high summer temperatures.

Brachychiton acerifolius (flame tree). Inhabiting forest edge situations from Queensland to New South Wales in Australia, and ranging from 17 ft. (5 m) in rocky situations to 80–100 ft. (25–30 m) in deep soil, this plant, from my northern hemisphere perspective, looks for all the world like *Acer macrophyllum* (bigleaf maple). The bright green, somewhat pinstriped young twigs (in all but the older trunks), along with the very maple-like leaves, could fool almost anyone—until the red, flame-like tubular flowers appear, sometimes while the plant is still winter- or otherwise drought-deciduous. The leaves measure from 5–7 in. (13–18 cm) and up to 10 in. (25 cm) across in vigorous growth and have five fairly sharp lobes.

Brachychiton acerifolius is at home in both moist garden situations and those experiencing drought at any time of the year, though in an extensive summer drought occasionally deep watering should be provided. Because of its somewhat succulent quality, it can be confined to surprisingly small areas of real estate, even surviving in containers for a great length of time, though 100 ft. (30 m) in height should not be expected there. A plant for warm climates, it is suitable for the mild parts of the Mediterranean, coastal southern California, and certainly its homeland in the milder areas of Australia. Outside the native habitat the species is nearly pest-free and again, certainly drought resistant. The biggest drawback is lack of frost tolerance: temperatures below 20°F (–7°C) or briefly into the upper teens (16 to 18°F, –9 to –8°C) would spell doom.

Propagation is easiest from seed, and stratification is usually not necessary. Cuttings have been successful in early to mid summer with careful use of mist and bottom heat.

Brachychiton acerifolius. Photo © Global Book Publishing Photo Library

Brachychiton populneus. Queensland to New South Wales. More popular outside its native Australia than *B. acerifolius*, *B. populneus* is a popular landscape subject in such areas as the U.S. Southwest and especially coastal southern California to the milder parts of the Oregon coast. Though growth has exceeded 60 ft. (18 m) in the wild, it is rare to see specimens over 35 ft. (10.5 m) in cultivation. The leaves are 2–5 in. (5–13 cm) in length and either single or three-lobed with five lobes possible in youth. They are glossy and deep green, often purple-tinted, and the single leaves are wide-based, quickly tapering to a sharp point. The leaflets are often irregular. The flowers are small and creamy yellow, very lightly fragrant, but otherwise insignificant.

The most striking feature is the thickened trunk, with bark that remains a succulent greenish color for many years. The tree becomes a nicely shaped tall pyramid as an adult. *Brachychiton populneus* has an even greater ability than *B. acerifolius* to be kept in small garden spaces, and the more confined the space, the larger the trunk can become in relation to the rest of the plant. Young plants are often used as insta-bonsai and can be kept in small pots for many years. Regardless of the situation and even in great drought, the leaves remain a healthy, shiny green, making this species all the more useful for dif-

Brachychiton populneus. Photo ©
Global Book Publishing Photo Library

ficult situations. Plants can withstand temporary inundation but can become stunted over time with lack of soil aeration. As with most plants, regular watering and deep soil provide the best situation if a tree form is desired and, under ideal conditions, over 3 ft. (1 m) of growth per year is possible.

Again this is not a broadleaved evergreen for northern climates. But nearly anywhere temperatures rarely drop below 18 to 20°F (–8 to –7°C) for more than a night, it is suitable. Plants have resprouted from the succulent trunk after periods of 10 to 12°F (–12 to –11°C) but remained shrubby for some time.

Callistemon	bottlebrush bush	Myrtaceae

Nearly all Australian, some venturing as far as New Caledonia or Southeast Asia (where they might likely be placed in another genus). There are about thirty species, related to both *Melaleuca* and *Leptospermum*, all having tough leathery lanceolate leaves and flowers attached directly to the stems with greatly exserted (read "long") stamens branched evenly around the entire stem, indeed very much like a bottlebrush.

Though the majority would be considered shrubs, including the most hardy of the genus, some grow to be tree-like or are easily manipulated into such, and a few of these are sufficiently frost hardy to be included here. As well, the following species are all surprisingly tolerant of extended drought though often found growing next to water in their native habitat.

All appreciate sun, especially for good flowering, and an occasional well-rounded fertilizer for luxuriant growth. Careful trimming back or thinning as well as removal of dead twiggy material helps avoid the leggy look associated with older specimens.

Mid to late summer cuttings have been most successful for propagation, with heat and mist or within a closed container. Seed, produced in abundance in tiny capsules, is best picked while just slightly green, dried in an envelope, and sown in early spring.

Callistemon citrinus (crimson bottlebrush). One of the most commonly used species in the genus, ubiquitous in warm desert communities, Mediterranean climates, and other warm temperate zones. The smallest forms grow to only 6–8 ft. (2–2.5 m) but most, especially with the removal of side branches, can easily obtain 20–25 ft. (6–7.5 m) in height after a number of years, the flaring and weeping branches clothed in narrow leaves up to 3 in. (8 cm) in length and ¼ (6 mm) to ½ in. (1.5 cm) in width which emerge with a silky, pinkish tint. The flowers are most often brilliantly red, sometimes pink or white;

Callistemon citrinus

each flower spike is about 1½–4 in. (4–10 cm) long. Most common in spring and summer, flowers can appear nearly year-round in milder places. *Callistemon citrinus* 'Superba' has prominent yellow anthers, giving a rather luxuriant appearance with the red of the flower.

Easy both in containers, beds with limited soil, and as street plantings where temperatures rarely reach 18°F (–8°C). Plants that are protected from the wind have taken 12 to 14°F (–11 to –10°C) if such a cold snap does not come too early or too late in the season. At temperatures of 5 to 10°F (–15 to –12°C), specimens have resprouted from the base, losing tree stature at least for a time.

Callistemon pallidus (lemon bottlebrush). Widely distributed in New South Wales, from Tasmania to Queensland in the north at higher altitudes. Smaller in stature than *C. citrinus*, an upright, few-branched, large shrub to small tree with quick growth to 9–12 ft. (2.7–3.5 m) by 6–8 ft. (2–2.5 m) in width. Easy to grow, the abundant foliage is often blue-green and the new growth replete with silky hairs. The flowers, also abundant, are fragrant, about 3 in. (8 cm) long and 1–2 in. (2.5–5 cm) wide, and range from cream to chartreuse to sometimes pink. The goldish brown seed capsules remain on older stems, an attractive feature that adds texture.

Castanopsis   Fagaceae

Over 100 species, all evergreen, are thought to exist. Numerous in central and eastern Asia, mostly in subtropical and warm temperate woodlands. Only one close relative exists in North America—*Chrysolepis*, occasionally included in the genus *Castanopsis* but currently listed separately in the nomenclature and, therefore, described separately here.

Easy in cultivation, all *Castanopsis* species are relatively fast-growing and tolerant of summer water as well as some drought. The tree forms have a flexible structure and root system, making them ideal for urban plantings. The upright, catkin-like flowers form in late spring into early summer and occasionally again in autumn; they sometimes occur in such abundance as to give the tree a halo when backlit. The only minor drawback that comes to mind is that of a very heavy floral fragrance or, as some would say, odor, that reminds one of . . . well, *Castanopsis*. Some do find it distasteful, but fortunately the aroma is short-lived and a small price to pay for the beauty of the tree.

Castanopsis cuspidata (Japanese chinkapin). Southern China and Japan. For those having fallen in love with *Chrysolepis* in the western United States, this plant is a much easier relative. A denizen of wet summer monsoon forests of Southeast Asia, it is well adapted to the various cooties associated with growth in heat and moisture. A somewhat larger tree, to 80 ft. (25 m), it is easy in cultivation, requiring little care except occasional irrigation in dry-summer places. As a garden specimen, it reaches 30–35 ft. (9–10.5 m) within five to eight years—eventually becoming substantially larger—with gently arching, upright branches, silver-gray bark, and glossy green leaves about 4 in. (10 cm) long and 1 in. (2.5 cm) or so wide, tapering to a long, narrow, drip-tipped point so common in plants from wet-summer places. Most beautiful are the undersides of the leaves that, although not as densely coated with golden indumentum as *Chrysolepis*, are nonetheless reflective and an almost brassy color. The leaves often curl somewhat upward on the sides, giving the tree a reflective quality, especially when light comes in from a low angle. The whole aspect of the tree, especially when young, is reminiscent of the common, subtropical *Ficus benjamina*.

Seemingly capable of growing in any soil as long as it is reasonably well drained, *Castanopsis cuspidata* performs equally well as a sun tree or an understory tree in medium shade. Though the species has a wide range, all in cultivation so far have taken short periods of –10°F (–23°C) with no damage and suffer leaf drop or twig damage only approaching –15°F (–26°C).

Castanopsis cuspidata. Photo © Global Book Publishing Photo Library

The striking *Castanopsis cuspidata* 'Variegata' has been available; a nice specimen can be seen at the JC Raulston Arboretum in Raleigh, North Carolina. This variegated form is slow-growing; probably only 15–20 ft. (4.5–6 m) can be expected in ten or fifteen years.

An added benefit is the relative ease of propagation: acorns, which often form at about five years of age, germinate quickly and, as with all oak relatives, should be planted as quickly as possible. Autumn and winter cuttings on current season's growth usually strike. When propagating from cuttings, however, excess callus tissue can occasionally form. This should be checked for, and at least partially removed, as it can inhibit root attachment.

Of the few species in cultivation, *Castanopsis cuspidata* is the best, possibly by default as few others have even been trialed. The genus seems promising, and more effort should be made to test other species for garden-worthiness.

Ceanothus   Rhamnaceae

About fifty species, almost entirely from the West Coast of North America, a couple having escaped to the Eastern Seaboard and into eastern Mexico. Although mostly a shrubby genus, a few reach tree size. In general, *Ceanothus* species prefer open situations with good light exposure and, except for the few species living away from the Mediterranean West Coast of North America, insist on scant summer irrigation and a lack of humidity coupled with heat. As well, those being cultivated along the immediate West Coast (within the reach of fog) or in places such as Great Britain (where summer temperatures never bake the ground, forcing the plants into dormancy) are more tolerant of summer water, having been seduced into believing they are living in perpetual early spring. In hot, interior places, or areas experiencing the dreaded heat-with-humidity, much more caution is necessary, with very little summer irrigation or irrigation only during the coolest weather.

Several species other than the eastern native *Ceanothus americanus* and its hybrids have been tried in the U.S. Southeast, with some success, usually with shelter from summer rains and the use of sand beds and the like.

Clearly best for Mediterranean climates, the evergreen species are almost no-brainers for the West Coast of the United States and, especially, southern England, where, despite summer rain, summer temperatures rarely warm the soil enough to activate the various fungi that accompany warm soil with moisture, a combination they are not accustomed to.

That said, propagation is pretty easy. Seed of various species usually collected in mid to late summer, given some stratification via the veggie-crisper method, and planted in late winter to early spring in mineral soil are usually successful. Cuttings are best in the cool season from mid autumn to mid winter, put briefly under mist until callused then quickly moved to cool drier conditions. Otherwise, place in a mineral substrate and cover so some general humidity is retained but little directly on the leaves. One quick method has been the removal of new shoots in early and mid spring with cuts made to include both the newest growth and just a nick of the previous season's growth. With warmth and mist they can be rooted quite quickly, showing roots in a week to ten days. But the narrow window of root to rot must be watched closely as the difference can be only a couple of days.

Ceanothus arboreus

Ceanothus arboreus (Catalina lilac). Endemic to Catalina Island off the coast of southern California, *C. arboreus* can be a large shrub to about 10 ft. (3 m), but also as high as 20–25 ft. (6–7.5 m) and definitely tree form. The leaves are relatively large, 2–4 in. (5–10 cm), and rounded with some teeth toward the tip. A pleasing matte green color above, they have a delightfully blue cast on the underside, sometimes in the form of a fine indumentum. The vigorous stems easily reach

4–5 in. (10–13 cm) in diameter, retaining an almost succulent green bark.

One of the most handsome *Ceanothus* species, it is also one of the most tender, succumbing, or at least being damaged, at temperatures around 13 to 14°F (–10.5 to –10°C) and during freezes of any length. We were pleasantly surprised in our garden, in the wake of a windy cold spell when temperatures dropped to below 20°F (–7°C), to find blackened leaves quickly give way to a bright new shiny set of leaves and normal flowering, as if nothing at all had happened.

Trained to single trunk or allowed to grow several, *Ceanothus arboreus* makes a wonderful foreground plant where it can be walked under or at least viewed from beneath, taking full advantage of the reflective leaf undersides. The flowers are rather large, in 3–4½ in. (8–12 cm) thyrses of silver-blue to a good lilac-blue, with a typical but strong *Ceanothus* fragrance reminiscent of grapes. Usually appearing in March or April, the flowers are sometimes thrown out sporadically all year long.

Ceanothus arboreus 'Trewithen Blue', a selection from the famous Trewithen Garden in Cornwall, has a strong, good blue flower and uniform growth rate. Plants in our garden reached 12–16 ft. (3.5–5 m) in five years.

As with all North American Pacific Coast ceanothus, good drainage and a gritty, if not sterile, soil are musts. In cool maritime climates, *Ceanothus arboreus* tolerates year-round water; in the warmer interior, water should be kept to winter only. Either way, plants given summer drought and lean soil, though slower growing, will not exhibit rank growth and will be longer lived. As with other western *Ceanothus* species, it is intolerant of summer moisture coupled with heat and humidity, thus limiting (or, in reality, eliminating) this plant for use in summer rainfall/humid climates.

One of the best attributes of *Ceanothus arboreus* is its usefulness as a small garden or patio tree. It reaches its maximum height quickly, is easily kept in check with light pruning, and is relatively long-lived for a ceanothus: ten to fifteen years or more is reasonable.

Ceanothus arboreus 'Trewithen Blue'. Photo by Michael A. Dirr

Ceanothus thyrsiflorus (blue blossom lilac, coast California lilac). One of the major components of the coastal chaparral along the southern Oregon and California coasts, certain forms in favored places creating a *Ceanothus* woodland. With its wide distribution and relative ease in cultivation, numerous cultivars and hybrids have been named. Found in both immediate coastal and inland situations, *C. thyrsiflorus* is able to handle inland heat as well as cool, coastal conditions and is one of the best of the western ceanothus for its ability to accept at least some summer irrigation, though not enough to make it a given

in places that combine heat and high summer humidity, such as the U.S. Southeast.

Though often seen clipped into hedges or maintained as a large shrub, the plant's best use is as a small tree, to 15 or even 20 ft. (4.5–6 m), trimmed up enough to expose the greenish bark and a view of the lighter undersides of the dark, shiny, glossy, green leaves, to ½ in. (1.5 cm). Substantial, deep sky-blue flower clusters of 2 in. (5 cm) or more usually adorn the plants in early to mid spring, though, in areas of cool summers and mildest winters, they do so year-round, at least sporadically, with a sharp peak in the spring.

In general, most forms of *Ceanothus thyrsiflorus* can withstand winter temperatures of 10 to 15°F (−12 to −9.5°C) for at least brief periods, though such temperatures with drying winds can burn the foliage. They have resprouted from 0 to −4°F (−18 to −20°C). *Ceanothus thyrsiflorus* 'Victoria' is quite common along the Pacific Coast of

Ceanothus thyrsiflorus

Ceanothus thyrsiflorus 'Victoria'.
Photo by Michael A. Dirr

Ceanothus 'Ray Hartman'. Photo by Bart O'Brien

North America and, though not quite as large growing as the species, can attain 10–12 ft. (3–3.5 m) in six years. Additional height can be encouraged by early trimming of lower, wide-spreading branches. This cultivar has sailed through temperatures reaching close to 0°F (–18°C) for at least brief periods. *Ceanothus thyrsiflorus* 'Snow Flurry', with slightly larger leaves than typical and clean, white flowers, can also attain a height of 20 ft. (6 m). It is slightly more frost sensitive than *C. t.* 'Victoria', punishing its gardener with brown leaves and possible twig damage below 10 to 15°F (–12 to –9.5°C), depending on wind exposure. *Ceanothus thyrsiflorus* 'Oregon Mist' is a 2004 introduction from Greg Shepherd and Paul Bonine of Xera Plants, selected from Coos County, Oregon; it sports fine-textured leaves of an attractive blue-green and light blue flowers, and grows to 15 ft. (4.5 m). *Ceanothus* 'Ray Hartman', a hybrid with *C. thyrsiflorus* undoubtedly as one of its parents, has long been in cultivation; it has been reliable under ordinary garden conditions, given at least some summer water along the West Coast of the United States. Quickly reaching a rounded form of 10–15 ft. (3–4.5 m), eventually even 20 ft. (6 m), with mid spring pink-hued buds opening to cheery blue flowers in clusters of 1½ in. (4 cm) or more.

IN A GENUS SO FULL of possibilities, it is unfortunate that so few become tree size. *Ceanothus papillosus* (wartleaf ceanothus), with rhytid (leathery) and rather viscous leaves—a clear parallel to the stickiness of Mediterranean *Cistus* species—grows in the California Coast Ranges and can easily exceed 18–20 ft. (5.5–6 m). Flowers are generally a good to almost purplish blue. It needs careful drainage and is a tad less frost hardy than some of the others, to 10 to 15°F (–12 to –9.5°C).

Another, *Ceanothus incanus* (coast whitethorn), has a picturesque

Ceanothus papillosus.
Photo by Michael A. Dirr

Ceanothus papillosus, flowers. Photo by Michael A. Dirr

shape and can also reach 15–20 ft. (4.5–6 m) with gray-green leaves, very pale beneath, and often nearly white bark contrasting with the twiggy branch growth. The flowers are white or creamy white as well. Uncommon but with some work can be a picturesque small tree.

With such a wonderful genus where adapted, these should, of course, be grown with many of the other shrub and ground cover species.

Cercocarpus	**mountain mahogany**	Rosaceae

Six or seven deciduous to evergreen shrubs and small trees from western North America south to central Mexico. Most at home in dry country from the Mediterranean chaparrals to Baja California, Mexico, California, and Oregon and associated with *Arctostaphylos*, *Ceanothus*, and sclerophyllic oaks (*Quercus*). Further inland the genus often becomes an upland denizen of rubble slopes or islands of damp areas in the mountains of the Great Basin to the Rockies. Some species live in broadleaved evergreen purgatory, being neither completely deciduous nor completely evergreen. The one species confirmable as truly evergreen, as well as easily available, is described below.

Cercocarpus ledifolius (desert mahogany). Interior western North America, often in sites just above the driest valleys of the Great Basin along with western juniper (*Juniperus occidentalis*) or piñon pine (*Pinus monophylla*). It is one of the first arborescent encounters where moisture is just plentiful to allow such, seemingly above 10 in. (25 cm) of precipitation or nearly so. Two striking features stand out: the first is olfactory and the second, structural. Often, in its desert habitat, where the aroma of sage or other harsh desert scrub is a familiar association, the sweet smell of vanilla foreshadows an encounter with *C. ledifolius*, as the leaves, either in warm weather or when crushed, exude a most refreshing fragrance. In addition, at maturity specimens are strikingly flat-topped and picturesque, conjuring images of the African savanna with their horizontal branches, which seem to invite browsing by the nearest giraffe.

A small tree—rarely over 25 ft. (7.5 m)—that, especially where browsing is prevalent, spends many a decade as a very dense, intricately branched shrub. The leaves are tiny—usually less than ½ in. (1.5 cm) and rarely over 1 in. (2.5 cm) in favored conditions—narrow and a very dark green, sometimes with a reflective backing. After the flowers—minute, typical of this branch of the rose family, and significant, really, only to the desert mahogany and its pollinators—come the masses of attractive seed heads, resembling those of clematis and particularly beautiful when backlit.

A superbly adaptable small tree in desert and interior climates, where trees of any type have difficulty getting established whether because of warm-season frost, wind, drought, or general pestilence. In cultivation the long, shrubby period can be shortened by encouraging apical growth and trimming lower branches to keep the bunnies away. One individual specimen at our second home in the Oregon desert—grown from seed and collected on the peaks of the Diablo mountains high above Christmas Valley in the middle of Oregon's Great Sandy Desert—is indeed reaching its picturesque best complete with beautifully flaking mahogany-colored bark in but ten years with good irrigation to push it a bit. In places such as Bend, Oregon, or Santa Fe, New Mexico, desert mahogany should be a mainstay in the landscape.

Cercocarpus ledifolius var. *intricatus*, found mostly in the eastern reaches of the species distribution, is a smaller, more intricately branched plant that might take a few years longer to reach tree size, but the small, usually under 1 in. (2.5 cm), and very narrow leaves and the tufted appearance of the branches make it a variety worth pursuing. This fine-textured plant has slightly rolled and sometimes upturned leaves that display their silvery undersides, harmonizing nicely with other silvery leaved, dryland shrubs.

Cold hardiness is another plus, not only to severe drought and all the aforementioned hazards but also to temperatures dipping below −30°F (−35°C), possibly even to −40°F (−40°C)—not bad for a broad-leaved evergreen, even if the leaves aren't really all that broad. Performs well in milder climates but suffers greatly in areas of high humidity or poor drainage.

Propagation from cuttings is possible, though it can often be difficult to find lengths of recent (late summer to late winter) past season's growth sufficient for use. Seed, however, is not difficult after some stratification and early spring sowing in mineral soil and bright conditions. Seed is often available from collectors' lists, and the occasional plant can be obtained from nurseries that specialize in plants native to the western United States.

A FEW SPECIES that are not necessarily reliably evergreen or fully tested—or for that matter readily available—are nevertheless interesting enough to mention here.

Cercocarpus montanus is one such species, mostly shrubby and deciduous but having western relatives that can become more tree-like and semi-evergreen to nearly complete evergreen. A close relative, *C. betuloides*, now widely accepted as *C. montanus* var. *glaber*, can form trees upwards of 10 ft. (3 m) with 2 in. (5.cm) leaves, heavily veined and somewhat silky. Possibly the most interesting form sur-

Cercocarpus montanus

rounding the Rogue Valley of southern Oregon and into the Siskiyou Mountains is *C. montanus* subsp. *macrourus*, forming a narrow, vase-shaped tree to 25 ft. (7.5 m) or even more with similar, rather birch-shaped leaves that can be 5–6 in. (13–15 cm) and semi-evergreen. Indeed a beautiful small tree, but a bit too deciduous some years to be included in the "official" list of broadleaved evergreens.

Cercocarpus montanus var. *traskiae*, a southern California endemic, can reach significant size as well, up to 20–25 ft. (6–7.5 m), with narrow, oval leaves, somewhat hairy, but dark green above and quite pale beneath. Seems frost hardy. Spends a significant amount of time as a relatively dense shrub, possibly attempting to avoid being browsed, but eventually can make a rather picturesque, small tree with any deciduousness being more drought related than because of winter cold.

Cercocarpus fothergilloides, native into remote areas of northeastern Mexico, is another small tree to about 25 ft. (7.5 m), with a deep green leaf, rather shiny above and a reflective silky pubescence beneath. Trials have indicated frost hardiness into the upper teens (16 to 18°F, –9 to –8°C) or the warmer parts of zone 8 (and indeed, it seems evergreen). Our 1991 collection has remained evergreen for us in our garden, producing exquisitely corrugated leaves in almost a perfect oval.

Chrysolepis	chinkapin	Fagaceae

Two or three species along the immediate West Coast of Oregon and California. (While some botanists maintain there is only one species in the genus, still others include *Chrysolepis* in *Castanopsis*, from which genus it differs mostly by having a particularly thorny receptacle that nearly encloses the acorn.) For its limited range, a variable plant—one of the reasons nobody seems to know just how many species there are. Ranging from a fairly small shrub under 6.5 ft. (2 m) in the Sierra Nevada of California and the Oregon Cascades to the southern Oregon Siskiyou Mountains and the Coast Ranges of northern California, to a large tree, reaching as high as 80–100 ft. (25–30 m)—there is even a specimen of *C. chrysophylla* recorded at 150 ft. (46 m)—in the most damp, sheltered sites.

Unfortunately, in areas of California and southern Oregon large populations have been decimated by diseases brought in through logging and road building, much as happened to the Lawson cypress (*Cupressus lawsoniana*). As well, the ridiculous habit of spraying herbicides and broadleaved evergreen defoliants to promote conifer growth has killed some of the largest stands along with numerous others species in these areas of some of the greatest diversity in North America.

Chrysolepis chrysophylla (golden chinkapin). The form varies from a rounded, dense pyramid to a tall, straight-trunked tree with an oval crown where mixed with other trees. To come upon this tree, or better yet a grove of them, in southern Oregon's Siskiyou country, is like finding buried treasure. Frequently found in association with other rare and wonderful delights of the region, this large tree can reach over 80 ft. (25 m) in cool, undisturbed situations; with its deep green, glossy leaves, often held up to reveal dazzling undersides coated with a golden powder, it is truly one of the most attractive evergreens in existence. The stems, branches, and trunks are a clean silver, eventually aging to a texture of shredded wheat, circling around the tree where conditions permit the trees to get large, mostly in the redwood belt. In the rare garden situation where the tree can be entirely happy, it is likely to remain under 30 ft. (9 m) for several decades.

In autumn, the fruit is formed among the leaves in clusters of chartreuse spines, revealing its relationship to the chestnut (*Castanea*). As with a few other plants in this work, it is a "look but can't have" species for most because of its habitat requirements—sterile soil and parched summers—and its limited tolerance for many gardens pathogens. It can be quite difficult in cultivation even in areas within its natural range and, as with other plants native to the Mediterranean West Coast of North America, it is intolerant of summer garden irrigation. *Chrysolepis chrysophylla*, much like *Arbutus menziesii* which comes from similar or even drier areas of the West, is not only unwilling to have a garden hose pointed in its direction but also seems able to predict a gardener's intention to merely approach the spigot, responding by dropping dead before the handle is even reached.

Chrysolepis chrysophylla,
Siskiyou Mountains, Oregon

That said—perhaps even overdramatized—this is indeed a plant only for severely Mediterranean climates with low humidity, cool nights, and a low probability of even a summer thunder sprinkle. In most situations sun is best, though woodland planting is fine, even possibly best in hot climes so as to avoid overheating the soil. It has been successful in native plantings along the Pacific Coast, especially where heat accumulation is low and where no organic amendment is used and ground is shaded from direct sun, again, avoiding soil warming. If Pacific madrone (*Arbutus menziesii*) is worth trying, and it is, well, why not golden chinkapin?

Frost hardiness, of course, varies a bit, coastal forms being hardy to close to 0°F (−18°C) and mountain forms being good to −10 to −20°F (−23 to −29°C), should they live until winter!

They are, as one might expect, nearly impossible from cuttings, though they have been successful in autumn using ripened wood and high hormone levels. Planted in autumn, the tiny edible "chestnuts" germinate easily over the winter if successfully extracted from the massive spines in which they form.

Chrysolepis chrysophylla, flowers.
Photo by Michael A. Dirr

| *Cinnamomum* | camphor | Lauraceae |

A large genus of over 250 species from eastern and southeastern Asia growing, most often, in mixed broadleaved evergreen forests—another genus in a splendid family of which so many genera are underrepresented in cultivation. The camphors are handsome and, for the most part, tall-growing trees, all evergreen and mostly natives of tropical or subtropical regions. Fortunately, a few species occur far enough north or high enough in altitude to warrant inclusion here.

The leaves of the genus are the most notable characteristic, usually pointing to a long, thin taper and displaying three prominent veins on their shiny surface. They are aromatic in all species. The flowers are typical lauraceous little cream-colored puffs, usually less than 2 mm across. En masse among the dark green leaves, they are appealing and, in some species, fragrant. The fruit is also small, under ⅓ in. (1 cm), and dark blue to blackish.

Although propagation varies a bit by species, most can be rooted in late summer through winter on ripened, previous season's wood. They require slightly higher hormone levels than average and appreciate bottom heat and mist.

The generic name, apparently derived from both Hebrew and Greek, is the ancient name for cinnamon, which, indeed, comes from the tropical species *Cinnamomum verum.*

Cinnamomum camphora. Widespread in warm temperate and subtropical Southeast Asia, from China, Japan, Korea, and Taiwan into Vietnam. Fast-growing, medium to large tree, reaching 90–100 ft. (27–30 m) with ample moisture. This species, widely planted throughout the warm temperate world, features dark gray, furrowed bark, and shiny, spring-green leaves, narrow, oval in shape to about 3 in. (8 cm), that always appear to have just emerged from a recent rain. In mature trees the leaves become more rounded with an abbreviated tip, almost like those of *Populus tremuloides* (quaking aspen), but remain just as shiny.

A most satisfactory tree for its quick growth, its tolerance of urban pollution and even periodic drought, and its acceptance of sun or shade, though because of its size, shade is eventually not an option. Certainly, the most widely available species. Trees planted in the latter half of the 1800s in the capitol grounds in Sacramento, California, and on several surrounding streets, have trunks that not only fill their 5 ft. (1.5 m) wide planting squares, but expand far beyond, supporting a height of 70–80 ft. (21–25 m). The Sacramento trees have been subjected, on occasion, to temperatures in the mid teens (14 to 16°F, –10 to –9°C), incurring frost damage that killed upper branches, but the plants have quickly recovered. In areas experiencing temperatures of 13 to 14°F (−10.5 to −10°C) on a regular basis, but rarely below, they can be grown as, essentially, perennials. The crown is replete with dormant buds, possibly as stooling or fire adaptation. In Happy Valley, Oregon, just east of Portland, plants in the wonderful private arboretum of Stan Lindstrom have frozen to the ground over the decades, each time growing 6 ft. (2 m) or more the following season.

Cinnamomum camphora makes a fine pot specimen; the somewhat succulent nature of its roots and wood allow it to dry to the point of appearing near death, only to revive quickly with water—a fortunate attribute discovered through personal experience. It can be repeatedly root pruned.

The clones available at this point are of unknown provenance; with such a large distribution in the wild as well as a great elevation range, it would be expected that strains more tolerant of cold are waiting to be found. One collection, now under observation in our garden, hails from over 11,000 ft. (3300 m) in southern China. After having had the luxury of becoming established without experiencing frost in the first few years of growth, our plants responded to a bout of windy 20°F (−7°C) with a little bit of discoloration on the tips of young growth. We await further testing at lower temperatures.

An allée of *Cinnamomum camphora*. Photo by Michael A. Dirr

Cinnamomum chekiangensis

Cinnamomum chekiangensis. Native of a small area of southcentral China near Chekiang and discovered in 1929. Although previously rare in cultivation, several collections have appeared in the last thirty years, the most notable by Cliff Parks of Camellia Forest Nursery in North Carolina. These specimens were obviously adapted to temperate climates—and fortunately awakened me to a beautiful species. The nursery's original plants, growing in a light woodland with some overstory protection, were damaged in the very long −8°F (−22°C) freeze in the late 1980s, but regenerated quickly and have not been damaged since by temperatures just below 0°F (−18°C). Examples in Vancouver, B.C., and Seattle, Washington, have survived temperatures a tad above 0°F (−18°C) with flying colors.

The 5½ × 1½ in. (14 × 4 cm) leaves taper gradually to an elegant drip-tipped point, often just a tiny bit off center, perhaps as if punched in the nose during childhood. In spring through mid summer, the new growth emerges a deep shrimp color, darkening toward red before turning a dark, shiny green. In the deepest shade the leaves emerge a lighter, almost chartreuse-green, aging to peach. For the first several years *Cinnamomum chekiangensis* grows quickly to 15–20 ft. (4.5–6 m) with a strong apical dominance and one or more central stems. Not as quick-growing as *C. camphora*: 3–4 ft. (about 1 m) per year is common while young. In garden situations, upward growth slows after six years or so, and the secondary branches begin spreading in exquisite layers, bedecked with gracefully hanging leaves on long petioles—though it should be noted that, in the wild, specimens of 50–60 ft. (15–18 m) and still growing have been recorded.

Tolerant of sunny conditions, the most graceful specimens always appear in dappled shade or with protection from hot afternoon sun, especially along the U.S. West Coast. Best planted in well-drained soil, and consistent water is a must. Anywhere moisture is available and winter temperatures seldom fall below 10°F (−12°C), *Cinnamomum chekiangensis* should be on the short list for the woodland garden. Fortunately, several nurseries have taken Camellia Forest's lead and are making it available.

Cinnamomum japonicum. Another widespread species from southern Japan across to East China and Korea, to Taiwan and the Ryukyus. Although it has been in cultivation for at least a century, it remains rare. Narrow in youth and a moderate grower to 30 ft. (9 m), with over 60 ft. (18 m) being reported in the wild, older trees, free of competition, broaden to a wide pyramid. The bark remains a pleasing green for several years before turning gray and furrowed.

As is typical with the genus, the leaves are narrow and slightly pendulant, 3½–4 in. (9 to 10 cm) long and 2–3 in. (5–8 cm) wide. They

emerge pinkish but quickly darken. The dense growth is amplified by the deep, almost black, green of the leaves. Tolerant of at least brief periods of drought, and apparently happy in as much sun as *Cinnamomum camphora*.

Specimens produced from seed by China's Nanjing Botanic Garden and distributed by Piroche Nursery of Vancouver, B.C., have proven to be tough, resilient, and handsome in form. Rated by Piroche as zone 7, they have certainly withstood temperatures near 0°F (−18°C) with no damage and might prove even hardier than *Cinnamomum chekiangensis*. These lowest temperatures might not work if the frost is of great duration (more than a couple of days), or accompanied by low humidity and drying winds. In areas where this is likely to happen on occasion, protection afforded by larger, tougher, sheltering evergreens will, if nothing else, avoid bark split from direct sun on the tender bark after a sudden temperature drop. Provenance should always be considered.

Cinnamomum japonicum 'Harlequin' is a variegated form introduced to us from Ted Stephens of Nurseries Caroliniana. Though we have not grown it for long, it appears vigorous and is most attractive, having nearly white margins and some splashing on its dark green leaves.

Cinnamomum japonicum. Photo © Global Book Publishing Photo Library

As with *Cinnamomum chekiangensis*, this species, once rare and obscure, is now frequently encountered at better garden centers along the U.S. West Coast and increasingly in the Southeast. Trials in the United Kingdom, at least in the south, have found it rewarding and not particularly in need of great summer heat. The yellowing that some other laurel family members experience in long, cold winters does not appear to be a problem. Several earlier introductions along the U.S. West Coast include specimens in southern California that have become multi-trunked, reaching 35 ft. (10.5 m) or more, and have been tolerant of drying winds and poor air quality. The size and shape makes *C. japonicum* a good, smaller tree candidate for street and courtyard planting, although it doesn't enjoy life in a container for any length of time.

CINNAMOMUM PORRECTUM, with tidy round leaves, 3 in. (8 cm) across and blue on the reverse, shows great potential, having triumphed through upper zone 7 winters in the U.S. Southeast. It reaches 25 ft. (7.5 m) in ten years.

Citrus   Rutaceae

Nearly twenty species of evergreen trees, mostly native to southern Asia but cultivated worldwide. Of the numerous species and cultivars grown, a few exhibit enough frost hardiness to be mentioned for use in temperate gardens. All possess shiny, deep green leaves and pleasant foliage scent with, of course, the added attraction of the blossoms. These alone are enough reasons to grow citrus trees, even in climates where they don't fruit reliably. Much effort has been made in recent years to bring the hardier species and hybrids into commerce. Many hybrids have been created, for example, with the deciduous *Poncirus trifoliata*, bringing its extraordinary cold hardiness into the mix. A few of these are listed at the end of the *Citrus* section.

In general *Citrus* species have a few necessities. In climates with intense summer heat, the protection of afternoon shade is a big help, along with regular watering where drought occurs. They are also great lovers of iron and fertile soil. Although all benefit from high summer heat to ensure fruit production, in climates prone to severe frost, allowing the plants winter shade can slow rank autumn growth, making the plants less prone to scorching and bark split during a cold event. In other words, plant them on the north side of the garage, and they might be a bit hardier.

For most species, propagation is quite easy with the newest, vigorous growth, taken in mid to late summer when the heat is high. The growth should be somewhat hardened but not mature and, under heat and mist, rooting can occur in as little as a week or two. Autumn and winter cuttings are possible, but cuttings are slow to produce callus tissue and roots.

Of those included here, many have been in cultivation so long or are derivatives of such a tangled web of hybrids that their origins or ancestry remain obscure—unless one were to have a handy, pocket DNA analyzer. The nomenclature used here reflects presently accepted usage.

Citrus ichangensis (Ichang lemon, Ichant papeda). From southern West China. A large shrub to very small tree that has garnered much attention in the West of late because of its great cold hardiness coupled with an attractive form. Approximately 10–15 ft. (3–4.5 m) tall with a rounded, somewhat flat-topped form, plants have small faintly lobed leaves with an attractive, expanded petiole that starts out to be nearly half the size of the leaf, the whole contraption being under 4 in. (10 cm) long. The bark is smooth, brownish green at the base with shiny green twigs and spines, as deadly as they are beautiful, emerging from the branches, thus making it a plant for less heavily trafficked areas. The white flowers in spring are smallish, around ¾ in. (2 cm) across but do carry the heady "orange blossom" fragrance so desired in the garden. The fruit that follows in mid to late autumn is thin-skinned, lemon-like, and small, only about 1½ in. (4 cm) by 3–4 in. (8–10 cm). Although acidic, it is flavorful and said to be edible out of hand, though the fruits produced in our garden have definitely induced a high pucker factor.

The tree's behavior varies as much with the amount of summer heat as with winter cold. Though rated cold hardy to 0 to –10°F (–18 to –23°C), that is only true where summers are hot and ripening of the wood has occurred. In cool coastal elevations, or higher, winter protection would be a benefit below 10 to 15°F (–12 to –9.5°C) and, as mentioned earlier, plants should be situated out of direct winter sun where temperatures are likely to plummet.

Citrus ichangensis. Photo by John Grimshaw

Citrus ×*meyeri* (Meyer lemon). South China, of probable hybrid origin (*C. limon* × *C. sinensis*). If one were to choose from the myriad of edible citrus offerings one of the hardier, most attractive and fragrant, the first choice would be the Meyer lemon. The compact, small tree barely achieves more than 15 ft. (4.5 m) and produces copious numbers of fruits with superior fragrance and taste. It adjusts well to the small patio space and pot culture and can be kept indefinitely with just an occasional root pruning and repotting. Those in cultivation seem to either be producing flowers or fruit almost all the time. Nearly full sun to dappled shade suits the plant just fine. If a specimen

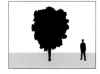

is to be kept in a pot anywhere where temperatures do not stay below freezing for long periods of time, it seems best to keep the plant on the porch or patio until (or if) cold weather arrives, bringing it inside only for short periods. The plants are then less likely to suffer from the shock of being put in bright light for the first time in spring and are much more likely to produce fruit. Although they will often "self" (produce fruit without a friend nearby), having more citrus specimens around, even if not a lemon, is beneficial, and an excuse to have more plants. As with most commercially produced citrus, zone 9 (or a cut off point at any prolonged temperatures under 20°F, –7°C) is regarded as the general limit of its tolerance, but *C. ×meyeri* is quite often found stepping outside those boundaries, lurking in protected courtyards and gardens well into zone 8, often surviving brief dips into the low to mid teens (13 to 16°F, –10.5 to –9°C) without noticeable damage.

CITRANGES ARE THE result of crosses between the edible *Citrus sinensis* (orange) and *Poncirus trifoliata* (trifoliate orange). Many have survived cold spells of 0°F (–18°C) if hardened for the fall. 'Morton' citrange, with 3–4 in. (8–10 cm) trifoliate, somewhat winged leaves and fruit a little over 3 in. (8 cm), has an appearance and flavor similar to that of a navel orange. Plants that came to us as citrumelos (*C. paradisi* × *P. trifoliata*) have made a 10–12 ft. (3–3.5 m) handsome, green-barked tree with 5 in. (13 cm) glossy leaves. Substantial whitish flowers spread their citrus fragrance throughout the garden in the spring. It has not set abundant fruit, yet its grapefruit parentage is obvious when the yellow, 5 in. (13 cm) spheres appear. It's no Ruby Red but edible nonetheless, and adding a little sugar never hurt anything. A very windy 20°F (–7°C) January freeze partially defoliated the windward branches, but the plants were fully flushed again by early spring.

We have tried dozens of cold hardy citrus crosses from such growers as Woodlanders Nursery in Aiken, South Carolina and Oregon Exotics in Williams, Oregon, and look forward to lots more experimentation in the future.

Comarostaphylis	summer holly	Ericaceae

Up to ten species of ericaceous shrubs to small trees, mostly from Mexico stretching into the chaparral of southern California. Each has small clusters of usually winter flowers, not dissimilar to *Arbutus*, followed by small red fruit. Some have young twigs that are quite shiny, with older bark orangish and shredding or sometimes in checkered patterns.

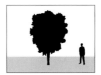

Comarostaphylis diversifolia. From the dry, winter-rainfall mountains of northern Baja California and southern California, including insular islands off the coast. This attractive small tree or large shrub might be thought of as a particularly drought tolerant strawberry tree that resembles a more hardened *Arbtutus unedo*. It usually remains under 15 ft. (4.5 m), with picturesque leaning trunks, orange shredded bark, and narrow, rounded to nearly lanceolate leaves, typically with finely toothed edges except in the mainland form, where the edges are somewhat cupped and toothless. The flowers are pale pink to nearly white in short racemes, followed by fractal, delicate orange-red fruit. Fine specimens can be seen at the Rancho Santa Ana Botanic Garden in Claremont, California, and the Carl S. English Jr. Botanical Gardens in Seattle.

Though certainly not as frost hardy as some forms of *Arbutus unedo*, plants in cultivation have withstood 12 to 15°F (−11 to −9.5°C) and are probably most useful where conditions are simply too dry for *Arbutus* to thrive. Sadly, this tree does not meet the "readily available" requirement, and obtaining plants may require advanced search engine techniques. Worth the effort.

Propagation is from late summer to early winter cuttings, where the take is rather low, or by seed stratified and planted in early spring.

Cornus	dogwood, cornel	Cornaceae

The family Cornaceae takes many forms worldwide, but the cornels are almost exclusively northern hemisphere, spread throughout, mostly in climates with abundant rainfall. Probably, of just over a zillion species in the genus, only a few can be considered evergreen. These add the same grace and texture to the garden as deciduous species but keep doing it year-round (though most will never be planted for beautiful twig contrast against the neighbor's snowbank). The evergreens tend to be most suited to milder woodland situations with ample moisture and little, if any, blowing snow. Many do add the gift of richly colored leaves and flowers that arrive later than the predominantly early to mid spring flowering of the deciduous species.

The evergreen species reproduce quite satisfactorily in private. However, if voyeuristic tendencies prevail, fairly well-ripened, current season's wood—in late summer through winter, with medium to slightly above medium hormone levels, and with the help of bottom heat—produces the desired results in two to four weeks or so. Seed is best stored cool and moist and sown in early spring. Still, for most, cuttings are the best way to ensure desired traits, as several evergreen species are indeed quite variable in flower size.

Comarostaphylis diversifolia in fruit

Cornus capitata. Photo by Michael A. Dirr

Cornus angustata (syns. *C. kousa* var. *angustata*, *C. capitata* subsp. *angustata*). Southern Asia. Related to the deciduous *C. kousa*, it has a denser habit and often reaches only 18–20 ft. (5.5–6 m) after several years. The leaves, shiny and attractive, retain their deep, lustrous green throughout the year. They can be narrow and pointed, 3½ in. (9 cm) long and ½–1 in. (1.5–2.5 cm) wide, or in some forms more rounded, 3 in. (8 cm) long and 2½ in. (6 cm) wide. The form and the ability to grow in either sun or shade are features more redeeming than the flowers, which tend to have relatively small, rather narrow bracts, the whole show being only about 3 in. (8 cm) across (though this is not something about which we think the species should feel self-conscious). The fruit is similar to but smaller than the following species, *C. capitata*, and less easily set.

Cornus angustata performs best on the U.S. West Coast with at least dappled shade and generous additions of organic compost to help retain soil moisture; it does require a bit more consistent moisture than *C. capitata* and is also a good deal hardier in general than that species, having taken temperatures to –12°F (–25°C) with only leaf discoloration. John Elsley selected the superb heavy-flowering *C. a.* Empress of China (= 'Elsbry').

Cornus capitata (evergreen dogwood). Himalayas into China, growing in mixed damp forests to rocky slopes, sometimes directly adjacent to running water. Rather large for a dogwood, from 25 ft. (7.5 m) in open, exposed situation or with less than ample water, and to 50 ft. (15 m) or more under the best conditions. This handsome tree tends to be apically dominant or have a single main trunk, developing a strong pyramidal form with graceful side branches and a very layered effect in time. The leaves, ranging 3–4½ in. (8–12 cm), are leathery and a medium green, somewhat lighter beneath, and the creamy, spring flowers, typical of bracted dogwoods, are small, appearing in late spring to mid summer in clusters about ⅓ in. (1 cm) across. However, the bracts (the petaloid leaves most people think of as the dogwood flower) are 1¼–1½ in. (3–4 cm) across to 2–3½ in. (5–9 cm) long and colored cream or white, sometimes blush pink. The fruit, an aggregate of cornels occasionally measuring 2 in. (5 cm), one of the larger of the genus, is fleshy and sweet and sometimes used in preserves or, being particularly big and splatty, as substitutes in water balloon fights.

Tolerant of full sun in all but the hottest, driest climates—think Phoenix, Arizona—its only requirement is a plentiful supply of water. It is graceful in the shade, but fewer flowers are produced and those, generally, toward the top of the plant. Though the species is tolerant of a fair amount of drought, garden seedlings seem to appear mostly in or near permanently damp or even wet ground. A vigorous, fast-growing species, it quickly indicates too much drought by leaf shed and production of fewer and smaller leaves. This shedding isn't to be confused with the spring leaf drop often associated with a push of new growth.

Because of its wide range, form and cold hardiness do vary greatly. Some have died to the ground permanently with temperatures of 17°F (–8°C), whereas others seem fine to 0°F (–18°C). A wild-collected form grown by Tony Avent of Plant Delights Nursery near Raleigh, North Carolina, exhibited complete hardiness to –2°F (–19°C) in his garden but split under a heavy coating of ice. Oh, well.

Cornus capitata 'Mountain Moon'.
Photo by Michael A. Dirr

Probably the most rewarding selection has come from Bhutan: *Cornus capitata* 'Mountain Moon', now widely available in the nursery trade, is a vigorous plant that reaches 22 ft. (7 m) in five years from a one-gallon container and then slows dramatically. The form is handsome and narrowly pyramidal, and the numerous flowers are something to behold, reaching well over 5–6 in. (13–15 cm). These flowers occur somewhat later than other forms, often not until late May and June in our garden, and last through the summer even with heat. They begin life a very pleasing, creamy chartreuse and age to nearly white. The abundant fruit is larger as well, sometimes 2½ in. (6 cm), a warm pink and also very attractive, hanging on late into winter if the birds don't find them too soon. The fruit is edible, possessing all the qualities of such fruits as *Arbutus unedo* or *Duchesnea indica* (Indian strawberry)—crunchy water with a little sugar added. More enterprising or stubborn people use them anyway.

Cornus capitata 'Yoko' has large reflexed bracts and has been successfully grown at the Mountain Horticulture Crops Research and Extension Center in the mountains of North Carolina.

Cornus omeiense (syn. *C. capitata* subsp. *emeiensis*; Mount Omei dogwood). Endemic to the middle slopes of Omei Shan, this species is one of a number of fabulous plants to have come from the slopes of this mountain, referred to in China as the "mother of gardens." This handsome small tree has, in cultivation, stayed under 18 ft. (5.5 m) in the form of a narrow, rather tightly branched pyramid with some weeping branchlets. Consistently, the deep green glossy leaves are tinged red; the new growth and winter color are often deep maroon, sometimes tinged shrimp-pink. Although Arthur Lee Jacobson (1996) described the color as "liver," I much prefer "kidney to pancreas pink."

Flowers are variable. My first experience with the plant was of a species bearing narrow, bracted flowers of only about ½ in. (4 cm) and not in the least impressive. Recently, however, forms have been selected with substantial, wide bracts, creating a "flower" of well over 3 in. (8

cm) and a pleasing creamy white, setting off beautifully the nearly maroon foliage. Clearly an understory tree, plants in full sun seem a little stunned, whereas in dappled or even fairly solid shade, they loosen up and are more graceful. Consistent water is also preferred.

Cornus omeiense Summer Passion (the trademark for seedling trees, not a clonal name), an introduction from Piroche Nursery in Vancouver, B.C., is a fine if rather loose tree, represented by numerous, individual clones, each possessing distinct characteristics, including flower size, plant shape, and even frost hardiness. The clone grown by Tom Ranney did not tolerate the winter lows (well below 0°F, –18°C) of his zone 6 location in the mountains of North Carolina, but he has hybridized his plant with *C. kousa* 'Satomi', a pink-flowered Chinese dogwood, with hopes of developing a pink- or red-bracted evergreen dogwood with greater frost hardiness. Although *C. omeiense* and *C. o.* Summer Passion are now considered by most to be included in *C. hongkongensis*, I am interested here in presenting the particulars of these forms; the final nomenclature with the new species designation will be sorted out later.

Cornus hongkongensis

CORNUS HONGKONGENSIS is another voluptuously evergreen species now being trialed in cooler climates than that of its steamy origin. So far a low of 18°F (–8°C) has not resulted in anything but some leaf loss. More experimenting will determine how widely it can be used, but certainly it is most worthy of trial in southern climes (or northern, for those gardening in Australia, New Zealand, or South Africa!), where excessive heat and humidity rule out standard dogwoods.

The Norman Hadden group are plants originating in England between the Chinese species *Cornus kousa* and *C. capitata*. These exhibit evergreen characteristics and the vigor of *C. capitata*, including tolerance of persistently wet ground, and suggest good potential for garden use in shade or sun. *Cornus* 'Porlock' is one of the most common with large white bracts—in my experience sometimes tinted pink—and a fast rate of growth to about 25 ft. (7.5 m). With temperatures dipping below 15 to 18°F (–9.5 to –8°C) it can be partially deciduous, but its *C. kousa* parentage renders it apparently frost hardy to below –8 to –10°F (–14 to –12°C).

Another dogwood worth pursuing is the Mexican species *Cornus floccosa* (syn. *C. disciflora* f. *floccosa*), a sort of New World *C. capitata*. An upland species, it grows among other typically Laurasian associates, where the mountain summer monsoons create mesic areas in the Mexican Sierra Madre ranges. The petaloid bracts are missing or nearly so, but the central aggregates are quite attractive and light up the branches with generous silvery pompoms. Though a lover of summer water, it resists periods of summer drought well and attains

Cornus 'Porlock'. Photo by Michael A. Dirr

15–20 ft. (4.5–6 m) in only three years. So far, it has retained its dark green leaves down to temperatures of –1°F (–18.5°C).

Crataegus	hawthorn	Rosaceae

A genus of up to 200 species, all of the temperate northern hemisphere. Nearly all are winter-deciduous, but the one described next is sufficiently evergreen to be included here.

Crataegus mexicana (syn. *C. pubescens* f. *stipulacea*; Mexican hawthorn). Central and northern Mexico. Found in the wild in both mixed woodland and as single specimens in the open. Although another variable plant, several forms in cultivation not only retain their leaves during the winter months but do so infused with purples and other mottled colors, depending on the amount of frost received. A pleasing small tree to about 25 ft. (7.5 m) in height with horizontal branches spreading easily to 15 ft. (4.5 m) across, sometimes suckering a bit. The bark is silvery and a good contrast to the very shiny and deep green leaves, which are large, to about 1 × 2 in. (2.5 × 5 cm), and slightly lobed. By the end of the year, especially with frost, they begin to take on purplish overtones, not shedding, however, until the new leaves begin to emerge in spring. Only a sharp frost below 15 to 18°F (–9.5 to –8°C) forces early leaf drop, the plant itself being hardy to at least 0 to –10°F (–18 to –23°C).

The flowers, appearing mid spring in clusters, are white and each a little under ¾ in. (2 cm) across, a bit larger than a typical crataegus, but with the same heavy, sweet scent. One of the nicest characteristics is the warm yellow fruit, more reminiscent of a small apple than

Crataegus mexicana. Photo by John Grimshaw

Crataegus ×lavallei. Photo by Michael A. Dirr

a hawthorn. They begin to color in early autumn and hang on till mid winter, when birds or people descend. The fruit is, in fact, a popular source for a tasty jelly throughout its native range. In climates where even light frosts occur through the winter and the leaves take on purple and bronze tones, the brightly colored fruit is a wonderful contrast.

It is tolerant of both sun and shade but most handsome and most productive with bright light and good air circulation. Though the species is more drought tolerant than many other hawthorns, maximum growth rate is supported by regular water, at least until the desired size is achieved. With its ease of cultivation and manageable size, it should be a far more common garden plant. The specimen in the Mexico section of the University of California Botanical Garden at Berkeley has been the subject of positive comment for many years.

One form used in the trade and commercially available, *Crataegus ×lavallei*—a hybrid of *C. mexicana* with *C. crus-galli*—is a delightful small tree often well over 30 ft. (9 m) with the same glossy aspect to the leaves, having the distinction of ½ in. (1.5 cm) orange-red fruit set among the deep green leaves. Young trees have nail-like thorns; old branches are virtually thornless. The trees are deciduous but often not until after the beginning of the new year in warmer zones. The hybrid is hardier, often rated to zone 6 or at least to –10°F (–23°C).

Propagation from mid summer cuttings, on new wood, is usually successful as is somewhat older wood toward the end of summer. Sucker growth can also be removed, often with roots or root initials already attached. It seems the most rewarding cuttings are those that have already rooted. Seed after cool dormancy is easy and, with the Mexican species, exhibit only moderate variability though seedlings do go through an extended period of shrubbiness before finding their inner tree.

Crinodendron   Elaeocarpaceae

Three or so species inhabiting Chile and Argentina and a bit north. Those who have visited the temperate rainforests of southern Chile and experienced the thousands of hanging maroon bells of *Crinodendron hookerianum* or spent time in the gardens of southwest Ireland, where similar, though maybe out of context, sights may be seen, can already appreciate the beauty of the genus. Crinodendrons range from large shrubs to significant trees, and all are evergreen. The leaves range from glossy and narrow, ¾ in. (2 cm) by 2½ in. (6 cm) or more, to more rounded and matte green. All are appreciative of even moisture and prefer cooler summer areas. In cool, coastal regions of the world, where temperatures seldom fall below 10°F (–12°C), crinodendrons thrive in full sun, but inland, where temperatures climb, afternoon shade is warranted, especially for *C. hookerianum*. The warmer the summer, especially when coupled with high humidity, the more care should be taken to ensure a relatively low-fertility soil.

Seed is easy enough with or without substantial cool stratification. Early spring sowing, again, in mineral soil is preferable. And cuttings strike readily under cool, damp conditions from hardened, current season's growth, preferably in autumn and winter.

Crinodendron hookerianum (Chilean lantern tree). From temperate rainforests of Chile. Small tree with a dense pyramidal shape especially when young, 10–30 ft. (3–9 m) or more in size, but only after a long time and under perfect conditions (such as mild, fog-shrouded slopes in Chile). The narrow leaves are somewhat curled downward and sharply pointed, measuring ½–¾ in. (1.5–2 cm) wide and 1½– 2 in. (4–5 cm) long. They are glossy green, reminiscent of polished leather. Adding to the graceful shape of the tree itself, the mid spring flowers—sometimes repeated in autumn—having formed small buds attached to rather long stems at the branch ends, suddenly expand to an exquisite carmine, aging to maroon. These lantern-shaped flowers, 1¼–1½ in. (3–4 cm), hang beneath the branchlets sometimes in great numbers, giving the appearance of a highly decorated Christmas tree. Occasionally in the spring a few buds form on new growth, and a smaller crop of flowers rewards the gardener in the summer.

Forms of the species have survived 12 to 15°F (–11 to –9.5°C) with no damage, and with bouts of 0 to 10°F (–18 to –12°C) have resprouted from the ground or from larger limbs, reaching flowering size again within two years. In areas prone to freezes below 15°F (–9.5°C), placement under larger evergreens and out of cold winter winds is an advantage. At least in areas with warm to hot summers, the south wall method is not advisable as they are prone to yellowing and spider mite if too stressed.

Crinodendron hookerianum.
Photo by John Grimshaw

Crinodendron patagua (lily-of-the-valley tree). A plant from the southern Andes of Chile and Argentina, it can be found as a large shrub to 6½–10 ft. (2–3 m) or a handsome, medium tree to 45–50 ft. (14–15 m), though in garden situations it takes its own sweet time to reach 20–25 ft. (6–7.5 m). Unlike *C. hookerianum*, the branch pattern is somewhat more irregular, especially in young trees, perhaps an adaptation against browsing. As an older plant it is round-crowned, with leaves somewhat lobed and rounded to about 1¼ in. (3 cm). The white flowers, appearing in June and July, are ¾–1¼ in. (2–3 cm); they are more open than the bell-shapes of *C. hookerianum* but just as numerous, and also hang gracefully beneath the branches. The sub-

Crinodendron patagua. Photo © Global Book Publishing Photo Library

sequent seedpods, looking to me like flattened red bell peppers, are an attention-grabbing feature; they form in late summer and hang on into winter, eventually opening to expose the tiny (1 mm) dingly-dangly black seeds. These can be collected when they transition from the dingly to the dangly and make for easy harvest.

Tolerant of sun or shade and a bit more tolerant of drought than *Crinodendron hookerianum*, *C. patagua* affords more opportunities for placement in the garden. But because of its variable native range, forms or selections with the hardiest provenance should be used where gardens are prone to frost. One plant at the University of Washington Arboretum in Seattle has withstood numerous winter assaults to below 10°F (–12°C) with no visible damage.

CRINODENDRON TUCUMANUM presents new possibilities. A species found in the narrow rainforest belt on the eastern flank of the Andean cordillera from Tucumán, Argentina, several hundred miles north, it grows at elevations high enough to receive not only significant frost but also significant heat and humidity during the summer. Having made several shimmies up the large (40 ft., 12 m, or more) trees, I found them to have shed their white, cup-shaped flowers and, apparently, every seed as well—creating incentive to return and climb again.

Daphniphyllum   Daphniphyllaceae

Fifteen species, though possibly many more, all from Southeast Asia, including Korea and Japan. Named after the genus *Daphne*, and indeed, resembling the form—albeit a very large daphne. Though at first glance most daphniphyllums appear to be oversized rhododendrons, one look at the minuscule flowers clears up any confusion. A polymorphic (really, really variable) genus: each mountain range seems to have its own form, many of which have been segregated into their own species. Essentially, all the plants within *Daphniphyllum* have handsome leaves, often glaucous especially on the undersides, with petioles and current year's stems infused with pink and red tones. The plants are either male or female with quite small flowers, usually under 1 mm, in attractive springtime clusters of purple-red (in the male) or green (in the female). The tiny flowers nestled among the exuberant growth create a pleasant contrast to the large scale of the leaves. More attractive, however, are the clusters of dusty blue fruits on the female plants—and yes sometimes on the males as well, but that's another story—of ⅓ in. (1 cm), often ready by late summer to early autumn. Daphniphyllums have a reputation for being somewhat allelopathic (i.e., they kill off their neighbors, or at least plants under the canopy). Although I have not found the problem to be significant, I do tend to clean up extra leaf debris, just in case.

Propagation is easiest from seed, preferably with a cool stratification; in my own case, this involves a complicated procedure of forgetting about the seeds on the plant, allowing them to ferment and fall into neighboring pots while being very careful not to weed that entire section of the greenhouse for weeks at a time, then being surprised that there are seedlings germinating when all attempts on the seed benches have failed. Cuttings can be rooted with some difficulty in late summer through autumn with warmth and mist or, at least, a closed atmosphere and a high hormone level. Callusing is slow, and many attempts have resulted in roots forming only after a year. Grafting of desired forms, such as the even-more-difficult-to-root variegated clones from Japan, is successful on seed stock—if you ever got around to collecting those wayward seedlings.

Daphniphyllum macropodum. Large shrub but more often a small tree to 35 ft. (10.5 m), though 50–60 ft. (15–18 m) examples exist in the wild. With wide ranging distribution from Japan to Korea and into China, the form can vary considerably. The showy leaves are 3–4 in. (8–10 cm) wide and 6–12 in. (15–30 cm) long, reaching their greatest size in shade. They have all the attributes of the genus and, in most forms, display the pink petioles and beautiful arrangements of stems toward the ends of each burst of growth, creating a bold whorl of leaves and a very tropical effect. The flowers are those described in the genus (and, really, something a mere 1 mm across, if that, ought not to be described too many times). The relatively fast rate of growth, up to 3 ft. (1 m) or more a year when young, provides a quick reward. Within ten years, a well-grown plant can easily reach 15–20 ft. (4.5–6 m) and a nearly equal spread if grown in the open. Some training when young can encourage a single trunk and an attractive umbrella shape, allowing a view from below and, of course, room for even more plants under the canopy.

Plants are not particularly tolerant of drought and appreciate regular summer water and a place in the garden that retains reasonable humidity. As with so many other plants, good drainage is preferred. Winter yellowing and the dropping of older leaves is reason to check the drainage. Tolerant of heat and even thriving in it as long as humidity is retained, they are successful in areas receiving winter chill as low as zone 6, to –10°F (–23°C) or lower with wind protection during freezing weather. In colder climates, provenance should be sought: with the great range of the genus, cold hardiness should be expected to vary as well. In western Oregon, performance is quite adequate in the sun, but the leaves are smaller and can occasionally become a bit puckered from sudden heat or dryness.

Daphniphyllum macropodum

Daphniphyllum teijsmannii.
Photo by Tony Avent

Daphniphyllum macropodum var. *humile* tends to be more of a shrub, to under 6 ft. (2 m) tall, with slightly smaller leaves that can be quite green and glossy or glaucous.

The less common *Daphniphyllum teijsmannii* is also a fine garden tree, having been tested cold hardy at least to the upper end of zone 7. This 10–15 ft. (3–4.5 m) creature is somewhat more open than *D. macropodum* and presents narrow (2 × 6 in., 5 × 15 cm., or longer) leaves that are both shiny and tinted rose, especially in the new growth.

For all *Daphniphyllum* species, many variegated sports, both splashed and margined, have been introduced in Japan and elsewhere, though few are named or easily available: most have to be grafted as cuttings, having proven exceedingly difficult, and most are awaiting names and stability before introduction. As well, there are selections from China that accentuate either blue foliage or red stems; but, again, most are unnamed and still rare in nurseries. One from Monrovia Nursery in Azusa, California, is available, but, again, without having been given a specific name.

Dendropanax   Araliaceae

A large genus of possibly eighty or more species, trees and shrubs, nearly all tropical or subtropical, spread throughout Southeast Asia and into the tropics of the New World. These and other members of the ivy-on-a-stick family are among the most graceful and textural plants to be found. All have the telltale sputnik-like terminal inflorescences, consisting of florets radiating from a single point and followed, eventually, by either bluish or black berries. The leaves can be simple or schefflera-like, a palmate leaf compound. Of all the *Dendropanax* species only one, proven frost hardy in temperate gardens, has made its way into commerce.

Dendropanax trifidus, from the wet subtropical to temperate forests of southern Japan, has proven its worthiness for many years, certainly in many gardens in its native Japan as well as in the U.S. Southeast and an occasional garden along the Pacific Coast of North America. A small tree to an eventual 12–15 ft. (3.5–4.5 m) with one or many trunks and a rounded crown. The leaves on juvenile plants often have two or three lobes (hence, the epithet); eventually, roughly upon the first flowering, plants produce a single long-petioled leaf, oval to nearly triangular, 4–6 in. (10–15 cm) long and a half to two-thirds as wide. Though older wood produces a grayish bark, the twigs and young growth maintain shiny green stems that, along with the bright shiny leaves, create an airy presence, countering the subtropical effect of the arrangement and presentation of the leaves such that the plant is never coarse.

Rated by many to zone 8, it is to be seen in a number of zone 7 climates, having withstood temperatures of 5 to 10°F (–15 to –12°C) with only a little leaf damage when somewhat protected overhead, and surviving slightly below 0°F (–18°C) with quick recovery in Raleigh, North Carolina. Appreciative of summer warmth, *Dendropanax trifidus* also desires summer dampness so, where summers are dry, adequate moisture must be provided, or growth can be yellowed or stunted. In the humid U.S. Southeast and similar climates, they are right at home in either full sun to moderate shade. In climates with lower humidity or those prone to heat and dryness, dappled shade, or at least afternoon shade, is recommended. This is an underused plant making a rebound. Old plants can be seen in such places as the JC Raulston Arboretum in North Carolina and the Elisabeth Miller Botanic Garden near Seattle, Washington.

Dendropanax trifidus. Photo by Michael A. Dirr

IT WOULD SEEM that any plant with the suffix "panax" is worthy of interest. Many aralia relatives have become available and have proven surprisingly frost hardy outside of the tropics, providing an array of textures from beautiful to bizarre. Some that can be coaxed to tree size are included briefly here.

The genus *Pseudopanax* has produced amazing plants in New Zealand, many having anti-browsing adaptations resulting in their juvenile leaves being strangely colored and sometimes tubed. *Pseudopanax ferox*, for instance, produces juvenile leaves that are linear, extremely narrow, and purply pink with tan brown mottlings and random bumps and bulges. Eventually producing compound leaves, *P. ferox* grows to over 20 ft. (6 m) as a very narrow, umbel-shaped tree that has proven frost hardy to 12 to 15°F (–11 to –9.5°C) or even a little colder out of the wind. *Pseudopanax crassifolius* is similar, possibly even slightly more frost hardy, having juvenile leaves as narrow as *P. ferox* and purply pink with a light midriff—but minus the warts. Other species such as *P. arboreus* make small trees as well to over 25 ft. (7.5 m) that, again, look very much like typical scheffleras with leaves often having deep purple tints. Tolerates cool climates but often succumbs to frost below 20°F (–7°C). Though relatively rare outside its native region, beautiful *P. arboreus* specimens can be found in such cool, mild climates as western Ireland and in the occasional garden on the U.S. West Coast. In general, *Pseudopanax* species respond best to cooler summers and maritime climates.

Other "panaxes" worthy of cultivation are in the genus *Metapanax*. With the aid of a pair of secateurs, *M. davidii* can attain small tree size, to 12 ft. (3.5 m) or so. This attractive, umbel-shaped adult with its two- or three-lobed leaflets of matte green has proven hardy to slightly below 0°F (–18°C) with protection but safely to 8 to 10°F (–14 to

Pseudopanax ferox

Pseudopanax crassifolius. Photo ©
Global Book Publishing Photo Library

Pseudopanax arboreus

−12°C). And in the genus *Nothopanax*, *N. delavayi* displays amazingly graceful and glossy marijuana-like (*Cannabis sativa*) leaves but is universally evergreen and legal. It is hardy to slightly below 0°F (−18°C) and, although mostly a multi-branched shrub, can be trained to a very attractive, upright small tree—to at least 10–12 ft. (3–3.5 m)—if provided fertile soil and consistent moisture.

Tetrapanax (rice paper plant), from Taiwan possibly through Southeast Asia but so long in cultivation that its exact original distribution is not known, is represented by *T. papyrifer*, a suckering shrub or small tree to 10 or even 20 ft. (3–6 m), fast-growing for the first few years then slowing after its first autumn flowering. The most distinctive feature is its gigantic leaves, which can be 3 ft. (1 m) or more across, providing a most tropical appearance. The plants are often single-stemmed and palm-like, but upon flowering or injury can produce multiple branches. Root disturbance—or even the mere fact of existing—can induce suckering, which is annoying to some but a source of joy to the nurseryman. One form, introduced from Japan through Ed Carmen of Carmen's Nursery in California and presented to us by plantsman Roger Warner, we named *T. p.* 'Steroidal Giant' for its larger pointed lobed leaves to over 5 ft. (1.5 m) as well as its larger stature overall. It has proven stem hardy to well below the roughly 15 to 20°F (−9.5 to −7°C) expected for the species but becomes deciduous at 8 to 10°F (−14 to −12°C). Where temperatures in general drop below 0°F (−18°C) for short periods, the plant can be grown as a perennial.

Though not a "panax," the genus *Fatsia*, another aralia group from Southeast Asia, is well worth mentioning along with its relatives. One of the most commonly used evergreen aralias in warm-temperate climates, *F. japonica* from Japan and possibly China, seems to be required decoration in front of most dentist offices in Portland, Oregon. Though most often planted as a shrub, it is one that will undoubtedly become too big for its space. A multi-stemmed shrub that can be thinned and lifted to 10–12 ft. (3–3.5 m) or more, it deserves inclusion as a no-nonsense yet texturally useful component of any courtyard where temperatures rarely fall below 15°F (−9.5°C). Desirous of summer water and at least afternoon shade in hot climates, the leaves can span 10 in. (25 cm) and are entire but deeply lobed. The flowers, produced in autumn, are in great white umbels, 10 in. (25 cm) tall or more, followed by fruit clusters 2–3 in. (5–8 cm) across of berries that are blackish purple through the winter and add even more texture to the plant. If a small, standard tree is desired, it is best to search in the local nursery for a single or few-trunked specimen. Plants that have been headed back can produce awkward branching and a less attractive trunk. *Fatsia japonica* has been crossed with *Hedera* to make an

Nothopanax delavayi

Tetrapanax papyrifer. Photo by John Grimshaw

Tetrapanax papyrifer 'Steroidal Giant', looming large in the border. Photo by Michael A. Dirr

Fatsia japonica 'Variegata'

Schefflera delavayi, goldish indumentum

Schefflera delavayi

Schefflera delavayi, foliage

attractive, clamoring hybrid ×*Fatshedera lizei*. Variegated selections of both are on the market. *Fatsia oligocarpella*, though slightly less frost hardy, is increasingly making its way into gardens; it can be differentiated by its very narrowly lobed leaves, appearing as delicate as snowflakes.

Members of another genus, *Schefflera*, though also lacking "panax" anywhere in the name, might be called the matrons of the family, possessing the archetypal palmate leaf associated with so many of the arborescent aralia. The fact that more and more species are proving frost hardy in temperate climates is a special thrill for lovers of bold foliage. Some, such as *S. digitata*, are on the verge of frost hardiness and widely grown; others are becoming better known. I first saw *S. delavayi* in a magical Cornwall garden where, even after a winter of heavy frost that had damaged the *Fatsia japonica* nearby, plants had produced 5 ft. (1.5 m) whorls of exquisitely serrated leaves covered with goldish indumentum. Love at first sight. Subsequent cultivation of the plant has proven frost hardiness to below 0°F (−18°C) with no apparent damage, so it might prove hardier even than the ubiquitous *Fatsia*. With pruning and time, 10 ft. (3 m) is possible. From Taiwan, *S. taiwaniana* produces 6–10 in. (15–25 cm) leaves ranging from bright, shiny green to those delicately covered with purplish hairs. Ooooh! Higher-elevation forms have also proven quite frost hardy, but they have not been subjected to temperatures to 0°F (−18°C) to my knowledge. *Schefflera taiwaniana* must be trained to achieve small tree status of 10 ft. (3 m) or more. Many other evergreen aralias await introduction to horticulture (or extraction from the realm of collectors).

Dendropanax trifidus and many other evergreen araliaceous plants respond well to propagation by cuttings from mostly ripened, current season's wood or even wood from the previous year if the bark still appears green. New wood cuttings, though sometimes successful, are prone to collapse. In the more difficult species, layering is often successful. Seeds, when available, should be fresh, preferably cool stratified with some moisture after cleaning; they will germinate immediately the following spring.

Schefflera taiwaniana

Drimys   Winteraceae

Thirty or more evergreen trees and shrubs from Australia to South America and extending into Mexico. They are primarily inhabitants of mesic (damp) places with never too much drought, though *Drimys winteri*, reaching into the northern range in Chile, experiences some drought. Most species have aromatic leaves, some very spicy, some more like peppers, and all species encountered so far have been attractive, though few are in widespread cultivation. More species should be attempted in temperate gardens.

If growing from seed, a cool damp stratification is helpful prior to sowing; an autumn sowing in cool soil also works. Cuttings can be taken as early as mid to late summer on mostly ripened growth, and success is frequent on previous season's growth taken through late winter, though rooting might take longer. Not unlike the genus *Daphniphyllum*, however, callusing might be quite successful, with the cuttings coming to resemble a paperweight as the callus continues to grow. Roots do eventually form with quite adequate attachment.

Drimys lanceolata (mountain pepper). Southeastern Australia including Tasmania. Though mostly thought of as a shrub, older garden specimens, or those encouraged into tree shape by removal of lower branches, can make fine small trees for the garden, growing relatively fast to 6–8 ft. (2–2.5 m), eventually to 12–15 ft. (3.5–4.5 m). Its handsome, narrow pyramidal shape with leaves, under ½ in. (1.5 cm) wide by 2–3 in. (5–8 cm) long and a shining dark green, coupled with deep red stems, makes mountain pepper attractive both up close and from a distance. The flowers, somewhat small for the genus, are only 2 mm wide and white in color, appearing in clusters. Both the leaves and fruit (like peppercorns) can be used as pepper substitutes, and a small dose of leaves actually makes a fine addition to a salad.

Inhabiting higher elevations with cool summer temperatures and occasional hard frost and snow in winter, *Drimys lanceolata*, in its higher-elevation forms, exhibits hardiness to about 10°F (–12°C), with the least amount of damage if grown in full sun. They are at their best with regular summer water and, although resilient to some drought, are much happier with abundant moisture as long as they are not actually sitting in it. Also tolerant of hot weather in areas where nights are cool but not thrilled by regions with hot, humid summers.

A wonderful complement or color echo to gardens with maroon foliage, and a perfect vertical accent where an exclamation point is required rather than a towering tree.

Drimys lanceolata. Photo by Michael A. Dirr

Drimys winteri (canelo, Winter's bark). An Andean plant of Chile and western Argentina, it varies from a small shrub to a large tree, over 65 ft. (20 m), depending mostly on moisture availability or elevation. The leaves are roughly 2–2½ in. (5–6 cm) wide and 8 in. (20 cm) long, very shiny above and glaucous beneath—very much so in some forms. In prime habitat on damp west-facing slopes in central and southern Chile, they reach their peak. There they are compact yet slender trees, often making a column to well over 60 ft. (18 m) but only 10 ft. (3 m) across. In central Chile's Altos de Lircay National

Reserve and surrounding areas, *D. winteri* is especially narrow with some specimens remaining under 10 ft. (3 m) in width while ascending to over 50 ft. (15 m) in height.

The thickly petalled, star-like white flowers are about 1¼ in. (3 cm) across and hang off the ends of the branches in numerous, fragrant clusters in early to mid spring, with an occasional autumnal afterthought. The purple-aging-to-black fruits that form in late summer and autumn also add interest and, with luck, more plants. Climbing through the incredibly diverse forests of central Chile, so rich in broadleaved evergreens, a stand of *Drimys winteri* is a beacon. Thick-textured leaves shine from a great distance, their undersides reflecting to the ground what little light is available.

Though subject to seasonal drought in their habitats, adequate moisture is appreciated in the garden. Happy in shade, they are equally happy if their lives begin in the sun, though rather more compact for not having to reach for the light.

Speaking of plants that look like rhododendrons and aren't, young plants of *Drimys winteri* in the garden can be so confused until a closer look is taken. The leaves have a more succulent texture, and the flowers appear to resemble much more the genus *Illicium*.

The somewhat more diminutive *Drimys winteri* var. *chilensis* seldom exceeds 25 ft. (7.5 m), with 10–15 ft. (3–4.5 m) being most usual, and is a very dense grower with leaves that are also smaller and somewhat more compact. The numerous, nearly white flowers combine beautifully with the particularly silvery undersides of the leaves. The flowers have from twenty to forty flowers per umbrel, topping the fewer than half that number in the species as a whole. This variety is increasingly common in horticulture.

There is also an exquisite dwarf form from higher elevations, *Drimys winteri* var. *andina*, though the separation of varieties is fluid. Remaining under 3–5 ft. (1–1.5 m) and, therefore, too small to be truly included here—it is too wonderful to ignore completely, as it retains the flower size and leaf color of *D. winteri* var. *chilensis* in miniature. Possibly one could train it into a very, very small, knee-high tree.

It should be said that the more one observes the genus *Drimys* in nature, specifically *D. winteri*, throughout its range in Chile, the more one is likely to doubt exacting, presently accepted subspecies and/or varieties. One comfort is that the forms discussed here have been in cultivation for some time and, though perhaps taxonomically questionable, maintain their characteristics as garden plants.

Cold hardiness varies, of course, with provenance. As one would expect, the shrubbier forms from higher elevations have withstood the coldest temperatures, with the taller plants at lower elevations and farther to the north being the most sensitive to frost. Of the largest

Drimys winteri. Photo by John Grimshaw

Drimys winteri var. *andina.*
Photo by Michael A. Dirr

forms, the beautiful aforementioned columnar form from the mountains near Vilches, Chile, has withstood 13 to 16°F (−10.5 to −9°C) with little damage save a few frostbitten leaf tips and would likely stand short periods of temperatures even lower, providing absence of drying wind. Another as yet unnamed form occasionally encountered along the U.S. West Coast was introduced years ago by the Saratoga Horticultural Research Foundation. This elegantly weeping tree seems to be injured by temperatures below 15 to 18°F (−9.5 to −8°C). *Drimys winteri* var. *chilensis*, at least in the forms I have observed, has withstood temperatures of about 10°F (−12°C) in exposed situations and brief dips below if protected from wind and with some overhead shelter. Plants have recovered from below 0°F (−18°C). None are particularly fond of the hottest, driest climates or, for that matter, anywhere away from Mediterranean or cool, coastal conditions.

Elaeocarpus	blueberry tree	Elaeocarpaceae

New Zealand, Australia, north into Asia. Over sixty evergreen trees and shrubs, at least twelve of which have great potential for warm temperate gardens. The entire genus possesses attractive leaves, often with a rich green sheen. The leaves are usually long and narrow, though of variable size, either entire or gracefully toothed, and appear at the ends of layered branches, giving a very elegant, tufted appearance to the entire plant. The exception, however, is with some New Zealand species. As the New Zealanders can do divarication like no one else, species of *Elaeocarpus* there can be wiry-stemmed and have tiny, toothed leaves that no large ostrich relative in its right mind would attempt to eat.

The fragrant spring flowers, frilly lanterns of pink or white, emerge from the leaf clusters in long, graceful racemes. Blueberry trees get their name from the attractive, rough, ⅓ in. (1 cm) fruit, often black, purple, or indeed blue. Potential for pie-making unknown.

All species come from wet forested habitats, with a few in scrub communities experiencing a bit more drought. All prefer consistent summer moisture in the garden. Though all can tolerate some drought, prolonged dry spells can stress plants beyond recovery. Like so many others, they require well-drained soil. All seem satisfied in full sun, though most begin their natural lives as an understory plant, and also seem quite happy in, at least, dappled shade, often achieving a somewhat more delicate structure there. A common assumption with many New Zealand plants (*Elaeocarpus hookerianus*, for one) is that with divaricating form and small leaves, they are drought tolerant. In many cases, however, it is a browsing adaptation and not one for drought, so appearances can be deceiving.

Thy neighbor's coveted specimen can be acquired, though not as easily as some of the broadleaved evergreens, usually in late summer and autumn on ripened wood of current season's growth (permission having, of course, been sought and received!). Cuttings are sometimes slow to root, and many batches will not achieve fifty percent.

Elaeocarpus decipiens. East Asia. A variable small tree, 20–35 ft. (6–10.5 m) in height, occasionally reaching 60 ft. (18 m) or above with great age. The form is narrow and upright, showing the graceful branch pattern typical of the genus; leaves are 4–6 in. (10–15 cm) in length and roughly 1½ in. (4 cm) wide, with an almost puckered pattern above. As spring arrives, the tree sheds some of the previous season's leaves while new growth emerges. The old leaves turn to shades of deep red and orange, while the new growth emerges bronzy and deep green. The flowers are white, and the fruit a deep, almost cobalt, blue. This species appears to be somewhat more drought tolerant than most and tolerates more sun exposure.

On the West Coast of North America, *Elaeocarpus decipiens* has been in common cultivation only since about 1995. An unnamed form imported from Nanjing, China, by Piroche Nursery in Vancouver, B.C., is now the most frequently encountered (and keys most likely to *E. sylvestris*); thus far, it has been decidedly more frost hardy than the type. These have achieved 20 ft. (6 m) in height, have had no noticeable frost damage in the low to mid teens (13 to 16°F, –10.5 to –9°C), and have survived near 0°F (–18°C) in Vancouver with minimal damage, though an event in the upper teens (16 to 18°F, –9 to –8°C) with strong freezing winds caused significant leaf burn. *Elaeocarpus sylvestris* appears related, ahem, and has also popped up of late; it seems to be a somewhat larger-growing plant with larger leaves. More observation is needed before the distinctions become entirely clear.

Elaeocarpus decipiens

Elaeocarpus dentatus. New Zealand. Medium to large tree, 50–65 ft. (15–20 m) tall, spending many years as a small tree under 20 ft. (6 m). The leaves are 3–4 in. (8–10 cm) long, narrow and toothed with a very leathery texture above and a downy texture beneath. The racemes of flowers hang gracefully downward to about 4 in. (10 cm) and are particularly fringed. The fruit is lavender-purple. The most striking or outstanding feature is the reflective, felty undersides of the leaves with their zigzag margins. The plant in our garden lights up a space in an area of dappled shade that would otherwise be drab. Alas, it is not the hardiest elaeocarpus to extremely low temperatures. With forms thus far experienced, temperatures below 18 to 20°F (–8 to –7°C) can tatter the leaves, and plants can be killed to the ground in the low teens (13 to 14°F, –10.5 to –10°C).

For those who love, enjoy, need, and crave divarication—legal in most states—*Elaeocarpus hookerianus* is a smaller species that reaches tree size only after many years spent as a thickly divaricated shrub with tiny purplish gray leaves, finally loosening up a bit but maintaining its dense appearance. Picture the opening scene of *Jurassic Park*, the movie, only instead of dinosaurs, large, hungry ostrich-relatives are running as fast as they can toward your plant, where, upon arrival, they are disappointed, unable to get their beaks around the wiry stems and tiny foliage. This characteristic is not only useful against thundering hordes of giant birds, should such occur in your garden but also (because wonderful forms have evolved to defend against these creatures) accounts for some of the most attractive architectural forms available. The colors of plummy purples and even browns and blacks, though seen elsewhere in the world, can easily be outdone by New Zealand plants. *Elaeocarpus hookerianus* has a particularly wonderful texture as a young plant, with its tightly knitted branches and densely conical shape. Very slow to attain tree size, it can remain a well-defined garden specimen for years. It might be at its best as a very small tree and 10–15 ft. (3–4.5 m). Frost hardiness has ranged from 12 to 15°F (–11 to –9.5°C) with little or no damage, but records have 10°F (–12°C) leading to loss of the plant.

Elaeocarpus japonicus. A delicate species from Japan, where it occurs in warm, humid forest situations. Plants can reach over 30 ft. (9 m) but achieve this height quite slowly in cultivation. Forms in cultivation here from southern Japan have one to several upright trunks with attractive spreading branches; these have reached about 15 ft. (4.5 m) in height by 8 ft. (2.5 m) across in a little under five years, slowing considerably thereafter. They have a shiny green leaf, 2–4 in. (5–10 cm) long, with overtones of coppery red in both the new growth and in older leaves and a graceful, narrow shape, exhibiting the typical drip tip of plants from warm, wet climates. Absolute cold hardiness is as yet unknown, but temperatures of 16°F (–9°C) nearly defoliated our Portland plants, although growth was quick to resume in the spring. Dappled shade with adequate summer water seems to please. Planting this species in conjunction with *Trochodendron aralioides* and evergreen members of the family Araliaceae has created a very lush look in our garden.

Embothrium	Chilean firebush	Proteaceae

Up to eight recognized species of trees and shrubs. Part of a large, mostly southern hemisphere family, this is one of the relatively few genera in South America but one of the most spectacular. Its members share the dislike, peculiar to their family, of phosphorous fertilizers and are really not too fond of potassium either. Their proteoid roots do, however, have the ability to fix nitrogen. This—combined with the fact that much of the family, including *Embothrium*, grows on very old and/or sterile mineral soils—suggests that fertilizing should probably be kept to a minimum.

Species occasionally grow in a mixed forest along with *Araucaria araucana*, *Nothofagus* and *Eucryphia* species, and other choice Chilean woodlanders. Even though some plants are also found growing on what appear to be hot, rocky slopes, all these plants share one trait of climate: that of preferring a cool maritime influence or sufficient elevation to ensure that the soil never reaches great warmth, to much more than about 60°F (15.5°C). As with so many broadleaved evergreens (and much of the family Proteaceae), exposure to warm soils with moisture can lead to quick fungal attack and death. They will forever be solely suited to either Mediterranean climates, with little summer moisture availability, or relatively cool coastal climes. Anywhere they are tried, the adage often used for clematis applies: faces in the sun, feet in the shade. Cultivation on a gentle north slope and use of mulches, ground covers, and shrubs to cool the soil can be helpful.

Pollinated by hummingbirds, *Embothrium* is part of a well-adapted flora that also includes *Fuchsia*, *Escallonia*, tubular-flowered *Lobelia*, and scads of additional taxa producing red and orange tubular flowers. It is truly a sight to see *E. coccineum* in its habitat, surrounded by other hummingbird-adapted plants, all with their showy flowers creating a hummingbird heaven.

While *Embothrium coccineum* is the lone inclusion here as the hardiest to frost and by far the most popular and available in cultivation, others are well worth pursuing, especially in very mild climates.

Embothrium coccineum (Chilean flame tree). A species inhabiting high slopes of the Andes from central Argentina and Chile south to the Magellanic region, reaching sea level there. Although nearly all forms are evergreen, a few in the south will lose their leaves in cold weather. The leaves are lanceolate in some forms, nearly rounded in others, and a very dark green. The flowers occur in late spring to early summer and often turn the entire plant an eye-crossing crimson to lipstick orange. They are produced in both terminal and axillary clusters and, individually, have four somewhat twisted petals, fused to form a tube with the style extending outside—a perfect fit for a hummingbird chin. Occasional rebloom occurs in autumn.

In cultivation in the United Kingdom and along the immediate West Coast of North America, many trees now exceed 30–40 ft. (9–12 m). Numerous forms exist: the jury is still out on the number of rec-

Embothrium coccineum

ognized subspecies. *Embothrium coccineum* var. *lanceolatum* from the south is a stout, rather narrow plant with good flowering habits and a proven degree of cold hardiness, having survived temperatures near 0°F (–18°C) with no damage and resprouting vigorously after bouts of –10°F (–23°C). *Embothrium coccineum* 'Norquinco Valley' was selected for these same characteristics and its particularly bright, scarlet flowers. *Embothrium coccineum* 'Inca Flame' is somewhat more rounded in form with more rounded leaves as well, and a vibrant, orangey red flower. It is also rhizomatous, forming a thicket in time, a fact suggesting that they are easily propagated from root cuttings, especially in winter and spring. Current season's late summer through autumn growth seems to work well with a minimum of bottom heat.

A fabulous plant for the garden in accommodating climates, but, where excess summer heat might be a problem, the following techniques to keep the ground cooler—watering only during cool weather, keeping the soil rather mineral (i.e., little organic compost), providing some afternoon shade or ensuring ground cover—can increase the chances for success.

On the lower slopes of Aconcagua in western Argentina there exists a rather low-growing, yellow-flowered form. Many of us have paid homage to this plant, and cuttings were finally taken and successfully rooted (mine came in the mail!). Fingers crossed, the plant will succeed in the garden.

Eriobotrya	loquat	Rosaceae

An east Asian genus of a dozen species of trees and shrubs, most with a pleasing umbrella shape and large leathery leaves, some with attractive felt. Flowering in winter to early spring with fleshy fruit following in autumn, all seem to be equally happy in blazing sun to about half shade, the main difference being an airy or more graceful form with at least afternoon shade especially in hot summer places.

Propagation is easy from seeds (nearly 6 mm) produced singly in the tasty fruits. Cool stratification helps but is not necessary. Cuttings are not a great challenge either, with success common from late summer through winter on newly ripened to ripened, current season's wood.

Eriobotrya deflexa (bronze loquat). China and Taiwan. Small broad-crowned tree, to about 35 ft. (10.5 m), with 10 in. (25 cm) long, narrow leaves, pleasingly toothed and red-tinted, with brown indumentum on both the leaves and the stems. Flowers are far showier than those of *E. japonica*. Used occasionally in the South and extensively in warmer, coastal areas of the United States, this is one of the most

Eriobotrya deflexa

attractive loquats where it can be grown and makes a fine houseplant or conservatory tree. Try as we might to show otherwise, we have found this to be frost hardy only to about 20°F (−7°C) or briefly a bit below. Plants were severely damaged here by a December freeze of 18°F (−8°C). The 1 in. (2.5 cm) fruit is attractive, covered with rusty pubescence, giving the appearance of a small kiwi, but is not frequently observed on the West Coast of North America.

Eriobotrya japonica (common loquat). Southeast Asia but so common in cultivation that the exact range is difficult to know. Large shrub to small tree to 30 ft. (9 m) with a broad form, sometimes becoming wider than high. The leaves are oval and pointed, from 8 in. (20 cm) to nearly 16½ in. (42 cm) by 5½ in. (14 cm) in shade, with shiny, attractive, leathery ridging and often pleasing pubescence of creamy golden brown beneath. The tree's spreading, vase shape com-

Eriobotrya japonica. Photo by Michael A. Dirr

bined with the large leaves clustered near the ends of the stems creates a tropical presence and a wonderful contrast when used in front of fine textures. An adaptable species, it responds well to generous garden water, growing in excess of 3 ft. (1 m) a season, but tolerates a surprising amount of drought, though slower growing. Plants grown in a courtyard or any small space can, in the autumn, late winter, or early spring, bring us into close contact with the small clusters of white flowers, each about ⅓ in. (1 cm), with their sweet scent hinting of baby powder. Most often grown for their fruit, large-seeded with a tangy, sweet, orange-yellow flesh, which appears in late summer to late autumn, depending on the amount of summer heat.

Hardy into the warmer areas of zone 7, plants are generally completely undamaged above 15°F (−9.5°C), not showing significant leaf damage at short periods as low as 10°F (−12°C). Because the plants flower in winter, the same temperatures can destroy new buds, thus a significant cold spell might nix the chances of fruit. As well, in cooler coastal or short-season areas, fruit does not always ripen.

Some intrepid gardeners are succeeding in protected areas of zone 6, where temperatures often fall below 0°F (−18°C), by plastering the plant against a south wall and sometimes using winter protection. In these colder zones it is certainly worth the extra effort, as few broad-leaved evergreens of such a large and attractive leaf can be found.

One of the numerous available cultivars, *Eriobotrya japonica* 'Christmas', is becoming popular in the Gulf Coast states. It seems to flower and set fruit more reliably, consistently shrugging off winter cold snaps that "deflowered" other cultivars.

A plant received from the Shanghai Botanical Garden as *Eriobotrya cavaleriei* has thrived and sailed through 8°F (−14°C) in North Carolina at Juniper Level Botanic Garden, where, after eight years, it was 7 ft. (2.1 m) tall with a typical umbrella form. This specimen produces 8–10 in. (20–25 cm) long leaves, glossy above with a particularly thick indumentum on the underside; as well, the new growth is fur-covered and an eye-catching reddish bronze in color. Definitely deserving of further observation.

Eucalyptus   Myrtaceae

A large genus of over 500 species, including small shrubs to stately trees, often aromatic, many producing very attractive foliage and bark, native throughout Australia with some extending northward into Malaysia and the Philippines. Some species from south Australia are contenders for the largest trees in the world, winning or losing the contest with *Sequoia sempervirens* (coastal redwood) from the West Coast of North America, depending on which hopeful has had its topmost branches knocked out in the most recent storm. *Eucalyptus* species inhabit a wide range of soils and climates from cool, high-elevation swampy places to sterile, desert scrub.

If misplanted they can seem strangely out of place in "foreign lands," but wherever there is desperate need for fuel wood, or of vegetation to stabilize soil or serve as windbreaks, eucalypts have been a boon. Our purposes here are more about entertainment and ornamental value than practicality, but it would be hard to find a better or quicker screen than a number of these species. Whether in a native grove or in one's own garden, the silver tones and graceful shapes of eucalyptus foliage, the clean, spicy fragrances, and the movement in a breeze of both leaf and branch create a presence like no other plant group. The light dappled shade created by most species is just enough to cut the glare in hot climates, and in our Portland garden, for example, understory plantings, often of shrubs and perennials that prefer full sun, perform very well, even better in most circumstances, for having the harshest of summer glare taken away. Brightly colored bark in so many patterns and hues along with the reflective foliage of most species cool a hot summer day and warm the winter by their mere presence outside the window.

Though many are adapted to surprisingly swampy conditions, many will also be found to be invaluable for use in the harshest of urban settings as street and parking lot trees, even in places thought too temperate. Exceptions are the most alpine species, such as *Eucalyptus pauciflora* and its subspecies, which suffer with too much drought. Most indeed tolerate a wide range of soils in cultivation, with some resenting heavy clay, especially in hot climates where alkalinity could be a problem and yellow from chlorosis might occur. Hardly a more amiable plant exists for a wide range of purposes, from very quick, if temporary container plants (the smaller mallees or lignotubered species are best) to quick screens and pollarded plants where that new apartment building has just been built on the property line and must be hidden quickly. The shapes and sizes vary greatly from fast-growing, tall, and narrow to wide-spreading, short, and stout. Though some species have stunningly beautiful flowers—yellows, oranges, reds, and pinks—most of those adapted to cooler climes, as with so many other plants, are whitish to cream and under ½ in. (1.5 cm). Many produce abundant nectar or honey and a pleasing fragrance. The variety of fragrances, whether foliar or floral, can provide endless entertainment, from the fruity aromas of *E. nitens* and *E. glaucescens* to the spicy peppermint of *E. coccifera*, to the pungent *E. gunnii* and *E. neglecta*, which smell of something to seek out while suffering a bad cold.

The limiting factor here (as there is not room for 500 species)—

aside from suitability to cultivation in general and attractiveness to the human eye—is their adaptability to cold winter temperatures. In recent years much practical research has been undertaken on cold hardiness in areas outside their native habitat in order to extend the range of their cultivation and availability for gardeners. The findings come in both scientifically plotted data and somewhat hopeful fixations as to their potential hardiness. Those of us living in climates where freezes occur even occasionally dwell on cold hardiness at least as much as on the ornamental advantages. And there is no exception to that here. Of all the species available for discussion, at least thirty are both reasonably frost hardy into zone 8 or even 7 and in general cultivation. Chosen from among those thirty, the species included here are those I feel possess the best combination of frost hardiness and reasonable size for most gardens and esthetics.

Multiple factors contribute to a species' potential for success. Several species are described as quite cold hardy but often have a wide range, both geographic and elevational. Provenance is especially crucial as *Eucalyptus* species are not generally easy from vegetative propagation; seed is the primary source. Therefore, collections from colder habitats (i.e., high elevations or cold air drainages within their native ranges) are preferred, in addition to cultivated strains from areas that have experienced low temperatures or other adverse conditions. As well (as with all plants), forms vary, and seed should be collected from plants with attractive features.

Some eucalypts are mallees, many-branched plants with a special feature by which a basal burl or lignotuber possessing dormant buds forms at the base of the plant (we should all be so lucky), an attribute generally understood to be a fire adaptation. In particularly fire-prone areas, numerous species also have these buds just under the outer layer of bark allowing them to resprout quickly after a fire. This feature comes in handy with freezes as well, so a plant rated to 5°F (–15°C) might well survive –10°F (–23°C) resprouting quickly from the main stem or trunk in the spring. Standing as good examples are the many *Eucalyptus globulus* specimens that, after the 1991 Oakland, California, fire (again in common with redwoods), resprouted from the main stems although the side branches were killed. For the first couple of years they resembled very tall Italian cypress (*Cupressus sempervirens*), until the scaffolding once again formed. Many mallees rely mostly on their basal burls and are more likely to simply resprout from the base after such a disaster. In cultivation they are sometimes coppiced purposely every year or two and used as perennials that retain their often very attractive, juvenile foliage. The ability to regenerate quickly is a trait that growers of cut foliage look for and appreciate.

In general, for those wishing to grow *Eucalyptus* species in the colder areas of their potential, many tricks of the trade exist. Aside from selecting for good provenance, a situation out of cold, dry wind, the protection of a south wall, and the application of a heavy autumn mulch are all useful techniques. Planting against walls can be a bit tricky, however, as most species tend to lean away from any shade or nearby objects, even if not in the shade. Another sleight-of-hand used when attempting to ensure survival in a colder winter is withholding water late in the summer. Observations indicate that, for almost any of the species, hardening off induced by drought in late summer into autumn seems to allow more frost tolerance, up to ten degrees more in Fahrenheit (approximately six degrees more Celsius). Plants grown "hard," with minimal garden irrigation seem, in general, a bit longer lived though somewhat slower growing.

If dieback does occur during the winter, it is best to wait until spring is well underway, even until new growth is seen either along the stems or at the base, before cutting back. Once the dead material is removed, allow all the sprouts to grow: they will do so vigorously, essentially creating a large dense shrub. Often the second spring is the time to begin thinning the new trunks into the desired number, choosing the strongest among them.

When choosing and planting a new addition to a eucalyptus collection, it is best to find the youngest plant possible in a given-sized container, difficult as it is to resist a big plant in a small pot. The roots of eucalypts circle easily in containers and are difficult to unravel without injuring the plant. Root-bound plants, though they often establish quickly enough, are subject to falling once any size has been attained. Though supposedly knowing better, I have been guilty in my own garden of planting for instant effect and, indeed, with the first rain and wind of the following fall, have suddenly acquired ample material for holiday decorations. If these trees do begin to lean or fall, it is possible to reestablish them by cutting to the ground in the spring, allowing the plant to reestablish a top while growing a more stable root system. However, it is better not to try this technique at all.

Be aware when choosing a plant that many are quite fast-growing, often stretching out 10 ft. (3 m) or more a season for the first few years. Be particularly wary if the species' size or frost hardiness is unknown, as a towering plant might become firewood by the first winter. Renowned British plantsman W. J. Bean, upon observing a planting of *Eucalyptus globulus* in a climate too cold, noticed a dead, two-year-old tree of up to 60 ft. (18 m) and dubbed it "the world's largest annual" (Bean and Clarke 1991)—an apt description and one to avoid in one's own garden.

Eucalypts, outside of their native Australia and surrounds, have generally been pest- and disease-free though, as one would expect, cooties eventually find them. In southern California, at least two insects have become pests, shredding the leaves and disfiguring the trees. It has so far not been a big problem elsewhere. Aphids (greenfly) can distort young growth of plants anywhere, but the problem is easily controlled by a mild soap solution or even a squirt with the hose. Mildew can be nuisance to young plants in enclosed environments so, even when young, as much air circulation as possible is best.

Although success with cuttings, especially from juvenile wood, is increasing, it is a long way from being standard practice, and grafting of select forms is rare. Therefore, seed is still the way to go. Even with its inherent variability, germination is usually quite fast (under a week) if seed is previously stratified for a month or so in cool conditions, though sown any time of year, it eventually sprouts. If producing one's own seed, just a few seedpods not only store the seed in dry capsules for years but also produce enough to forest the entire planet. Eucalyptus are not prudes so, when collecting seeds where other species are present, be aware that hybrids are likely to occur. Pricking out of young seedlings should be done within a few weeks of germination and, as stated earlier, young plants should not be left in containers for any great length of time, as growth is rapid.

Eucalyptus archeri (alpine cider gum). Tasmania, in areas of year-round, high rainfall in sterile, stony ground to permanently swampy soil. Mallee or small, single-trunked tree from under 10 ft. (3 m) in high elevations or windswept places to 35–40 ft. (10.5–12 m) at the lowest elevations in habitat or particularly happy garden situations. Attractive, bluish gray newer stems and leaves, the round, opposite, juvenile leaves, 2–3 in. (5–8 cm), becoming more oval and alternate in adulthood and sometimes a bit more of an olive-green. The bark, in patches of smooth cream and tan turning to nearly white, can also be pale green and pink. The flowers are white to cream in three-flowered umbrels, each about ⅓ in. (1 cm) to ½ in. (1.5 cm) in diameter. Although usually spring-flowering in habitat, plants along the West Coast of North America often flower in late autumn and winter as well.

Eucalyptus archeri has a significant elevation range in its native Tasmania, growing in relatively low elevations up to 4000 ft. (1200 m) or more on the tablelands of the central plateau, where it inhabits cold, swampy conditions and is often buried by snow for several months. That said, even the harshest areas of Australia aren't as extreme as one might assume, and temperatures below 0°F (–18°C), even in the colder, mountainous areas, are rare. Plants from the highest elevations, however, have survived –4°F (–20°C) with no damage. Others, from low elevations, have frozen to the ground at 14 to 15°F (–10 to

Eucalyptus archeri. Photo by John Grimshaw

9.5°C). Either way, it is an attractive species and does not quickly outgrow its space in a small garden.

The blue-tinted leaves catch the light, seeming to cool the garden in the summer and suggest warmth in the winter. The shade cast is light, and plants requiring full, or nearly full, sun seem to thrive under them. Despite its boggy habitat, this species seems to tolerate significant drought, though it would be unsuitable in areas of unirrigated desert. In our garden, *Eucalyptus archeri* eclipsed 20 ft. (6 m) in about three years with a straight narrow trunk and bark gleaming white. It then began to round out into a very pleasing broad oval with a much slower growth rate.

Eucalyptus cinerea (argyle apple, mealy stringybark). From New South Wales in Victoria, in grassy country, often in clay soils but inhabiting a wide range of substrates. One of the more common species in cultivation in warm climates and one of the most striking. The juvenile leaves, about 3 in. (8 cm), are round and perfoliate or nearly so, while the adult leaves are broader but still quite compact. The young leaves and branches are covered with mealy white powder; the older branches and trunk, with persistent, red, fibrous bark.

The flowers, appearing in mid spring, are about ⅓ in. (1 cm) across, white and sometimes tinted pink in the center, and held neatly above the plane created by the clasping leaves. Branches bearing flowers or seedpods are both used frequently in floral arrangements, and the leaves themselves are high in essential oils, making their decorative use as cut foliage an olfactory as well as a visual experience. After wandering in the garden, cup of coffee in hand, I can attest to the flavor-adding qualities of the flower stamens, having bumped into the tree and been showered. The flavor enhancement is not to be recommended!

This species is more commonly used in frostier areas of Australia, simply as utility trees, than it is abroad. In the western United States, plants are often found in the culinary herb sections of nurseries and are, therefore, seen growing from many an inappropriate place in the garden, having undoubtedly surprised the owner with their size and rapid growth. Given adequate space, bright light, and at least decent drainage, *Eucalyptus cinerea* grows into a picturesque medium tree to 50 ft. (15 m) or more with age, but more like 20–25 ft. (6–7.5 m) in several years, becoming nearly equal in height and spread.

As with many eucs, the quick growth rate can lead to lankiness in its first few years, as will cultivation in or near shade. *Eucalyptus cinerea* might need a bit of discipline to ensure a shapely mature specimen and occasional thinning so the beautiful bark can be seen in contrast with the pale leaves. Can be stooled to maintain juvenile growth.

Eucalyptus cinerea. Photo © Global Book Publishing Photo Library

Although one of the more frost hardy species, plants with poor provenance can succumb below about 15°F (–9.5°C) for any length of time, so in colder areas, seed should be sought from chillier climes. These have been found to tolerate 5 to 10°F (–15 to –12°C) briefly with no visible damage and have been known to resprout from 10°F (–12°C). Propagation, as with others, is best from seed.

Eucalyptus coccifera (Tasmanian snow gum). Tasmania, from low-elevation mixed forests to higher elevations, both in well-drained and permanently wet soils. A well-behaved large shrub to small tree, to around 35 ft. (10.5 m). Young growth is upright, occasionally many-branched in cold climates but, either way, spreads to a rounder, broad oval shape. The small, rounded, juvenile leaves are alternate and a deep matte green or grayish, with adult leaves becoming broadly elliptic to nearly rounded, about 2½–4 in. (6–10 cm), and a deeper, attractive green. The bark peels in pleasing jigsaw-puzzle patches, often emerging a creamy yellow or pink, aging to pale gray. The flowers number about a half-dozen in small clusters in mid to late spring; they too are a pleasant creamy white with a noticeable honey scent in abundance. They are profuse enough to be quite attractive.

Another very adaptable plant, growing at a wide elevation range, from somewhat rocky, sterile soil to swampy, peat-rich soil. Though *Eucalyptus coccifera* is said to grow only rarely above 35 ft. (10.5 m) in habitat, plants in Portland, Oregon, have achieved nearly 30 ft. (9 m) in four years, thereafter quickly decreasing in growth rate and becoming broader. It is proving an example of yet another *Eucalyptus* species that, when pulled from its cool habitat and taken to one with higher summer temperatures and a longer frost-free season, experiences accelerated growth rate in parts of the western United States.

Experience has shown that it is not quite as drought tolerant as other species; though often surviving extended periods of summer drought, it begins to look ratty, losing lower branches and leaves. Because of the quick rate of growth, it has been used, along with other species, as a pulp tree in parts of the western United States and even in areas a bit too cold for its permanent cultivation. After an unusual freeze or being cut back, *Eucalyptus coccifera* also can resprout quickly from the base. The seed or plants from good provenance have taken 0 to 5°F (–18 to –15°C) with little damage and as low as –10°F (–23°C) with vigorous resprouting from the base.

It is a very pleasant experience on a warm summer day, preferably with a breeze, to stand in a grove of this eucalyptus, with the leaves rustling and a distinct scent of peppermint in the air.

Eucalyptus coccifera

Eucalyptus crenulata (silver gum, Buxton gum). From the cooler, wetter reaches of Victoria, Australia, most in one very localized area northeast of Melbourne, growing in wet sites, often as an understory tree of *E. ovata*. A small tree with a narrow form, spreading to pyramidal, it reaches an eventual 35 ft. (10.5 m) but often stays under 20 ft. (6 m) in the open. *Eucalyptus crenulata* is a rather unusual eucalypt for its true-blue to purple-blue foliage color and relatively small leaves, which are undulate, somewhat powdery, often covered with a bit of a bloom, and densely held against the branches. Both juvenile and adult leaves are under 2 in. (5 cm) and arrow-shaped, and their crinkled margins make them appear even smaller.

The bark is smooth and silver-gray, shedding into patches of cream and tan but persisting on older wood. *Eucalyptus crenulata* flowers at a relatively young age. Sometimes by the end of the second year, cream to white blossoms appear that, though only ⅓ in. (1 cm) across, are profuse and held pleasingly amid the leaves—their light fragrance masked by that of the highly aromatic leaves. For those of us who grew up in western North America, the fragrance is reminiscent of sagebrush (*Artemisia tridentata*), a desert plant inhabiting millions of acres of arid uplands. *Eucalyptus crenulata*, however, not only tolerates both water and drought but also has the somewhat unusual willingness to grow in at least dappled shade, doing so without growing away from nearby shade as if frightened by the merest thought of the dark.

Eucalyptus crenulata grows quickly when young, which does make it prone to branch breakage or random leaning, so careful pruning to balance the plant and, if possible, a little drought administered toward the end of each growing season will help keep it in check.

As it inhabits cool but not cold areas in nature, it is not the absolute cold hardiest species but seems unharmed by short periods of 10 to 15°F (–12 to –9.5°C) with many records of 8 to 10°F (–14 to –12°C) showing little damage. Has resprouted from –4°F (–20°C). Propagate from seed.

Eucalyptus glaucescens (tingiringi gum). This species from southeastern Australia makes a large shrub, under 15 ft. (4.5 m) in some forms, to a large handsome tree of over 130 ft. (40 m). Upright in youth, becoming tall, oval in time. This very quickly growing tree has the outstanding feature, in youth, of having both bark and rounded leaves coated with a chalky blue indumentum. Though beautiful as adult specimens, the juvenile form is the more outstanding presence. *Eucalyptus glaucescens* responds well to periodic stooling, allowing it to be grown where a large specimen cannot be accommodated. Regardless of size or shape, the stunning silver-blue juvenile foliage makes

Eucalyptus glaucescens. Photo by John Grimshaw

it a good candidate for such. The adult plant, while retaining the blue cast to its newer stems, transforms into a more open form with narrow leaves hanging gracefully from older branches. If allowed to grow into adulthood, the leaves become much longer, 4–6 in. (10–15 cm), and a shiny olive-green, complementing the mint-green and cream patches of the bark and the open branch structure. The flowers, indeed cream-colored, stand out nicely against the darker foliage and often occur at the very end of summer through fall; in warm climates, they can occur sporadically any time.

With a significant elevation range in its native habitat, frost hardiness has been an issue with some clones. Those with higher-elevation provenances have been unaffected by 15°F (–9.5°C), though most have been cut to the ground below 8 to 10°F (–14 to –12°C), thus saving the trouble of pollarding. Tolerant of average garden conditions as well as drought, this is the species that seems to specifically benefit from the withholding of water late in the summer.

Eucalyptus gunnii (cider gum). Tasmania. Tree to 80 ft. (25 m), related to *E. archeri*, with a tall, narrow form in youth becoming a very broad oval in time (seemingly about three months): a specimen in favorable climates reaches 20–25 ft. (6–7.5 m) in three to five years, after which the growth rate slows greatly. The juvenile leaves of 2½–4 in. (6–10 cm) have the perfoliate (stem-encircling) form of many a florist's eucalyptus. A pleasing silver-green, this plant is commonly cut back hard every year to keep the juvenile form. After, usually, less than two to three years, if left alone, the adult leaves become gray-green and "somewhat crenulate, emarginate, elliptic, ovate or broadly lanceolate, acuminate or apiculate" (to quote the Royal Horticultural Society's *Index of Garden Plants*). If this description fails to conjure up a precise image, they are long, narrow, somewhat curved leaves with a sharp point. The white flowers can be as large as ¾ in. (2 cm) and rather frilly; they are in clusters of three, often flowering in late autumn. This is another plant that makes a vigorous, handsome garden specimen quickly, and the shades of blue-gray, sometimes with maroon overtones, add a great deal, either as contrast in the garden or, in Mediterranean style borders, with such plants as *Melianthus major* and *Rosa glauca*.

Provenance, again, is important, as many seed sources, especially in North America, have come from somewhat tender populations. Numerous specimens have taken 0 to 5°F (–18 to –15°C) with little or no leaf damage; others have been cut to the ground at 15 to 18°F (–9.5 to –8°C). Seed strains have proven to be reliable. Again, it is important to make sure seed or plants have come from parents at high elevation in the wild or from parents having withstood the coldest temperatures possible, if the intended site is a garden prone to hard frost. Among the most frost resistant and solidly cold hardy forms is *Eucalyptus gunnii* subsp. *divaricata*. It is only slightly slower growing than the type but with a reliable, silvery pink hue to the leaves. Several references refer to the higher-elevation forms of *E. gunnii* as being greener, but, so far, all provenances reported to be *E. gunnii* subsp. *divaricata* have been quite beautifully colored with light blues and pinks overlaid with a nearly white powder. It is my high-elevation form of preference.

Eucalyptus gunnii. Photo by Michael A. Dirr

Eucalyptus mitchelliana (Mount Buffalo gum). An exceedingly graceful small tree, endemic to the Buffalo plateau in northeastern Victoria, Australia, growing in sterile, granitic soil at about 4000 ft. (1200 m). In the most exposed areas they remain stunted trees under 15 ft. (4.5 m); in protected gullies they reach over 40 ft. (12 m). Rising from a lignotuber, *E. mitchelliana* can be multi-trunked and quite spreading but stays narrow in youth, forming an upright oval, eventually becoming rounded if out of the wind. In youth the leaves, 1–3 in. (2.5–8 cm) long and about ½ in. (1.5 cm) or less wide, sit amid the weeping branchlets, their narrow form enhancing the weeping appearance of the young

plant. They emerge a deep maroon, turning a rich gray-green later in the season. The young twigs are deep red, and the reddish brown bark peels in flakes while each trunk is still under 3 in. (8 cm) in diameter. The flowers are white, as with so many of the more frost hardy *Eucalyptus* species, and most often seen in late spring. Vigorous enough, with about 5 ft. (1.5 m) reached from seed in a couple of seasons. Eventually the trees take on a less weeping aspect, with undulating branches and only the branch ends sniffling quietly.

New to the horticulture scene even in Australia, *Eucalyptus mitchelliana* is quickly becoming a mainstay in the world of small, frost hardy eucalypts and should soon take its place as one of the most popular gums for the small garden. Frost hardiness so far has ranged to slightly below 10°F (–12°C), though even lower temperatures might be tolerated for brief periods. The lignotuber, of course, means the plants can resprout after unusual cold spells, or when coppiced as a garden perennial or hedge. As with other species from rocky soil in high elevations, *E. mitchelliana* grows more rapidly in a loving environment with well-drained soil and occasional irrigation in dry-summer places. Plants in the Cistus garden have reached 15 ft. (4.5 m) in four years, with the growth rate slowing appreciably in the fourth year when flowering has begun.

Propagation should be from seed, now more readily available. It is not known whether stratification would increase germination.

Eucalyptus neglecta (omeo gum). Victoria, Australia. Though often rated as a small tree to only about 20 ft. (6 m), examples in our garden planted at 4 in. (10 cm) tall stood at 45 ft. (14 m) after five years. They are quite a bit slower-growing in more stressful climates, places that actually include a lot of their native habitats, where temperatures are cooler year-round, the frost-free season is short, and the soils are low in nutrients.

Among the most outstanding in both form and texture at whatever its eventual height, this handsome tree grows into a round specimen with large, 4–6 in. (10–15 cm), stem-hugging, juvenile leaves of steely blue tinted pink in newest growth. Eventually, at three to five years, it may produce stemmed and somewhat lanceolate adult leaves. The juvenile leaves are a wonderful presence in the garden, and the adult leaves, though not as vibrant in color, remain bold-textured but are pendulant and a shiny, deep olive-green with just a hint of blue. The bark sheds in strips of a grayish brown, revealing light green and gray patches beneath. The flowers, though pleasing, are not the best feature of the plant; they are white in five- to fifteen-flowered clusters, about ½–¾ in. (1.5–2 cm) in diameter. They might be fragrant, but as they are 30 ft. (9 m) in the air in our garden, I've never found out.

Eucalyptus neglecta, adult leaves.
Photo by John Grimshaw

One of the best characteristics of this species in general is the "eucalyptusy" fragrance, very strong and seeming to elicit a feeling of good health or at least clear sinuses in those standing nearby. Good foliage for flower arrangements. Interestingly, though the tree grows to high elevations in its southeastern Australian haunts and is predictably cold hardy, it has become known as a species with some of the greatest tolerance for the wide temperature swings of the U.S. Southeast, where many other species can't handle summer heat and humidity or the sudden drops in temperature. *Eucalyptus neglecta* has proven a serious contender in many temperate gardens, having, for example, thrived in the garden of Tony Avent near Raleigh, North Carolina, surviving not only the heat and wet of summer but also temperatures of –9°F (–23°C), quickly recovering from leaf and some twig damage. Reports, as well, from such unlikely places as Cincinnati, Ohio, have this tree frequently dying to the ground but recovering from nearly –20°F (–29°C) with mulch. (It is presumed that no giant cloches were involved there.) This ultimate cold hardiness was tested in the garden of Frank Calia, who has experimented with many other species in that cold climate. (Frank has moved to western Oregon, and we can only hope that many of the species eucalypts that made the trip with him will not be relegated to the world of mulched perennials.) Strangely, even with such proven hardiness, numerous specimens around Portland experienced leaf burn after a windy 18 to 20°F (–8 to –7°C), presumably because they had not achieved proper dormancy in the normally mild climate.

Eucalyptus nicholii (narrow-leaved black peppermint, willow peppermint). Native to the tablelands of New South Wales to Queensland, Australia, at relatively high elevations in areas of periodic drought with well-drained to somewhat clayey soils. Introduced to cultivation early, it has one of the finest textures of any species. A surefooted, small to medium tree of 30–50 ft. (9–15 m) by 15–30 ft. (4.5–9 m) or a little more, with a growth habit that is often picturesque—that is to say, crooked.

The somewhat sickle-shaped leaves, indeed peppermint-scented, are blue-green to bluish, tinted pink to maroon in newer growth, and only 1–2 in. (2.5–5 cm) long by 3 mm as juveniles. Adult leaves are about 3–5 in. (8–13 cm) long and 5 mm to ⅓ in. (1 cm) wide, and often a bit more on the green side. The leaves' purple tint increases in winter, especially with some frost. The bark is persistent and a good orange-red, with individual strips twisting around the furrowed trunk. The flowers, numbering four to seven in umbels, are—no surprise—white and about ⅓ in. (1 cm) across.

Best suited to areas of lower summer humidity, it has been a com-

Eucalyptus nicholii

mon character in the western North American landscape for many years—possibly even too common in many a California coastal garden, where it stands up well to wind. Plants from the most common provenances are successful down to temperatures of 15 to 20°F (–9.5 to –7°C) but will often resprout from 10 to 15°F (–12 to –9.5°C), though not as vigorously as those with heftier lignotubescence.

To recap: fragrance, great color, texture, cool bark, takes wind—must have. The fine texture and purply gray color are great complements to such creatures as *Cotinus coggygria* 'Purpureus' (purple smoke tree) and *Melianthus major*. Add anything maroon, and the tableau is complete.

Some success has been had with cuttings, though the strange and intricate rituals that must be performed are cumbersome and, apparently, variable. So, as with the others, seed is best. Stratification does not appear to make much difference, nor does leaving the seed capsules to dehisce on a very hot dashboard seem to help germination.

Eucalyptus parvula (syn. *E. parvifolia*; kybean gum, small-leaved gum). New South Wales, Australia. Tree to about 35 ft. (10.5 m) with a broad graceful form, sometimes nearly flat-topped with age. The tree begins life with small, orbicular (rounded) leaves to about ¾ in. (2 cm), then quickly produces 1½–2¾ in. (4–7 cm) narrowly oval leaves.

Eucalyptus parvula

Like other preferred species, the leaves are a deep, matte green with purple and blue overtones. The bark is a rich brown, peeling to green and pink patches. The flowers (yes, small and cream-colored) are axillary, occurring toward the branch ends, with several showing at any given time (late winter in our garden). The branches bearing seedpods are used locally as attractive components of floral arrangements.

Another tolerant species, being rated to about 5 to 10°F (–15 to –12°C), plants have resprouted from bouts of –10°F (–23°C). They have proven tolerant of rather poor drainage as well as drought and possess the ability to resprout quickly after freezes, fires, or weed whacker attacks. Trees planted in the late 1950s or early 1960s near Woodburn, Oregon, along Interstate 5 persist despite multiple grass fires; out-of-control, giant lawn mowers; and coppicing to the ground by maintenance workers.

As a specimen in a more plant-friendly environment, the tree's fine texture and graceful form, as well as reasonable size, make it a superb urban garden addition. Where the texture or look of an olive (*Olea*) is desired, *Eucalyptus parvula* makes a fine and much faster-growing substitute, though it is to be presumed the seedpods make a somewhat less suitable condiment.

Eucalyptus pauciflora (snow gum). A widespread and variable species, occurring from southeastern Queensland, New South Wales, and Victoria south to Tasmania, Australia. Several subspecies grow in somewhat isolated mountainous ranges and are quite distinct. All have creamy white flowers that are scented of honey and in clusters of up to a dozen or more; flowers are at least ⅓ in. (1 cm) in diameter and held pleasingly among the leaves. Because of the wide range, not only the forms but also the hardiness vary greatly, some showing hardiness of not much under 20°F (–7°C), while others are arguably the cold hardiest of the entire genus. The following two subspecies are best suited to warm temperate gardens.

Arguably the cold hardiest of them all, *Eucalyptus pauciflora* subsp. *niphophila* (alpine snow gum) from southeastern Australia is a medium tree up to 36 ft. (11 m) in height, ranging down to a shrub of 6.5–13 ft. (2–4 m) in its most alpine habitats. In the garden, it is one of the slower-growing eucalypts, rarely exceeding more than 3–4 ft. (about 1 m) in a season, then slowing after three to four years. In its mountain habitats, most notably in the area of Mount Kosciuszko, Australia's highest peak at over 7000 ft. (2200 m), it is the main component of the highest-elevation woods. Even at low elevation, the tree's stout appearance—with wide trunks and limbs growing often in a twisted manner, forming picturesque flat-topped trees—makes it one of the most appealing subspecies. The bark, although peeling in patches that

Eucalyptus pauciflora. Photo © Global Book Publishing Photo Library

Eucalyptus pauciflora subsp. *debeuzevillei*

reveal the typical pinks and greens, has an overall appearance of ivory when exposed to the elements. Although the leaves don't possess the deep silvers or blues of the type, they are a pleasing gray-green: both the juvenile and adult leaves have a rather broad lance or sometimes nearly oval shape, 2–4 in. (5–10 cm) in length. The white flowers, six to ten or so in number, make a significant presence among the leaves in spring.

In climates without excessive summer heat, *Eucalyptus pauciflora* subsp. *niphophila* is probably the most reliable form. Sudden freezes have taken individuals to the ground at about 0°F (–18°C), while many a specimen has withstood –10 to –15°F (–23 to –26°C) with little more than temporary leaf blemish. In cultivation it requires fairly consistent moisture and, as with many plants from mountainous areas, would prefer cool soil. This can often be achieved by planting on a north slope (at least in the northern hemisphere), mulching, and adding ground-covering plants. Unfortunately, in areas such as the Gulf Coast states and elsewhere in the U.S. Southeast that are subject to periodic cold, gardeners have not had success with snow gums because of summer heat and humidity.

Eucalyptus pauciflora subsp. *niphophila* is no less complicated than the complex and variable type. Within its range in southeastern Australia, numerous valleys and mountaintops are adorned with this plant, each having characteristics important to their pollinators and eucalyptiphiles. To those of us seeking particular traits, especially from these mostly unnamed forms, seeds with good descriptive provenances should be sought.

Eucalyptus pauciflora subsp. *debeuzevillei* (jounama snow gum) is native to the northern reaches of *E. pauciflora* country. Along with *E. p.* subsp. *niphophila*, it inhabits mountaintops and frost pockets subject to cold winter temperatures. While this somewhat taller subspecies—to nearly 60 ft. (18 m)—has not been in gardens as long as others, it is proving a tough and reliable addition. Somewhat faster-growing, with chalky blue stems and larger leaves, to 6½ in. (16 cm), hanging gracefully on rather long petioles, the ghostly silver-blue cast in all its parts and more open appearance make it a stunning specimen. Tolerant of somewhat warmer summers and probably only slightly more tender to winter cold than most forms of *E. p.* subsp. *niphophila*, this tree should rate among the most popular once more people are able to pronounce its name!

Several additional forms of *Eucalyptus pauciflora* are in commerce. *Eucalyptus pauciflora* var. *pendula* can be strongly weeping to upright in form with weeping branchlets and leaves—leaves that are particularly shiny in adulthood. Another form, loosely allied with *E. p.* subsp. *niphophila*, comes from the summit of Mount Buffalo and is simply referred to in the trade as the Mount Buffalo snow gum, having, as yet, no proper nomenclature. It has an upright growth habit similar to *E. pauciflora* subsp. *debeuzevillei*, but long petioles and rounded leaves infused with aquamarine coloring and flushes of orange-red in new growth.

Eucalyptus perriniana (spinning gum, silver dollar gum). Australia, New South Wales to Victoria. A mallee or single-trunked tree to 20–35 ft. (6–10.5 m) or larger, in time. Shaggy at the base, the bark flakes to a tannish green or gray higher on the tree. The juvenile leaves are perfoliate, surrounding the stem, giving the appearance of stacked,

Eucalyptus perriniana

silver beads from a distance. The adult leaves are 3½–6 in. (9–15 cm) long and lanceolate, with a very long tip; they are gray to bluish green, often with maroon petioles in very young growth. Like many others, this tree grows quickly for the first few years, becoming a rounded, or nearly flat-topped, manageable garden specimen. An interesting characteristic—the leaves with each season's growth often begin as juvenile, switching later to the long, narrow leaves of adulthood. The early season's round leaves often detach, creating an almost tambourine-like look to the stems and, on windy days, they move around, creating a rasping sound as they rotate. A little kinetic energy in the garden.

Eucalyptus perriniana is a particularly good species to stool for use in perennial borders where its full size cannot be accommodated. The new growth is quick in spring, and the colors of the vigorous growth are stunning. At least somewhat tolerant of summer drought and rated to 0 to 5°F (–18 to –15°C), plants have been known to freeze to the ground at extended periods of 10 to 15°F (–12 to –9.5°C) but resprout after –10 to –15°F (–23 to –26°C).

Eucalyptus pulverulenta (silver-leaved mountain gum). From the tablelands of New South Wales at mid to high elevation. One of the most popular smaller species in cultivation, with angled branch pattern and growth only to 15–20 ft. (4.5–6 m) or so, with ever so slightly pointed, clasping leaves, roughly 2 in. (5 cm), giving the appearance of having been stacked on the stems. Extensively used for cut foliage. The powdered blue leaves, the waxy blue-green stems, and the abundant white flowers, ¾ in. (2 cm), set with buds on upper side and seedpods on the lower branches, create a statuesque presence.

Though not the most frost hardy, plants from colder provenances have easily withstood 12 to 14°F (–11 to –10°C) and have resprouted from even lower temperatures. Good candidate for coppicing, whether intentional or caused by weather.

Eucalyptus pulverulenta

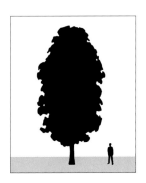

Eucalyptus subcrenulata (alpine yellow gum). Tasmania, from areas of high rainfall but variable soils. An unusual eucalypt in that, unlike so many with blue and gray foliage, this species has striking, deep green leaves. A small tree, in most garden situations quickly reaching about 30 ft. (9 m), but 120 ft. (36 m) or more has been achieved. Narrow and upright in youth, then spreading to a generous oval form. Both juvenile and adult leaves are glossy, almost appearing varnished. The juvenile leaves are about 3 × 2 in. (8 × 5 cm), nearly round and somewhat clasping, with a fanciful crisping around the edges. The adult leaves, 4 in. (10 cm) or more long and 1–1¼ in. (2.5–3 cm) wide, remain a dark to yellowish green. The bark is equally striking: in youth, a dark reddish brown, and in adulthood, silvery gray striped with cream and peeling in late spring and summer to reveal patches of yellowish orange and green.

The flowers are about ½ in. (1.5 cm) across and a clean to off-white in small clusters that stand out nicely against the dark leaves in mid summer or as late as autumn, often flowering in October and November in our Portland garden.

A sturdy, confident tree in its upright form with, in my experience, one of the more stable root systems. *Eucalyptus subcrenulata* also possesses a lignotuber, which qualifies it for membership in that special group of plants that are good candidates for coppicing because of their ability to sprout from the base. Used either as a small screen or even as a coppiced garden perennial, over years it makes an exquisite background thanks to its leaf texture and depth of color.

With some elevation range in its native haunts, cold hardiness varies a bit, but in general 10 to 15°F (−12 to −9.5°C) has presented little in the way of problems. Below 10°F (−12°C) trees have been taken right to the ground; others have survived down to about 5°F (−15°C). However, records of −10 to −12°F (−23 to −25°C), with recovery from the lignotuber, are fairly common. So obviously, if garden temperatures reach 0°F (−18°C) on a regular basis, the species is a perennial, like it or not.

The species can be used to great effect when planted with other saturated colors such as an understory of *Anemanthele lessoniana*, *Libertia peregrinans*, and a very dark, purple-leaved *Acaena inermis*.

Eucalyptus subcrenulata should be in full sun, as it can be a leaner if forced to reach for the light. Able to accept fairly long periods of drought and also temporary inundation. With this plant, as with most of the others, we do withhold water in the autumn to toughen it up a bit for the coming frost.

Propagation is from seed after about a month of cool stratification. While some references indicate that cold stratification is not necessary, I have found it increases germination by at least thirty to fifty percent and makes it more consistent.

A closely related species, *Eucalyptus vernicosa*, a shrub to small tree, makes a wonderful slow-growing addition to the garden. It takes its time to reach its 15–18 ft. (4.5–5.5 m) maximum (in the warmer garden), but at least the gardener knows that's about where it's going to stop. It retains the same characteristics as *E. subcrenulata*, deep shiny leaves and dark stems, but the leaves are narrower and the plant has a much more spreading habit. Another alpine from the tablelands of Tasmania, it prefers regular summer water and has been frost hardy to at least 10°F (−12°C).

Eucalyptus urnigera (Tasmanian urn gum). Tasman tablelands. Named for its rather large urn-shaped seed capsules, this is another

Eucalyptus urnigera. Photo by Michael A. Dirr

candidate for the blue garden. The small to medium tree ranges from 20 ft. (6 m) to over 140 ft. (40 m) in height by about half that in spread. In the warmer garden about 20 ft. (6 m) can be expected in several years with a very slow rate of growth thereafter. The plant has a graceful, open, pyramidal shape with weeping branches and slender leaves that abandon their 1½ in. (4 cm) round, juvenile form within a couple of years, turning into their lance-shaped adult selves, 3 in. (8 cm) long by ½–1 in. (1.5–2.5 cm) wide.

The three-flowered umbels produce white to cream flowers about ¾ in. (2 cm) across on long petioles. Even more attractive, however, are the large, glaucous fruits displayed amid the branches. Harvested, these can be used for decoration and in flower arrangements, though perhaps not fine jewelry.

Eucalyptus urnigera is tolerant of a wide range of soils, able to withstand fairly long periods of drought once established, and prefers full sun. In our garden the tree's most pleasing aspects are the true-blue of the foliage, especially glaucous when young, and the white of the early bark that lasts several years, eventually aging to a reddish color before shedding to reveal white and yellow green underneath.

When acquiring this species from the wild, or from cultivation for that matter, it would be prudent to secure those from high-elevation sites. Plants from seed collected at higher elevations have, in my opinion, the much more attractive foliage just mentioned—perhaps deeper blue—while seeds from lower elevations produce plants with leaves leaning toward matte green. Collections from lower elevations are also less frost tolerant, able to withstand 9 to 14°F (–13 to –10°C) with little damage, while those from higher elevations have been unharmed at an astounding –7°F (–22°C). Both forms have withstood winds well.

Propagation is from seed. A three- to four-week stratification has increased and stabilized germination.

WITH A NEARLY endless list of species from which to choose, even for the frost-prone garden, a number of other eucalypts warrant use and still more experimentation.

Eucalyptus bridgesiana (apple box) from the New South Wales tablelands tops out at 35–40 ft. (10.5–12 m) in the garden and is graced with the bluest of foliage—pink in its new growth—along with fragrant white flowers. It has withstood 7 to 10°F (–14 to –12°C) with little or no damage. Plants have resprouted from temperatures as low as –10 to –12°F (–23 to –25°C) as long as the cold spell is of short duration. *Eucalyptus nova-anglica*, also from New South Wales and slightly smaller, has similar blue leaves with silver new growth, white flowers at an early age, contrasting white bark, and frost hardiness to at least 5°F (–15°C) in any soil.

Eucalyptus camphora (camphor gum) has rounded, deep green leaves on long petioles that appear much like the northern hemisphere's quaking aspen (*Populus tremuloides*) but for the dark brown bark. Most seem frost hardy to about 10°F (−12°C); some have frozen to their lignotuber at 15 to 18°F (−9.5 to −8°C) but resprout quickly.

Eucalyptus gregsoniana (wolgan snow gum), from 5 ft. (1.5 m) to about 25 ft. (7.5 m), is a small wispy tree, often multi-stemmed with willowy, matte green leaves of only about 3 in. (8 cm). This blue mountain species seems great for any soil and a good candidate for the patio garden. It has withstood 8°F (−14°C) with no damage but rises quickly from its lignotuber after temperatures even below 0°F (−18°C).

Another species with dark green leaves is *Eucalyptus stellulata* (black sally), a small tree only about 20 ft. (6 m) tall with, eventually, a rounded crown and nearly black, furrowed bark, at least in the lower trunk. Also a small garden possibility, easy to coppice and tolerant of a fair amount of drought and wet soil. Cold hardiness is generally to about 8°F (−14°C), though the plant responds quickly from the lignotuber after lower temperatures.

Eucalyptus globulus subsp. *bicostata*. Photo © Global Book Publishing Photo Library

Although this discussion of *Eucalyptus* species leaves out some of the more glamorous species with their brightly colored flowers or those that are particularly large, at least one large species is worth mentioning, *E. globulus*, at least in one form. Members of this group of closely related subspecies from both Tasmania and the southern mainland of Australia have been planted worldwide, in the Mediterranean, much of Africa (extensively in South Africa), and in coastal California and southern Oregon, where it is the skyline tree of many a view. If planted in a region likely to experience frost beyond its tolerance, one might end up with firewood for life. Regardless, they are one of the cheap thrills of the botanical world simply by their rate of growth, 15 ft. (4.5 m) or more in a season not being unusual when young. *Eucalyptus globulus* subsp. *bicostata* is no exception, with exquisite, rounded, purply gray juvenile leaves and a beautiful cast to the adult foliage. The leaves can be 5 in. (13 cm) or more broad, and the plant itself makes a fine coppice plant with quick dense growth. One collection from above Wee Jasper in New South Wales comes from a particularly cool site where the 100 ft. (30 m) trees have withstood a recorded 12°F (–11°C) with no apparent damage. The similar and closely related Tasmanian *E. nitens* is another large and worthy addition with narrow, shining leaves, 5 in. (13 cm) or more long in adulthood, and hardiness to 12 to 15°F (–11 to –9.5°C).

Eucryphia   Eucryphiaceae

A genus of five or six species of trees and shrubs, often multi-trunked with a slender, upright growth habit, from Australia and southeastern South America. These are cool mountain and coastal growers, most at home in areas without excessive summer heat or dry winter winds, especially below freezing. All are evergreen with one exception. Sadly, these beautiful plants are destined to remain only in milder gardens. Where they can be grown, however, they are exquisite garden additions with glossy leaves, single or pinnate (multiple leaflets), varying in texture from rough and leathery to polished. As well, the arborescent species' narrowly pyramidal form makes a graceful presence in the garden and, of course, allows for more of them, even in small spaces.

Another advantage and one of the greatest selling points of the genus is that eucryphias flower in high summer, often June and July, when many others have finished or not yet begun. The flowers are, most often, a very cooling white and offered in generous clusters. Though a few double forms exist, even single, each flower appears substantial. The abundant stamens, filling the center of each flower, add to their exuberant appearance.

Oddly, eucryphias are little known and underused. At least two species (*Eucryphia cordifolia*, *E. lucida*) are used for high-quality honey in their native haunts. With all species the "southern hemisphere" rules seem to apply: many species come from old soils, low in fertility, and from places not having high summer heat and humidity at the same time, though receiving plentiful rainfall. Hence, the often repeated mantra of frugal care—low octane fertilizers, even watering, and cool soil temperature. Although cold hardiness varies, with some species being buried in snow for periods of time, none so far seem programmed to withstand long durations of cold, especially accompanied by drying winds, as can be experienced in western Europe and North America. In climates where such unfortunate phenomena occur, all should be placed under shelter of larger evergreens or out of harsh exposure—admittedly somewhat easier with the very small species than with 80 ft. (25 m) trees.

Plants raised from seed are rather fast-growing, possibly to a rate of 18–24 in. (45–60 cm) a season, but are slower to begin flowering, sometimes taking five years or more. Seed, though rarely available, loves a good cool stratification with a spring sowing in mineral or peaty mix, again, avoiding high heat. Individual clones raised from cuttings sometimes take as long as a couple of years to break away and begin reasonable growth, but flowering can be assured sooner than later, sometimes the same season if the cuttings were taken from wood of a mature tree. The trees themselves tend to begin flowering on lower branches, where the growth has slowed, leaving upper limbs in the dominant leader free to make more eucryphias. The cuttings themselves are best done from late summer to early winter on reasonably hardened growth. High heat is not necessary and even discouraged in some circles. Most make good container plants, and the accompanying stress of being rootbound in a container promotes earlier flowering.

Eucryphia cordifolia (roble de Chile). South and central Chile. Handsome, columnar tree to over 80 ft. (25 m) in height, eventually spreading to 50–65 ft. (15–20 m) wide in good light, though 25–35 ft. (8–10.5 m) by 16–20 ft. (5–6 m) is a reasonable expectation in cultivation. The leaves are simple, oval to oblong, with wavy or serrated margins, shiny with prominent veins above and a felty, brownish gray beneath. The flowers are white, 2 in. (5 cm) or more in diameter, and occur in late July through early September in the northern hemisphere.

The largest of these magnificent eucryphias—either a forest tree or an imposing specimen in the open—inspire awe when seen in the fertile, broadleaved evergreen forests of southern Chile. The shiny well-defined leaves cast a beautiful shade of gray-green even from a distance and, if caught while in flower, a sweet honey scent can be

Eucryphia cordifolia. Photo by Michael A. Dirr

detected from far away. Not the hardiest species: though plants with good provenance (from higher elevations) are proving to be quite tough, leaves remain uninjured only down to temperatures of about 15°F (−9.5°C), a bit lower if protected from wind. Shelter from wind and the overhead protection of large trees help a great deal in areas, such as along the Pacific Coast of North America and coastal western Europe, where occasional arctic outflows create cold, dry winds. One of the more heat-tolerant species: its frost hardiness actually increases where there is enough summer heat to ripen the wood.

Eucryphia ×*intermedia*. A hybrid between the deciduous *E. glutinosa* and *E. lucida*. A small upright tree eventually to about 25 ft. (7.5 m), having, in younger years, three to five leaflets bearing undulate and toothed margins, then, later, single, deep green leaves. The 1½–2½ in. (4–6 cm) flowers, in clusters, appear in mid summer. This hybrid has been one of the most reliable flowering eucryphias in our garden. The most commonly grown form is *E.* ×*intermedia* 'Rostrevor'. Foliage has been undamaged at 15 to 18°F (−9.5 to −8°C) without wind, and plants have resprouted from near 0°F (−18°C).

Eucryphia ×*intermedia* 'Rostrevor'

Eucryphia lucida (leatherwood). Tasmania, in mixed woodlands of high, year-round rainfall. Narrow, upright tree with a dense habit, 15–25 ft. (4.5–7.5 m) in height—even taller from ancient plants in habitat. Easily kept as a large shrub in cultivation. Narrow, oblong leaves to 2 in. (5 cm) by ⅓–½ in. (1–1.5 cm) are simple and entire (smooth-edged), though leaves on very young plants can be trifoliate. The leaves have a very fine, silvery blue pubescence on the underside and, especially in young growth, can be somewhat resinous. A favorite garden tree of mine, young plants have an aspect almost as narrow as an Italian cypress (*Cupressus sempervirens*), but with, instead, the very pleasing texture of shiny, rounded leaves, often held somewhat upright, showing the contrasting glaucous undersides.

The flowers, usually white, vary to light pink and are 1 in. (2.5 cm) or so in width. They often occur in voluptuous clusters held above the leaves. The symmetry of the round flowers makes a beautiful frame for the armies of black-tipped stamens. Like other species, *Eucryphia lucida* seems to have to be quite comfortable to flower well and consistently. Even plants having already set flowers might skip a year. As the tree becomes older, flowering becomes more consistent.

Cold hardiness has been proven to the upper teens (16 to 18°F, −9 to −8°C) to as low as about 10°F (−12°C) with overhead wind protection. *Eucryphia lucida* climbs to relatively high elevations in central Tasmania, and it would be well worth finding seed with higher-elevation provenance.

Though excessive summer heat in places such as the southeastern United States will limit their success, two selections have proven particularly garden-worthy. *Eucryphia lucida* 'Leatherwood Cream' has leaves consistently edged with a creamy yellow variegation. *Eucryphia lucida* 'Pink Cloud' has flowers blushed with pink with a darker pink center; it is said to be somewhat more frost sensitive but not in my experience.

Eucryphia 'Penwith' (*E. cordifolia* × *E. lucida*) has the upright aspect of *E. lucida* but significant pubescence on the stems, especially on new growth and the leaf undersides. The 1–1½ in. (2.5–4 cm) flowers and the narrow upright growth make it a particularly handsome garden specimen. More common in Britain and Ireland than the western United States.

Eucryphia lucida 'Pink Cloud'.
Photo by Michael A. Dirr

***Eucryphia* ×*nymansensis*.** A hybrid between *E. glutinosa* and *E. cordifolia*. This is a distinctly larger-growing cultivar with a dense, upright habit, achieving 50 ft. (15 m) or more fairly quickly with adequate water. The 2½–4 in. (6–10 cm) leaves—also often single in young plants, becoming three-leafleted and a bit larger with age—are shiny and green, distinctly paler beneath, with serrated margins.

The flowers begin later in the summer, often early to mid July on the West Coast of North America, and seem particularly undisturbed by sudden hot spells, which is kind of nice. Probably the main distinction between this hybrid and the previous one is that the flowers on *Eucryphia* ×*nymansensis* are fewer but larger. In some gardens, several years pass before the plant seems brave enough to put forth flowers; then it suddenly does so reliably.

Eucryphia ×*nymansensis* 'Nymansay' is the most common cultivar. *Eucryphia* ×*nymansensis* 'Mount Usher' is equally vigorous, perhaps more so, but possibly less floriferous, although it does have the reputation of throwing out occasional double flowers. Minor cautions aside, if a substantial garden presence is desired in a relatively short amount of time, *E.* ×*nymansensis* 'Mount Usher' is a reliable grower and fills its niche quickly. Plants now approaching fifty years of age in the Lady Ann MacDonald garden in Portland, Oregon, though not rivaling the majesty of specimens in the southwest of the British Isles, have remained handsome and vigorous, not showing the least bit of decline even with the occasional drought that follows the inevitable breakdown of ancient watering systems. Inheriting some of the frost hardiness of *E. glutinosa*, these cultivars have experienced temperatures at least briefly to 10°F (–12°C) without severe leaf burn and won't show significant damage at 8 to 9°F (–14 to –13°C), with the presumed protection from drying winds, assuming the temperatures don't last very long.

Eucryphia ×*nymansensis*.
Photo by Michael A. Dirr

Euonymus   Celastraceae

A widespread genus, from Eurasia to North and Central America and, in the southern hemisphere, to Australia and Madagascar. A genus of over 150 species, both deciduous and evergreen, with much to offer from plants not yet widely cultivated. Often thought of as shrubs, the evergreen forms seeming to be variegated with various sorts of mildew, plants can range from low mats to, indeed, trees. The flowers on all are small, either individual or in cymes, and, usually, a chartreuse-green. Many are valued for their fruiting capsules, which are often a vibrant yellow to orange to pink; these split apart late in the summer and autumn, exposing three to five orange-red seeds.

Few evergreen tree types are in common cultivation and, of those, the following species is most easily found.

Euonymus myrianthus. From mixed forests of western China. Often described as a large shrub, but many plants in cultivation are 10–12 ft. (3–3.5 m) or more in height within ten years. And unlike *E. japonicus,* another large evergreen species, one of infinite variation in horticulture that in time can become tree-like, *E. myrianthus* is easily trained to a single- to multi-trunked, small evergreen tree. The 3–4 in. (8–10 cm) leaves are narrow and drip-tipped with small uneven dentations. They are a rich, shiny green and are carried on the branches in what appear to be layered sprays.

Though *Euonymus* species are not known for spectacular flowers, the dense, multi-flowered cymes set about the branchlets of *E. myrianthus* are over ½–1 in. (1.5–2.5 cm) in diameter and are an exciting, if somewhat jarring, moss green, aging to the yellow end of chartreuse. The resulting fruit in autumn through winter is clustered amid the leaves though not hidden. Each is about ½ in. (1.5 cm) across with the deep reddish pink seed surrounded by carpels ranging from melon pink to nearly coral or orange-yellow, making a wonderfully colorful contrast to the green leaves.

The overall shape of the plant is broad-topped, with arching branches creating a light texture. At home in full sun to dappled shade and tolerant of long periods of drought once established, *Euonymus myrianthus* is a fine candidate for small urban gardens where a fine-textured background is important. Its use as a street tree, however, is limited, as the branches tend to weep and are brittle enough to be easily damaged.

A lover of heat, plants thrive at Peckerwood Garden in Hempstead, Texas, but also at the University of Washington Arboretum in Seattle, where specimens thirty years old or older appear quite

Euonymus myrianthus. Photo © Global Book Publishing Photo Library

healthy though being encroached upon by a thicket of maples. They have withstood temperatures of 5 to 10°F (–15 to –12°C) unharmed. Cold hardiness might increase with summer heat.

Though we have experienced random failures in propagation from cuttings, they should, by all accounts, be as painless as other *Euonymus* species from current season's wood, fairly well ripened from late summer through fall. Seed is easy as well, especially with the help of some cool stratification, but cuttings are the way to go if a certain fruit color is desired.

Fraxinus	ash	Oleaceae

A large genus of over sixty-five species of shrubs and trees spread through the northern hemisphere from riparian to quite dry zones, most deciduous but a few reliably evergreen. The leaves are usually compound though single in some (especially desert) species. The small flowers are carried in small panicles or racemes; the winged fruit (samara) is sometimes more attractive than the flowers.

Fraxinus greggii. A lovely small tree or large shrub, 12–20 ft. (3.5–6 m), from Trans-Pecos Texas to southeastern Arizona to southern Sonora, growing in dry oak woodland or desert canyons. Specimens achieve a compact oval form, with a tight branch pattern, silver bark, and 1–2 in. (2.5–5 cm) leaves with conspicuous flattened petioles and shiny, minuscule leaflets. The flowers are small, but the seeds are held at the branch ends and remain a cheery yellow-green for a long time, adding texture. In contrast to *F. uhdei*, this is still a much underused plant, tolerant of some of the harshest conditions, and just now becoming more common in the desert southwest of North America but happy further north, including along the West Coast. This is a very good candidate for courtyard, patio planting, or container.

Though clones with greater frost hardiness will undoubtedly be introduced, most presently in cultivation have withstood between 5 and 10°F (–15 to –12°C) with no damage save for leaf drop, plants remaining evergreen only to 12 to 15°F (–11 to –9.5°C).

Cuttings have been successful though small from mid to late summer growth, with seeds germinating easily for spring planting. Sometimes grafted on *Fraxinus velutina*.

The related *Fraxinus scheidiana*, a larger and more vigorous species from further south in Mexico, is also deserving of attention. Though we have planted this in our garden, its frost hardiness is as yet unknown below 20°F (–7°C).

Fraxinus scheidiana

Fraxinus uhdei (Mexican ash, shamel ash). From Central America into southern Mexico. Though resembling several other American ashes, its southern origins dictate an evergreen or nearly evergreen tree with large leaves, up to 6 in. (15 cm), consisting of up to seven shiny and somewhat serrated leaflets.

Vigorous and fast-growing, to 25 ft. (7.5 m) in ten years and eventually to over 50 ft. (15 m), with deep roots, the species is able to withstand prolonged drought though also tolerant of temporary inundation. Often used in warmer climates of the world, some leaf drop can occur toward the end of winter, or with temperatures approaching 18 to 20°F (−8 to −7°C). For most cultivars experienced so far, temperatures between 12 and 15°F (−11 and −9.5°C) have caused damage to the branching structure. *Fraxinus uhdei* 'Majestic Beauty' has a dense round crown and particularly glossy leaves; *F. u.* 'Tomlinson' is somewhat smaller and used less. All prefer sunny conditions but can be used between shaded buildings.

Propagate by cuttings from mid season's semi-hardwood growth, or by graft on *Fraxinus velutina*.

Though an obviously useful tree, I have difficulty recommending it with more than faint praise as in my wanderings through the mild West Coast of North America, I have found it to be much overused. Perhaps a time will come when it is no longer in fashion or, apparently, the only tree available, and we'll again promote its planting.

Gevuina	Chilean hazelnut, Chilean macadamia	Proteaceae

An intriguing and beautiful genus of only one species from damp, cool places in coastal and Andean foothills areas of Chile.

Gevuina avellana. This species is, indeed, a relative of the highly regarded macadamia nut (*Macadamia integrifolia*) of subtropical Australia and Madagascar. The fruit of this amazing plant, though often smaller than the true macadamia, has a very similar taste with, sometimes, a grainier texture. For purposes of this work, its ornamental potential is being emphasized but, unfortunately, only for the limited climates that can accommodate it.

My first experience of *Gevuina avellana* was a small specimen of about 5 ft. (1.5 m) in height at the University of Washington Arboretum in Seattle. The plant was in an exposed situation and somewhat yellowed, but because of the species' reputation for trickiness in cultivation, I was pretty much happy it wasn't dead.

Camping among the species in the Vilches area of central Chile was a rather more meaningful experience, even in a blinding rainstorm. In this cool mountain situation, they appeared as shrubs of

8–10 ft. (2.5–3 m), exposed on rocky sites, to woodland trees rising to 30 ft. (9 m) or more, with leaves up to 16 in. (40 cm) across, consisting of just a few to over thirty widely oval leaflets, each 3–5 in. (8–13 cm), depending on the juvenility of the plant or sun exposure. Later, hiking in the upper reaches—and riches—of the Altos de Lircay National Reserve, we found them among *Drimys*, *Colletia*, *Luma*, and *Nothofagus*—a most wonderful tableau. Plants in the higher elevations, in the park and elsewhere, appear a bit stunted from more frequent cold—3 to 7°F (–16 to –14°C) having been recorded at the nearest weather station significantly downhill—but maintained their bright shiny leaves and comb-like flowers so typical of the protea family, these being 3–4 in. (8–10 cm) and ivory in color with tips of copper-orange. As luck would have it, in one of the high mountain retreats we were shown a form with particularly large fruit, up to nearly 1½ in. (4 cm), in the midst of ripening to a deep red and black. (For future reference, about twenty-six of these will fit in a Pringles potato chip container.)

Gevuina avellana

Even for collections from high elevation with cold periods that might allow *Gevuina avellana* to be grown where temperatures fall to 0°F (–18°C), the horticultural range is still limited to areas having dry summers and those not receiving extreme heat, especially if accompanied by humidity and rainfall. In our Portland, Oregon, garden we have succeeded with this species in light shade and mineral soil with light mulches and ground cover to keep the soil as cool as possible. Though no winter damage has occurred, we occasionally lose a plant quite suddenly on a hot summer day.

Outside their rarified home, their ideal situation is immediately along the West Coast of North America, north of central California to southern British Columbia; the United Kingdom and Atlantic Europe; and, certainly, cooler areas of New Zealand and Australia. Where it can be made happy, it can be kept shrub-like through pruning, or, in its most elegant presentation, become a wide-spreading umbrella, though, in its first few years, spurts of growth give it a coarse and open form. Well worth fussing over, *Gevuina avellana* provides a wonderful subtropical texture, fruit that is amazingly flavorful, and a good story for the horticulturally curious.

Propagation from seed is best after cool stratification and with fresh seed. Cuttings have not been difficult in a cool mist or an enclosed environment in autumn and winter. Newly rooted cuttings should be transplanted early so fragile roots do not break. And it is always helpful to remember that this species and its entire family are sensitive to phosphorus and should only be fertilized in a light-handed manner with nitrogen-providing materials. Alfalfa pellets have been a good source.

Gordonia   Theaceae

Over seventy species of *Camellia* relatives, evergreen trees and shrubs, inhabiting Southeast Asia and the southeastern United States, especially along the Gulf of Mexico. Although recent taxonomic work places the Asian section of the genus into the more closely "tea" related genus *Polyspora*, for the purposes of this book I am staying with the name *Gordonia*, still commonly recognized by most. Pleasing aspects of all the species encountered so far are the very shiny, nearly succulent quality of the leaves and the bronzy red color of the newer growth. As well, many acquire *Stewartia*-like, silvery patchwork bark with age. And, unlike many other tea-family plants that have flowers infinitely smaller than one would associate with a relative of the camellias, *Gordonia* can have axillary flowers that are both substantial and colorful, from white to nearly ochre-yellow. More and more species have turned up on our horticultural radar, each seemingly more handsome than the last. It is a wonder more are not common in cultivation.

The genus as a whole requires consistent heat and moisture in the summer months, despite varying cold hardiness that limits their usefulness in cooler places. They do well in either sun or shade, though in cool, coastal climates in the northern hemisphere, they require a southern wall. Those discussed here are the frost-hardiest of this largely tropical genus.

Propagation has been easy and—unlike camellias, for which cuttings are often taken later in autumn—gordonias root readily and quickly from cuttings taken from late summer on, not requiring semi-hardened or hardened growth.

Gordonia axillaris (syn. *Polyspora axillaris*). Southeast China, Taiwan. Large shrub to small tree, with a rounded form, 30–40 ft. (9–12 m) tall and taking its time to achieve those measurements. The dark, glossy green leaves, 4–7 in. (10–18 cm), are entire to finely toothed. The flowers are substantial, 6 in. (15 cm) or even more in diameter. The single flowers occur at the leaf axis with notched rounded petals of a mellow, creamy white. Their numerous stamens are a deep, cheerful yellow, adding lively contrast. Reported as winter-flowering, plantings in the United States bloom from early February through March, often producing sporadic flowers throughout the year.

This plant resides in the twilight zone between shrubs and trees. With a little pinching (of the plant!), it is easily kept to 5–8 ft. (1.5–2.5 m). Thinning of the lower growth, the aforementioned warm aspect, and ample water, allows 15 ft. (4.5 m) in a reasonable time, thus making it officially a tree upon which one does not easily bump

Gordonia axillaris. Photo © Global Book Publishing Photo Library

one's head. Plants respond to high iron and nitrogen fertilizers and seem to love the same treatment as gardenias and other southern favorites. Cold hardiness does vary according to the amount of heat provided the plant in the previous summer. In low-heat areas such as the United Kingdom and the immediate West Coast of North America, 20°F (–7°C) can damage newer growth, but a plant placed in a warm aspect—not necessarily as warm as New Delhi but at least on the south side of the house, where any reflected heat will ripen the wood—seems unhurt by 12 to 15°F (–11 to –9.5°C) for short periods.

Gordonia lasianthus (loblolly bay). Southeastern United States, mostly in sandy soils immediately adjacent to water. A small to medium tree, reaching 20–25 ft. (6–7.5 m) in twenty years in the garden; specimens have achieved 65 ft. (25 m) over time in the most favorable conditions. A handsome species with pyramidal growth when young, eventually spreading, with the typical *Gordonia* deep, glossy green leaves and *Ternstroemia*-red new growth. The flowers, occurring in early to mid summer, are a clean, crisp white with, usually, five rather wide petals and contrasting yellow stamens. A faster-growing species than *G. axillaris* and somewhat more open in youth, with flowering usually delayed at least five years if grown from seed. Tolerant of cooler maritime conditions outside of its steamy habitat, but, as with other heat-loving plants, the lack of ripening makes it somewhat more prone to winter cold; rated to zone 9, it is shy of flowering and frost sensitive to the low 20s Fahrenheit (–6°C) in the United Kingdom, for example. Specimens in their native southeastern United States and plantings in hot-summer regions of the U.S. West Coast have withstood near 0°F (–18°C) with little permanent damage. A wonderful inland form, selected by Ted Stephens of Nurseries Caroliniana from near his nursery in North Augusta, South Carolina, seems to have both a frost hardiness edge and extra vigor. At his nursery, *G. lasianthus* 'Swampy' (named for its mushy habitat) has remained solidly evergreen to temperatures of –4°F (–20°C).

Gordonia lasianthus. Photo by Michael A. Dirr

For the more intrepid gardener willing to put up with a temporary hole in the landscape, damaged plants resprout quickly, making *Gordonia lasianthus* worthy of use where hard freezes are not frequent.

OTHER SPECIES, increasingly in commerce, are all worth trying in warm climates such as the Deep South of the United States and certainly many of the South Asian cities.

Gordonia sinensis (syn. *Schima sinensis*) makes a handsome, dense, evergreen tree with large (4–5 in., 10–13 cm) glossy green leaves and contrasting white flowers; *G. yunnanensis* (syn. *Camellia taliensis*) is similar, with new plantings from high elevations having taken 20°F (–7°C) with little damage on the West Coast of the United States.

Another smaller species worth considering is the very attractive *Gordonia chrysandra* (syn. *Polyspora chrysandra*). Though rarely over 10–12 ft. (3–3.5 m) in height, the dark green leaves, red tinted in new growth as are the branchlets, and the creamy yellow, fragrant flowers with dark yellow anthers make it an excellent standard wall shrub or dwarf garden tree. As with all the species, ample summer water is imperative, as is as much warmth as possible.

Tom Ranney in his work through North Carolina State University is making magic with multiple intergeneric crosses between *Gordonia* and *Franklinia*. The rumors of the resulting plants' lack of vigor and subsequent demise have been greatly exaggerated, as new crosses have been not only vigorous but also evergreen and brimming with potential, bringing the cold hardiness of the *Franklinia alatamaha* to an evergreen plant. Introductions are eagerly anticipated.

Grevillea   Proteaceae

Large genus of over 230 species, most in Australia with a few in New Caledonia. This amazing family, mostly confined to the southern hemisphere, reaches its greatest diversity in South Africa and Australia, with several genera in southern South America. The title of most familiar genus in the family belongs to the proteas themselves, which bear pinecone-like flowers of multiple colors and look more like a florist's fantasy than a real plant. Grevilleas, with somewhat more subtle floral displays, are no less beautiful, with flowers in multiple colors as well as highly variable leaves from large and oval, to deeply lobed, to needle-like. The flowers are in paired comb-like racemes with a small bract carrying a tubular perianth.

There are many, many garden-worthy and even surprisingly frost tolerant *Grevillea* species, but most are in the shrub category, not reaching the minimum size for inclusion in this book. The one species here described seems to have escaped not only the diminutive form taken by the majority but also, to some degree, has escaped or left behind the sensitivity to warm temperatures and nutrient-rich soils.

Grevillea robusta (silk oak). From eastern Australia in milder, low-elevation habitats in areas of ample, year-round rainfall, this handsome fast-growing tree reaches a broad, conical 100 ft. (30 m) in height. The leaves are 9–10 in. (23–25 cm), pinnately compound, and a deep green but covered with a silky, copper-colored indumentum, particularly on the underside and especially in the young growth.

Flowers—about 4½ in. (12 cm), one-sided combs of a coppery orange, sometimes varying to cream—usually appear in mid spring but often only after the tree reaches five to eight years of age or more. Though satisfactory in dappled shade, *G. robusta* flowers only in sun and, especially in climates where frost is a problem, much prefers a sunny site.

Because of its tall straight stature, handsome leaves, and tolerance of some phosphorous and potassium in a normal garden situation, this tree has become quite widely planted in near tropical to warm temperate climates throughout the world. Surprisingly drought tolerant considering its eastern Australian origins, it also has the ability to tolerate or accept warm to hot summer temperatures in combination with moisture, a pairing that often makes other species prone to fungal attack; indeed, it is one of very few proteaceous plants seen in warmer regions of Florida. *Grevillea robusta* is a common street and garden tree throughout southern California and California's Central Valley and along the Oregon coast. Further north, where temperatures fall below 18°F (−8°C) or so, or where the occasional cold spell remains for more than a day or two, plants are often cut to the ground but resprout quickly. In Sacramento, California, for example, majestic plants over 40 ft. (12 m) in height were frozen by several days of temperatures reaching the low teens (−10.5°C). Some took up to two years to begin resprouting in earnest but were tree size again within three to four years. Ease of propagation and availability make these good temporary garden plants or pot specimens where freezes occur too quickly or frequently to justify permanent garden use.

Grevillea robusta. Photo by John Grimshaw

Grevillea robusta is one of the easier species to propagate. Unlike many other cool temperate grevilleas, which prefer to be propagated under the cover of late autumn, this species can be propagated any time the wood is ripened or mostly ripened. Seed can be sown in spring or fall.

Serving as a good indicator plant, *Grevillea robusta* signifies departure from, or entrance into, a milder climate. On the Pacific Coast of North America, along with the even more common *Acacia dealbata*, it indicates, when traveling north, the increasingly narrow strip of land where one can assume many subtropicals are safe and probably in the inventory of the local garden center.

Heteromeles	toyon	Rosacea

Though taxonomically challenging (by some lumped with the genus *Photinia*, or split, adding Asian components), *Heteromeles* is for this work maintained in its strict sense, with one evergreen species occurring from southernmost Oregon to northern Baja California and an outlier (probably bird-carried) in southernmost Baja California Sur.

Heteromeles arbutifolia.
Photo by Bart O'Brien

Heteromeles arbutifolia (Christmas berry). This common component of the California Floristic Province can be found in mixed chaparral (dry shrub matrix) or in groves, each plant up to 20–25 ft. (6–7.5 m) with narrow, 3 in. (8 cm), lightly serrated leaves and panicles of white flowers that later produce orange-red berry-like pomes that ripen in late autumn and winter.

The plant's holly-like appearance, at least from a distance, gave way to another common name, Hollywood, as *Heteromeles arbutifolia* is a common feature on those southern California hillsides. In the garden, Christmas berry can be used as specimen shrub or easily trained to single-leader small trees. Tolerant of and even preferring summer drought and, in any case, enjoying good air circulation in bright light to deter leaf spot or mildew. Treated with tough love, with gritty soil and low summer humidity, *H. arbutifolia* can be an important garden component, at its best where conditions dictate tough Mediterranean plantings.

Few horticultural selections exist, which is unfortunate, as its distribution over nearly 2000 miles suggests great variability in frost hardiness. The yellow-berried *Heteromeles arbutifolia* var. *cerina* 'Davis Gold', displayed beautifully at the UC Davis Arboretum, is a southern selection that has sustained damage at 14°F (–10°C). *Heteromeles arbutifolia* 'Zenia', a selection of mine from near Zenia in the Trinity Mountains of northern California, has withstood temperatures nearing 0°F (–18°C) in its native habitat; chosen for its location in a cold mountain pocket, it is otherwise typical of the species.

Late summer through autumn and winter cuttings are slow but usually reliable, preferably with humid rather than mist conditions. Seeds prefer winter stratification and sowing in a mineral mix.

Hoheria	lacebark	Malvaceae

Five evergreen and two deciduous species from New Zealand, usually in mixed forest situations, though sometimes on forest edges or in mixed shrub associations in bright light. They are accustomed to ample year-round moisture and rarely experience any real drought in their native habitat: even at their most southern points and highest elevations, they receive some frost and snow but almost never temperatures that most of the temperate world would deem extreme.

The species range from large shrubs to small trees with somewhat serrated, rich green leaves, often with a coppery overtone. At first sight one would be hard pressed to place these in the same family as hollyhocks (*Alcea*) or flowering maples (*Abutilon*), as large, woody species are rare among the cultivated members of family Malvaceae. All *Hoheria* species, even those usually only reaching shrub size, can eventually become what one would consider a small tree, with delicate deep green leaves and silky, silver bark, a gracile presence in any garden situation. In western Oregon, they have performed splendidly along the immediate coast, where extreme heat and frost is rarely a problem. Inland, in our Portland garden, where summer heat and dry air (or, in winter, occasional cold with dry air) can damage them, they make an ideal background plant for dappled shade or for under light coverings in gardens where silvers and whites are important. We've used them under large *Eucalyptus* species or where such plants as white crapemyrtles (*Lagerstroemia*) can hide them from the brunt of the sun. As well, the contrast of white flowers and deep green leaves adds coolness to the summer garden.

The flowers, single or in small cymes, are campanulate with, often, overlapping white to cream petals and a typical mallow clusters of stamens. With their refreshing color at the height of summer, they are one of the best attributes of the genus.

Many in the genus are equally at home in sun or, at least, dappled shade, but none are fond of prolonged drought or poor soil. They are, indeed, at their best in coastal situations; they are not comfortable in desert areas or the U.S. Southeast and other areas that couple summer heat with high humidity. In places prone to even the slightest hint of freezing winter winds, the protection of buildings or overhead trees should be provided: plants are prone to bark split with sudden drops in temperature.

Propagation from seed is best with fresh collections; the germination rate is helped by a period of a few weeks of cool stratification. Cuttings are not difficult, from semi-ripened wood in late summer through hardened, current season's growth in mid to late winter. Some bottom heat and light mist speed the process along.

Hoheria populnea. From mild areas in the north end of the genus' range, *H. populnea* is a small tree, reaching a little over 30 ft. (9 m) in height in fifteen or twenty years under the best conditions. They are narrow in youth, eventually developing a rounded form with silver-gray bark peeling in narrow strips. The young leaves are broad ovals, ⅓–1¼ in. (1–3 cm), slightly reminiscent, as the epithet implies, of a poplar. The leaves on the mature specimens become more oval or even lanceolate, 3½–6 in. (9–15 cm) by 1½–2½ in. (4–6 cm). Occurring in late spring to early summer, the flowers are a particularly pure white, 1¼–1½ in. (3–4 cm), and provide a good contrast to the mature foliage, dark green in most forms (in some, blush purple).

This is a popular tree in cool, coastal areas, where temperatures of 18 to 20°F (−8 to −7°C) or lower are seldom experienced. Though, unfortunately, not the hardiest species—temperatures in the mid teens (14 to 16°F, –10 to –9°C) can severely damage even the most mature specimens—it is well worth growing in a protected spot even in a marginal climate. Rated a solid zone 9, plants have twice been damaged in Portland, Oregon, winters, when the temperature slipped below 20°F (–7°C), but do stunningly well on the Oregon coast and south to about the Santa Barbara parallel. Further south the frequent, dry wind can turn all but the most protected plants crispy. Much prefers evenly damp soils amid the security of dappled overhead shade or some protection from the western sun away from coastal areas. Fortunately, *Hoheria populnea* does have the ability to resprout well should it be hit by frost or stooled for use as a wall plant or border shrub.

Hoheria populnea 'Alba Variegata'—more common in its native New Zealand and, to some degree, in the mildest districts of the British Isles than it is on the U.S. West Coast—has leaves strikingly margined with white and makes a marvelous pot specimen if not in the garden. *Hoheria populnea* 'Variegata', also very attractive, has a mottled, yellow-green margin to the leaves. It should be noted that the variegated forms take longer to reach tree size than the quick four to six years of the greener forms.

Hoheria sexstylosa (ribbonwood). Fairly widespread in New Zealand, the species' range extends far enough south and at enough elevation to give it some of the greatest cold hardiness of the genus. A small evergreen tree, rarely reaching 20 ft. (6 m) but fast-growing to about 12 ft. (3.5 m), it maintains a narrow, pyramidal growth habit, and, as the common name implies, has bark that exfoliates in silvery strips, exposing a shiny, reddish brown underlayer. Pulling the bark is extremely tempting, but this should probably be avoided, as bruised and barkless plants thrive poorly!

The juvenile foliage begins as ¾–1¼ in. (2–3 cm), broadly oval leaves, some nearly round, eventually becoming narrow ovals to almost lanceolate, 2½–4½ in. (6–12 cm) by ¾–2 in. (2–5 cm) and a deeper, glossy green. As in the rest of the genus, the flowers are white, fragrant, and occur in some abundance in early June to early July, depending on the warmth of their placement. *Hoheria sexstylosa* 'Snow Flurry' is a particularly handsome, early-flowering plant gaining popularity on the West Coast of North America; because this upright clone is propagated by cuttings, one does not see the juvenile leaves in young plants.

In practice, *Hoheria sexstylosa* is as much as ten degrees Fahrenheit (about six degrees Celsius) hardier to frost than *H. populnea*. Particularly hard frosts, however, especially when accompanied by dry air, can damage the plant below 15 to 18°F (–9.5 to –8°C), although speci-

Hoheria sexstylosa 'Snow Flurry'

mens have survived 10 to 12°F (−12 to −11°C) in winter with the protection of overhead companions.

Hoheria angustifolia is a similar but a bit larger plant, with somewhat narrower leaves; in my experience, it is not reliably hardy in frost or even a hint of drought.

Hoheria 'Glory of Amlwch', a hybrid between *H. sexstylosa* and the deciduous *H. glabrata*, can in time reach 25 ft. (7.5 m), producing leaves that are rounded with an almost fan-like shape, gracefully attached to long petioles and about 2½–5½ in. (6–14 cm) in diameter, depending on the vigor of the plant. Eventually, on older trees, the leaves become narrower but retain a very pretty sheen. The flowers, about 1½ in. (4 cm) in diameter, are large, in loose panicles, and a very rich creamy white. The anthers can add richness to the flowers as they tend toward a rose-purple. Also hardy to about 12 to 18°F (−11 to −8°C) with protection from wind.

Ilex	holly	Aquifoliaceae

The family Aquifoliaceae is made up of only two genera, *Ilex* and *Nemopanthus*, but the small number of genera is more than made up for by the volume of species in the very large genus *Ilex*, over 400 throughout the northern hemisphere, though shy in Mediterranean zones, and extending into northern South America. Some species in the genus are deciduous, but a great number are evergreen and possess an astounding breadth of texture, the range of which has not been taken advantage of in the temperate world. Hollies vary from very dwarf shrubs to large, handsome trees, and from tropicals to some of the cold-hardiest broadleaved evergreens in existence. Many have multiple medicinal uses and traditions.

For myself, whose boyhood bare feet were too often spiked by the spiny leaves of thuggish trees that seemed to dominate every fifth house, acquiring a positive feeling for *Ilex aquifolium* (English holly), and for hollies in general, took a long time. (That the leaf spines penetrate bare feet, not to mention bare fingers, is not surprising since, indeed, the epithet comes from the Latin *acus*, meaning "needle," and, of course, *folium* for "leaf.") Later, having been witness to the exquisite leaf shapes and colors of not only some of the North American species but also the Asian species, and then, indeed, coming back to some of the forms of *I. aquifolium*, my prejudice was overcome in the face of such diversity and garden-worthiness. Among the most popular characteristics of English holly are the brightly colored berries produced by the females of most species. The flowers of most species are small, however, usually creamy in color though sometimes tinted purple. Their main horticultural attribute is a wafting, sweet fragrance in many species.

Most hollies occur naturally in places of frequent summer rainfall, though some, such as *Ilex vomitoria* from the American South and some forms of *I. aquifolium*, occur naturally where prolonged drought can occur. As a general rule, however, the species described here perform best with, at least, periodic deep watering in the summer months where drought is a yearly event. Most tolerate a surprising amount of drought, however, once established, and are equally at home in full sun or with dappled shade or an overstory.

Ease of propagation is certainly one of the reasons hollies are so widely cultivated and, indeed, have escaped in places. Certainly if the characteristics of the individual plant are to be carried on, cuttings are best. They can be taken early, any time from mid to late summer, after current season's growth has hardened somewhat, to around mid to late winter with mist and some heat preferred.

Ilex ×altaclerensis 'Golden King'. Photo by John Grimshaw

Ilex ×altaclerensis. A hybrid with *I. aquilifolium* and *I. perado*, a combination that has led to numerous crossings and a number of large and vigorous shrubs and trees, often with larger and less spiny foliage, the spines tending to decrease with age as with some others in the genus. One vigorous upright form, *I. ×altaclerensis* 'Golden King', a plant that John Grimshaw especially loves, has gold leaves, particularly beautiful in winter; *I. ×altaclerensis* 'Atkinsonii' is robust with deep green leaves sometimes tinted an attractive purple in new growth; *I. ×altaclerensis* 'Balearica' is another green-leaved form, particularly free-fruiting; and *I. ×altaclerensis* 'Camelliifolia' has rounded leaves tinged a dark glossy purple. These plants seem to thrive with low heat and on marginal soils if provided summer rainfall and, though reportedly more successful than *I. aquifolium* with high heat, they can suffer in extremely hot and humid places.

Ilex aquifolium (English holly). A wide-ranging species from western Europe with outliers in northwest Africa. Although there is a temptation to exclude species in such common use as *I. aquifolium*, especially since they have already been covered in many tomes, *I. aquifolium* is a variable and important economic plant. This is the holly best known for its ubiquitous presence in the winter holiday season. As one of the very few broadleaved evergreens native as far north as the British Isles, the species and a few of its most interesting variants should be mentioned here. As well, with such a wide distribution and long history—at least 1000 years in cultivation—numerous forms and cultivars, some both exquisite and underused, have been brought into cultivation. Besides, one has one's own favorites. Interestingly, at least for us Oregonians, numerous cultivars and hybrids were named by Teufel's and other nurseries in western Oregon.

Ilex aquifolium can range from a dense shrub, taking decades to reach the smallest definition of "tree," to large pyramidal trees of over 80 ft. (25 m). In cultivation a well-tended specimen of one of the typical tree forms can attain a size of over 30 ft. (9 m) in under twenty to thirty years. Though pollarding is rarely suggested for most trees, hollies resprout quickly after being "hat racked," or taken back to rather large limbs (preferably to a shape resembling a pyramidal form), a procedure done frequently in commercial operations so as to produce as much foliage as possible in a limited space.

The flowers, produced on second year wood, are surprisingly fragrant. Though their size is insignificant, they can be produced in enough mass that the pale creamy color contrasts well against the leaves. The signature red berries appear only on female plants, of course, with at least some fruit forming even if no males are present. But, if fruit is desired, at least one male clone should be within bumblebee distance.

When choosing among the many *Ilex aquifolium* cultivars, select those not subject to phytophthora, a fungal disease evident in various forms in areas with extended winter wet. Local agriculture extension services should have information on resistant species based on local information. Phytophthora can defoliate the lower branches and even affect the whole plant if unchecked by pruning out any affected material, removing any dead leaves from under the plant, and, if necessary, lifting the branch skirt to above the splash line made by dripping water. As well, concern exists about the species spreading into adjacent woods via bird-carried seed, especially in damper areas of the Pacific Northwest. If this is a problem near one's home garden, it is best to plant only male clones or a less prolific species. In the American Southeast, *I. aquifolium* often has a great deal of trouble with high summer humidity combined with heat, though some coastal areas of the mid Atlantic have had notable success.

Most *Ilex aquifolium* cultivars are easily hardy to 0 to 10°F (−18 to −12°C), with some surviving −10 to −15°F (−23 to −26°C) without significant foliar burn. It would take a book in and of itself—and indeed several good ones exist—to describe the overwhelming number of these cultivars, both historic and presently available, many produced for their berries, others possessing brightly variegated leaves or unusual forms. Those included here are just a sampling of my favorites.

Ilex aquifolium. Photo by John Grimshaw

Ilex aquifolium 'Angustifolia'. In cultivation since the early 1830s, a form with narrow, pyramidal growth and densely held leaves of only about 1½ (4 in.) by 6 mm. Both male and female clones exist. Either way, it is a handsome garden subject and slower growing, eventually to about 15 ft. (4.5 m), filling the same niche as a trimmed yew, though with the advantages of maintaining its compact form and having highly attractive and very glossy leaves.

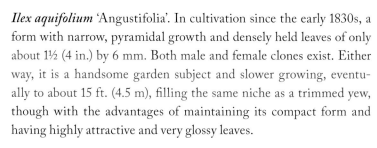

Ilex aquifolium 'Bacciflava Group'. A lumping of several attractive yellow-berried forms, including *I. aquifolium* 'Fructuluteo' and *I. aquifolium* 'Yellow Berried', a Wieman's Nursery clone. The late autumn, clear yellow fruit stands out effectively against the deep green, more or less typical holly leaves and also lasts well into the winter season.

Ilex aquifolium 'Beacon'. Originating in a French holly plantation and introduced in the 1940s by Wieman's Holly Nursery in Portland, Oregon, it bears bright green twigs and large glossy leaves with less obnoxious spines and particularly large orange-red berries in consistently large quantities.

Ilex aquifolium 'Ferox' (porcupine holly). A very early form, known since the 1600s, the convexly formed leaves have numerous spine-like appendages on the leaf surface, making an unusual and attractive presence. Much smaller and slower growing than the typical *I. aquifolium*, this cultivar can reach about 15 ft. (4.5 m) tall by 10–15 ft. (3–4.5 m) wide in ten years. Slower growing yet is *I. aquifolium* 'Ferox Argentea', with leaves that are blotched and edged silver.

Ilex aquifolium 'Ferox Argentea'. Photo by Michael A. Dirr

Ilex aquifolium 'Integrifolia' (syns. *I. a.* 'Rotundifolium' and, in local Oregon circles, *I. a.* 'Screw Leaf'). Again, smaller in general form, beginning life as a pyramid, then rounding in age. The leaves are spineless and very glossy with a twist about mid leaf. A pleasing plant both up close and at a distance. Like so many other cultivars in the holly world, this also seems a lumping of several clones, including one affectionately known as *I. aquifolium* 'Variegated Screw Leaf' with a creamy gold splashed throughout the screw!

Ilex aquifolium 'Marginata'. Although the number of names put to this plant and those very much like it is daunting, Jacobson (1996) did a very concise grouping of them under this cultivar. The bold leaves, to about 2½ in. (6 cm) long, are dark green, mottled and edged creamy white with bold and regular spines and a slightly undulate form. This is a male form, so one is not confronted by the seizure-producing effect of the bright red-orange berries against the silver-variegated foliage.

Ilex aquifolium 'Pinto'. Another discovery by Wieman's Nursery in the 1930s. Pleasingly shaped, glossy leaves, with a consistently golden center. The berries are a brilliant red and remain attached through the winter season. It has also exhibited good cold hardiness into zone 6 or well below 0°F (–18°C). As a garden plant, the warm, chartreusey gold holds up, and the tree, without much effort, remains a compact pyramid to 20–25 ft. (6–7.5 m). Unfortunately, a bit susceptible to phytophthora.

Ilex cassine (dahoon). This very southern holly inhabits a large area in the coastal southeastern United States to central Mexico and much of the Caribbean. Tolerant of poorly drained soil as well as heat and

Ilex cassine. Photo by Michael A. Dirr

Ilex cassine 'Angustifolia'.
Photo by Michael A. Dirr

humidity, it also tolerates a surprising amount of cold, especially those forms from the U.S. mainland, often withstanding –10°F (–23°C) without damage. Except where noted, it and its forms are slender upright growers, spreading only with age. Although records exist to 70 ft. (21 m) in height, 20–30 ft. (6–9 m) can be expected in average garden situations. The compact leaves—under 1½ in. (4 cm) wide and 3–4 in. (8–10 cm) long in typical forms—are slender, pointed, and very neat, with almost no teeth, save for, occasionally, fine serrations near the apex of the leaf. *Ilex cassine* 'Angustifolia' (syn. *I. c.* var. *angustifolia*) is popular in the American Southeast. The shiny, narrow 2–3 in. (5–8 cm) leaves are set about numerous small branches, giving the entire plant an easy demeanor. In some ways a very unholly-like holly, *I. cassine* is relished in gardens for its exuberant clusters of berries, from 6 mm to ⅓ in. (1 cm), varying from red to orange to yellow.

Ilex cassine '**Lowei**'. This cultivar is derived from a colony of yellow-berried specimens found in the wild in Georgia. Specimens observed in the U.S. Southeast have been vigorous and spreading.

Ilex cassine var. *myrtifolia*. Accepted by some as *I. myrtifolia*, this variety, with narrow leaves less than 6 mm to ⅓ in. (1 cm) wide by about 1½ in. (4 cm) long, is a tidy, compact plant, comfortably to about 15 ft. (4.5 m) in height and about 5 ft. (1.5 m) in width though, with age, plants can reach 30–40 ft. (9–12 m).

Ilex cassine 'Lowei'. Photo by Michael A. Dirr

Ilex cassine var. *myrtifolia*. Photo by Michael A. Dirr

Ilex cassine '**Pendula**'. This cultivar somewhat resembles *Maytenus boaria* or a small, compact weeping willow, though remaining shorter to under 10–15 ft. (3–4.5 m) with an 8 ft. (2.5 m) spread. Shaping this form in its youth can promote a more graceful adult. These plants have survived close to –10°F (–23°C) with no apparent damage at the JC Raulston Arboretum in Raleigh, North Carolina.

Ilex latifolia (lusterleaf holly, magnolia leaf holly). Southeast China to Japan. Narrow pyramidal tree to 25–30 ft. (7.5–9 m), occasionally 40 ft. (12 m) or more, with records near 50 ft. (15 m) in its native China. In Europe since the early 1820s and North America since the late 1800s, this remarkable holly has leaves that can be nearly 10 in. (25 cm) long and 3–4 in. (8–10 cm) wide. Noticeable spination along the leaf margins can occur, but often, especially in older specimens, the leaves are entire, emerging in spring as a deep mahogany, aging to dark green with a most striking reflective quality. The size of the leaves alone makes this species a welcome addition where a larger texture is needed, and the narrow habit fits easily into most garden situations. The flowers, often purple or purple-tinted, are also large for the genus—up to ⅓ in. (1 cm) wide!—and lie in dense clusters beneath the leaves. The berries, from an orangey red to true red, and ranging up to ⅓ in. (1 cm) in diameter, are also plentiful and easily visible between the leaves.

Ilex latifolia, foliage. Photo by Michael A. Dirr

Ilex latifolia. Photo by Michael A. Dirr

Though *Ilex latifolia* prefers summer heat and plentiful moisture, lightly irrigated specimens in western Oregon have remained attractive for dozens of years, though growing slowly and becoming somewhat sparse. With reliable summer water, either applied or from the sky, it's an amazingly tolerant plant and, though not the hardiest of the hollies, specimens can be seen in areas rated as the middle of zone 7, where temperatures routinely fall below 10°F (–12°C). I have used them on several occasions in courtyard plantings where the large texture, even on a small plant, attracts immediate attention.

Ilex opaca (American holly). Southeastern United States, mostly in coastal areas. This species is the North American equivalent of English holly, and many of its forms are similar in outline. The most striking difference—as the epithet implies (*opaca* means "dull")—is the more matte surface of the leaves. Spination also can be less intense. Often a small tree, 20–30 ft. (6–9 m) in height, in the garden, but in the wild, with time, can on rare occasions grow to nearly 100 ft. (30 m).

Though in some respects not as outrightly attractive as *Ilex aquifolium* and its cultivars (and having *only* about 1000 published selections, compared to multitudes more in the English hollies), it is often a graceful plant and, most importantly, a good deal more cold tolerant, most forms being rated to zone 6 and some surviving zone 5 (–10 to –20°F, –23 to –29°C). The leaves are similar to but a little larger than *I. aquifolium*, about 1½ in. (4 cm) across by 4–5 in. (10–13 cm) long. The small, often greenish flowers produce berries that vary from about 6 mm to ⅓ in. (1 cm) and exhibit the typical range of colors from nearly red through oranges to yellow, maturing in late autumn and, unless discovered by a flock of celebrating robins, hang on well into the winter.

All are tolerant of a diversity of soil types, even poor drainage, and compete better than *Ilex aquifolium* in high summer heat and humidity.

Ilex opaca. Photo by Michael A. Dirr

Ilex opaca, fruit and foliage. Photo by Michael A. Dirr

Ilex opaca 'Canary'. Typical in all respects, save for the deep yellow berries produced in some abundance; it was introduced in North Carolina in the 1930s and is one of the most easily obtainable cultivars. *Ilex opaca* 'Cardinal', a Massachusetts selection from the same era, has a similar silhouette with a compact habit and plentiful clusters of bright red berries; it is a particularly frost hardy form.

Ilex opaca 'Hampton'. A 1940s introduction selected in Hampton, Virginia; a vigorous grower with deep red berries and an almost undulate leaf texture of alternating marginal spines. It exists in several collections on the U.S. West Coast and appears vigorous over long periods, surviving even periodic drought.

Ilex pedunculosa (longstalk holly). A forest and forest-edge plant from the rich woodlands of Japan, southeast China, and Taiwan. Though the species straddles the line between a tree and a shrub, I prefer to think of it as a delicate, small tree, particularly attractive when grown with lifted skirt, showing off both the graceful branch pattern and the glossy, rounded leaves floating on very long petioles. In gardens the plants quickly reach 8–10 ft. (2.5–3 m) and, with a little corrective pruning and reliable water, can reach 30 ft. (9 m).

The leaves—sometimes exhibiting slightly purple-tinted new growth—are a rounded 2–3 in. (5–8 cm) wide and about 4 in. (10 cm) long and have no teeth. June flowers produce autumn berries of a light to medium red and about 6 mm.

Ilex pedunculosa, fruit and foliage.
Photo by Michael A. Dirr

Ilex pedunculosa. Photo by Michael A. Dirr

One of the best potentials for this small tree is as a standard, either in the garden or as a superb street tree. The foliage is consistent, and the height means that, in areas of smaller storefronts or with power lines, size is not a problem. It is also tolerant of compacted soils.

Ilex pedunculosa 'Vleck', introduced from Illinois in the early 1990s, seems even more frost hardy than this notably hardy species has already proven, remaining evergreen into zone 5, accepting temperatures to nearly −20°F (−29°C) with only bronzing of the foliage, although in colder climates, tree size may be reached very slowly.

Ilex purpurea (purple holly). Japan and China. Handsome tree with forms varying from shrubs under 10 ft. (3 m) to broad pyramidal trees of over 35 ft. (10.5 m) with shiny leaves, rounded at the base and sharp-tipped, and often tinged, yes, a true purple. The small clusters of flowers are also tinted purple-red, while the fruit approaches fire-engine red and is 6–8 mm in diameter—of course, on female plants. As with so many of the better hollies, the muscular bark is a fine-textured silver-gray. The tree, with little fussing, can attain beautiful structure.

Ilex purpurea is quick-growing in youth and even moderately drought tolerant. It can be kept in containers for great periods of time and will maintain color and vigor if well fertilized. Underused, it is still seldom seen even in the Deep South of the United States, where its cultivation should be common; numerous large specimens, some now over 25 ft. (7.5 m) in height, exist there, the females producing a particularly brilliant display of deep red fruit lasting through the winter. In southern and Southeast Asia, where it has long been used medicinally, it is a much more common garden and utility tree.

One of its few drawbacks is the assumed lack of frost hardiness. Rated by most to zone 8, temperatures in the low teens (13 to 14°F, −10.5 to −10°C) over long periods have indeed caused yellowing, die-

Ilex purpurea. Photo by Michael A. Dirr

Ilex purpurea, flowers. Photo by Michael A. Dirr

Ilex purpurea, fruit. Photo by Michael A. Dirr

back, or even some bark split. However, many new collections have come to light in recent years that have withstood at least close to 0°F (–18°C) with little or no damage. Some overhead cover by larger trees is always a plus in areas prone to winter rough spells. A form introduced by the U.S. National Arboretum some years ago, though tending to be shrubby, has withstood everything that Washington, D.C.'s zone 7-ness has wrought.

Illicium   Illiciaceae

A genus of about forty species, all broadleaved evergreen shrubs or trees closely allied to the family Magnoliaceae. The genus is represented in great numbers in Southeast Asia north into warm temperate regions and also occurs in Mexico north to the southeastern United States, appearing most often as understory shrubs in summer-moist woods, frequently associated with other broadleaved evergreens or, rarely, mixed deciduous forests. A few attain tree size, and some can reach a height of 50 ft. (15 m) or more—thereby becoming overstory.

Long a favorite group of plants, they easily attract gardeners to their layered branches of succulent, often drip-tipped leaves and shiny, bright green presence, especially when growing in deep shade. The leaves have a spicy fragrance, noticeable to varying degrees among the species and sometime evident even without their being crushed. The flowers, with petals that are actually petaloid segments, from ⅓–¾ in. (1–2 cm) to over 2½ in. (6 cm), can be cup-shaped or very large and star-like, with colors ranging from white or green to pink to deep burgundy.

One drawback is the flower fragrance or shall we say odor, best described in most species as dog-breath on a hot July day and a bit overpowering right by the front door. Luckily, the pollinators attracted to this distinctive aroma are needed only for a very short time, and the problem is short-lived. Planting away from the prevailing wind or at a distance, where they can be easily seen, can provide some mitigation. Given the exquisite beauty of *Illicium* species, inventing solutions is very worthwhile.

In cultivation, most species—all those described here—prefer moist soil but with sharp drainage. Though species such as *Illicium floridanum* can be seen in the Deep South of the United States or immediately adjacent to water, they are usually in sandy soil that drains quickly.

There are hardly better candidates to meet the ever-increasing demand for small, delicate trees and courtyard specimens, especially in those species with the least heavy flower scent. Each member of the genus is beautiful in its own way, and new species and forms appear every year, though many are rare or nonexistent in cultivation. The following are a few of the best tree forms.

Illicium anisatum (aniseed, Japanese star anise). Native from Japan at the Ryukyu Islands to South Korea and Taiwan. A large shrub to small tree that can reach 30 ft. (9 m), though 15–20 ft. (4.5–6 m) in ten years is good going. The leaves, 2–4½ in. (5–12 cm) long and ½–1½ in. (1.5–4 cm) wide, are largest in deeper shade and exude a spicy sweet fragrance on particularly warm days or when crushed. The flowers occur from late winter to late spring and are small, ⅓–¾ in. (1–2 cm), and creamy white to yellowish green with green, star-shaped seed capsules that eventually brown, becoming decorative and remaining on the plant through the following season.

Though many *Illicium* species prefer high heat and humidity for ultimate growth, *I. anisatum* is right at home in cool maritime climates, producing even more vigorous growth in the south of England and the maritime Pacific Northwest if given adequate summer water. Plants are happy in full sun immediately adjacent to the coast, but where fogs are infrequent or humidity is low, at least dappled shade is preferable; fairly deep shade suits the species well in any garden situation. In sun the growth habit is rather tight but as a background specimen or small garden tree in shade, the eventual habit is graceful and layered.

Temperatures of −10 to −12°F (−23 to −25°C) have had little effect other than some leaf mottling on understory plants. *Illicium anisatum*, one of the most frost hardy species, is more subject to frost and wind damage in an exposed sight or in an area with lower winter humidity.

Though propagation is somewhat rare from seed, cold stratification is helpful with an early spring sowing; germination readily occurs

Illicium anisatum. Photo by Michael A. Dirr

Illicium anisatum, foliage. Photo by Michael A. Dirr

Illicium anisatum, flowers. Photo by Michael A. Dirr

with warming of the soil in spring. Cutting propagation seems best from late summer using newly hardened, present season's growth. It is also possible, though slower, with more mature growth through the autumn and winter. Fairly generous hormone levels, bottom heat, and mist are helpful.

The related *Illicium verum* produces the edible anise. Also a small to medium tree that can reach 50 ft. (15 m), it has 4 in. (10 cm), narrow, pointed leaves and flowers that are yellowish pink to nearly red and somewhat cupped. Its habitat in southern China and Vietnam make it a bit less frost hardy than *I. anisatum*, though it has been successful to temperatures of about 10°F (−12°C) for brief periods.

Illicium floridanum. An exquisitely beautiful shrub or small tree from the Deep South of the United States, *I. floridanum* can be wide and sprawling or an upright pyramid. Plants can form a near thicket, achieving 6–7 ft. (2–2.1 m) in height in exposed situations or as much as 10–12 ft. (3–3.5 m) when planted in the understory or "persuaded" to uprightness by the removal of lower branches and competing terminals. They are easily cultivated in shade or in all but the most glaring afternoon sun except in particularly hot and dry regions, where it helps to have the overhead protection and increased humidity provided by a woodland situation.

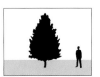

The leaves are very showy ovals and often over 4–6 in. (10–15 cm) in length with a curved and sharp terminal. The flowers can be upwards of 1½ in. (4 cm), held out gracefully on multiple petioles. The color can vary from maroon and red to pink and salmon. *Illicium floridanum* f. *album*, slower growing than the species and, in truth, not reaching tree size, is worth mentioning for its flowers, which emerge chartreuse-green, fading to white.

Illicium floridanum f. *album.*
Photo by Michael A. Dirr

Illicium floridanum. Photo by Michael A. Dirr

Illicium floridanum 'Variegatum'.
Photo by Michael A. Dirr

Illicium 'Woodland Ruby'.
Photo by Michael A. Dirr

That this species is the poster child for odoriferousness is unfortunate, but, because of the plant's beauty, it is definitely worthwhile to create the distance that lessens the aroma problems. Several variegated forms exist. Woodlanders Nursery in Aiken, South Carolina, offers at least one good cultivar, *Illicium floridanum* 'Variegatum'. As well, they offer a hybrid of *I. floridanum* × *I. mexicanum*, the shrubbier *I.* 'Woodland Ruby', a beautifully shaped, upright plant with luxuriant leaves and rich ruby-red, maybe-with-a-drop-of-salmon flowers over 1½ in. (4 cm).

One of the more frost hardy species, *Illicium floridanum* and its hybrids have been rated to zone 7 and have withstood temperatures slipping below 0°F (–18°C) without noticeable damage, though even with protection, –10 to –12°F (–23 to –25°C) has caused injury.

Propagation is among the easiest for the genus. Seed, with up to thirty days of cool stratification, is easy; spring sowing is best. Cuttings may be taken any time from late summer through fall, though rooting is quickest with the highest percentages in late summer or early autumn.

Illicium henryi, foliage. Photo by Michael A. Dirr

Illicium henryi. Another Asian species, from southwestern and central China, usually growing in woodlands though sometimes exposed to brighter sun. *Illicium henryi* attains small tree size to 25 ft. (7.5 m) or more over time, though 10–15 ft. (3–4.5 m) can be expected in the garden. Leaves are 3–6 in. (8–15 cm) long and only ¾ in. (2 cm) in diameter, narrow and oval with an abrupt and sharp tip. Both the stems and leaves appear rather succulent; they are bright spring-green, though they can be tinted coppery red in bright light. The flowers, though only ¾ in. (2 cm) in diameter, are brightly colored—dark, pinky red to an orangey, almost copper color—and a very pleasing cup shape, gathered in numerous clusters. The leaves, when crushed, have a sweet, spicy fragrance. The flowers are also spicier and more pleasingly fragrant than other species—and, thankfully, the fragrance is light.

Though, as with most of the genus, plants can be maintained as shrubs, in a woodland situation or with removal of bottom branches, a delightful, small tree can be developed in only a few years, one with a delicate pyramidal shape from which the outward leaning clusters of flowers can be easily seen. For best growth, as with the other species, *Illicium henryi* should be provided with reliable summer moisture and, in hotter or drier places, dappled or at least afternoon shade. Summer heat speeds its growth. But in coastal areas—such places as the southern United Kingdom, coastal southeastern Australia, and the West Coast of the United States—upward mobility has been maintained at a good clip—again, with water provided while temperatures are high. Though temperatures near 0°F (–18°C) have been endured, the plants have had to resprout from damaged wood, reducing vigor, and the leaves have become mottled and yellow. Only where temperatures rarely drop to the low to mid teens (13 to 16°F, –10.5 to –9°C) can *I. henryi* be expected to attain small tree size.

Propagation is the same as the other species from seed. Cuttings have proven successful in mid to late summer to autumn on newly ripened wood.

Illicium henryi, flower. Photo by Michael A. Dirr

Illicium simonsii. A beautiful species from Southeast Asia, growing in rich, mixed broadleaved evergreen woodlands. Slow to attain a height of 20–25 ft. (6–7.5 m); 30–40 ft. (9–12 m) is not unknown. This small tree maintains a rather dense, pyramidal shape, though like *I. henryi* it remains looser and a bit more layered in deeper shade. The leaves are narrow and oval, 3–4 in. (8–10 cm) by 1–2 in. (2.5–5 cm), with a sharply pointed tip and a very dark, shiny green color.

The flowers are the most exciting attribute of this plant, new in cultivation to most of the world. Appearing as multi-petalled stars, they are 1–1½ in. (2.5–4 cm) in width and a rich cream to deep yellow in color. And they have a scent that is more spicy than stale—not unpleasant.

Illicium simonsii has a moderate growth rate, achieving upwards of 18 in. (45 cm) per year when not stressed by drought. Ten-year-old plants at the Quarryhill Botanical Garden in Glen Ellen, California, were exceedingly handsome, narrow pyramids over 12 ft. (3.5 m) tall. A plant, several years older, at the University of California Botanic Garden at Berkeley was larger and somewhat rounder, sited as it was in a substantial amount of shade.

Doubtless not as frost hardy as some in the genus, *Illicium simonsii* has withstood 12°F (–11°C) with little damage but has been entirely cooked at 0°F (–18°C). Provenance will undoubtedly play a role in selections yet to be made, not only from among the locations from which a plant is collected in the wild but also the possible forms and flower colors.

Propagation has been the same as the others from seed, but cuttings have been more difficult. Late summer, early autumn cuttings are again best, but they are slow: percentages, for me, have been an eventual thirty percent. Cuttings taken later in autumn and winter have been even less successful. Grafting onto more vigorous species has been successful, though the expense still restricts plant distribution. Let's hope clones will be found that not only possess desirable horticultural characteristics but are also easily enough reproduced to make them commercially viable.

Laurus   Lauraceae

A genus of but three to four evergreen trees or shrubs from southern Europe and the Canary Islands to the Azores. Though the genus *Laurus* is small, it has a rather high profile among Mediterranean plants, both as a garden tree and a culinary flavoring, not forgetting its handiness on those special occasions where a laurel wreath is required upon a noble head. All *Laurus* species are native to areas of the true Mediterranean, with only one, *L. nobilis*, being reliably frost hardy in cooler zones.

Fossil records place the genus in mesic climates, both in the Mediterranean and, for its close relatives worldwide, in what are termed Laurasian associations. *Laurus nobilis* now inhabits areas with at least pronounced summer drought. In cultivation all seem tolerant of water at any time of year as long as the drainage is good. Certainly easy in containers and long used in kitchen gardens, they are also easy to shear and don't seem to mind perpetual plucking for evening meals.

As with many members of the family, propagation can be tricky. Late summer newly ripened wood seems best, but what worked last year might not this year. It has proven useful to take a series of cuttings from mid summer through winter in hopes that at least some root well. Fairly strong hormone levels and a steep wound are also helpful, along with mist or an enclosed damp situation and a bit of bottom heat. Seed is generally easy, and if a specific clone is not sought, passive collection of the seedlings in early spring under desired trees might be the way to go. Otherwise, seeds can be sown in autumn or winter in a cool situation or stratified below 40°F (4.5°C) for a few weeks to a month and sown in early spring. As seed is not long-lived, earlier sowing seems to work well.

Laurus nobilis (true laurel, sweet bay). A medium tree to 50 ft. (15 m) in height and, rarely, as tall as 60 ft. (18 m), in winter-rainfall areas of southwestern Europe, often adjacent to the Mediterranean Sea in association with other horticultural symbols of the area—*Cupressus sempervirens* (Italian cypress), *Olea* (olives) and *Arbutus* species—and found as well to the northwest in mixed forest associations. Some dwarf or shrubby forms are in cultivation. A common sight in western Europe and along the Mediterranean, where temperatures rarely fall below 15°F (–9.5°C), the most common forms are dense and narrowly pyramidal with deep green, rather shiny leaves, most often narrowly oval and 3–4 in. (8–10 cm) in length. Indeed, it is these leaves that supply the wreath-makers of ancient and modern times. Aside from that and its obvious use to sweeten and add distinct flavor to foods, *L. nobilis* makes a fine garden plant, providing either a good solid background or a well-behaved, single garden specimen. Plants do well in long periods without water in the summer, though they respond with more rapid growth to regular irrigation—sometimes 3–4 ft. (about 1 m) per year when young. Although there are some dwarf or shrubby forms in cultivation, gardeners should be aware that the small sweet bay from the local nursery, purchased in a 4 in. (10 cm) pot and tucked into the garden, can become a bit more than was bargained for—a fairly common surprise, much like the tiny, potted, flocked Christmas tree that turns out to be a 90 ft. (27 m) Italian stone pine (*Pinus pinea*).

Although pleasing in a smaller garden (especially in a spot where the spicy fragrance of the leaves can be experienced on a warm day), this species is possibly better as a background plant, whose shedding leaves can fall harmlessly into the shrubbery—or possibly into the neighbor's garden. Its shedding, rather coarse leaves have a propensity to collect both dust and scale in its very dense canopy. Plants can be shorn or carefully guided into the form of an attractive pyramid and kept in check, thereby making particularly stout garden bones that don't take up too much space.

The attractive creamy yellow flowers, the largest of which can be nearly ⅓ in. (1 cm) in width, are produced in axillary clusters on the previous season's growth. They arrive early in the spring and provide a sweet, honey-like scent as well as a very nice contrast to the deep green of the leaves. (The flowers are not as likely to be produced on shorn specimens as the reaction growth that follows pruning is quite vigorous and does not often form flower buds.) The berries are a bluish black and begin to color in the early autumn, hanging on fairly late into winter on female specimens. Males, having more showy flowers, are far more often grown.

Cold hardiness can be an issue, as both its native and cultivated ranges in the Mediterranean vary widely. Some forms have easily withstood temperatures between 0 and 10°F (–18 and –12°C), with others showing leaf damage at 10°F (–12°C). In Portland, Oregon, several large specimens exist that show no signs of damage from the notorious winters of 1950 or 1972, when temperatures slipped below 10°F (–12°C) or even 0°F (18°C) in many suburban spots. Some local gardeners actually took such freezes as a hint and now regularly stool their plants, making them into large shrubs. We are now growing a number of clones with clever names attached like "Tree from SW Macadam Avenue" or "Tony Avent's Friend's Collection from Turkey," as it is always useful to have a clone growing with a predetermined cold hardiness. A seedling taken from a particularly small

Laurus nobilis, foliage and flowers. Photo by Michael A. Dirr

Laurus nobilis, trained as a standard. Photo by Michael A. Dirr

Laurus nobilis f. *angustifolia*

Laurus nobilis 'Aurea'

adult remained, at eight years of age, less than 3 ft. (1 m) in height with leaves of about ½ in. (1.5 cm), thus revising, once again, my definition of a very small tree.

Laurus nobilis f. *angustifolia* has proven to be frost hardy to near 0°F (–18°C) with very little damage. Its graceful leaves are far less imposing than the typical form, and the crown tends to be rounded rather than pyramidal. For many years I thought of this as a large shrub, but after seeing specimens nearing 50 ft. (15 m) in western Cork in Ireland, I have revised my definition of a shrub.

One plant I find most attractive is *Laurus nobilis* 'Aurea' which, when grown in bright light, looks like yellow crushed velour, the innermost, shaded areas of the tree remaining spring-green, while areas exposed to sun turn a golden yellow (that doesn't at all resemble the yellow of iron deficiency). This form, unfortunately, seems a bit less frost hardy—undamaged at Hillier Arboretum in the United Kingdom below 10°F (–12°C) but severely damaged by the same temperature in the U.S. Southeast. Several incidents have led me to believe that autumn frosts shut down the plant's system gently, whereas sudden freezes in an otherwise warm climate can do much more catastrophic damage when the plant has been in active growth.

Laurus nobilis 'Crispa' has a narrow, upright form with nicely undulate, indeed crinkly, leaf margins. A marbled, variegated leaf form, *L. n.* 'Sunspot', is also floating among local hortheads. Though attractive, it is a bit more of a curiosity as green reversions must continually be culled.

Tolerant of nearly any soil, provided water does not stand, and benefits from planting against a west or south wall should the climate be marginal. All forms make fine pot specimens, surviving many years in confined spaces. As well, bays and a favorite form of rosemary (*Rosmarinus officinalis*) in their fresh form are an advantage when placed as close as possible to the kitchen.

Another relative that deserves mention is *Laurus* 'Saratoga', a large, somewhat awkwardly spreading tree to over 30 ft. (9 m) in just a few years. It occurred, apparently spontaneously, at California's Saratoga Horticultural Research Foundation and was sold as a hybrid between *L. nobilis* and *Umbellularia californica* (California bay). But although those hybrids do exist, and several have made nice garden specimens with intriguing if not altogether pleasant fragrance, *L.* 'Saratoga' is more likely a hybrid with *L. azorica* and *L. canariensis*. Both the floral and leaf forms as well as its tenderness much below 20°F (–7°C) support that assumption.

Leptospermum   tea tree   Myrtaceae

This genus of close to eighty species (limited by some to only a little over thirty) is primarily native to Australia but ventures north into more tropical Austroasia and west into New Zealand. The vast majority are shrubs or even ground covers, but a few reach tree form or can easily be pruned into such. The fine, often fragrant foliage creates an unusual texture found in few other genera, and the small seed capsules, held against the stems in multiple generations, add an additional textural element. The flowers, typically myrtaceous and varying from under ⅓–¾ in. (1–2 cm), are overwhelmingly white; the most color is found in *Leptospermum scoparium* and New Zealand forms.

All the larger species can be kept as standards or trimmed into screening hedges. Though most tolerate periods of drought in ground, they are ill adapted to excessive dryness in containers. As well, few revel in high heat with humidity; they are best grown in cool maritime or Mediterranean climates with irrigation.

Propagation is from semi-ripe to ripe, current season's growth with mist and some bottom heat helpful. The small seed capsules can be collected when just turning brown and ripened in a paper bag or on a warm surface, with the very fine seed sown immediately or the following early spring. Germination is usually easy.

Leptospermum grandifolium. This southeastern Australian species is quite variable, some remaining under 6–8 ft. (2–2.5 m), others attaining 15 ft. (4.5 m) or more. The one we grow was obtained some years ago from Spinners Nursery in Hampshire, England. There a speci-

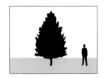

Leptospermum grandifolium. Photo by Michael A. Dirr

men at 14 ft. (4 m) is nearly forty years of age. In our nursery, seven years in the ground gave us over 10 ft. (3 m) from planted seedlings.

The most striking characteristics of this plant, often allied with *Leptospermum lanigerum*, are its shredding, straw-colored bark and leaves of silver-gray, measuring up to ¾–1¼ in. (2–3 cm) in length. The flowers are white in early spring though, in our garden, flushing whenever the mood strikes. Plants can easily be pruned into standards, thus revealing the attractive bark and delicate, arched branching pattern.

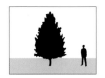

Although tolerant of dappled shade, *Leptospermum grandifolium* is most fit in direct sun with regular irrigation to push upward growth. Among the most frost hardy of tea trees, this species has withstood temperatures to 10°F (–12°C) in the United Kingdom with no apparent damage.

Leptospermum lanigerum

Leptospermum lanigerum (woolly tea tree). Another species from southeastern Australia, often found growing near water's edge at mid to high elevation, and among the easiest in cultivation. At first instinct, it is a sprawling shrub; but, when encouraged to maintain a central leader, it easily reaches 8–10 ft. (2.5–3 m) or taller, with bark more finely textured than that of *L. grandifolium* yet still straw-colored and an arching branch pattern with weeping branchlets, particularly attractive as most forms have silvery gray leaves and pink newer stems. The early spring flowers are white and often produced in some abundance. As a patio specimen or against a simple wall, a specimen plant makes a very nice silhouette.

Tolerant of both summer drought and winter inundation as well as reasonably cold temperatures: in our garden, *Leptospermum lanigerum* has been unaffected by 18°F (–8°C) and is reported to be frost hardy to between 0 and 5°F (–18 and –15°C) for brief periods.

Leptospermum sericeum is closely related and of equal horticultural merit but with a tighter, more upright branching pattern and smaller leaves of olive-green. Of similar frost hardiness and culture, and a fine garden plant.

Leptospermum scoparium. Certainly the most common of the tea trees in cultivation, with multiple selections available. Native of both New Zealand and southeastern Australia and ubiquitous among coastal gardens in western North America and other warm maritime climates. The size is variable over such a wide range of native habitats, but the larger forms attain 6–8 ft. (2–2.5 m) rapidly and 10–14 ft. (3–4 m) with age.

Light brown shredding bark with an abundance of flowers set among small foliage, usually under ⅓ in. (1 cm), creates a pleasing contrast, and the entire plant is useful as a small garden specimen or fine-textured background, lending an almost coniferous look. The leaves are more or less shiny but quite silky when they first emerge and, in some forms, somewhat to deep burgundy in color. The flowers are typically white to very pale pink, with forms in New Zealand providing multiple selections from rose to salmon to red.

Frost hardiness is the biggest issue. Most plants are damaged below 18 to 20°F (−8 to −7°C) or with sudden early or late frosts, bark split often occurring before other noticeable signs.

Many, many cultivars are available and increasingly produced with regional names attached. *Leptospermum scoparium* 'Washington Park Hardy'—our name for a Tasmanian collection from the University of Washington Arboretum of narrowly upright form with purple-tinted leaves (liver-colored, really) and white spring flowers—has withstood temperatures below 12°F (−11°C) in that garden and has proven a valuable garden exclamation point in ours.

Leptospermum scoparium, flowers.
Photo by Michael A. Dirr

Ligustrum	privet	Oleaceae

A variable genus of over fifty species of shrubs and trees, both deciduous and evergreen, native from North Africa through southern Europe, Southeast Asia, and Australia and from nearly Mediterranean to summer-wet regions. A few (including *Ligustrum japonicum* and *L. lucidum*) easily attain tree size. And many species used throughout the temperate world as hedge screens and foundation plantings can also reach tree size in time. Most are at home in full sun to dappled shade and even tolerate fairly deep shade, though growth will be lanky. Some accept saturated soil for long periods, but those discussed here prefer to avoid standing water.

As successful as the genus can be in difficult sites—enduring drought, root competition, and in some cases, cold—they can be a serious weed problem, especially in areas of ample summer rainfall. *Ligustrum sinense* has become very troublesome in the woodlands of the southeastern United States, and many species are a bit too well adapted to be used everywhere.

As one might expect, the evergreen species are quite easily propagated, though they do seem to have some "issues," which have been uncovered in my attempts to increase them. *Ligustrum japonicum* is easiest from semi-ripe cuttings in summer, whereas *L. lucidum* seems easiest from well-ripened wood of current season's growth. Both enjoy bottom heat and humidity but low mist. However, the ratio of root to rot can fall to only seventy to eighty percent success, especially with the variegated cultivars of less vigor. It seems ironic that *L. lucidum*, such an obnoxious garden weed in a few places, can be miffy about rooting from cuttings.

Leptospermum scoparium, bark.
Photo by Michael A. Dirr

Ligustrum japonicum, foliage and flowers. Photo by Michael A. Dirr

Ligustrum japonicum. Photo by Michael A. Dirr

Ligustrum japonicum (wax privet, Texas privet). Though most often used as a shrub or pot specimen, plants can reach small tree size, to 10–15 ft. (3–4.5 m) in a few years. The leaves are glossy green and somewhat more succulent in texture than those of *L. lucidum*, and the plants certainly maintain a more compact appearance. Frost hardy to similar temperatures or even slightly more tender, 0°F (–18°C) can seriously injure them, especially if roots are frozen in pots. *Ligustrum japonicum* 'Variegatum' is yet more compact but would take many years to prune into a small standard tree.

Ligustrum lucidum (glossy privet, tree privet). China and Japan. Mention of this species often draws moans of angst rather than squeals of delight. In some areas of the United States—the Deep South and, to some degree, urban areas of the West Coast—it is an ambient, woody weed. The plant, with its 20–30 ft. (6–9 m), occasionally 40 ft. (12 m), umbrella shape, rather clean branching structure, and attractive leaves—subject to few insects or diseases—is like an evergreen version of *Ailanthus altissima* (tree of heaven): it either represents a noxious weed, an unwelcome denizen of vacant lots worldwide, or a savior, one of the few green things willing to grow in inhospitable urban places. (Does privet grow in Brooklyn? Yes!)

Glossy privet flowers in May and June, producing a rather strong scent from swarms of tiny white flowers, and forms purple-blue berries in late summer and autumn that hold into winter if the birds don't find them first. In the right situation, as a small street tree or garden specimen, it can be quite valuable. However, in areas where this or other privets have become a problem by escaping the garden, careful

Ligustrum lucidum

Ligustrum lucidum 'Excelsum Superbum'. Photo by Michael A. Dirr

consideration should be given as to whether another, less fecund plant might be a better choice.

Several cultivars exist, many not as free-flowering as the species, but most being easier to manage due to their smaller size and, often, lack of fruit set. *Ligustrum lucidum* 'Aureovariegatum' has leaves streaked in yellow throughout, especially in spring; *L. lucidum* 'Excelsum Superbum' is a rather upright form with highly variegated leaves of deep cream and pink, quite striking in the shade; and *L. lucidum* 'Tricolor' has nearly white variegations, streaked pink especially when young, and is also superb in the shade.

As the earlier discussion would suggest, *Ligustrum lucidum* is tolerant of many soils short of standing water. It also tolerates significant periods of drought at any time of the year. One of the hardier of the evergreen species, temperatures of –5 to 0°F (–20 to –18°C) cause little damage. Temperatures much lower for any extended period of time produce red blotching or leaf drop, and wet heavy snowfall causes much branch breakage.

Ligustrum lucidum 'Tricolor'

Lithocarpus	tan bark oak	Fagaceae

Lithocarpus includes up to 300 recognized species, nearly all native to southern and eastern Asia, with one tan bark oak appearing along the North American Pacific Coast. All are evergreen with leathery leaves, usually oval and entire, rarely with some dentations. The fruit is acorn-like, as one would expect, with the receptacle usually covering a fair amount of the seed.

Both males and females flower in bunched, sometimes creamy

golden, erect spikes that distinguish the genus *Lithocarpus* from the closely related genus *Quercus*, with its downward-dangling, catkin-like flowers. They also represent a potentially negative attribute of the entire genus, in that the flowers, though attractive in appearance, emit a strong odor, usually in May or June, that some find oppressive.

That being said, tan bark oaks are among the most beautiful in the wide array of broadleaved evergreens, often exhibiting an upright stature, many having silver bark and lovely leaves coated powder blue and with varying degrees of coppery indumentum. Perhaps the most pleasing aspect among the many species is the appearance in spring of the decidedly pubescent, new growth, emerging in colors ranging from the deepest pinks to golden and silver.

Though most species come from warm temperate and tropical regions, a number inhabit areas with significant winter frost. Those listed here are among the most cold hardy and are known in cultivation.

Lithocarpus densiflorus (tan oak). Santa Cruz in central California north to Douglas County in southwestern Oregon in coastal mixed forests, including the redwood belt, inland to drier interior slopes from sea level to about 6000 ft. (2000 m). Medium to large tree; in forest conditions to 35 ft. (10.5 m) tall and slowly to over 150 ft. (46 m) by 25–45 ft. (7.5–14 m) wide; slower and usually smaller in cultivation. Plants in woodland conditions are narrowly conical, often with a single leader.

The tree is deep-rooted with strong, flexible branches. The leaves—narrow, pointed, and 1½–4½ in. (4–12 cm) long—are striking, glossy above, often silvery or cream-colored beneath and decidedly tomentous with, sometimes, a hint of indumentum. The new growth of spring can be entirely covered with a glittering light tan or copper felt. Bunches of small, creamy yellow flower spikes, to about 2 in. (5 cm), reach upward in late spring from the previous season's growth, their handsome appearance countered, somewhat, by their rather strong odor, as with the entire genus. The acorns begin to form quickly after flowering and, by early to mid fall, ripen in greenish brown clusters supported by attractive fur-covered receptacles.

This single North American representative of the genus *Lithocarpus* is a relic of an earlier time when, along with the more famous coastal redwoods (*Sequoia sempervirens*) and numerous West Coast endemics, they were pushed to the edge of the continent by the last ice age. One of North America's most magnificent natives, the largest and, most often, the purest stands remain alongside the redwoods, where they are bathed by the moisture and protection of the Pacific Ocean. Gazing upon these primitive oak relatives, with their patchy white bark and reflective leaves casting a blue-tinted shadow from high overhead, makes one wonder what other ancient species were pushed beyond their limits, no longer to enrich our flora or adorn our gardens. As one of the treasures not lost, *L. densiflorus* is still too uncommon in gardens and public plantings. Some of the finest specimens in cultivation can be seen in Portland, Oregon's Hoyt Arboretum, along with other oaks and their relatives.

The plants are accepting of sun or shade, trees in the wild having often begun life in forest conditions and spent many years as part of the understory. Though not as fussy as some other Mediterranean-climate western North American natives, they are often displeased by summer irrigation or particularly high humidity, especially while temperatures are high. This fact probably limits their cultivation to mostly cool maritime or Mediterranean parts of the world. For western North American gardeners, they are perfectly at home with such contemporaries as *Garrya elliptica*, *Arbutus menziesii*, and *Ceanothus*

Lithocarpus densiflorus. Photo by Bart O'Brien

species, and plants from similar climates (*Rhamnus alaternus*, *Viburnum tinus*), all of which grow quite happily beside, or in the dappled shade of, *Lithocarpus densiflorus*.

Although, again, sensitive to abundant watering especially in hot summer areas, *Lithocarpus densiflorus* is a fine tree if left to its own devices and is among the most, if not *the* most cold hardy of *Lithocarpus* species. Even forms from the lowest elevations seem unaffected to near 0°F (–18°C), and plants from provenances higher in the mountains have reported tolerance of under –10 to –15°F (–23 to –26°C). Too, the strong flexible branches hold up well under heavy loads of snow or ice.

Although, as with many oaks and their relatives, they don't root easily from cuttings, they do germinate quickly from fresh acorns, available from a number of seed sources in the western United States. Alas, since 1995 sudden oak death (*Phytophthora ramorum*) has killed thousands of tan oaks.

Lithocarpus densiflorus f. *attenuato-dentatus*, discovered in the early 1960s in the Southern Cascades of Yuba County, California, has too many syllables but beautifully serrated leaf margins with a marvelous, silvery white indumentum beneath. This form has been amenable to garden cultivation, growing quickly. The largest specimens on the West Coast have now exceeded 40 ft. (12 m) in height and 15 ft. (4.5 m) in width. It blooms only rarely and may be sterile. Propagation is unusually easy from cuttings of current season's growth in autumn or winter.

Lithocarpus densiflorus subsp. *echinoides* grows mostly on serpentine soils in the Siskiyou Mountains of southwest Oregon and northwest California; it displays stunning blue leaves and new growth covered with golden indumentum—making it worthy of mention despite its small stature, sometimes to under 3–5 ft. (1–1.5 m).

Lithocarpus densiflorus subsp. *echinoides*

Lithocarpus densiflorus subsp. *echinoides*, foliage

Lithocarpus densiflorus f. *attenuato-dentatus*. Photo by Bart O'Brien

Lithocarpus edulis (Japanese tan bark oak). From southern Japan and in cultivation in the West since the mid 1800s. The epithet ("edible") refers to the numerous acorns produced by this tree, said to become edible quickly, bypassing the long ripening process of other acorn-like fruits. The untoothed leaves are shiny and a brilliant green with a pale green underside cast in light, coppery fur; large and slender, they can measure 9 in. (23 cm) in length by 2–3 in. (5–8 cm) wide, creating a wonderfully tropical effect that is one of the tree's best attributes.

Though reported to be 50–60 ft. (15–18 m) in the wild, the largest trees in North America have yet to attain 30 ft. (9 m), having remained rather bushy for many years. Growth seems a bit more rapid in dappled shade than in sun and is best supported by evenly moist soil, well drained and well supplied with organic matter. Plants used for stock in our nursery grew rather slowly—under 1 ft. (30 cm) a year—until placed in the ground and given the above conditions. Then, shoots of over 3 ft. (1 m) appeared in the first spring, resulting in over 6 ft. (2 m) of growth during the first season in the ground, surely a testament to the plant's capacity to become tree-like quite quickly, given the right incentives.

Appearing clean and green in the southeastern United States, where they revel in summer heat and humidity, plants must be more carefully placed in drier climates such as the West Coast. Experiences in Portland, Oregon, have shown that in unrelenting summer sun and without regular water, the leaves are noticeably smaller and yellowing can occur. However, they thrive in Vancouver, B.C., with no sign of the winter yellowing that can occur on some evergreen oak relatives from lack of a season's accumulated heat. Wonderful specimens can be seen at the University of British Columbia Botanic Garden.

Lithocarpus edulis has taken winter bouts of 0°F (–18°C) in stride with protection of larger, overhead trees, but those temperatures

Lithocarpus edulis

Lithocarpus edulis, foliage

Lithocarpus edulis 'Variegata'

or below in exposed areas have resulted in leaf scorch and twig damage.

Lithocarpus edulis 'Variegata', with elegant dark, leathery foliage splashed creamy white in the leaf centers, was first offered by Woodlanders Nursery and is similar to the species in form, habit, and frost hardiness.

Propagation is easy from acorns and also relatively easy from cuttings taken from current season's growth in autumn and winter.

Lithocarpus henryi. Introduced to the West from China about 1900; as with *L. edulis*, still rather rare in cultivation but becoming less so. Another lithocarpus with handsome glossy foliage: leaves can be 9–12 in. (23–30 cm) long by 2½–3 in. (6–8 cm) wide when grown in dappled shade. In youth, *L. henryi* is upright, becoming broad and pyramidal later on, and rather fast-growing as well, nearly 3 ft. (1 m) a year in the first ten years or so. Specimens have been recorded growing to 60 ft. (18 m) or more in the wild, and plants of over 50 ft. (15 m) can be seen at Caerhays Castle in the United Kingdom. Many 30 ft. (9 m) or taller specimens exist in the southeastern United States and along the West Coast.

Useful as an understory tree where the leaves attain their largest size, plants also perform well in the open, where the intense green and polished shine of the long leaves adds a striking, year-round lushness to a streetscape or a tropical effect in the garden.

Lithocarpus henryi has proven hardy to 0°F (–18°C), even below, in the southeastern United States, without leaf damage. In marginal places that are subject to bouts of cold, an area out of drying wind would be preferred.

Cuttings have been quite successful from late summer through

Lithocarpus henryi

Lithocarpus henryi, foliage

mid winter using the most recent season's growth and relatively potent hormones. Seeds are also easy but not as readily available.

Lithocarpus variolosus. In contrast to *L. edulis* and *L. henryi*, with their bright green leaves, this handsome species from southeast China has leaves of brilliant silver. Somewhat smaller than others mentioned here—to about 4 in. (10 cm) long and 2 in. (5 cm) wide—the leaves are also somewhat undulant, which adds to their already silky texture.

First introduced to the North American Pacific Coast in about 1990 by Quarryhill Botanical Garden, this plant (which at first glance looks like a giant *Elaeagnus pungens*, without those annoying thorns) in time reveals pewter-colored bark and an upright, conical habit no evergreen elaeagnus achieves. Six-year-old plants are well adapted to their mixed planting, already showing off their reflective leaf undersides and silvery bark. Specimens shared with the University of British Columbia Botanic Garden have quickly achieved 20–25 ft. (6–7.5 m), while plants at Quarryhill have seemed a little less happy in northern California's intense summer sun.

From experiences so far, it seems a bit of light shade, especially in hot, dry areas, would be appropriate. Otherwise, regular summer water, as with the other Asian species.

Lithocarpus variolosus appears at quite high elevations in China, and all indications are that it will be among the hardiest of the genus. Though some flaw in its character could still appear, because of its ease of growth and propagation (cuttings and seed), there is no reason it should not be among the most popular broadleaved evergreens in zones 7 and above.

For propagation by seed, acorns should be collected in early autumn and sown immediately . . . or as soon as there is available potting soil. Cuttings are the easiest, with a good result, seventy to eighty percent, if taken in late autumn or winter from ripened, current season's growth with low hormone levels, bottom heat, and mist.

Lithocarpus variolosus, foliage

Lithocarpus variolosus, flowering spikes

Luma	Myrtaceae

Having previously been bounced in and out of the genus *Myrtus*, *Luma* is now a genus of at least four and probably more shrubs and trees, all evergreen and primarily native to the western slopes of the Andes from central Chile south, in any place where abundant rainfall is received, a region shared with six, possibly seven, recognized genera of the family Myrtaceae. Yet other myrtles can be found east of the Andes, further north in the damp belts catching Atlantic moisture, from northwestern Argentina north. Most of these myrtles grow alongside, and sometimes in, running or standing water, filling a rather important ecological niche, as they are particularly good at holding soil, thus preventing erosion. The genus *Luma* is no exception. In numerous locations skirting the Andes of southwestern Argentina and Chile (Los Alerces National Park, for example)—among the southern beeches (*Nothofagus*), *Fuchsia*, and other wonders—there are gravelly outcrops reaching into high, inland lakes and lapped by their cold surf where fat-trunked, small trees as tall as 20 ft. (6 m) or more are displayed, with cinnamon-brown and nearly white, patched bark and ample spring flowers catching the eye from some distance. Often multi-trunked and shrubby in youth, they may take many years to reach tree size, but, without the perils found in nature, a specimen can achieve small tree size quite quickly under good garden conditions and with the help of a pair of secateurs to encourage upward mobility.

Propagation is not difficult for any of the southern South American myrtles. Seed germinates readily with the help of cool moist stratification, and cuttings are best at the end of summer through autumn from mostly ripened, current season's growth.

Luma apiculata (arrayán, palo colorado). Widespread in Chile and southwest Argentina, this species ranges from a small shrub on windswept hillsides, growing not much more than 3 ft. (1 m), to a medium tree, in either mixed woodland or in its own bosks, reaching over 30 ft. (9 m), though reports of 50 ft. (15 m) specimens suggest even greater possibilities. The mahogany-red bark, with a little "basketball" orange (vibrant, brownish orange) and white in patches, is very attractive, decorating the tree's stout, muscular presence.

If trained at an early age to one or only a few main trunks, the tree maintains apical dominance for some years, eventually becoming a round-topped specimen with naturally layered branches. Careful thinning enhances the outline and exposes the rich colored bark and older twigs.

The rounded-oval leaves—usually under 1 in. (2.5 cm) long and ½ in. (1.5 cm) or more wide—are dark and shiny with a pointed tip, creating a fine texture that makes *Luma apiculata* useful not only as a small specimen tree but also as a clipped hedge. The spring to early summer flowers begin appearing when the tree is only a few years old, each flower white and about ½ in. (1.5 cm) across, with a large boss of stamens, and in enough quantity to nearly cover the plant. The fruit, though only about 5 mm in diameter, can be produced in abundance and usually appears just beyond the leaves, dressing the tree in the shiny, dark purple-blue typical of the myrtles, in late summer or fall.

Numerous wonderful specimens exist in New Zealand gardens. In the southern United Kingdom and in Ireland, especially the south-

Luma apiculata. Photo by Michael A. Dirr

west, plants in cultivation can be seen in possibly their greatest glory outside their native habitat. Near Garnish, in western County Cork, Ireland, one specimen measured well over 25 ft. (7.5 m) in height with a nearly equal spread and an 18 in. (45 cm) buttressed trunk of screaming orange-red. These are climates of ample rainfall where *Luma apiculata* does particularly well, a fact underlined for me at the University of California Botanic Garden, where my daily route took me past one specimen that was flourishing, as were its seedlings, within the wet zone of a very old sprinkler leak. Plants will succeed with moderate summer drought but take a rather long time to achieve any size. In wet climates such as the west of the British Isles, seeding can be a problem; it is less so along the North American Pacific Coast, except in irrigated areas.

Luma apiculata, foliage.
Photo by Michael A. Dirr

For one's own garden a better small tree could hardly be found. With its small, solid stature; aromatic flowers, fruit, and leaves; bark that is appealing as well as peeling, it is a delight. One small caveat is the fruit, not as attractive when staining the garden furnishings as when dressing the plant. However, it is edible.

Historically many collections have been made immediately along the Pacific in Chile, and plants grown have often not been frost hardy much below 20°F (–7°C). Increasingly collections from higher elevations are proving hardy at least into the 8 to 10°F (–14 to –12°C) range, providing they are not subject to cold, blasty winds.

Luma apiculata, flowers.
Photo by Michael A. Dirr

A couple of forms of *Luma apiculata* with quite recognizable characteristics are under cultivation by Michael Remmick in McMinnville, Oregon. Plants from the high country near Nahuel Huapi on the Argentine side of the Andean cordillera, where upright specimens with somewhat rounded, matte, shiny leaves and a very dark brownish tan bark reach 40 ft. (12 m) tall, have had great success in his garden, growing in seven years from seed to over 15 ft. (4.5 m) with a 2½ in. (6 cm) caliper trunk and beautifully exfoliating bark. Two bouts of temperatures well below 20°F (–7°C) have wrought no damage.

Collections of *Luma apiculata* from near Vilches in central Chile are somewhat shorter, to 20–25 ft. (6–7.5 m), with glossy, rather downward-pointed leaves and wide-arching branches. Grown in McMinnville near such other broadleaved evergreens as *Drimys winteri*, *Gevuina avellana*, and *L. chequen*, and occupying a streambank adjacent to the Nahuel Huapi form, seven-year-old plants of the Vilches form are 8–10 ft. (2.5–3 m) tall and, as in habitat, more widely spreading. In one winter cold spell, a windy dry temperature of 16°F (–9°C) frazzled tender branch ends but did not inflict lasting damage. Both of these collections are being made available to the nursery trade, identified by their place of collection—Nahuel Huapi and Vilches.

The exquisite *Luma apiculata* 'Glanleam Gold' deserves mention, but it is slower, being likely to stay under 6–8 ft. (2–2.5 m) over time.

Luma chequen (chequén, arrayán blanco). Another western Andean species, usually at mid elevation to the north and low elevation to the south, growing among a rich assembly of broadleaved evergreens. The species is often found in somewhat drier conditions than *L. apiculata* but is still quite happy to get its feet wet and is surprisingly resilient to at least moderate summer drought conditions. *Luma chequen* populations do not quite reach the altitude and, therefore, don't have quite the cold hardiness of *L. apiculata* populations.

It is grown as a large shrub to pyramidal small tree, with densely flattened sprays of branches sporting lanceolate leaves, 5 mm to 1 in. (2.5 cm), sometimes rather shiny and often rhytid (leathery) and covered with a fine pubescence. The overall look of the plant is more ascendant than *Luma apiculata*, although individual populations and certainly clones within those populations vary greatly. Some are not destined to grow beyond wide-spreading shrubs; others, such as forms collected near Vilches in central Chile, maintain a dense, pyramidal shape and can reach 12–15 ft. (3.5–4.5 m) in under ten years from cuttings. The aptly named *L. chequen* 'Vilches Clone', selected by Michael Remmick, has achieved this size from a specimen in the wild, apparently of great age, measuring under 25 ft. (7.5 m).

As *Luma chequen* is not common in cultivation, there is, unfortunately, little evidence from which comparisons can be made. Experience suggests less frost hardiness (five to eight less Fahrenheit degrees, approximately four less in Celsius) than the examples of *L. apiculata* collected in the same location. We know that *L. chequen* particularly dislikes sudden, early frosts, having suffered bark split on even fairly old twigs during an early November, 20°F (–7°C) surprise in Oregon's Willamette Valley. This same unusual event caused similar problems with several budding olive (*Olea*) orchards, where young, vigorous specimens had not slowed their summer growth.

In compatible climates, both Mediterranean and cool coastal, *Luma chequen* deserves attention. It has a tighter habit and greater drought tolerance than *L. apiculata*, together with attractive white flowers, dark bluish fruit, and reddish, patchy bark, all fine attributes for a small garden tree. The plant has performed best in bright light, if not full sun. Growing in any degree of shade, where it is often found in habitat, its unripened growth is potentially susceptible to damage from hard frosts.

Luma chequen should be assumed reliable where temperatures rarely dip below 10 to 20°F (–12 to –7°C) and, like other semi-hardy members of its clan, will resprout handily from temperatures even as low as from 0 to 10°F (–18 to –12°C). Cold, drying winds, its main winter enemy, can inflict severe damage.

As with others in the genus, plants root reliably from late summer through winter from semi-ripened or current season's growth or from harvested seed, preferably given a month or two of cool stratification. In our garden, *Luma chequen* is shy to produce unsolicited seedlings, thus making it potentially less worrisome as an invasive species in cool, wet climates.

Amomyrtus luma

AMOMYRTUS LUMA, a little-known relative found in the wet, southern Andes and coastal forests, is worthy of mention here. An exquisite, small tree, it can reach over 35 ft. (10.5 m) producing small, dry fruit from clusters of white scented flowers that appear to be a flattened spray at the ends of the branches in spring—earlier than the genus *Luma*, which flowers later in summer, depending on the temperature. So far, in cultivation, growth has been quite slow, but hope springs eternal: plants observed in their native riparian, if not swampy, habitats have become striking, narrow but round-crowned trees, the silvery barked trunks furrowing beautifully with age—an age that, unfortunately can't be predicted under conditions of cultivation.

Since the species inhabits both coastal and cold mountain habitats, plants with good provenance might be frost hardy in the 10 to 15°F (–12 to –9.5°C) range or even lower if there are no dry, freezing winds. Coastal forms should be avoided for colder gardens.

Amomyrtus luma, flowers

Lyonothamnus Catalina ironwood Rosaceae

A monotypic and rather narrowly endemic genus, growing in a limited area of southern California, the common name alluding to its habitat on Catalina Island. Related to the genus *Vauquelinia*, which grows inland in the desert mountains of the U.S. Southwest into Mexico—and tends toward shrubbiness, Catalina ironwood is a true example of island gigantism, whereby plants and animals living in isolation and without competition or predators can reach unusually large proportions in comparison to their relatives on the mainland.

Lyonothamnus floribundus. Truly one of California's most handsome natives, this evergreen tree is fast-growing to 20–25 ft. (6–7.5 m), occasionally reaching 40 ft. (12 m). The narrow crown broadens with age, becoming a very wide oval if out of the wind. The leaves are remarkably shiny, and, depending on the form, either single and entire, or pinnate with serrate margins. They are 6–7 in. (15–18 cm) in length, sometimes persisting for a couple of years before they fall. The late spring or early summer flowers are in terminal panicles, 6–8 in. (15–20 cm) in diameter, with each tiny, white, campanulate flower of about 6 mm giving out a pleasing, almost musty, fragrance reminis-

Lyonothamnus floribundus.
Photo by Bart O'Brien

cent of a very special crataegus. The bark, also an outstanding feature, is produced in gently swirling strips of cinnamon-brown which give the trunk and branches a shaggy, picturesque texture—if everyone resists the temptation to pull off the long strands. Though the entire-leaved type exists in horticulture, *L. floribundus* subsp. *aspleniifolius* (fernleaf ironwood), with its twice-compound leaves, each about 4½ × 2 in. (12 × 5 cm) and beautifully serrated, is the most common in cultivation, though the genus could hardly be called common at all. It is increasingly available in western North American nurseries and occasionally grown in the United Kingdom, where it has survived outside at Kew for a number of years. Solidly hardy to 18 to 20°F (−8 to −7°C), temperatures of 8 to 12°F (−14 to −11°C) have frozen it back, even to the ground in some cases, with vigorous resprouting from the base.

Lyonothamnus floribundus subsp. *aspleniifolius*

The species thrives in full sun except in the extreme heat of interior climates. In shade, plants stretch for the light, becoming tall and narrow with well-spaced branches. Examples of both sun and shade specimens can be seen at the Rancho Santa Ana Botanic Garden in Claremont, California.

Catalina ironwood prefers a mineral soil and, to ensure a longer life for the tree, a light touch with the fertilizer. Experience has found the species to be fairly tolerant of summer garden water along the immediate Pacific Coast of North America, where summers, or at least summer nights, are cool. But, as with so many other western North American natives, it can collapse in inland heat if water is applied. Thus *Lyonothamnus floribundus* fits the pattern of not being suitable for growing outside Mediterranean or coolish summer climates.

A fabulous small garden specimen, trees should be placed where the handsome shaggy crimson bark can be admired, always remembering that, even in the garden, the species tends to a late-summer purge of leaves which drives even the less compulsive among us to clean the canopy; the brown seed clusters are unsightly as can be.

Propagation can be accomplished from mid summer cuttings on into winter without mist; plants grown from seed are fairly uniform and should be sown in autumn in mineral soil that can remain cool and moist throughout the winter.

Magnolia   Magnoliaceae

A genus of some 125 to nearly 200 species of deciduous, as well as evergreen, shrubs and trees, the number of species depending on whether one includes the once-separate genera *Michelia*, *Manglietia*, and *Parakmeria*. Richard Figlar, a well-respected student of the magnoliads, now, convincingly, includes all three in the genus *Magnolia*. If indeed this "lumping" is accepted in the long run, the entire family will have only two genera—*Magnolia* and *Liriodendron*, the tulip tree of eastern Asia and eastern North America. Since the plants described here and once listed in separate genera are now likely to be found in other texts under the genus *Magnolia*, I've chosen to do so here as well. However, I continue to identify michelias and manglietias and parakmerias alongside, in order to be able to discuss their differences as groups and, perhaps, minimize the absolute importance of nomenclature.

Both the genus and family show the greatest diversity in southern and eastern Asia, with another pocket in southeastern United States and northeastern Mexico. All have the same love of rich soil and object to any prolonged drought. The flowers can be star-like or cupped and, except in the michelia group, are terminal, at the tips of twigs. The decorative seeds, when ripe, are often exhibited on the outside of a rather primitive cone-like structure of carpels and are frequently a bright orange-red.

Like many other broadleaved evergreens, the evergreen magnoliads are all best propagated by cuttings with mature, current season's growth, often in late autumn through winter; success may be had with the original magnolia group in mid summer to early autumn as well. Seed of all species is best if sown directly and either sprouts immediately or the following spring after cool stratification.

The manglietia group includes, roughly, twenty-five examples, their distinction being primarily that the seed carpels consist of four to six rather than the two ovules of the genus at large—a small difference, but one that gives the writer an excuse to highlight these wonderful plants.

Predominantly native in moist, broadleaved evergreen woodlands that are very high in diversity, manglietias are only one component of a number of primitive family members reaching their greatest numbers from central and southern China, south into Vietnam and into the Himalayas. Whether working with manglietias as a mere subset of the genus *Magnolia* or as a stand-alone genus, it is a very interesting group of plants even though relatively little is known about the range and diversity of its members. All share the characteristic of at least beginning life as understory trees, growing quickly when young and eventually reaching canopy size. As growth matures and the plants reach sunlight, the leaves often become smaller and capable of taking nearly full to full sun. Without the crowding of nearby forest or woodland trees, they remain narrow and pyramidal for many years, becoming broad-crowned in age.

Unlike other magnolias, manglietias lack the propensity to flower for long periods or sporadically throughout the year. Nearly all seem to flower for a relatively short period in late spring. Accustomed to plentiful moisture, plants in cultivation, whether in containers or in the ground, display discontent with any long-term drying or starvation by quickly reducing speed of growth and yellowing.

From the multitude of magnolias and their relatives in southern and Southeast Asia, it is obvious that that continent has served both as a refuge for and as a birthplace to the great diversity of the magnoliad family. The michelia group—in which I include about fifty different plants, though the numbers fluctuate as various botanical interests study them—is found there in tropical, subtropical, and warm temperate, broadleaved evergreen forests of high rainfall.

The michelias differ from the rest of the genus in that, while members of the magnolia and manglietia groupings are terminal-flowered, tending to produce a single flower at the end of a given branch, those in the michelia group can have a dozen or more flowers on a single branchlet, often unfurling over a period of many weeks and offering a lot more floral "bang for the buck." Careful scrutiny has shown that these apparently axillary flowers are, in fact, produced from what is termed proleptic branching—meaning that what appear to be axils are technically the ends of tiny branches. Go figure. While this attribute is clearly significant to people interested in taxonomic details, it is also important horticulturally, for a multitude of flowers is produced where there would otherwise be only one.

Culturally, these wonderful plants require generally the same conditions as others in the genus: a love of rich soil and a dislike of any prolonged drought. Much like citrus and gardenias, they like a snifter of nitrogen after a hard day's growing work—with an iron chaser to keep them green and growing vigorously. All michelias seem to love warm weather, and ample nutrients give them fortitude during the cool season, especially in areas such as the United Kingdom and along the immediate West Coast of North America, where spring seems to last for nearly half the year and heat-lovers have a problem getting kick-started. Retailers, on occasion, have poor luck convincing the public of a michelia's worthiness, as the plant can yellow and even partially defoliate during long stints in a container, especially if nutrient-depleted or allowed to dry out.

With so much horticultural sleuthing over the last hundred years or so, and so many plants having been brought into cultivation, it is a wonder so few michelias have made their appearance in Western horticulture or, for that matter, Eastern. *Magnolia doltsopa, M. champaca, M. figo* (a shrub, but an important one), to some degree *M. maudiae*, and a very few others have been used in Asia for centuries and found to be culturally indispensable. Others have only recently emerged from their remote, often mountainous, retreats, with many more waiting to be "discovered" horticulturally. For myself, when I encountered my first michelias, having been told numerous times that even the species then available were not cold hardy in western Oregon, I fell into an all-too-common horticultural trap: the assumption that if a plant isn't already here, it surely must have been tried and failed. Upon further investigation, I found that most people who confidently relayed that michelias were not frost hardy had, in fact, never planted one in the ground. Since then, in the Willamette Valley and coastal Oregon gardens, significant examples have come to my attention: large specimens of *M. figo*, *M. compressa*, and even *M. doltsopa* have been spotted in old gardens, having survived the worst this climate can offer. I have come to realize, again, that some things just haven't been planted yet in sufficient numbers to be noticed. Many other michelias, some coming from even colder provenances in the wild, are proving exceedingly garden-worthy—for their flowers' longevity, mass, and exquisite fragrance; for their highly variable leaves, with a great array of textures and colors; and, for many, their compact size, which fits very well into urban and small gardens.

As a group—or perhaps a lifestyle—michelias are fairly easy to propagate. Seeds have been successful with immediate sowing or after chilling in a damp cooler for up to two months. Those sown very soon after dehiscence should germinate immediately. Older seeds might germinate sporadically and take longer to do so. Cuttings are best taken from vigorous, nonflowering branches, preferably close to the main trunk, in what is often called a zone of juvenility, or—better yet—from sucker growth at the base of the plant. Cuttings taken in late summer are often successful, but the best results are from November to February with bottom heat and mist as well as a fairly high concentration of hormone.

Though michelias are among the easiest rooters, propagation can be a source of frustration because of one small conundrum—the plant's ability to easily root decreases significantly once the plant reaches flowering size and displays characteristics worthy of selection and reproduction (i.e., the size, shape, abundance, frequency, and fragrance of the flowers). This technical problem can be overcome by taking advantage of the majority of the species' propensity for sprouting from what appears to be a permanent burl at each plant's base. Whether it is an adaptation to enable resprouting after fires, browsing, or, indeed, constant coppicing by humans, these sprouts remain juvenile and much easier to propagate. We have taken cuttings from sucker growth or other vigorous material, then kept that named or numbered individual in a juvenile state by continually cutting back the mother plant to maintain vigorous shoot growth. Be sure the desired subject is not grafted, however! Adult plants can be coerced into sprouting from the base by cutting back the top or, if pruning courage fails, opening the base to sunlight.

In the greater world of magnolias, the inclusion of these many evergreen species has added great diversity of texture and flower. If anyone were to think of the true magnolias as mostly deciduous—those specimens that we who are biased toward evergreens think of as either the pink one or the white one, used to create enough shade for a hosta, the green or, perhaps, variegated one—this large group suggests otherwise and rewards our inner magnolia with ever greater diversity of choices.

Of the increasingly large number of evergreen species available, the ones chosen here exhibit both the most attractive characteristics for the garden as well as the greatest hardiness to frost. The genus as a whole tends to be pest-free, and all magnolias are somewhat tolerant of at least short periods of drought once established.

Magnolia champaca (syn. *Michelia champaca*). Southeast China to the Himalayas and northern India and tropical and subtropical forest. Plants have been in cultivation for so long the exact, original range is not known. A relatively large evergreen tree to nearly 100 ft. (30 m) in the wild, often 30–40 ft. (9–12 m) cultivation. The large, slightly pointed oval leaves to 11 in. (28 cm) long by 4½ in. (12 cm) wide are a rich spring-green, and slightly felted beneath.

The flowers are creamy yellow to nearly orange and thin-petaled, with the entire inflorescence measuring only 1 in. (2.5 cm) or less. However, what they lack in size, they make up for with intense fragrance and long bloom season. An important plant in the culture of much of Southeast Asia, and a plant few would be without if there were a bit of room in the garden or in a pot. Often, where they grow or can be shipped, the flowers are made into necklaces, their fragrance increasing as they are warmed by the heat of the body. Cutting-grown plants often flower their first or second year; those grown from seed might take five or six but can be induced to flower earlier when grown in a pot.

One of the most tender species, frost of more than four or five degrees Fahrenheit (roughly two degrees Celsius) below freezing can damage the plants. In North America they have been successful in southern California, usually within view of salt water, and are grown out of pure stubbornness further north along the coast with the knowledge that they may be frozen back every so often. They are increasingly popular as an indoor/outdoor pot plant. Needing dampness and nutrients, the same conditions as other michelias, they can be kept in a large container, slightly root pruned every few years, and can survive inside, at least in winter, if given bright light and a careful transition to the out-of-doors whenever spring occurs. As with any houseplant spending the summer outside, a shift to several days in the shade before spending any time in the sun is necessary so the current crop of leaves doesn't burn. Whether inside or out, dappled shade, or at least protection from afternoon sun, seems preferable.

Propagation is relatively easy, preferably from stems, suckers, or branches that have not flowered. Late autumn to mid winter is best.

Magnolia compressa (syn. *Michelia compressa*). Southern China, Taiwan, southern Japan, from sea level to relatively high elevations in warm temperate to near tropical, mixed forest, always damp, though sometimes with some winter dryness.

Both widespread in habitat and one of the earlier species in cultivation, plants were introduced to the western United States in the 1950s or before and were grown at various arboreta from Vancouver, B.C., to southern California. But the plants never caught on commercially and many disappeared, one exception being a 30 ft. (9 m) specimen that remains strong and floriferous to the present in an old garden in Salem, Oregon.

A vigorous tree to 40 ft. (12 m) or more, *Magnolia compressa* maintains a relatively narrow, pyramidal shape, rounding with age. Leaves are somewhat linear, 3–4 in. (8–10 cm) by 1–2 in. (2.5–5 cm), and lacking any significant indumentum; they too become more round as the tree grows older. The silvery gray bark, with its telltale rows of attractive lenticels, contrasts nicely with the bright green leaves.

Flowers average about 3 in. (8 cm); they are white to pale pink, sometimes with a rose center. On occasion, the inner tepals will all be of a dark color, giving the flowers a bicolor effect. If *Magnolia figo* is the banana shrub, then *M. compressa* should be the pineapple guava shrub as, to my nose, they smell just like my childhood memories of *Acca sellowiana*. Other noses might find it otherwise. The flowers occur in such great abundance, it is a mystery the plant has so nearly disappeared from horticulture in the United States. Of late, wonderful specimens have drawn attention in the University of California Botanic Garden in Berkeley, and the Quarryhill Botanical Garden in Glen Ellen, California.

Additional features—a good sun tolerance and a slightly greater tolerance of drought—make them fine street trees and candidates for urban planting. As well, the frost hardiness of selections brought from higher elevations makes them viable in areas receiving too much winter chill for other species. The Salem, Oregon, plant, for example, withstood −11°F (−24°C) during a particular cold winter spell and remained vigorous.

Propagation has been comparatively easy from very late summer to mid winter cuttings, even from flowering wood.

Magnolia compressa

Magnolia delavayi. South and southwest China and northern Vietnam. Named in 1889 for the French Jesuit missionary who discovered the plant in 1886. Just prior to 1900, E. H. Wilson sent seeds to England, and plants reached North America as early as the 1920s. They have been included in gardens since, in milder areas in Britain, in both southeastern Australia and New Zealand, and, of course, in China and Japan. Examples in western North America remain rare and, until recently, appear to be of only one form.

A bold evergreen tree from 20 ft. (6 m) to a fairly quick 30 ft. (9 m), with known specimens over 60 ft. (18 m). Wilson reported it to be the largest-leaved evergreen tree that can be grown in a cool, temperate climate, with leaves measuring from 8 × 4 in. (20 × 10 cm) to over 15 × 8 in. (38 × 20 cm), depending on the form—larger and bolder even than *Magnolia grandiflora* and nearly as leathery. Their rather dull, olive-green color is spruced up by a slightly bluish cast.

The flowers too are of great size, forming a white to creamish cup that can be over 10 in. (25 cm) across. Some forms exhibit bronzy red new growth and light to deep pink flowers, though these are still very rare in cultivation. The flowering habit is much more sporadic than one might expect in a magnolia. Although they reach their floral peak in early summer, many plants have some flowers throughout most of the year, especially in milder climates. A double-bracted form, for example, given (without cultivar name) to Portland's Classical Chinese Garden by Gossler Farms Nursery of Springfield, Oregon, is a local legend, having had one, if not two, flowers open every weekend for months on end. Spectacular as the flowers are, their longevity can sometimes be measured in hours rather than days. It is best to judge the opening of your plant's flower, then have a cocktail party for its duration, so all can see—hoping, of course, it does not open too early in the morning. Additional attractions are the seeds, or "cones," often over 6 in. (15 cm) tall by 3 in. (8 cm) wide, and the bark on aged trees, which can attain a supple, almost elephantine texture, with silver-gray coloration.

Often a fairly high mountain plant in its native haunts, it seems to prefer mild summers and does not thrive in the gardens of the southeastern United States, for instance. On the other hand, in particularly cool summer regions, such as the United Kingdom and along the immediate northwestern coast of North America, the plants, though appearing healthy, may maintain a shrub form for many years. Perfect conditions seem to include ample humidity, warm days, cool nights, and possibly a little dappled shade. Like many of the magnolias, addition of iron and nitrogen greens them up if they have become yellowed by extended winter cool. That said, even in the relatively cool

Magnolia delavayi

Magnolia delavayi, flower.
Photo by Michael A. Dirr

though winter-mild climate of Caerhays Castle in Cornwall, plants have attained heights of over 60 ft. (18 m). Though usually reported as a zone 9 plant, taking temperatures no lower than 20°F (−7°C), specimens have withstood short periods of 10 to 12°F (−12 to −11°C) with no damage when grown in a warm situation where they have not been allowed to yellow. As the species' native habitat consists of a great range of altitudes, forms with greater cold hardiness could be expected.

California specimens include a magnificent (30 × 45 ft., 9 × 14 m) plant at Huntington Botanical Garden in San Marino, and a 45 × 40 ft. (14 × 12 m) multi-trunked specimen at the University of California Botanic Garden at Berkeley. A specimen planted against a north wall at Elk Rock Gardens in Portland has for years struggled with great vigor to escape its keepers' apparent desire to keep it espaliered. In recent years, a red-flowered form has appeared; at five years of age, the plants in our Portland garden, from seeds sent from the Kunming Botanic Garden in China, were vigorous, with leaves narrower but flushed pink in new growth. Ours have yet to flower, but pictures and reports suggest their color as more of a blushed pink than a true red.

Propagation from cuttings is best done in autumn and winter, using current season's growth, preferably with a little bottom heat. Seeds, though rarely available, should be planted immediately or kept in damp storage until sown. Grafted or cutting-grown plants from mature trees will flower in as little as two or three years. Seedlings can take several additional years to flower.

Magnolia delavayi is truly a stunning plant. Though not for the small garden, its presence should be felt in every municipality where it can be grown.

Magnolia doltsopa (syn. *Michelia doltsopa*). Unlike other very fragrant magnolias of the michelia group, such as *Magnolia champaca*, *M. doltsopa* occurs over a wide range of habitat, from the Himalayas to southwestern China, as well as having been extensively cultivated in southern Asia, and many forms have been surprisingly tough. Trees often approach 35–40 ft. (10.5–12 m), and many become a pleasing, somewhat narrow pyramid. The leaves are a slightly pointed oval shape, about 4 in. (10 cm) by 5–6 in. (13–15 cm), with a pleasing, matte green top surface and a pale blue-green underside. The bark, with some maturity, attains a very reflective silver-gray sheen.

The flowers, varying in size according to the clone, can be as small as 2–3 in. (5–8 cm) or as large as 4½–5½ in. (12–14 cm) across, and often a little longer. They are consistently white to a very pale cream, rarely with a little pink in the center, and most have an outstanding fragrance. This michelia-of-choice in southern California gardens is

Magnolia doltsopa. Photo by Michael A. Dirr

Magnolia doltsopa. Photo by Michael A. Dirr

planted with surprising success at least as far north as western Oregon. Increasingly common in the milder districts of the United Kingdom, it is also one of the most common in milder areas of New Zealand and Australia and a given in east and south Asia, where it is a regular component of parks and gardens.

Tolerant, once established, of short periods of drought and confined situations if adequate nutrients are applied, a number of forms have proven frost hardy, or at least frost resistant, to 15 to 18°F (–9.5 to –8°C), with little bud or leaf damage. *Magnolia doltsopa* 'Silver Cloud', introduced by Duncan & Davies of New Zealand and relatively common in coastal California, is a bit more tender, having exhibited bud and stem damage with long temperatures below 20°F (–7°C); and a high-elevation seed form collected in southern China's Gaoligongshan mountain range at over 8500 ft. (2600 m) had its new growth significantly nipped by an early cold spell of 23°F (–5°C) at our Sauvie Island, Oregon, garden.

Several clones of a hybrid made some years ago between *Magnolia doltsopa* and *M. figo* are in cultivation as *M.* ×*foggii*. *Magnolia* ×*foggii* 'Jack Fogg' has the pyramidal shape of *M. doltsopa* but maintains its height under 20 ft. (6 m) with the influence of the shrubby *M. figo*. The hybrid has good relative frost hardiness, rarely having been cut back at near 0°F (–18°C) in the southeastern United States. In our Portland, Oregon, garden a seven-year-old specimen planted as an 18 in. (45 cm) whip approached 17 ft. (5 m) and, although probably planted in a bit too much sun, has thrived with abundant water, showing only the slightest yellowing of its shiny green, 4 in. (10 cm) leaves; it produces its flowers in great abundance from early March through

Magnolia ×*foggii* 'Jack Fogg'

May, then again sporadically through the summer and often into the next winter. Creamy white flushed with pale pink toward the center, they maintain a rather narrow tulip shape, opening to a full 2–3 in. (5–8 cm) only just before shattering. The fragrance is much like that of the banana shrub, *M. figo* (imitation banana candy), with just a bit of the pleasant sweetness of *M. doltsopa*. Even when not in flower, the dark, rust-colored pubescence on the stems and flower buds stands out, especially when backlit. This is one of the relatively few magnolias of the michelia group available in standard nurseries.

Magnolia ernestii (syns. *M. wilsonii*, *Michelia sinensis*). This species from western China is still suffering whiplash from a multitude of name changes. *Michelia sinensis*, a more valid name when michelia was a genus, was eclipsed by the pre-existing *Magnolia sinensis* and, therefore, a new name was created by cleverly adopting Ernest Wilson's first name. By any name, *M. ernestii* is a medium to large tree to 60 ft. (18 m). Vigorous and fast-growing when young, gaining upwards of 3 ft. (1 m) a year, the youthful pyramidal shape broadens with age. The leaves, 5½–7 in. (14–18 cm) long by 1½–2½ in. (4–6 cm) wide, are medium green and completely lacking indumentum. The flowers are soft ivory to nearly butter-yellow, depending on the clone, and rather open, to as large as 2–3 in. (5–8 cm). They are lightly fragrant but, seemingly, never in great abundance.

The primary attractions of *Magnolia ernestii* are its vigor and lush green color: where a large tree or garden structure is needed, a small plant from a one- or five-gallon container makes a substantial presence in three to five years. Cultivation requirements differ little from the other species except that, with adequate moisture, it is tolerant of full sun in most areas. Plants introduced by Piroche Nursery in Vancouver, B.C., have quickly made *M. ernestti* both available and reasonably common, both along the West Coast and in the southeastern United States.

Common wisdom has the cold hardiness at a little under 10°F (–23°C), though plants experiencing temperatures slightly below 0°F (–18°C) have recovered, looking a little stunned but quickly resuming growth. It is possible that in areas lacking summer heat, winter hardiness might be slightly less, as indicated by the grand specimens at Caerhays Castle in Cornwall, which suffered great damage in 1962, when winter temperatures approached 0°F (–18°C). Provenance might also play a part.

Easy to propagate, they should be treated as the others, concentrating on juvenile growth.

Magnolia figo var. *skinneriana* (syn. *Michelia skinneriana*). Southern China, mid to high elevations in mixed broadleaved evergreen forests. A variety of the shrubby *Magnolia figo* but larger in all parts, this small tree reaches 30 ft. (9 m), a broad pyramid with darkish branchlets and shiny, spring-green leaves. The branch structure is delicate, with relatively thin stems and a narrow trunk displaying the typical silvery gray bark. The flowers, to about 3 in. (8 cm), are pale cream, sometimes with pink or even a hint of maroon in the center. They are sweet-smelling, occasionally even carrying a hint of banana—another *M. figo* indication.

Magnolia figo var. *skinneriana*.
Photo by Michael A. Dirr

Among the easier michelias in cultivation, provided adequate water and a little afternoon shade to avoid yellowing in the hottest of climates, it makes a fine small garden tree and is suitable for replacing *Magnolia figo* where a small canopy is preferred over a large, rounded, ground-hugging shrub. *Magnolia figo* var. *skinneriana* has proven as frost hardy as *M. figo*, tolerating −4°F (−20°C) with little or no damage. It thrives with summer heat but performs well in cool coastal areas as long as attention is paid to its need for nitrogen and iron, both helping perk up and green the plant after a long winter lacking warmth. Propagated as are the other magnoliads.

Magnolia figo var. *crassipes* (syn. *Michelia crassipes*) is another important variety. Essentially a shrub that can be pruned into a small standard, it is often confused with *M. laevifolia* (syns. *M. dianica*, *Michelia yunnanensis*). A lovely, glossy-foliaged plant with dark hairs on the buds and stems and flowers in varying shades of rose to blood-red. Our form, *M. figo* var. *crassipes* 'Nanjing Red', flowers for a month or more in late winter to late spring, depending on sun exposure and, of course, temperatures. It has proved frost hardy to the lowest edge of zone 8.

Magnolia floribunda (syn. *Michelia floribunda*). Yunnan and southwest Sichuan provinces of China, between 4250 and 8800 ft. (1300 and 2700 m), in damp, summer monsoonal forest. Small tree to 25–35 ft. (7.5–10.5 m) in cultivation, but reaching an eventual 65 ft. (20 m) in its forest habitat. With its narrow trunk and small-diameter twigs, both silver-gray, the tree has a rather delicate stature. A medium to narrow pyramid when young, specimens remain narrow when surrounded by larger trees but become rounded if grown in the open.

The leaves have a graceful, oval shape and, although small, 1½–2 in. (4–5 cm) wide and 3–4 in. (8–10 cm) long, they look substantial compared to the gracile twigs. Among the most textural of the michelia group, leaves have an almost chalky blue farina on their underside and, especially when young, a silky pubescence above. This is one plant in our garden that gets stroked every time someone passes. It is also one of the fairly select group of plants with a light at its base, to show off its undersides in the evening.

I hope this description places *Magnolia floribunda* in a must-have category. It has been in cultivation no more than a dozen years, as far as can be verified. As is common in the michelia world, the flower buds are also covered with a pubescence, in this case, of a warm, brassy yellow. Plants in cultivation for five years in Portland, Oregon, have, in late February, produced a few, quite lovely, roughly 2½ in. (6 cm) silvery-white flowers with a custardy, sweet fragrance, but not, as yet, the "floribunda" described in the literature as occurring the wild. Other species have begun flowering with great abandon in as little as two years. Possibly, indeed, this is a late bloomer that may still live up to its name. But even if not, the graceful form and the beauty of the leaves make the tree worth growing. It is just as drought intolerant as other michelias and has withstood temperatures as low as 12°F (–11°C) with no discernible damage. Intuition suggests *M. floribunda* will prove to be a species able to withstand 0°F (–18°C).

Magnolia fulva var. *calcicola* (syn. *M. xanthantha*). Southern China. This high-altitude species, often growing in rocky soil and narrowly restricted limestone habitats, takes various conditions in the garden, seeming to suffer from none. Growth is somewhat angular, but with good soil and abundant water a bright tree to 30 ft. (9 m) or more eventually emerges. Excessive trunks and lower branches should be removed from young plants to predetermine eventual shape and expose the flaking, brownish gold bark. Leaves, longer than 1 ft. (30 cm), are broad ovals with a powder-blue farina on the undersides; veins, petioles, and the surfaces of newly emerging leaves are studded with brass-colored hairs. The flowers emerge from, yes, golden, fully covered buds as flattened 3–4 in. (8–10 cm) light yellow disks. A most attractive plant that sends tingles up and down the spines of magnolia lovers, it is a particularly good candidate for garden uplighting and courtyard planting. Not a fan of dehydrating winds; as with many evergreen magnolias, this is a plant for protected sites with light overstory or protection from hottest afternoon sun.

Seemingly tolerant of cold temperatures of 18 to 20°F (–8 to –7°C) with no foliage damage. Plants in Victoria, B.C., have withstood temperatures close to 0°F (–18°C), and reports are the same at Kew Gardens in the United Kingdom. Again, it is best to choose selections derived from such provenance if cultivation is being attempted in a colder zone.

Magnolia fulva var. calcicola

Magnolia grandiflora. Photo by Michael A. Dirr

Magnolia grandiflora, foliage.
Photo by Michael A. Dirr

Magnolia grandiflora. This species is a great symbol of the American South, along with Virginia live oak (*Quercus virginiana*) and possibly bald cypress (*Taxodium distichum*). It is among the most majestic components of the woodlands of the southeastern United States, from coastal North Carolina to east Texas. These forests often receive in excess of 50 in. (20 cm) of rain annually, much of it in the summer, with very high humidity and heat accumulation. Though drought does occur in these places, it can be sporadic, usually short in duration and often mitigated by moist air flowing north from the Gulf of Mexico. *Magnolia grandiflora* may be seen growing in association with such recognizable trees as *Liquidambar styraciflua*, tupelos (*Nyssa*), elms (*Ulmus*), dogwoods (*Cornus*), the often-evergreen *M. virginiana* and other deciduous magnolias, and its relative, *Liriodendron tulipifera*. The species is sometimes found growing nearly in water but is often perched above, on limestone ledges or in sand, either as an understory or a freestanding specimen in full sun; it almost never occurs in solid groves.

A medium to large tree, ranging from as small as 15 ft. (4.5 m) to over 100 ft. (30 m), this is the most recognizable of the evergreen magnoliads, and the most loved—and hated. The leaves are generally large, 6–8 in. (15–20 cm) in length or more, and 5 in. (13 cm) in width, with smaller and larger forms occurring. They are also very tough, shiny above with an almost waxy and leathery consistency, with indumentum below varying from very little to completely lanate and colored silvery cream to deep rust-brown. The large white flowers, 5–8 in. (13–20 cm) across, have a citrusy scent and can be seen in abun-

Magnolia grandiflora, flower.
Photo by Michael A. Dirr

Magnolia grandiflora, fruit.
Photo by Michael A. Dirr

Magnolia grandiflora 'Little Gem'.
Photo by Michael A. Dirr

dance in early summer, standing out starkly against the deep green foliage. In warmer climates, flowers can be seen throughout the year; in cooler areas, they begin later, more often in mid summer. If freezing weather occurs in winter, the flowering period is abbreviated.

Magnolia grandiflora can be seen both in the wild and in gardens, creating a more than substantial presence. In truth, some smaller gardens both in the South and along the West Coast of North America are indeed composed of only one plant, and this is it. In the garden, whether the space is large or small, there is a cultivar that is right for the situation. The falling leaves, which some liken to paper grocery bags (remember them?) descending from the heavens en masse, can be mitigated, not necessarily by hiring a full-time gardener, but by planting in a situation where large, architectural shrubs will hide them and under which the leaves will eventually break down—or they can be removed periodically and used as building materials. *Magnolia grandiflora* is also the cause of numerous run-on sentences.

In reality, the "problem" of *Magnolia grandiflora* leaves isn't a serious one. The leaf debris can be easily managed, whereas the presence and individual quality of the tree and its foliage and flowers is unmatched, as is the cold tolerance of many of its forms. The sight of *M. grandiflora* offers the sense of being in a forgiving place of abundance. As well, ownership (or at least proximity to a specimen) often ensures a flower at almost any given time for that big last-minute centerpiece. Clearly, if *M. grandiflora* did not possess great qualities, it would not have become one of the most widely grown trees in the warm temperate climates of the world. In almost any city with a sufficiently benign climate, they are to be seen in both municipal and private plantings—tolerating urban pollution quite amiably. Even in South Asia and China, where numerous evergreen members of the magnolia family occur naturally, it is a common sight in southern cities.

An easy plant to grow in most garden situations, *Magnolia grandiflora* does prefer at least some regular water in summer in Mediterranean or other summer-dry climates and soil free of standing water. In cool climates, such as along the immediate Pacific Coast or the milder areas of western Europe, they should be situated where as much heat is available as possible; in the southern United Kingdom, for example, it is often sited, even espaliered, against a south wall, ensuring that little bit of extra heat that keeps plants from yellowing and induces better flowers.

Numerous forms have been selected, not only for appearance but also for tolerance of low winter temperatures, some surviving in such unlikely places as central Michigan and Ohio. The popular *Magnolia grandiflora* 'Little Gem', often sold as a dwarf, can reach 30–40 ft. (9–

12 m) in time and, unfortunately, becomes rather weak and gangly. The small leaves that provide a becoming texture in its youth are not a plus with age. However, *M. g.* 'Little Gem' is a fine plant for container use, remaining more compact in root-bound situations and attractive with its pyramidal form, its ever-flowering habit in mild climates, and small, 3–5 in. (8–13 cm) leaves, with contrasting deep green above and light brown beneath. *Magnolia grandiflora* 'Exmouth' has been successful in low-heat areas such as the United Kingdom.

Pat McCracken of Raleigh, North Carolina, has amassed hundreds of cultivars as well as many unnamed forms. His criteria for selection include cold hardiness in northern climes, ability to withstand urban conditions, strength of the tree's structure and, of course, overall ornamental value. Pat, like myself, has a great interest in, if not fixation on, the color and amount of indumentum on the undersides of the leaves. In the best forms it can be cinnamon-brown, golden, or silver in color and creates a striking presence. One of Pat's favorites—and one that we too have found quite beautiful in the few years it's grown in our garden—is *Magnolia grandiflora* 'Kay Parris', a seedling of *M. g.* 'Little Gem'; it has particularly glossy leaf surfaces and a pyramidal form with upturned leaves that show off its deeper, more richly colored indumentum. The overall structure is tighter than *M. g.* 'Little Gem' and less likely to become shaggy and fall apart with age. In North Carolina, it reached 20–25 ft. (6–7.5 m) in height in ten years, and then put on slow but measured growth. Plants have been undamaged at −2 to −4°F (−19 to −20°C), which should make it more widely available than at present, especially given its relative ease of

Magnolia grandiflora 'Exmouth'.
Photo by John Grimshaw

Magnolia grandiflora 'Hasse'.
Photo by Michael A. Dirr

Magnolia grandiflora 'Kay Parris'. Photo by Michael A. Dirr

Magnolia grandiflora 'Majestic Beauty'. Photo by Michael A. Dirr

propagation with late summer cuttings, another attribute in which it differs from the much more difficult *M. g.* 'Little Gem.'

More difficult to propagate and therefore still rather rare is *Magnolia grandiflora* 'Hasse', another of Pat's selections. A tight columnar form with very dark green leaves and a dark chocolate indumentum, it makes a stunning garden plant. It is a little shy flowering, but the leaf texture and form are worth the space. Its growth rate also slows greatly after 20–25 ft. (6–7.5 m), and it is frost hardy to well below 0°F (–18°C). For a larger tree with a similar indumentum, *M. g.* 'Brown Velvet' (apparently the same clone as the more recently introduced *M. g.* 'D. D. Blanchard') reaches 40–60 ft. (12–18 m) or more and is more spreading; for chillier climates, it is a good candidate, as it has done well where winters often fall below zone 6 levels.

Selections from elsewhere include the, indeed, majestic *Magnolia grandiflora* 'Majestic Beauty', an exceedingly large tree—an 80 ft. (25 m) specimen is achievable in one's lifetime—with leaves nearing 1 ft. (30 cm) or nearly so in diameter with almost no indumentum. The flowers fit the scale, over 14 in. (36 cm) in width, making flower arranging extremely easy. Drawbacks are the rampant growth and large leaves, which catch any frozen precipitation, such that the unlucky gardener has been left with nothing but a utility pole after a fall of snow or ice. So, although they are rated as hardy to well below 0°F (–18°C), they should be planted where heavy snowfalls or ice accumulations are not likely, or where their scaffold branches can be tied or propped up so as to relieve weight.

With so many cultivars from which to choose—too many to include here—it can be an enjoyable project to research what forms have succeeded in one's local area and then to compare and contrast their features with newly available selections.

Magnolia grandis (syn. *Manglietia grandis*). Yunnan Province, China, in rich, mixed forest at 5200–5700 ft. (1600–1700 m) elevation with ample year-round rainfall—a very limited range. Ever on the lookout for new and bold textures for the garden, I found this creature to be stunning at first sight, in Roger Warner's fabulous Camellia Mountain Botanical Garden in northern California; I thought I was looking at *Ficus elastica* (rubber tree). His plants are growing at a hefty 3–4 ft. (about 1 m) per year; data from the wild suggest that 50–100 ft. (15–30 m) is this species' mature limit. Among forest companions, trees develop a relatively narrow, spreading crown, but in cultivation, at least so far, have remained very narrow.

The flowers are a wide cup shape, 5–6 in. (13–15 cm) in width, cream to white in color. The slightly glaucous stems hold leaves over 1 ft. (30 cm) long and 6–8 in. (15–20 cm) wide; these have the texture of hard plastic, deep green and glossy above, underneath, the same pale blue color as the stems.

Certainly, a plant new to cultivation outside of China and remaining very rare even there. We are still learning about its range and tolerance; what we do know is that, as with so many of its relatives, it begins life as an understory tree and, in many cases, remains so for many years. Young plants, grown in the shade, have the propensity to shoot vigorous stems into the air on a trial-and-error basis, each one leaning over, then making way for the next. The strongest grows up and away, forming the eventual main trunk of the tree. *Magnolia grandis* has the same habit in cultivation, so the tidy main stem staked in its pot might be superseded by another vigorous stem.

The biggest question is the plant's ultimate frost hardiness. Because of its limited natural range, we probably can't expect a great deal of variability. Roger Warner has maintained his plants through the upper teens (16 to 18°F, −9 to −8°C), with only some showing bronzing or leaf drop. In Portland, Oregon, the same temperatures produced no damage on plants well protected in an urban courtyard. However, temperatures near 10°F (−12°C) killed young plants outright in Vancouver, B.C. Regardless of their ultimate frost tolerance, which is assumed to be somewhere in the low teens (13 to 14°F, −10.5 to −10°C), it seems these plants need consistently ample humidity and a drought-free situation to thrive. Several in a group of Portland plants, having gone without water for only about three weeks their first year in the ground, lost leaf and stem tissue during the month of August.

Propagation from fresh seed, kept moist and either sown directly or cool stratified for thirty to sixty days, results in at least fifty percent germination. Cuttings are fairly successful taken in late autumn to mid winter.

Inclusion of *Magnolia grandis* in this book is not necessarily an endorsement but, rather, recognition of the fact that an intriguing and, indeed, a grand plant has appeared in our midst. Its ultimate horticultural range isn't known certainly, but we can assume it's safe in protected gardens along the U.S. West Coast from Oregon south, and in the Deep South, especially central and southern Florida. Potential use in warm temperate to subtropical Asia and coastal western Europe would seem likely, especially where that rubber tree just won't grow.

Magnolia ingrata (syn. *Michelia calcicola*). A recently discovered (late 1980s) species from a narrow region of limestone mountains in Yunnan Province in southern China. This member of the michelia group is the stuff of those air-brushed catalog pictures we all had as children. Photos show us a plant with a butter-yellow flower, and leaves and stems both stunningly blue and covered with a long, pale cream to golden indumentum.

Too good to be true? Not so far. Having received seed material from this plant in the late 1990s and grown it under various conditions, we have found the leaves and eventual flowers to be every bit as attractive as pictured without, apparently, having been airbrushed. Native to only a few locations, the limestone mountains of both mixed woodland and open sun, one might assume specialized requirements. This has not been the case, as they have taken to both nursery conditions and "average" dappled shade garden conditions with no complaints. The rate of growth has been relatively fast, creating a 10–12 ft. (3–3.5 m) plant in four years and flowering in the fifth. The leaves, as in so many evergreen magnolias, are the most attractive feature. Upwards of 9–10 in. (23–25 cm) long, or even longer, and 5 in. (13 cm) wide, they are, as just described, both colorful and textural. The flower buds, also with a lanate covering of a warm, creamy gold, develop into short-petalled flowers of about 3 in. (8 cm), lightly but sweetly fragrant and a warm, creamy yellow, contrasting beautifully with the blue in the leaves. So far in the garden, flowering has occurred in April and May, lasting for about four to six weeks.

One possible drawback is the young plant's gawkiness. Whether that is because nursery conditions can be less than perfect or just because of its vigorous youth, we hope the characteristic is temporary. Although we cannot say what its final shape and presence will be in the garden, our plants have mellowed a bit and are sending out smaller branches, especially those that flower, as opposed to the earlier 6 ft. (2 m) whips from the base. Accounts of the adult contour in its native range vary, mostly according to whether it has been found in the open or in mixed woodland, but it appears to make a rather open specimen and maintain under 30 ft. (9 m).

Also a mystery is its ultimate frost hardiness. Its southern range and relatively low altitude would indicate cold sensitivity, but, as with so many others, there seems to be a memory of colder times, and temperatures a little below 20°F (–7°C) have caused no damage. Whether it will take "real" cold remains to be seen. It would be a fine indoor/outdoor, or conservatory plant.

It has been said that, because of the limestone habitat in which it is native, it might need to grow in calcium-rich soils. Again, this has not proven true so far, although it might make a fine parking-lot tree in southern Florida with its limestone soil and warm climate. While it is a little bit more at home in full sun than others of the michelia group, still, a bit of shade in the afternoon—along with a mint julep—allows the leaves to achieve a larger size and the plant, seemingly, a little more robustness. Moisture, of course.

Propagation has been among the easier of the genus, even from flowering wood. Because of the large stems and leaves, they do require a lot of space. Mid autumn to mid winter has been best for cuttings, with some success had from just ripened wood in late summer. This plant has been rather taxonomically confused, and though it might be found under the name *Magnolia ingrata*, *M. calcicola*, or even *M. xanthantha*, with its relatively easy propagation, it will be making the rounds sooner than later.

Magnolia insignis (syn. *Manglietia insignis*; red lotus tree). Found from the Himalayas and Burma to Tibet, western China, south to Vietnam, this widespread species has been the longest in cultivation of the manglietia group and remains one of the hardiest to cold. Relatively fast-growing (1½–3 ft., .5–1 m, a year when happy), becoming a rather dense, pyramidal tree to 30 ft. (9 m) in a reasonable time, *Magnolia insignis* has reached over 65 ft. (20 m) in cultivation and over 120 ft. (36 m) in the wild.

The shiny leaves, narrowly oblanceolate, range from 7 in. (18 cm) to nearly 1 ft. (30 cm) long and 2½–3½ in. (6–9 cm) wide, tending to be larger and longer when younger and under shady conditions. They don't possess the indumentum underneath the leaves or the reflective qualities of some other members of the family, but the shape and size of the leaves create a memorable texture in the garden.

Magnolia insignis

Their terminal flowers are 4–5 in. (10–13 cm) across, in tulip shapes. Thought at one time to take many years to flower from seed, container-grown plants have flowered in under five years. The color varies from the palest of pink (nearly white) to a deep, almost ketchup-red, the most common color being Pepto-Bismol pink. Although, as a collector, it is often plant minutiae I find most intriguing, the wait for the first flowering buds to open on a *Magnolia insignis* can be torturous. Plants from seed often take between five and ten years to set flowering buds. Eventually what appears to be a little green egg on a stick sitting atop the growth sheds several layers of sepals before unfurling into a delicate flower—long after any such transformation seems possible.

In the last several years, most noticeably thanks to Piroche Nursery in Vancouver, B.C., this species has become relatively common, especially along the North American Pacific Coast, and with enough seed-grown plants flowering, selections are beginning to appear. Though the flowers are attractive, they often last only a couple of days and are never particularly numerous. The real beauty is the dense, deep green growth and the long, narrow shape of the leaves.

Plants have been brought from many provenances, but those from the highest elevations are now the most common, placing them among the hardiest of the evergreen magnoliads. Temperatures of −9°F (−23°C) in the U.S. Southeast and near 0°F (−18°C) on the West Coast have not fazed them, and they have succeeded for dozens of years in the cool-summer climate of the southern United Kingdom, also remaining robust.

Seed collected in September and sown immediately will often germinate, but some cold stratification, preferably in peat to keep them moist, might enhance the results. Though varying by clone, mid autumn to mid winter cuttings often strike relatively easily with mist and bottom heat.

Magnolia lotungensis (syn. *Parakmeria lotungensis*). From Yunnan, China. Formerly all but nonexistent in Western horticulture, this species is now widely available along the Pacific Coast, thanks mainly to importation of seedlings from Piroche Nursery in Vancouver, B.C., in the early 1990s. A tree reaching 60 ft. (18 m) in the wild and probably 40 ft. (12 m) with some ease in cultivation, considering that plants in our Portland, Oregon, garden had grown to a height of just under 20 ft. (6 m) in eight years. The trunk is stout, a little over 3 ft. (1 m) in diameter on mature specimens in nature. The bark remains a fine silvery gray throughout the tree's lifetime. The leaves are elliptic, 2–4 in. (5–10 cm) long and 1½–2 in. (4–5 cm) broad. Compared to *Magnolia nitida* var. *nitida*, the articulations of the veins are a bit more visible and the leaves are not quite as shiny. The new growth is often nearly maroon with the leaves aging to what can be termed *Rosa glauca* grayish pink. This coloration is probably the finest quality of the plant, although the literature is filled with descriptions of their pleasingly fragrant, creamy yellow flowers.

Experience thus far has led us to believe that *Magnolia lotungensis* is a good deal hardier to frost than *M. nitida*, as near 0°F (−18°C) has not made a blemish on any known plantings. Where decent water is available, this would make a rewarding garden or street tree.

Once from a batch of seedlings, I selected a form with stunningly orange-red new growth and red-infused older leaves. Enthusiasm for this unnamed cultivar was slightly dampened when a (formerly) well-respected colleague glanced at this stunning, new addition to our garden and announced its resemblance to *Photinia ×fraseri*, a plant I have since, as a consequence, grown to appreciate.

Magnolia maudiae (syn. *Michelia maudiae*; smiling forest lily tree). Native over a wide area of southern China, from near Hong Kong west to Guizhou, in a great range of elevations. Long used as a garden and even as a street tree near its native ranges, *Magnolia maudiae* is a superb garden tree for warmer temperate climates. The numerous seedlings brought by Piroche Nursery in Vancouver, B.C., from Nanjing have spread far and wide on the West Coast and the southeastern United States. Having so many seed-grown plants available allowed for observation of the great variety of leaf, flower, and tree shape, and improved selections are now appearing.

A small tree, reaching an eventual 20 ft. (6 m) and maintaining a rounded, pyramidal shape, it seems equally at home in containers or in the garden. The oblong leaves are 3–4 in. (8–10 cm) wide and 5–6 in. (13–15 cm) long, with a dull matte green above, sometimes having a bluish cast, and, most often, with a white-white underside. The leaf size in comparison with the small stature of the tree creates a bold textural presence.

Magnolia maudiae

Plants can flower the third or even the second year from seed, if pushed a bit, even in containers, putting them in the "instant gratification" category of the magnoliads, some of which take some time to produce flowers. What is more, these are not just any flowers. As is typical with the michelia group, the flowers are produced at nearly every leaf axil of the prior year's growth, beginning in February (at least in Portland, Oregon), with a few still sputtering open as late as June. In hot summer areas where good growth has occurred on the tree, there is also an autumn showing. The flowers, ranging from cream to stark white with, sometimes, a rose center, are held upright, opening fairly wide after several days and possibly reaching an astounding 6 in. (15 cm) across. The fragrance on many forms is very sweet, falling somewhere between lilies and daphnes. A row of *Magnolia maudiae* planted in 1997 along NE Fremont Street, in Portland, Oregon, draws heavy traffic and the occasional camera crew during the spring extravaganza. Their fragrance can be detected blocks away.

Again, belying its natural range, *Magnolia maudiae* has withstood slightly below 0°F (–18°C) near Vancouver, B.C., and has had no bud damage in the mid teens (14 to 16°F, –10 to –9°C) elsewhere. They have also maintained great vigor at the Quarryhill Botanical Garden in northern California with adequate moisture provided. What's more, this species is equally at home in the heat of the U.S. Southeast: in Hayes Jackson's garden in Anniston, Alabama, a tree well exceeded 30 ft. (9 m) at fifteen years of age and flowers exuberantly. His excitement generated a little plant rap: "Don't be dumb. Get you some." I agree.

Like its brethren, *Magnolia maudiae* is a little greedy for nutrients and, along with consistent moisture, would like regular feedings, being especially fond of nitrogen and iron. Cottonseed meal is a good, slow-release organic fertilizer.

Propagation has been relatively easy, both from seed and cuttings.

Seeds sown fresh or stored in a damp cooler for about two months germinate readily, and cuttings taken in early autumn to mid winter, preferably from juvenile branches on late, previous season's wood, are usually successful.

Magnolia maudiae var. *platypetala* (syn. *Michelia platypetala*). Southern China in mixed forests. Another graceful michelia, now a variety of *Magnolia maudiae* but with a more open growth pattern and taller, to a rounded 40–50 ft. (12–15 m), though 25 ft. (7.5 m) is probably the norm in horticulture.

When first introduced to this plant, a fresh import from China's Nanjing Botanic Garden by Piroche Nursery in Vancouver, B.C., I was struck by the coppery indumentum on both the stems and leaf undersides as well as a spattering on the leaf surfaces. This indumentum stands out nicely against the very dark green leaves, 4–5 in. (10–13 cm) by 2–3 in. (5–8 cm), which are so gracefully set on rather narrow petioles and fairly thin branches that they appear to float. When backlit, the plant seems to have a warm brassy halo that literally glows.

The flowers are not as overpowering in their presence as those of the type, being slightly smaller and not quite as numerous, but they are sweetly fragrant and a handsome contrast to the dark foliage. They are generally white, sometimes with a bit of cream or a very light pink in the center, and have very wide petals, to about 4 in. (10 cm), which appear from a distance to be slightly ruffled.

Seemingly best in medium to light shade, though in coastal areas where there's high humidity, it can stand full sun and not look stunned. Constant moisture is a must, along with, of course, good drainage. If plants have been sitting in a container for too long, they can take a season or two to adjust to garden conditions and begin vigorous growth. It is best not to starve young plants or allow them to dry out, as reinvigorating them can be difficult. *Magnolia maudiae* var. *platypetala* is one plant that is unlikely to become common in the nursery trade, if only because of the consistent care it needs in containers.

That aside, *Magnolia maudiae* var. *platypetala* is one of the hardier magnolias, having withstood –2°F (–19°C) without appreciable damage. Propagation is easier when taken from juvenile shoots or, otherwise, growth that has not yet flowered. As with all magnolias, propagation material taken from plants not yet of flowering size is almost always easier to root.

Magnolia megaphylla (syn. *Manglietia megaphylla*). From China in Wenshan at 3200–5200 ft. (970–1600 m) elevation. Imagine *Magno-*

lia grandis covered with orange fur. Though the leaves are thinner in texture and a tiny bit more oblanceolate, they have the same astounding presence. Another tree of very limited range and, as with *M. grandis*, endangered by human activity, it also begins life as a component of a very lush understory, growing eventually to 65–100 ft. (20–30 m), though 45 ft. (14 m) seems more reasonable in the garden. As the plants grow, they send up stronger and stronger "canes" until the strongest succeeds. As with *M. grandis*, the trees in habitat eventually become part of the upper canopy; in the meantime, young plants are able to grow upwards of 2 ft. (60 cm) a year. Another showstopper!

The leaves of *Magnolia megaphylla* do live up to their name, measuring at times over 14 in. (36 cm) long and 6–8 in. (15–20 cm) wide, soaking up every bit of light they can get from their position deep in the canopy. As the plants age and gather more light, the leaves become somewhat smaller, and, sadly, a bit less furry. The petioles, the undersides of the leaves, and even the surface of the leaves when young—all the new growth—have a fine, coppery indumentum, which makes them shimmer in even the dimmest of dappled sunlight. The flowers in early spring are white, sometimes with a maroonish center, and a rather wide cup, more than 5 in. (13 cm) across.

One of the most pleasing qualities of this species (indeed, of so many of the evergreen magnoliads) is the great diversity of leaf textures, both visual and tactile, it offers the gardening world. With *Magnolia megaphylla* the exquisite texture also provides a hint of the conditions it requires. The paper-thin leaves seem to need constant humidity in order not only to maintain their size, but also to avoid burning. They also need protection from direct sun, especially in the afternoon, and protection from wind as well. Plants shared by Roger Warner with the Quarryhill Botanical Garden in Glen Ellen, California, have suffered greatly in the low humidity and heat of the garden's interior location.

Ultimate cold hardiness is still something of a mystery. Though records near its native habitat indicate only light frost, many members of the family Magnoliaceae have delivered surprises, withstanding much colder temperatures than their current natural ranges now experience. A temperature of 10°F (–12°C) killed plants in both North Carolina and British Columbia, but the mid 20s (–4°C) in Portland, Oregon, left no scars, and temperatures between 10 and 12°F (–10 and –11°C) did little to deter plants in a protected situation at the Atlanta (Georgia) Botanic Garden. Placement in a breezy situation, however, has left the leaves in tatters by spring.

The ability of both *Magnolia megaphylla* and *M. grandis* to sprout quickly from basal buds and put on phenomenal growth in a season makes them prime candidates for cut-back shrubs, possibly making them the wildest perennials your neighbor has ever seen. Propagation is not particularly difficult. Late autumn and winter cuttings are preferred as is, of course, juvenile growth. The large size of the cuttings, leaf, and stem require "mucho" propagation space, even with the leaves trimmed (a step not preferred by this author).

Magnolia moto (syn. *Manglietia moto*). Another magnificent species from the rich candy store of southern China. This 100 ft. (30 m) tree is a forest dweller, though tolerant of much more light in youth than its closest relatives, *Magnolia megaphylla* and *M. grandis*. For many years it remains a narrow pyramid with a dark silvery gray bark, the small rings or lenticels of which, so common in the magnolia family, add a decorative touch.

This plant has been in cultivation for some years now in the United States, possibly the first specimen a collection from North Carolina's Cliff Parks. His collections remain among the most attractive of the several at the JC Raulston Arboretum in Raleigh, North Carolina, having flowered after about ten years in cultivation. Though protected from cold winds by a lath structure, *Magnolia moto* withstood a few degrees below 0°F (–18°C) there with little, if any, visible damage. This species, again, might not prove to be the very hardiest of evergreen magnoliads but should prove useful over a fairly wide range from warm zone 7 to humid areas of zone 10. The flowers, creamy white and averaging a little under 5 in. (13 cm) across, have a sweet, almost lily-like fragrance.

It seems that, as well as being a bit more sun tolerant than *Magnolia grandis* and *M. megaphylla*, *M. moto* is able to withstand brief periods of drought without calamity. With a somewhat wider distribution in its natural habitats, attention should be paid to provenance if cultivating in frostier locales.

According to the law of inverse proportions, this plant, though easier in cultivation, has proven rather difficult from cuttings. I have achieved twenty percent at best. Plants have been successfully grafted, and time will tell us about the long-term compatibility.

Magnolia nitida (syn. *Parakmeria nitida*). Southwest China and eastern Tibet, especially in summer-wet forest situations. It was this species that set off my current fixation on the evergreen magnoliads, precisely at the moment I came upon a 15 ft. (4.5 m) specimen at Caerhays Castle in the United Kingdom, where I'd spent the afternoon, wandering and wondering through the more than impressive collection of broadleaved evergreens, magnolias included. I spotted a distant triangle of what appeared to be nearly black, extremely reflective leaves. Prepared for the same disappointment I experienced when a fantastically exciting apparition turned out to be an entire greenhouse full of English laurel (*Prunus laurocerasus*), I nevertheless rushed onward. Here, what I found was fairly recognizable to me as a magnolia but an unfamiliar one that didn't resemble any pictures in my mind or descriptions I had read. With some careful pawing, the label was uncovered and yet a new fervor was born. I considered the great possibilities in the genus and began to wonder what other treasures awaited my further investigation. I haven't been disappointed.

Magnolia nitida ranges from a large shrub to medium tree, to 40–50 ft. (12–15 m), with pyramidal growth that becomes rounded with age in some forms. To name just a few of its attractions: the silvery gray bark is extremely lustrous, having the mirror-like quality of a dark pool of water; the leaves are a very, very deep green, 4–7 in. (10–18 cm) broad and about half as wide, with all forms tapering to a rather elegant and sharp tip; and the fragrant flowers, 2½–3 in. (6–8 cm) in diameter, bloom on the branch tips, a creamy white to nearly yellow in some forms (though they appear only after the plant is several years old).

Magnolia nitida is definitely a contender for the title of Most-Beautiful-Plant-One-Could-Have-in-the-Garden (as are the other parakmerias included in this book). As in choosing among fine wines, the characteristics should be examined carefully, with frost hardiness being the most important—at least in the plant world. *Magnolia nitida* var. *nitida* is the least cultivated form in the United States. Seedlings from plants at Caerhays, planted in the University of British Columbia Botanic Garden, did not survive temperatures of just a little above 0°F (–18°C), but the plants were young and the freeze particularly severe. We are hoping that new trials will prove hardiness to at least 0°F (–18°C) on established plants. Tolerant of short periods of drought and deep and stoutly rooted, they, like the rest, can become sparse or a bit yellowed with lack of summer moisture. Nutrient-rich soil is preferred, and they seemingly are less subject to yellowing due to lack of summer heat.

Propagation from seed, when available, is assured given fresh seed or cool damp stratification for a couple of months. Cuttings have proven more difficult. Even from juvenile plants—with luck, in my experience—the success rate is under twenty percent. I have had some success with late summer cuttings from mostly ripened wood, with slightly less from the more typical cutting time of late autumn to mid winter. It is hoped that through development of cutting techniques or grafting, *Magnolia nitida* can be made more easily available.

Magnolia ovoidea (syn. *Manglietia ovoidea*). Southeastern China from middle elevations up to about 6500 ft. (2000 m) as a constituent

Magnolia nitida

of lush and very rich woodland. Not a huge tree, it reaches to about 35 ft. (10.5 m) with a straight, narrow trunk and graceful, rather lateral branches. As a form, it seems almost an exaggerated version of *Magnolia insignis*.

The leaves, for me the most wonderful feature, are very narrow, oval and a graceful 5–7 in. (13–18 cm) long if not longer, but sometimes as narrow as 1 in. (2.5 cm) wide, though rarely over 1½ in. (4 cm). They have a silky texture and seem to float on the branches. As they emerge, the growth is a pleasing shell-pink, with tones of shrimp or red remaining in the petioles and leaves until they are completely mature. Although they have been in cultivation only a short time in North America and are just now reaching western Europe, the plants seem vigorous, rather fast-growing and nearly as frost hardy as *Magnolia insignis*. The flowers are white, to faintly blushed pink, and, although known only from pictures in our part of the world, appear to be reasonably substantial.

Magnolia ovoidea is included here, in part, because so far it has been outstandingly attractive in youth, and I think it has great potential. Time will tell us if it is indeed as hardy to cold as *M. insignis*.

Magnolia tamaulipana. Native to northeast Mexico in one localized region of the Sierra Madre Oriental, where it grows in an exceedingly diverse mixed forest on limestone. Separated taxonomically from *M. schiedeana*, a more widespread plant with which it is often confused. One of the most majestic of the evergreen magnolias, the broad silvery trunk stretches through the mixed forest to the canopy of thick glossy leaves, occasionally to nearly 100 ft. (30 m). Visiting the native haunts of this lovely tree feels, out of context, as if one were visiting a botanical garden that had been misplanted. The mixture of species with many additional endemics suggests what one might think of as a typical southeastern U.S. woodland with *Carpinus*, *Liquidambar*, and even an endemic beech (*Fagus mexicana*). Yet, on the ground, a mixture of cycads, *Agave*, *Erythrina*, and even damp-loving cacti carpet the forest floor. Once one is used to such a great mix of plants, seeing this large, primitive-looking magnolia as well might not seem such a surprise.

When grown in a garden situation or otherwise not encumbered by competing trees, *Magnolia tamaulipana* remains a relatively narrow pyramid through its life, retaining branches to near ground level. The silver bark stands out regardless of the density of branches, and the very dark leaves often have an attractive indumentum on the underside and, to some degree, above—the surface of the leaves becoming hairless and quite shiny with some age. The large leaves, 9–10 in. (23–25 cm) long and 4–5 in. (10–13 cm) wide, have a graceful shape and persist through at least one season, with one set falling, often, in early spring. The sweetly scented, creamy flowers are produced in late spring to early summer—but they usually occur at night and are not longlasting. They form a very wide cup of tepals, to nearly 6 in. (15 cm) across, never seeming to overwhelm the tree en masse but, because of their size, creating quite a splash.

Although the species is somewhat drought tolerant, its native habitat is within one of the most northern areas of cloud forest so common further south in Mexico. The winters are dry with occasional hard frost; summers are misty and cool, punctuated by frequent thunderstorms.

One of the first collections of *Magnolia tamaulipana* was by F. G. Meyer and D. J. Rogers. Specimens were planted at the University of Washington Arboretum in Seattle, where they have been flowering regularly since 1971. The plants have reached nearly 30 ft. (9 m) in size there. In warm summer areas, these are relatively fast-growing plants, adding up to 3 ft. (1 m) a year in youth then slowing once flowering begins; along the immediate Pacific Coast, they are a bit slower, due to the lack of summer heat, but still reasonable.

Where humidity is low, regular summer watering is best. Though subject to drought, more often in the winter, the deep, limestone-creviced habitat ensures general moisture availability. As well, in milder areas, as witnessed along the West Coast of the United States, *Magnolia tamaulipana* can flower at any point during the year, often producing at least some flowers in the dead of winter.

As with many magnolias, seed-grown plants can take several years to flower; cutting-grown specimens from mature plants can flower in under five years. Cuttings taken by us from the plants in Seattle flowered the third season.

Cuttings from one plant in habitat were introduced by Yucca Do Nursery of Waller, Texas, as *Magnolia tamaulipana* 'Bronze Sentinel'. In cultivation this selection responds quickly from late summer to early winter cuttings, remains narrow and upright, and has leaves tinted a bronzy purple, especially in the new growth.

The mountainous habitat from which the species comes is, indeed, subject to occasional cold; fronts sweeping down through the Midwest, east of the Rocky Mountains, can plunge cold air well into Mexico, assuring us that this magnolia and, undoubtedly, a surprising list of other species from surrounding areas are worthy of consideration in areas occasionally reaching 0°F (–18°C). Though in general, the species in cultivation has had leaf loss and even stem damage as high as 10°F (–12°C), *Magnolia tamaulipana* 'Bronze Sentinel' seems evergreen to near 0°F (–18°C) and begins experiencing damage at –5°F (–20°C) if the temperature remains low for more than a day. *Magnolia*

Magnolia tamaulipana

Magnolia tamaulipana, foliage.
Photo by Michael A. Dirr

tamaulipana, though slightly lesser in scale, might rival *M. delavayi* for cold hardiness in the world of large-scale evergreens.

Magnolia virginiana (sweet bay magnolia, silver bay magnolia). Evergreen or deciduous tree from the eastern United States, primarily coastal Virginia south through Florida, with the northern-most populations tending to be deciduous, especially north of coastal Virginia. Often seen growing in swampy or sandy soils adjacent to water in places with high summer rainfall, it forms a small to large tree from under 15 ft. (4.5 m) to occasionally over 90 ft. (27 m) in the wild, the shape varying from wide and multi-trunked to tall and single-trunked. Both the tall-growing forms and the most evergreen forms tend to be found in the southern reaches of their habitat. One of North America's finest broadleaved evergreen trees, the creamy yellow flowers and spring-green, sometimes slightly glaucous leaves with (often) powdery blue undersides make the sweet bay magnolia not only a sight to behold in its native woodlands but also a fine specimen in any garden.

The leaves vary in size, 5–8 in. (13–20 cm) long by, usually, 3 in. (8 cm) wide. The flowers, 2–4 in. (5–10 cm) wide, make up for their rather small size with not only the color, which stands out well against the foliage, but also with their strong citrusy fragrance. The flowers occur most frequently from late spring to mid summer, but in mild places, some flowers can be seen for much of the year. They are tolerant of a wide range of conditions, perhaps the most attractive to gardeners being their tolerance of poor drainage (and yes, even poor gardeners!).

Magnolia virginiana, flower

In the North American West and summer-dry areas of western Europe, care must be taken to ensure at least some regular water during the summer months, especially in poorly drained soil, as the combination of wet feet in the winter and drought in the summer often leads to poor-looking specimens. In free-draining soils, where the roots can range more deeply, some degree of drought tolerance exists, though the rate of growth might be slowed with periods of summer drought.

Magnolia virginiana var. *australis* occurs in the southeast part of the species' range, as the name would imply, creating beautiful stands in northern Florida. Where this loosely described variety can be grown, it seems superior in many ways, though not exhibiting all the cold hardiness of the more northern forms, some of those having been successfully grown where temperatures have approached −20°F (−29°C). Specimens of *M. virginiana* var. *australis* are often taller, with a more upright growth habit, and seem more vigorous during periods of drought yet just as tolerant of poor drainage. They have even more intensely fra-

Magnolia virginiana, fruit.
Photo by Michael A. Dirr

grant flowers, and the more reliably evergreen leaves tend to be a bit larger, some over 9 in. (23 cm), often displaying particularly stunning, silvery blue undersides. One fifty-year-old planting of street trees in inner Portland, Oregon, has withstood years of neglect and, undoubtedly, periods with no summer irrigation and occasional hacking near power lines, yet consistently remains worthy of a several-block detour during a neighborhood walk. In eight years, only one pilgrimage yielded no flowers but the stunning canopy was worth the trip.

In general, the evergreen forms of *Magnolia virginiana* are less hardy to cold than the deciduous forms, which are from more northerly climes, some having been hardy to −20 to −30°F (−29 to −35°C) or even colder! The more southerly forms, including *M. v.* var. *australis*, do not come close, although most evergreen forms tested so far seem hardy to at least 0°F (−18°C). One cultivar, *M. v.* 'Henry Hicks', named in Long Island, has been evergreen to −10 to −15°F (−23 to −26°C), as has *M. v.* 'Milton', named by the Arnold Arboretum. Leaf drop has occurred during these coldest temperatures.

Magnolia virginiana 'Aiken County' was found and introduced by Nurseries Caroliniana, selected in habitat in nearby eastern South Carolina. The plant has exceptionally large leaves, often over 6 in. (15 cm) in length, with a bright gloss. It has shown leaf retention to −4°F (−20°C), and the stems on new growth can be an astounding purple-black. Ted Stephens, owner of the nursery, declares this selection to be much more fragrant than *M. v.* 'Santa Rosa'. Not the easiest of cultivars to propagate from cuttings but late summer semi-ripened wood has been satisfactory.

Magnolia virginiana 'Moon Glow', a patented Earl Cully selection and now reproduced through tissue culture, has quickly gained popularity. It is evergreen, or at least only partly deciduous, to at least 10 to 12°F (−12 to −11°C), and the tree itself lives, though mostly leafless, after −33°F (−36°C). Planted from a liner, it went from 2 in. (5 cm) to 8 ft. (2.5 m) in two years, and in that second year flowered abundantly and with the typical scent.

Magnolia virginiana 'Ned's Northern Belle' is another selection that is becoming more common in commerce. It can reach 60 ft. (18 m) in height, with small, closely packed leaves adorned with pleasing silver undersides; and, most impressive, it has remained evergreen in several places to close to −20°F (−29°C). There are even reports of cold hardiness, though with great leaf loss, at close to −40°F (−40°C)! Propagation from cuttings is slow but usually successful.

Magnolia virginiana 'Santa Rosa', a new and increasingly available selection, is a fast-growing evergreen that quickly achieves tree size. Though seen as possibly a bit rank in growth in the hot, humid summers of the U.S. Southeast, in the West it seems to maintain a pro-

Magnolia virginiana var. *australis*

Magnolia virginiana 'Henry Hicks'.
Photo by Michael A. Dirr

Magnolia virginiana 'Milton'. Photo by Michael A. Dirr

Magnolia virginiana 'Santa Rosa'. Photo by Michael A. Dirr

portional growth and will undoubtedly be a fine street and garden tree. Experimental plantings have shown leaf retention to near 0°F (–18°C).

Propagation varies greatly and, although some forms of *Magnolia virginiana* var. *australis* have been reproduced with relative ease using barely hardened wood or even semi-soft wood in late summer, many of the cultivars, including *M. v.* 'Henry Hicks', are often grafted on seedling stock of *M. acuminata*.

Magnolia yunnanensis (syn. *Parakmeria yunnanensis*). Yunnan Province, China. The tallest and most vigorous of the parakmeria group now in cultivation and just now becoming known in Western horticultural, though plantings in both gardens and on streets are common in southern China. A tall, vigorous pyramid, reaching 65 ft. (20 m) and even a reported 100 ft. (30 m) in its forest habitat. From the growth rates observed during ten years in cultivation, a height of 30–35 ft. (9–10.5 m) is likely in a reasonable time. Both literature and experience in cultivation have dictated providing at least light, dappled or afternoon shading when the tree is young. After a canopy has developed, full sun seems acceptable. Tall and narrow in youth, becoming a broad pyramid with age, its shape has been compared in literature to, of all horrors, a larger *Pyrus calleryana*. Fortunately, its good qualities—aside from not being as brittle or as unpleasant-smelling in flower—far exceed those of the Bradford pear.

The leaves, 3–6 in. (8–15 cm) long by 2–2½ in. (5–6 cm) wide, are glabrous, midway in "glabrosity" between its fellow parakmerias, *Magnolia nitida* and *M. lotungensis*, with a long, elegant shape. The leaves rest on petiole that is itself rather long, adding to the plant's overall elegance. The flowers, produced after a reported five to eight

Magnolia yunnanensis, flower

years of vigorous growth, are said to be very fragrant and a pleasing creamy to buttery yellow, a nice contrast to the orange-tinted leaves.

So far, so good in cultivation along the Pacific Coast. Plants obtained and grown by Monrovia Nursery in the Los Angeles area have coped well with salt in the soil and the sporadic, very low humidity, though regular water has been applied. Plantings in Portland, Oregon, lost some leaves that had been tossed by a winter breeze coupled with overnight temperatures in the mid teens (14 to 16°F, −10 to −9°C). Intuition suggests 10°F (−12°C) or so, for brief periods, will be this species' lower limit.

Another member of the parakmeria group worth pursuing and trialing is *Magnolia omeiensis* (syn. *Parakmeria omeiensis*), from the slopes of Mount Omei, China's famous mother of gardens. The leaves are said to be shiny and very attractive and the flowers a golden yellow. From its native location on the planet, the species should have a good deal of frost hardiness.

Magnolia yunnanensis, foliage.
Photo by Michael A. Dirr

| *Mahonia* | Oregon grape, holly grape | Berberidaceae |

Close to seventy evergreen shrubs, some indeed growing into small trees, others capable of being pruned into tree shape. Most have few branches and a growth habit that is sufficiently upright for our purposes here. The leaves, though technically alternate, appear in dense whorls toward the top of each season's growth, giving a rather subtropical appearance, almost palm-like with the multiply-pinnate leaves. (The genus is separated from *Berberis* by most authorities for,

Mahonia ×*media* 'Arthur Menzies'. Photo by Michael A. Dirr

Mahonia ×*media* 'Winter Sun'

among other differences, its pinnately compound leaves.) The flowers are usually yellow and appear from autumn through winter (in some species, more toward spring); they are followed by clusters of dusty blue to nearly black fruit.

All mahonias are tolerant of shady conditions but also of sun in all but the hottest climes. Even western North American species accustomed to summer drought seem amenable to garden water providing soil is well drained.

Larger plants most commonly seen in gardens are those of the *Mahonia ×media* group, consisting of hybrids between *M. japonica* and *M. lomariifolia*. Most of these ('Winter Sun' is one) top out at 6–8 ft. (2–2.5 m), though with age, even greater heights can be attained. *Mahonia ×media* 'Arthur Menzies', originating at San Francisco's Strybing Arboretum and selected at the University of Washington Arboretum, is easily over 10 ft. (3 m) in many gardens, with each compound leaf as long as 18 in. (45 cm); and its spikes of canary-yellow flowers create a bold statement in December and January. Any of these hybrids might be planted where they can be seen from indoors during the winter months: they make a fine focal point and a ray of winter sunshine during the darkest days.

Cuttings are best from matured current season's growth in autumn and winter and can be done with only single leaves and small, attached stems. Seeds can be winter stratified and sown in spring.

Mahonia chochoca (Mexican tree mahonia). From northeastern Mexico, growing amid oaks and woodland species of *Liquidambar* but also occurring in drier chaparral. This is one of the largest North American species, reaching over 25 ft. (7.5 m) with age, trunks having been observed over 18 in. (45 cm) in diameter. Often multi-trunked but easily pruned to a single, *M. chochoca* is upright and fast-growing, gaining 3 ft. (1 m) a year if given adequate summer water.

More delicate in appearance than some of its Asian counterparts, the spineless leaflets are up to 18 in. (45 cm) long and glossy green or barely matte blue. Winter flowers are light yellow, borne in panicles of 3 ft. (1 m) or more. The bark in this species is particularly corky, with raised light and dark brown ridges—one of its most striking features. Specimens can be pinched in early spring to maintain bushiness. Best out of strong or drying winds and proven hardy to below 10°F (–12°C) for short periods.

Mahonia chochoca

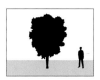

Mahonia lomariifolia (Chinese holly grape). From China, one of the parents of the *M. ×media* hybrids and valuable on its own. Early growth is upright, reaching 10–12 ft. (3–3.5 m) quickly and a possible 20 ft. (6 m) or more over time, with few branches even in maturity.

Mahonia lomariifolia

Mahonia lomariifolia, flowers

Can be multi-stemmed or kept to a single trunk. Spiny leaves consisting of multiple, light blue-green leaflets can be more than 2 ft. (60 cm) in length and create a beautifully symmetric rosette held horizontally toward the tops of the stems.

Best used where a sculptural or architectural specimen is wanted or a splash of winter color is needed, with consistent moisture and some shade protection provided in hottest areas.

This species is most reliably hardy in upper zone 8 and above. Exposed plants have been damaged at 12 to 14°F (−11 to −10°C), but those in woodland situations with overhead protection and out of drying winds have survived 10°F (−12°C) or a bit less unscathed. Plants have resprouted with some vigor from temperatures near 0°F (−18°C).

Mahonia siamensis (Siam holly grape). From Asia, one of the largest, to 12–15 ft. (3.5–4.5 m) tall with 18–20 in. (45–50 cm) leaves, tinged orange-red in spring, and magnificent, fragrant, yellow flowers in 1 ft. (30 cm), multi-branched, erect panicles. A robust grower, *M. siamensis* creates a lively texture as a multi-trunked small tree, planted where its corky tan bark can be seen.

Best suited for sheltered gardens where year-round moisture can be provided and temperatures seldom fall below 16 to 17°F (−9 to −8.5°C). Although leaning toward the high end of our limits for tenderness, this species is striking enough to be attempted where conditions warrant or a protected spot can be found.

Maytenus mayten Celastraceae

Over 250 species of evergreen trees and shrubs, many in South America and reaching into North America, though they can also be found in the Old World. As a genus, habitats and cultivation requirements are all over the map. Some are spiny shrubs; others possess glaucous or stunningly deep green and shiny leaves; and all have the attractive fruits so familiar to the bittersweet family. Few species attain tree size and, of those, surprisingly few are in cultivation. While some will forever remain components of desert scrub, others deserve inclusion, especially in dry climates where the palette is limited. Most likely to be successful in general cultivation are those whose habitats stretch into colder winter or mountainous areas and areas with greater rainfall, all factors that make them suitable for a wider range of cultivation.

Propagation is best from ripened (summer through mid winter) present season's growth; and, with a little mist and bottom heat, a high percentage of rooting can be expected. The desert and spiny forms can be a bit trickier, resenting mist and having little present season's growth with which to work. Seed, when available, can be sown any time, but a cool stratification for a month or so can increase the germination rate and make sprouting less sporadic. Sowing in a mineral soil is also helpful.

Maytenus boaria (Chilean mayten). In Chile, the common name *mayten* ("of cattle") is a reference to the hoofed mammals that browse these plants. The native range stretches from northwestern Argentina south and west through central and southern Chile, where they occur in a wide range of conditions, from the somewhat saline shrub country, or Chaco, to dry grasslands and wet mountain slopes, occasionally becoming one of the most alpine trees at high elevations. *Maytenus boaria*, one of the very few species to be found in cultivation outside public gardens, takes the form of a rounded, weeping tree, often resembling a miniature weeping willow. The slender, pointed leaves, under ⅓ in. (1 cm) wide and 1½ in. (4 cm) long, dangle from the branchlets like strands from a necklace. This texture, in an evergreen form, is difficult to achieve in the garden.

Although specimens have reached nearly 100 ft. (30 m) in both wild and cultivated locations, most forms remain under 30 ft. (9 m)—a graceful, small-scale addition to the garden. As suggested by their native habitat, they are tolerant of a wide range of conditions, from relatively poor drainage to stony soil and, once established, drought at almost any time of the year. Obviously, plants receiving more moisture and free-draining soil will achieve greater size.

Maytenus boaria

The range also suggests there will be great variations in cold hardiness. In years past, most commercially available plants were damaged by frost in the coldest years in the Pacific Northwest; now, numerous wild collections and trees with provenance from colder gardens mean that much tougher forms are available. One particularly beautiful specimen, planted in the 1950s in the Peevey Arboretum, which sits in one of the Willamette Valley's coldest pockets near Corvallis, Oregon, remains a fine 30 ft. (9 m) specimen having exhibited no frost damage in 0°F (–18°C). Our wild collections are from near the Biobio mine in central Chile, where they are the highest elevation trees, subject to long periods of snow and freezing wind.

Myrica	bay myrtle, wax myrtle	Myricaceae

Between thirty and thirty-five evergreen or deciduous shrubs and small trees, all with somewhat narrow, oval leaves and small catkin-like inflorescences, grown mostly for the foliage and often for the spicy fragrance of the leaves.

Propagation is from half ripened to mostly ripened current season's growth in summer to autumn or from seed—easy with some stratification.

Myrica californica (syn. *Morella californica*; California wax myrtle). From southern California to northern Oregon, all on the immediate coast in mixed chaparral. These medium shrubs to small trees, up to 25 ft. (7.5 m), have flattened sprays of narrow, fragrant leaves, small blue-black to purplish fruit held amid the leaves, and, when lifted into tree form, attractive silvery bark. Flowers are insignificant.

Tolerant of salt spray and wind, as well as a great degree of summer drought and poor soil. Not, however, a lover of high humidity accompanied by heat. One of the most useful woody natives for Mediterranean gardens in North America.

Myrica californica f. *buxifolia* has rounded, tightly held leaves and a more compact habit. Most forms have been hardy to between 0 and 5°F (–18 and –15°C).

Myrica cerifera (syn. *Morella cerifera*; southern wax myrtle). This is the California wax myrtle's eastern counterpart, from Florida to New Jersey, often in thickets and coastal sand dunes or glades, sometimes reaching a stout 30 ft. (9 m) or more, with 1–3 in. (2.5–8 cm) leaves, sometimes minutely serrated, always fragrant when crushed. Male flowers are yellow to green, 1 in. (2.5 cm) catkins; female flowers are tiny but produce abundant light blue-gray fruit, lovely to look at, beloved by birds. A gold-leaf form found by Pat McCracken, *M. c.* 'Soleil', combines the species' vigor with glowing color.

Myrica californica

Myrica californica f. *buxifolia*.
Photo by Bart O'Brien

Myrica cerifera 'Soleil'. Photo by Tony Avent

Accepting full sun to dappled shade, *Myrica cerifera* is easy, happily accepting wet, even swampy soils, and periodic drought, as well as salt spray and coastal conditions. Multi-stemmed specimens make wildlife-friendly screens; others, carefully trimmed, can be formal garden specimens. The most northern forms have withstood −20°F (−29°C), though perhaps deciduous at those temperatures; southern forms are reliable above 0°F (−18°C).

Myrica rubra (syn. *Morella rubra*; red bayberry). East Asian species reaching sometimes 35 ft. (10.5 m) or more, with upwardly held narrow leaves often with narrow lobes toward the tips. Easily lifted to expose the silvery bark. Small-flowered, like the others; the purplered fruit on female plants is most attractive, held in clusters against the dark leaves. Widespread, grown for its edible fruit, with most forms frost hardy to between 15 and 20°F (−9.5 to −7°C). The search is on for plants that might tolerate lower temperatures.

Neolitsea   Lauraceae

Up to sixty evergreen trees and shrubs, entirely native to East and Southeast Asia. All come from mesic areas with abundant summer rainfall and only short periods of winter drought; these, along with the rest of the wonderful and diverse world of laurels, make up an integral part of the exceedingly diverse broadleaved evergreen flora in warm parts of Asia. A very handsome genus, especially adapted to cooler areas but with few species in cultivation. The arborescent forms become umbrel-shaped trees with beautifully layered branches and highly textural leaves. They bear sweetly scented spring flowers and red or black fruit.

The genus as a whole appears very plastic, and the number of species might very well be reduced. For the most part, a neolitsea can be identified by its substantial three-veined leaf, with more than attractive bluish undersides, and coppery new growth, which looks so different from the plant's mature growth that, just after unfolding, it might not appear to be part of the same plant. Except in stature, many recognized species seem quite similar—at least to my eye, though, I suppose, not to each other. Hence, only one species—the best, of course—is included here.

Neolitsea sericea. Photo © Global Book Publishing Photo Library

Neolitsea sericea (silky laurel, Japanese silver tree). Upright and narrow in youth, becoming a layered umbrella after four to six years and ultimately reaching 15 ft. (4.5 m), possibly 35 ft. (10.5 m), depending on the form. It is fast-growing: cutting-grown plants can reach 5 ft. (1.5 m) in their second or third year and grow into a handsome small tree by their fifth. Possibly the most endearing feature is the golden to coppery fur-covered new growth, as shiny as a new penny, maturing into drip-tipped, oval leaves, 6–8 in. (15–20 cm) or more long by 2½–3 in. (6–8 cm) wide; leaves have a glaucous blue on their underside that complements the silvery bark, which is beautifully exposed beneath the branch layers. This glaucescence is one of the finest attributes a broadleaved evergreen can have, especially when placed in a shady situation, where the leaves seem to gather light, adding to the definition of the tree. The flowers, in relatively small clusters, occur in mid spring and are pale, creamy yellow. Although they complement the bluish color of the leaves, their real value in the garden is their fragrance, sweet and noticeable from some distance.

The tree is happy in the sun if more compact, as one might expect, but, given adequate water, shows little sign of yellowing. It seems at its best in afternoon or dappled shade, with which condition the leaves are larger and the overall shape comes into its own. Full sun, especially in low humidity, and hot summer climates can burn the

Neolitsea sericea, underside of leaf

new growth as it emerges and cause the tree to have a much shrubbier appearance.

If the tree is to be planted in a frost-prone garden, provenance should be checked to ensure selection of one of the hardier forms. One in particular, from Cliff Parks of Camellia Forest Nursery in North Carolina, originated in South Korea and has proven both attractive and particularly winter hardy, having received no damage there from −8°F (−22°C). In our nursery, this form is the only one we propagate: our original specimen, planted in 1995, is some 20 ft. (6 m) in height and underplanted with *Mahonia gracilipes*, another favorite whose leaves have reflective, silvery white undersides. (A garden light that just "happened" to land underneath this garden grouping extends the pleasure into the evening.) Another Korean collection, at the University of British Columbia Botanic Garden, is also approaching 20 ft. (6 m), grown in open shade; it is a full round-headed specimen of over 15 ft. (4.5 m) across. Obviously hardy, and alone worth a visit to this fabulous garden.

Again, consistent watering in dry-summer areas is a must, as is adequate drainage. They do respond to nitrogen-rich fertilizers and, if wet feet or lack of nutrients has been a problem and yellowing has occurred, a shot of iron is useful.

Propagation is a bit hit or miss. However, as with much of the family, late summer to autumn current season's growth has been moderately successful, with sixty to seventy percent rooting using medium to high hormones, mist, and bottom heat. Seeds are the preferred method of propagation, with reasonably consistent results. It is best to leave the seeds on the tree as long as possible and give them a cool stratification for a month or so before sowing.

IF IT WERE UP to me, three plants would be in everyone's garden: *Neolitsea sericea* and the two species next described.

Litsea japonica (so closely related, some lump it in the same genus) is a superb large shrub to small tree from the warmer climates of Japan. It has attributes similar to *Neolitsea sericea*, especially the stunning blue leaf undersides, but the leaf shape is a bit more oval and rhododendron-like, and the indumentum persists along the leaf margins and, to some degree, on the leaf surface. The plant becomes round-headed as an adult and remains under 20 ft. (6 m). It requires the same consistent summer watering as *N. sericea* and has proven hardy to brief bouts of 0°F (−18°C). So far appearing in only a few public gardens and private collections, one specimen, at Peckerwood Garden in Hempstead, Texas, commanded at least an hour of adoration. Because of the combined qualities of leaf and plant shape, it deserves being sought out for garden use.

Yet another closely related genus, *Phoebe*, offers *P. chekiangensis*, a species from East Asia, with leaves a bit more "avocado" in shape, 5–6 in. (13–15 cm) wide, tapering quickly to a drip tip. The leaf undersides offer the same blue, refractive qualities, but both the surface and the underside have an overlay of golden indumentum. Rather than rounded, the structure is layered like that of a dogwood (*Cornus*), with leaves appearing as whorls at the ends of the branches.

Whereas *Litsea* and *Neolitsea* appear to take bright sunlight in stride, *Phoebe chekiangensis* seems most graceful and colorful in at least dappled shade. Garden height should reach 25–35 ft. (7.5–9 m), eventually, and the plant has survived, with overhead protection of evergreens, at about −4°F (−20°C). My first introduction to this plant was not through seeing an adult specimen but rather from growing seed—initially received as another species—from China. The adoration quotient had to build while discovering the potential of this beautiful creature. Now approaching 20 ft. (6 m) in our garden, and suffering a bit from the untimely removal of a neighbor's very large Atlas cedar (*Cedrus atlantica* 'Glauca'), it awaits new overstory but remains stunning.

Nothofagus	southern beech	Fagaceae

More than forty trees and shrubs, over two-thirds of which are evergreen. Native to the southern hemisphere entirely, primarily New Zealand and Australia and Chile, this is a genus of handsome plants, often with striking branch patterns, leaf shapes, and colors. The bark, usually silvery gray, has patterns of lenticels that become more exaggerated, turning into a major feature as the tree ages. All inhabit relatively mesic sites, most with at least some degree of year-round moisture, though several species from Chile persist through dry summers. Deep watering and well-aerated soil are helpful in encouraging deep rooting as most species tend to have wide-spreading, shallow roots. The small beech-like fruit is attractive to wildlife. I have several times tussled with various fauna over recently deposited nuts lying amid the groves. Squirrels can be vicious.

Propagation has been successful with late summer cuttings, mostly hardened wood, and with seeds, when available, which germinate readily given a cool, preferably damp stratification.

Nothofagus cunninghamii (myrtle beech). Southeastern Australia, Tasmania. At low elevations, a tree sometimes exceeding 165 ft. (50 m) in height, especially when in mixed forest situations with *Eucalyptus* and other tall trees. At high elevations, this species is found as a shrub; in subalpine areas, it can be as small as 5–10 ft. (1.5–3 m). The

Nothofagus cunninghamii. Photo ©
Global Book Publishing Photo Library

⅓–¾ in. (1–2 cm) leaves are shaped somewhat like a small birch leaf and with their dark, glossy green color bear a striking resemblance to those of *Azara microphylla*; set in what appear to be rows along zigzagging branchlets, they create a charming effect of draped fans.

Specimen trees grown in the open are somewhat tall and narrow early on, eventually spreading into wide pyramids with horizontal layers of branches. Some thinning of basal suckers and interior growth enhances the shape. Although the habitat of *Nothofagus cunninghamii* is variable as to elevation and soil makeup—some in the high elevations grow at least on the edge of swampy areas, whereas other colonies are in rocky soil or relatively deep soils—its entire range is quite wet. Although specimens can put up with poor drainage, they would much prefer as little drought as possible.

Ratings of cold hardiness have differed, and it is assumed that provenance is the variable. Standard plants in cultivation have remained evergreen into the mid teens (14 to 16°F, –10 to –9°C) for brief periods, but suffered below those temperatures. It is to be expected that forms from higher elevations would be frost hardy to 0°F (–18°C). Where winter frosts seldom fall below 20°F (–7°C), *Nothofagus cunninghamii* is one of the most handsome, small-leaved evergreens, having a more compact, less rangy nature than evergreen Chinese elms (*Ulmus parvifolia*) but a larger and more substantial presence than *Azara microphylla*. It is tolerant of some summer heat but dislikes extended periods of low humidity even with irrigation.

A species that has been little used in gardens outside its native range, it deserves a closer look and possibly some work on selection to distinguish the better forms.

Nothofagus dombeyi (coigüe). Southern Chile and adjacent Argentina. Appears in mixed forests in the south, and in south-facing islands at mid elevations further north. Another large tree, with well-watered populations reaching 165 ft. (50 m) or more. The ¾–1½ in. (2–4 cm) leaves are oval, sometimes sharp-pointed and dentate, and a glossy, almost black green. One form, native near Vilches in central Chile and just now being brought into cultivation, has leaves with a pleasing glaucescence, giving the tree a bluish hue when seen from a distance. A massive tree, not for the smallest urban lot, this moderately growing species—3–4 ft. (about 1 m) per year when young—is relatively deep-rooted for a nothofagus and makes a magnificent park or street tree. As well, since the northern populations, especially, come from areas that experience summer drought, *N. dombeyi* is better adapted to Mediterranean climates, even if given only some summer supplemental water (though, as in its native habitat, well-watered specimens in deep soil grow the largest and most quickly).

Nothofagus dombeyi

Although frost hardiness depends on provenance, most have been found resilient in temperatures to 10°F (–12°C) or even lower. In several southern Andean places, *Nothofagus dombeyi* is the dominant timberline tree, forming a very dark green ring around peaks, having emerged from a mixed situation to a pure stand before the mountain habitat gives way to alpine tundra. As one would assume, plants from these provenances have proven easily frost resistant to 0 to –10°F (–18 to –23°C), while other forms, for example, from toward the Chilean coast, prove tough only to about 10°F (–12°C).

Nothofagus fusca (red beech). New Zealand, in mixed forest, sometimes in pure colonies at higher elevations. Medium tree of 30–50 ft. (9–15 m), occasionally reaching 100–115 ft. (30–35 m). The oval leaves, 1¼–2 in. (3–5 cm) broad with evenly spaced teeth, are set in flat sprays on herringbone-patterned, silver branchlets. The most beguiling fea-

Nothofagus fusca. Photo © Global Book Publishing Photo Library

ture is the color of the leaves, an orangey red that New Zealand has mastered in its vegetation. In the shade and with age, the leaves can fade to an olive tone and then, before falling, turn a coppery yellow or even deeper orange-red. *Nothofagus fusca* var. *colensoi* has somewhat more substantial leaves and, in general, is a somewhat more compact tree. Both it and the type have bark with very small lenticels and a gray color dark enough to appear almost black when damp.

A plant of moist situations, *Nothofagus fusca* is equally at home as an understory tree or in the sun, though its delicate pattern is more visible with shade. A bit tender for temperate gardens, it thrives where the air, at least at night, retains some humidity and where temperatures seldom fall below the upper teens (16 to 18°F, −9 to −8°C).

Nothofagus solanderi (black beech). New Zealand. To 100 ft. (30 m), it somewhat resembles *N. cunninghamii* but with more compact leaves and a broader spreading form. The leaves are 6 mm to ⅓ in. (1 cm) in size and glossy, dark green, with some overall pubescence when the growth is new, remaining underneath as the leaf matures. *Nothofagus solanderi* var. *cliffortioides* (mountain beech)—capable of like size but

Nothofagus solanderi var. *cliffortioides*. Photo © Global Book Publishing Photo Library

Nothofagus solanderi, "autumn" color in late spring

Nothofagus solanderi

generally smaller and even more compact, with undulate leaves and a more acute tip—is the alpine end of *N. solanderi* and can be shrub-like at the highest altitudes. If frost hardiness is an issue, this is the variety of choice. Whereas *N. solanderi* can receive at least tip damage in the low to mid teens (13 to 16°F, –10.5 to –9°C), *N. solanderi* var. *cliffortioides* has been unfazed by bouts of 0 to 10°F (–18 to –12°C), and even hardier forms doubtless exist. A specimen growing in the Portland, Oregon, garden of Stuart Fraser reached about 25 ft. (7.5 m) in fifteen years and has withstood, with no noticeable damage, temperatures of 13°F (–10.5°C) along with several days below freezing.

Olea	olive	Oleaceae

About twenty species of evergreen trees and shrubs from western Europe to South Africa, with a few eastward into Asia. Most are native to seasonally dry regions and can thus take periodic drought; they are especially suited to areas with strongly Mediterranean climates in the U.S. West. On all species, the spring and early summer flowers are nearly white to cream and are fragrant as well as allergy-inducing. The fruit is a single drupe, some very small, others, such as in *Olea europaea* (common olive), up to 1½ in. (4 cm) or more.

For the first 1000 years or so of cultivation, many desired forms were reproduced by chopping the heavily burled bases into pieces, pulling chunks out of the ground, then dragging them to the next area where, eventually, an olive tree would grow. Luckily, better methods have come about of late and require less room and effort. Well-ripened wood from the end of summer through winter is easy though sometimes a bit slow. A high . . . ish level of hormone is good, along with a steep wound. Also helpful is some bottom heat and only light use of mist, as the foliage under damp conditions is susceptible to cooties.

Seed germinates with varying results—poor, in my experience—yet seeds have sprouted in the garden where not desired. Go figure. I do know, however, that those that did germinate were sown in autumn and received stratification for at least a few months. Of course, unless the goal is to pique curiosity, it is best to propagate these from cuttings, to retain the known characteristics of the adult plant.

Although comparatively new to cultivation in North America and elsewhere outside the Mediterranean, olives are a permanent fixture of the built landscape in the true Mediterranean, having been part of the architecture for at least two millenia. Recently, trading of truly ancient specimens, 500 to over 1500 years old, has increased, most intensely in Spain. One cannot help but wonder if future generations will mourn the loss, whether of ancient growth cleared for development or individual specimens taken to faraway lands where they are, quite possibly, less likely to thrive.

Olea europaea (common olive). Native to the Mediterranean, the Black Sea area, and as far south as South Africa. Since this species, well known for its rich oils and cured fruit, has been in cultivation for thousands of years, it is hard to say where most of the forms originated, although the earliest plantations were undoubtedly produced from nearby wild stands. It is safe to say that the most common forms were planted for the qualities of the fruit. Although some are shrubby, most attain tree status and are single- to multi-trunked with a broad crown; some reach as high as 50 ft. (15 m), with a couple of records over 90 ft. (27 m).

In the wild, the branches are often spine-tipped, an adaptation that discourages browsing or, perhaps, plucking; many cultivated varieties are spineless. Once the plant has attained tree shape, the branchlets often weep a bit, making a very soft appearance. The rather stiff-textured leaves are ½–3 in. (1.5–8 cm) long and 6 mm to ½ in. (1.5 cm) wide. Although they can be dark green, most are, well, . . . olive, a light gray-green to nearly silver, often with silvery, or sometimes golden, undersides. For the purposes of garden cultivation, my favorites are those with the more reflective colors. Along with *Cupressus sempervirens* (Italian cypress), olives give the immediate sense of being in the Mediterranean. They induce the feeling that if these trees can grow here, then the climate is mild, and the living is good.

The fruit is seen as either a blessing or a curse. In the western United States, even in areas where olives are rare, one of the first questions asked is, "Are they messy?"—a legitimate worry, as the fall-ripening fruit, especially the black-fruited forms, *can* stain sidewalks as it falls and ferments. While clearly a problem when white shag carpets were popular, as that era has mercifully passed, so have the staining problems seemed to diminish.

In western Europe, of course, diversity of forms is great. In the western United States and elsewhere, the choices had been few, mostly confined to those brought here in the early days, when olive cultivation first expanded outside Europe. In California, for example, people who left the seemingly endless I-5 corridor and entered the town of Corning for an olive tasting were treated to such cultivars as *Olea europaea* 'Manzanillo' or *O. e.* 'Mission', both adequate though inferior in taste and texture to many other forms. As olive orchards have given way to tract housing, or just given over to other agricultural uses, many of these trees have made their way into business and home landscapes, since large specimens are easily moved. (Possibly the reason shag carpets went out of style.)

Olea europaea. Photo by Michael A. Dirr

Olea europaea in fruit. Photo by John Grimshaw

Olea europaea 'Arbequina'

In recent years, as plant interest has grown, so has the quality of available forms. Michael Remmick of McMinnville, Oregon, has been collecting and trialing dozens of cultivars, some of which are probably groups of clones lumped into one name. For example, *Olea europaea* 'Arbequina', a Spanish cultivar, is most likely several clones of similar quality, but all are small trees, 25 ft. (7.5 m), producing copious amounts of small brown-purple olives rich in flavor. The leaves are typical olive-green, and the weight of the olives in autumn increases the weeping form of the tree. *Olea europaea* 'Arbequina' also tends to be self-fertile. As an additional interesting benefit, it appears to be hardy to 0°F (–18°C) or even a little below and ripens fairly well in cooler summer climes. *Olea europaea* 'Empeltre' eventually becomes a somewhat larger plant and bears larger olives jet-black in color and attractive silvery leaves; in a freak, early November frost of 22°F (–5.5°C), it continued ripening, where the fruits of others suffered damage. The old reliable *O. e.* 'Mission', remaining under 30 ft. (9 m), has proven nearly as frost hardy as *O. e.* 'Arbequina', though fruit loss and some fruit damage has occurred near 0°F (–18°C). *Olea europaea* 'Manzanillo', a bit larger and faster-growing, to upwards of 35–40 ft. (10.5–12 m), and with larger leaves, has been damaged in the low teens (–10.5°C). *Olea europaea* subsp. *cuspidata* (syn. *O. ferruginea*), a subspecies from the south and eastern ranges in the Middle East, varies from a very twiggy, small-leaved shrub to a larger, weeping small tree, both well endowed with silvery to brown indumentum but having very small fruit; ultimate cold hardiness is not known, but it certainly comes from areas subject to brief, hard frosts.

Olea yunnanensis from China, as the name would imply, inhabits areas that, though subject to occasional periodic drought, have much more year-round moisture. The leaves are larger than those of *O. europaea*, to 2–3 in. (5–8 cm), occasionally with minute teeth along the edges. It can grow into a narrow pyramidal tree of over 30 ft. (9 m) with a branch structure and leaves more similar to and reminiscent of the genus *Osmanthus*, a relative of *Olea*. Collections in cultivation have withstood temperatures in the mid to upper teens (14 to 18°F, –10 to –8°C), with better results where there is some overhead canopy.

Osmanthus	sweet olive	Oleaceae

Also known as fragrant holly and devilwood. A variable genus of up to thirty (or as few as fifteen, depending on recognized relationships with other closely related species) broadleaved evergreens, ranging from shrubs to medium-sized trees and inhabiting summer-wet forests mostly in Southeast Asia, but also occurring in southeastern North America. A related genus, *Phillyrea* (which occurs toward

Europe in Mediterranean climes and is included by some in *Osman-thus*), enjoys its own section in this volume.

Many of my fond memories of autumn are associated with the wafting fragrance of sweet olives. Wherever they are encountered—whether in their native China, where they are also heavily planted, or in the U.S. Southeast, where Asian species are more frequently cultivated than native species—the aroma of warm, baked apricots follows. One's nose often leads toward a common species, *Osman-thus fragrans*, with the expectation that the flower size will match the abundant fragrance. It is a surprise to discover, instead, the small (1 mm) tiny-petalled bells, typical of all species, that appear in small, dense clusters held between the leaves. Though individually flowers are small, their collective presence is attractive. Luckily, the pollen does not have a reputation for sending people into sneezing fits, unlike their close relatives, the olives. The fruit, however, is olive-like, appearing as a small, dark blue or purple drupe on female plants.

Alongside the flowers, the leaves, lustrous and often exceedingly handsome, are one of the most outstanding features of the genus. Depending on species they can be nearly entire, completely lacking spines on the edges, or serrated nearly to the point of comedy. In nearly every species, the leaves become less spiny, less toothed, as the plants age. The 2½–8 in. (6–20 cm) leaves are opposite, making a particularly friendly pocket for the flowers. This characteristic is key in distinguishing the genus *Osmanthus* from the genus *Ilex*, with which *Osmanthus* species are sometimes confused: *Ilex* species have alternate leaves.

All species mentioned here enjoy full sun in all but the hottest climes; they are also quite at home in dappled shade, some even in fairly dense shade. As all are from places with ample summer moisture, reliable irrigation is needed where it does not fall from the sky. Although established plants do show some summer drought tolerance, specimens, particularly young plants, can become sparse and decline. One word of caution—in places with low heat accumulation, some yellowing can occur, so careful attention to nutrition should be maintained. As well, general frost hardiness might be decreased a tad, especially where growth occurs later in the season and might not be fully ripened before the first autumn frost. In these situations, the coveted south wall is the best location for the plant.

For all species, newly hardened, current season's growth in early to mid summer, to well-ripened wood through the following winter, provides abundant material for easy propagation. Seed, though not difficult with a modicum of cool stratification, preferably damp, is rarely used, as so many good clonal selections are available.

With osmanthus, the best suggestion might be to simply plant them all. But if space or attention span is limited, and choices must be made, the following attributes could be considered: bloom season (spring or fall); quality of flower fragrance, which (while always delightful) does vary from species to species; overall leaf texture, including size, serrations, and potential harmfulness to small toes; and mature size (some species can become quite large).

Osmanthus americanus (gray devilwood, American fragrant olive). An outlier of this primarily Asian genus, gray devilwood can be found growing in the woodlands of the U.S. Southeast, with some of the most handsome forms coming from north and central Florida. To 30 ft. (9 m) or more—though most garden specimens remain under 20 ft. (6 m), achieving large size only with great age—they occur at forest edges, often as understory, often in shallow soils.

Underused even in its native haunts, *Osmanthus americanus* is a handsome, pyramidal, small tree that is usually multi-trunked but can be trained as single. The leaves, more rounded when young, become elliptic to lance-shaped, reaching to over 5 in. (13 cm) in length, with an entire margin and a shiny, dark green surface. Though at home in the hot, humid summers of the Southeast, even there, when pulled from their woodland habitat, they enjoy some garden water. When put in drier climates, garden water is even more necessary, as they can become sparse with too much drought. Unlike most Asian species, *O. americanus* produces early to mid spring flowers, but, as with its counterparts, they are sweetly fragrant. The fruit, in small clusters, is purply black, resembling somewhat that of a mahonia.

It is always a pleasure to see these plants used in the native land-

Osmanthus americanus, flowers.
Photo by Michael A. Dirr

Osmanthus americanus, fruit.
Photo by Michael A. Dirr

Osmanthus americanus. Photo by Michael A. Dirr

scapes of the eastern and southeastern United States. Though rated in numerous publications as hardy only just below 20°F (–7°C), specimens, especially of northern provenance, have withstood 0°F (–18°C) and even –4°F (–20°C) with little noticeable damage. Some of the Florida forms have had leaf drop in the low to mid teens (13 to 16°F, –10.5 to –9°C) but have usually recovered. Some at the northern range experience bark split and have recovered slowly, if at all, remaining sparse and unattractive.

Osmanthus americanus is at its best used as a courtyard or close-in understory tree, where garden visitors can be surprised that a native North American osmanthus exists.

Osmanthus armatus. Though most often used as a shrub, its moderate annual growth of 18 in. (45 cm) puts *O. armatus* in the small tree category soon enough. From western China, in areas of ample rainfall in both summer and winter, specimens of over 30 ft. (9 m) have been observed. Narrowly pyramidal in youth, plants spread slowly with age to create a more rounded form with one to many trunks. In cultivation they reach 6–8 ft. (2–2.5 m) from a newly planted small specimen in only a few years, topping out at an average of 10–12 ft. (3–3.5 m). In regions of high summer heat, several flushes of growth per season might occur.

The leaves are possibly the most attractive feature. Pubescent young growth gives way to a leathery but shiny mature leaf of 2½–5 in. (6–13 cm). Although obovate to ovate, they are often strongly toothed, appearing sculptural in close view and very fine-textured in the distance. Some leaves can become entire, especially as the plants

Osmanthus armatus. Photo by Michael A. Dirr

Osmanthus armatus, flowers.
Photo by Michael A. Dirr

mature. The flowers, appearing most often in late September through October, are a clean white to the palest of creamy yellows and bear a sweet fragrance. The dark blue to deep purple fruit is rather large for the genus, to about ⅓ in. (1 cm), and hangs in small clusters amid the leaves.

Easy in the garden and, where conditions are not desert-like, happy in medium shade to full sun, they prefer good drainage, like all osmanthus, and, although resilient to occasional drought, perform their best with at least occasional deep waterings where the soil is likely to dry thoroughly. Rated to zone 7, *Osmanthus armatus* has performed admirably in cold spells, even nudging zone 6 and surviving from –5 to 0°F (–20 to –18°C) with mere leaf burn.

Osmanthus decorus. From the Caucasus leaning toward central Asia, the easterly mesic habitats more associated with the genus. Another species most often treated as a shrub yet making a lovely small tree if lower branches are pruned away and the plants are kept to one or a few trunks; often observed as such in older gardens, topping out at 10–12 ft. (3–3.5 m). It is often wider than tall. *Osmanthus decorus* is better adapted to summer drought than most *Osmanthus* species and has performed well in low-water gardens of western North America. The leaves, entire and only to about 4 in. (10 cm), form a pleasing, narrow triangle with a fairly sharp tip. They are matte green on top and a very light yellow beneath. Bluish black fruit of ½ in. (1.5 cm) follows the late winter to mid spring flowers, their sweet and custardy aroma a delight when carried by the breeze on an early spring day.

Osmanthus decorus is another resilient plant, having few pest problems and withstanding temperatures between 0 and 10°F (–18 and –12°C) with little damage, especially if planted out of the wind.

Osmanthus decorus, flowers.
Photo by Michael A. Dirr

Osmanthus decorus, foliage.
Photo by Michael A. Dirr

Osmanthus decorus. Photo by Michael A. Dirr

Osmanthus fragrans (fragrant olive, tea olive). Widespread from the Himalayas through China and Japan, this denizen of rich woodlands with ample moisture has also been used for centuries in gardens throughout warmer regions of Asia, and, more recently, in the West. Along with camellias and the michelia group of magnolias, *O. fragrans* is one of the iconic plants of Japan and China and the best bet for that deliciously fragrant baked apricot scent. Though sometimes treated as shrubs, heights of 20–30 ft. (6–9 m) or more are very common, with 40 ft. (12 m) not unheard of, especially in warm summer climates. The 4–5 in. (10–13 cm) leaves are long and narrow with a rounded tip and either entire or finely toothed margins; sometimes the leaves are almost quilted between the network of veins or are somewhat fluted. The flowers, typically white to creamy, are in small clusters but bunched at the leaf axils of the present season's growth.

As would be expected with a species having such a wide distribution and such a long history of cultivation, numerous forms exist. *Osmanthus fragrans* var. *aurantiacus* has dense clusters of orange-yellow to orange flowers heavily scented of apricots, though the effect may be psychological because of their color. Asian forms with nearly red flowers have begun to spill into Western horticulture as real rather than mythological plants; one from Japan, *O. f.* 'Benekei', was shared with us by Ted Stephens. *Osmanthus fragrans* var. *thunbergii*, with creamy flowers set in dense and particularly fragrant clusters, has the added beauty of purple flushes of new growth. An extra, extra bonus might be its apparent, increased frost hardiness, having withstood winters in the upper zone 7 range from 5 to 10°F (−15 to −12°C) with no more than superficial damage, whereas, in general, the spe-

Osmanthus fragrans var. *aurantiacus*

Osmanthus fragrans. Photo by Michael A. Dirr

Osmanthus fragrans var. *thunbergii*

cies is rated only to mid zone 8 or even zone 9. *Osmanthus fragrans* 'Fudingzhu', introduced from China and given to us by Ted Stephens, appears to be this subspecies.

Probably more than for any other *Osmanthus* species, frost hardiness is dependent on the amount of summer warmth received. In cool and coastal climates, new growth might appear late; flushes of new growth, having had no time to harden in autumn, are most subject to blackening from cold. Overhead cover or southern exposure to achieve more heat accumulation is certainly helpful.

Osmanthus ×*fortunei*, a cross between *O. fragrans* and *O. heterophyllus*, is a fast-growing broad plant either maintained as a large shrub or, in time, a very small tree, to 12–15 ft. (3.5–4.5 m) in warm summer climates. The requisite white, sweet-scented flowers appear in late summer to mid fall. The leaves are roughly 3 in. (8 cm) long and narrowly ovate, toothed when young and nearly entire with age. *Osmanthus* ×*fortunei* 'Hilliers Variegated' (also listed as *O.* ×*fortunei* 'Varie-

Osmanthus fragrans 'Fudingzhu'.
Photo by Michael A. Dirr

Osmanthus ×*fortunei*, new leaves.
Photo by Michael A. Dirr

Osmanthus ×*fortunei*

gatus'), with cream-splashed and -margined leaves, is slower growing and smaller, to only 8–10 ft. (2.5–3 m) in as many years.

Osmanthus heterophyllus (holly olive, Chinese holly). This species, the most common in cultivation, is found in Japan and Taiwan, in both rocky places and in woodland situations. It prefers full drainage with consistent moisture. Variable in habit and slow-growing, it is often seen as hedging or a small garden specimen; rarely is it thought that the cute little shrub just acquired at the garden center might eventually reach 30 ft. (9 m) or more. Young plants have leaves that are heavily toothed, indeed, much like *Ilex aquifolium* and just as dangerous to the bare foot. As the plants mature, they lose most of their marginal teeth, becoming nearly entire with only serrations. The fragrant white flowers form small clusters that can appear at any time of the year but are most reliable from late summer to mid fall. One of the frost hardiest species, plants are often seen in parks and gardens in areas as cold as zone 6 and can withstand −10°F (−23°C) or even colder for short periods.

Among the many cultivars, *Osmanthus heterophyllus* 'Purpureus' is one of the most common, with its rosy purple, new growth flush. A close second would be *O. h.* 'Variegatus', a large specimen of which was donated to the Portland Classical Chinese Garden, a transplant from a private garden (where it had been since before the turn of the twentieth century) into the entry courtyard (through the magic of very large trucks and cranes and with the disruption of many a power line through the city on its travels there). The courtyard is now called Old Gui ("spirit" in Pinyin) in honor of this lovely spreading

Osmanthus heterophyllus, flowers.
Photo by Michael A. Dirr

Osmanthus heterophyllus 'Variegatus', arriving at the Portland Classical Chinese Garden

Osmanthus heterophyllus. Photo by Michael A. Dirr

Osmanthus heterophyllus 'Purpureus'. Photo by Michael A. Dirr

Osmanthus heterophyllus 'Goshiki'. Photo by Michael A. Dirr

Osmanthus heterophyllus 'Aureus'. Photo by Michael A. Dirr

Osmanthus heterophyllus 'Gulftide'. Photo by Michael A. Dirr

Osmanthus heterophyllus 'Myrtifolius'. Photo by Michael A. Dirr

Osmanthus heterophyllus 'Rotundifolius'. Photo by Michael A. Dirr

tree, now 25 ft. (7.5 m), which has survived and flourished in its new environment.

Osmanthus heterophyllus 'Goshiki' is somewhat more compact and splashed with creamy yellow; *O. h.* 'Aureus' is still more compact and a bright cheery golden; and *O. h.* 'Gulftide' is dense and upright with particularly sharp teeth. *Osmanthus heterophyllus* 'Myrtifolius' is as dense and upright but has long narrow leaves and a very graceful presence. By contrast, *O. h.* 'Rotundifolius' has cloud-like layered branches with rounded, exquisitely undulating leaves without teeth.

The variegated forms thrive in dappled shade; as one might expect, those with the most variegation can burn in full sun or reflected heat and benefit from at least afternoon shade.

Osmanthus suavis, foliage.
Photo by Michael A. Dirr

Osmanthus suavis. A compact large shrub or small tree, from 9 ft. (2.7 m) to over 15 ft. (4.5 m), found in open and in mixed woodland situations from the Himalayas to southcentral China. In youth the growth is very upright and dense, with narrow leaves to 1–1½ in. (2.5–4 cm) with fine teeth along the margins. The leaves emerge faintly pubescent but quickly turn a shiny but leathery green; they are often somewhat crenulate or pleated on the margins. The flowers, also sweetly fragrant, are a clean white and occur from early to mid spring. The plant's dark green leaves, contrasting with the silvery bark and the clean white flowers, present a most pleasing sight early in the year.

With age, plants become more rounded but still maintain a narrower form than many other species, making them useful in tight spaces or where a narrow, upright plant is desired. Their frost hardiness is also of interest. Reported to be one of the toughest of the genus, *Osmanthus suavis* has performed admirably in zone 7, withstanding temperatures, at least briefly, between 5 and 10°F (–15 and –12°C) with no perceivable damage. Though far less common in cultivation, *O. suavis* may, with further trialing, come to rival *O. heterophyllus* as the toughest *Osmanthus* species.

Osmanthus suavis, flowers.
Photo by Michael A. Dirr

Osmanthus yunnanensis. Another species from western China, both in forest and open situations, *O. yunnanensis* is likely, at least at times, to itself become the forest overstory, albeit in a short forest! A strong, upright grower to 25–30 ft. (7.5–9 m) in favored situations, the large flattened leaf with spined margin makes a strong presence—especially on anyone walking underneath in bare feet. The shiny and somewhat leathery leaves are a very light green, with an almost yellow cast in bright light; both the petioles and leaf undersides can appear a dark gray. The leaves can be over 8 in. (20 cm) long, with sharp, evenly spaced teeth and apex. The early spring flowers, in substantial clusters of waxy, creamy white bells in the leaf axils, are, again very

Osmanthus yunnanensis, flowers and foliage. Photo by Michael A. Dirr

Osmanthus yunnanensis, Wakehurst Place, RBG Kew. Photo by Michael A. Dirr

fragrant but a bit more custardy, with not even a hint of stone fruit. The 15–20 mm fruit is purple to almost purple-red, with a very light powdery coating.

Unfortunately too rare in cultivation, *Osmanthus yunnanensis* makes a fine small street tree or broadleaved evergreen background plant. It is tolerant of some drought but best if at least occasional deep watering is received during dry summer months. Plants have survived 0 to 5°F (–18 to –15°C) with some damage; however, in Seattle, a tree growing in rather dense shade was frozen back nearly to the ground by temperatures near 0°F (–18°C). A particularly beautiful specimen over 25 ft. (7.5 m) in height can be seen in San Francisco's Strybing Arboretum.

Persea   Lauraceae

A rather large genus of over 150 trees and shrubs, all evergreen, widespread in tropical and subtropical America, Macronesia, and East and Southeast Asia. The leaves are entire; many are beautifully shaped with, often, the long drip tip that is frequent in summer monsoonal places. New growth emerges maroon or orangey, with attractive indumentum in some instances. The flowers can be either unisexual or single-sex, nearly always yellow-green and inconspicuous, sometimes highly scented. The vast majority of species are indeed tropical or denizens of the warm end of warm temperate climates, but a number have widespread potential in areas as cold as zone 7. Those included here—with the exception of the common avocado (*Persea americana*)—are necessarily in the "for external use only" category:

they have small, inedible fruit but many overall qualities that make them superior garden plants.

Seed, preferably after a cool stratification, germinates well in spring. Cuttings vary by species in ease of rooting, but are best in late summer through autumn on ripened, previous season's wood with mist and heat.

Persea americana (avocado, aguacate). Central America and Mexico. Occasionally large shrubs but most often trees, exceeding 65 ft. (20 m) in height. The leaves are a sharp-pointed oval, deep green and coarse-textured, 6–12 in. (15–30 cm) in length. The large, coarse plants are a common sight throughout tropical regions of the world, and a description of the fruit is a cliché (but here goes). Of various sizes, from 4½ in. (12 cm) to over 10 in. (25 cm) depending on the variety, the fruit is basically, well, avocado-shaped with a rather rough exterior that is . . . avocado-colored. Three main strains are cultivated in Central America and the West Indies; another, the distinct *P. americana* var. *drymifolia* often seen in Mexico, has spicy scented leaves and smaller, thin-skinned fruit that is particularly appealing in flavor.

As with olive associations, an encounter with *Persea americana* conjures a good association, if not a grand appetite, sending a message about place, telling of warm climates and great horticultural possibilities. That, along with the experience of eating a ripe avocado off a tree, maybe with a little salt and pepper and, on a hot day, maybe a local beer with a little lime. My recollection has the fruit overlapping its ripening time with the presence of flowers, their very sweet scent carrying on the breeze for some distance. Horticulturally, not a tree for the small garden, as the wide trunk and very coarse texture of the leaves tend to have their way with any space. If used as background or, preferably, as scenery borrowed from the neighbor's garden (with the potential of ripening fruit hanging over your fence), it can be useful; otherwise, cultivation might be better relegated to a rooting "pit" on the windowsill—in memory of the first plant many of us propagated.

Persea americana. Photo © Global Book Publishing Photo Library

The plants need at least partial sun and average to good drainage, and, although drought tolerant once established, prefer deep, regular watering in dry periods to avoid aborting the fruit.

Other than the places where one would expect to see them—the tropical and near tropical climes of the world—they can be spotted between freezes in such areas as London and most cities along the U.S. West Coast, where they will grow quickly between the occasional cold winters. They can be seen reaching maturity in mildest western Europe and its counterparts of warmest zone 9 and above. On the U.S. West Coast, for example, beyond the avocado belt of southern California, they can be seen as far north as the southern Oregon coast—usually planted way too close to the garage. Actual frost hardiness varies among many clones in cultivation, but, as one would expect, the Mexican forms show the most frost tolerance, often putting up with 20°F (−7°C) or so with no noticeable damage. That temperature or lower—early or late in the season or for more than a few hours—damages fruit, flowers, and leaves and begins to kill wood.

Propagation is not difficult. Although some favorite varieties are grafted, late summer and autumn cuttings of newly hardened wood are usually successful with warmth and mist. Seed is one method, of course, although the results are variable. It is not known whether insertion of toothpicks is truly of help in germination, although folk wisdom insists old peanut butter jars are far superior to mayonnaise jars.

Persea borbonia, foliage. Photo by Michael A. Dirr

Persea borbonia, fruit. Photo by Michael A. Dirr

Persea borbonia (red bay). From damp forests and well-drained sandy areas, especially close to ocean inlets in the southeastern United States into Mexico. Though a bit slow-growing in cultivation, to 25–30 ft. (7.5–9 m), *P. borbonia* can reach over 70 ft. (21 m) in its native woodlands. The leaves are roughly 2 × 5 in. (5 × 13 cm), tapering gently to a sharp point and colored a deep green with paler undersides, both sides being nearly hairless, poor bald things. When crushed, they emit that familiar, spicebush fragrance. A spring leaf drop turns the older set of leaves a brilliant copper-orange to almost red, an attractive feature that shouldn't suggest the tree is dying. The flowers are typically tiny, creamy white, and fragrant in a close encounter. And the avocados, borne on maroon-tinted stems, are also tiny, under ½ in. (1.5 cm) long. An entire grove would be required to produce a very small serving of guacamole.

Persea borbonia var. *pubescens*, widespread throughout the range, has a number of especially attractive forms. One from the high mountains of Coahuila in northeastern Mexico has leaves with a silvery covering of small hairs that make each leaf extraordinarily reflective. This variety is now undergoing trials and has proven hardy to at least 10 to 12°F (−12 to −11°C), whereas *P. borbonia* itself, especially the more northern forms, has survived −10 to −12°F (−23 to −25°C) with little damage.

Among the easier of the avocados to propagate, cuttings have been most successful in late summer to early autumn, but are usually successful in all but the time of pushing the spring growth. The seeds, far too small for toothpick insertion, germinate easily after a cool stratification. A pre-soaking to eliminate any excess flesh can be helpful.

Persea borbonia is a particularly pretty member of a loosely knit group of avocado-ish, laurel family creatures and is likely to perform better than a number of other family members in gardens further

Persea borbonia. Photo by Michael A. Dirr

north and in cooler places, especially those with ample summer moisture. In areas of high summer humidity, it performs well in full sun; in drier climes, such as along the U.S. West Coast, it prefers the company of a tall stranger to its south or west.

Persea podadenia, a related Mexican species, maintains a very pleasing oval form and has leaves similar in size to *P. borbonia* but adorned with particularly nice indumentum, especially on the undersides. It is represented, at least in the high-elevation Yucca Do Nursery collection, as growing quickly to 10–15 ft. (3–4.5 m), eventually to 25–30 ft. (7.5–9 m) or more. Plants have maintained vigorous growth in coastal areas of the U.S. West Coast, even with lack of summer heat, and have remained undamaged through temperatures of 8 to 10°F (–14 to –12°C) at the Juniper Level Botanic Garden and Plant Delights Nursery, both in Raleigh, North Carolina. Seems as happy as an understory plant as in full sun, provided adequate summer water.

Persea thunbergii (syn. *Machilus thunbergii*). From widespread areas —southern Japan, China, South Korea, Taiwan, and the Ryukyus. Although often placed in the genus *Machilus*, for purposes of convenience and getting away without additional genera listings, I recognize it here as a persea. It makes a stout, small tree in gardens, to 25–30 ft. (7.5–9 m) or so, though in its wet, monsoonal habitats it has been known to reach nearly 100 ft. (30 m). The central trunk is upright with ascending side branches carrying rather thick, strongly horizontal branchlets, creating the effect of a sturdy umbrella. The faintly sweet flowers are, yes, tiny, but bright chartreuse to cream, colors that would be all the rage in an arrangement if a hand lens were provided. The fruit, under ⅓ in. (1 cm) and longer than wide, is a purplish black and attractive among the leaves. The leaves are oval and entire, about 3 in. (8 cm) wide and 6 in. (15 cm) long, with a blunt taper; they appear as if in whorls at the ends of the branches. They are exceedingly shiny and emerge in the spring a rose-pink to shrimp color, the new leaves remaining so throughout the season except in areas of strong summer sun or low humidity, where the color fades quickly, suggesting a preference for afternoon shade or even full-time dappled shade. Specimens at the North Willamette Experimental Station south of Portland, Oregon, have remained healthy and lustrous in the shade with adequate water but have suffered terribly where underirrigated and in the full sun.

As with *Persea borbonia*, plants can react negatively to long, cool winters such as in the northern Pacific Northwest, responding with yellowing of the leaves and slow growth. The results can be counteracted, at least to some degree, with a few servings of iron and nitrogen in the spring and diligent summer watering to ensure adequate growth when the temperatures are warm.

With such a wide native range, frost hardiness will vary. Plants from more northern origins or high elevations should be sought where frost is an issue. The toughest forms have withstood –10 to –12°F (–23 to –25°C) with little damage, though they did have the protection of some overhead trees. Less frost hardy forms are prone to bark split and twig damage at even higher temperatures.

Propagation by seeds and cuttings is the same as for *Persea borbonia*.

Persea yunnanensis. From damp forests, occasionally from seasonally dry slopes, in China's Yunnan Province and surrounds. Though rare in cultivation, specimens brought to the U.S. West Coast in the late 1930s have been carted north and south and are in many plant collectors' gardens, both public and private. A tree to over 50 ft. (15 m) or more in the wild, specimens in cultivation reach 30 ft. (9 m) and begin spreading to a broad pyramid (as most of us do). The leaves are 2–3 in.

(5–8 cm) wide and 4–6 in. (10–15 cm) long, the narrow shape being quite noticeable. They are dark green above, paler beneath, and have an orange cast when first emerging. The flower is small and creamy white, with a pleasant fragrance that does carry a bit. The fruit is not the reason to have this plant; it is brown, with little flesh, and under 6 mm.

Persea yunnanensis holds a special place for me—beyond the pit-on-the-windowsill experience—having been the first species I understood as having the potential to grow in temperate places. The specimen in our garden, though shaded by numerous other trees (as one might assume thus far into the book), has spread beautifully, making an elegant backdrop and winding its long-leaved, drooping branches through the trunks of such compatriots as black bamboo (*Phyllostachys nigra*). A lover of summer water and fertile, free-draining soil, it does put up well with root competition (as is well illustrated in our garden) if provided generous water. Among the hardiest of the avocados, *Persea yunnanensis* has withstood below 0°F (–18°C) with some noticeable damage. The expected hardiness, with some protection from wind, would be about –10°F (–23°C).

A fine understory or even full-sun garden tree, plants at the University of British Columbia Botanic Garden attest to their long-term suitability in cultivation. There is also a specimen in Seattle's Washington Park Arboretum, planted in 1938 and now over 45 ft. (14 m); but some uncertainty exists as to the actual identity of this plant and its seedlings (and therefore, many planted throughout the Northwest). Upon inspection, these plants resemble herbarium specimens of *Persea ichangensis*, a species we are growing from other collections. It seems there are many closely related species, which can certainly add to taxonomic confusion but also attests to the great number of additional perseas with potential for warm temperate cultivation. Several of these have now appeared and are being trialed in West Coast gardens, bringing much potential to broadleaved evergreen-osity.

Propagation has been easy from both seed and cuttings, and the methods described earlier will suffice.

Phillyrea	mock privet	Oleaceae

Although sometimes referred to as the poor man's *Osmanthus*, the genus *Phillyrea* deserves better; here I would like to come to its members' defense and discuss their many positive attributes. Really! A genus of only two species—or four, by some definitions, depending on the continual tug of war with the genus *Osmanthus*, with which they are closely related. Phillyreas represent the Mediterranean end of the *Osmanthus* clan, much as *Olea yunnanensis* (another closely related genus), an olive outlier in summer-rainfall Asia, represents the eastern end.

Both *Phillyrea angustifolia* and *P. latifolia* inhabit dry shrublands and forest from Portugal to North Africa and east to Turkey; plants are shrubs to trees, depending mostly on exposure to wind and drought, with wide and narrow opposite leaves. They flower in winter and early spring with axillary clusters of greenish white, sweetly scented flowers, each not more than 1–2 mm, followed by purply blue fruit.

If grown in the sun, both species are broad pyramids in youth and easily trained quickly into small trees if provided with generous irrigation. Unlike a number of true Mediterranean plans, both respond well to summer irrigation if the soil is well drained and not too rich in organic material. Old specimens become quite picturesque, with leaning and gnarled branches. As early as the 1500s, the species were used for ornament and hedgerows in their native regions but became far less common as other broadleaved evergreens, especially *Osmanthus*, became increasingly available. Both species fall into the "between" category of large shrubs to small trees. At the nursery, we have found that people are uneasy buying small specimens, finding it difficult to place them in their mind's eye. Larger plants in five-gallon pots (roughly 30 cm wide), pruned up a bit into a standard form, seem better at showing off their garden potential.

Propagation is similar to that of *Osmanthus*. Most success is had with cuttings of fairly well-ripened current season's growth, taken from the end of summer through early spring and accompanied by a little heat and mist.

Phillyrea angustifolia. A fine-textured shrub to small tree, from only 8 ft. (2.5 m) with a wide, rounded form where exposed to ocean winds or in very rocky situations, to nearly 15 ft. (4.5 m) in mixed woodland or in protected places, where it can be narrowly upright. The narrow lance-shaped leaves are under 2–2½ in. (5–6 cm) in length and sometimes narrower than ⅓ in. (1 cm) in width, usually spineless, and a deep lustrous green, brushed with gray in some forms. The tiny flowers are a bit cleaner white than those of *P. latifolia* and, to my recollection, more intensely fragrant. The bark is fine-textured and silvery gray; on older specimens (especially those not in exposed situations), the branchlets and leaves weep at the ends, adding to the plant's attractions.

One of the most exciting features of this species (to those who live in summer-dry climates) is that plants are able to withstand much more summer drought—even preferring it—than their *Osmanthus* relatives. In our nursery's Mediterranean garden, the plants grew to about 8 ft. (2.5 m) in three years from cuttings. Having had opti-

Phillyrea angustifolia, foliage.
Photo by Michael A. Dirr

mal conditions in their youth, they then slowed, with only occasional summer irrigation. From spindly greenhouse specimens, they are now delicately branched, nearly columnar plants, with branchlets just beginning to show signs of weeping and spreading. A well-tended specimen, in which the structure has been opened and lifted, might very well make a fine substitute for *Maytenus boaria* (Chilean mayten), having many of the same qualities. It is to be highly commended as a small patio tree in the Mediterranean garden.

The most narrow-leaved forms of *Phillyrea angustifolia* seem to be relatively rare in cultivation, whether due to plant variability or the fact that it hybridizes with *P. latifolia* when grown nearby. Collections from one population on Mallorca, collected by Kevin Hughes of Britain, have the look of *P. angustifolia* f. *rosmarinifolia*. These plants came from a pure stand, with the entire population having very attractive narrow leaves and a shrubby form in their windswept habitat. We grew out seed from Kevin's collection and named the narrowest upright selection *P. angustifolia* 'Mallorca'—not very original but gets the job done. Though Mallorca, even at higher elevations, is not one of the world's colder places, the flora's Andalusian history dictates some memory of chill, and plants broadcast to other gardens have so far reported frost hardiness of below 10°F (–12°C).

Phillyrea angustifolia

Phillyrea latifolia. A larger plant that *P. angustifolia*, the habitat ranges further east in the Mediterranean and encompasses both the matorral association (the equivalent of the western North American chaparral) and mixed scleritic woodlands, including *Arbutus* and *Laurus*. Sometimes shrubs but often, eventually, small dome-shaped

Phillyrea latifolia. Photo © Global Book Publishing Photo Library

trees, up to 30 ft. (9 m) or so. They are stout and thick-branched, with oval leaves (sometimes nearly lanceolate, especially where seen hybridizing with *P. angustifolia*). Usually margins are very clean, but sometimes, especially in youth, leaves have fine or even pronounced dentations. The greenish white flowers are lightly scented but sweet and occur in mid to late spring.

Another superb plant for dry summer climates. Though rarely putting on more than 18 in. (45 cm) per year, *Phillyrea latifolia* can be spurred to faster growth in nursery conditions or with supplemental summer water. The matte green leaves contrast nicely with the grayish bark and twig color, and they do take well to shearing, although that doesn't do much for the overall form. This species has been at least as frost hardy, if not even a bit more so, than *P. angustifolia* and is a bit more widely available, at least in western North America.

Photinia	red tip, Christmas berry	Rosaceae

A genus of some sixty evergreen or deciduous shrubs and trees, all characterized by corymbs of small white flowers and orange-red fruit. Of all the broadleaved evergreens, two taxa in particular, *Photinia davidiana* and *P.* ×*fraseri*, have made large inroads into cultivation in recent decades, and another, *P. serratifolia*, deserves to be taken up again.

Propagation is from semi-hard to hard wood on current season's growth with heat and mist helpful.

Photinia davidiana. From western China. A large shrub to small tree, easily pruned into tree form, with narrow leaves of leathery texture, often emerging red-tinted and lacking the serrated margins of the two other taxa mentioned here. Small corymbs of white flowers appear in spring; the nearly scarlet fruit becomes evident by late summer, drooping in bunches along the stems. Specimens as tall as 15 ft. (4.5 m) can be seen in older gardens. Thinning inward-growing branches enhance the small rounded shape of the tree.

An interesting selection, *Photinia davidiana* 'Painter's Palette' has leaves marked cream, white, and pink; *P. davidiana* 'Fructuluteo' bears bright yellow fruit, particularly attractive in late autumn when the plant's mature leaves are showing off their dark, late-season hue.

Photinia davidiana takes temperatures to −10°F (−23°C) or so with little damage. It is somewhat prone to fire blight, exemplified by sudden browning of leaves and shriveling branches. Infected material should be removed, the clippers cleaned between each snip, and the clippings disposed of rather than used in garden compost.

Photinia davidiana, flowers.
Photo by Michael A. Dirr

Photinia davidiana. Photo by Michael A. Dirr

Photinia davidiana, fruit.
Photo by Michael A. Dirr

Photinia ×fraseri. These hybrids between *P. glabra* and *P. serratifolia*, introduced mostly as shrubs, are ubiquitous in western North America in almost any area where temperatures remain above 10°F (−12°C). Whether as shopping mall plantings or highway dividers, they are used often enough to have become a cliché. Mention of this hybrid is made not so much to suggest its use—others have already done that, and as it is now much overused—but rather as a gentle plea that it be grown as the attractive small tree it is destined to be. Although now susceptible to a mildew which causes leaf drop, *P. ×fraseri* can be successful and indeed useful, especially when not shaped into a box.

Photinia ×fraseri, yearning to be a tree! Photo by Michael A. Dirr

Photinia ×fraseri, new growth.
Photo by Michael A. Dirr

Photinia ×*fraseri*, flowers. Photo by Michael A. Dirr

Photinia ×*fraseri*, fruit. Photo by Michael A. Dirr

Though indeed shrubby when young, plants are easily trained to single- or few-trunked specimens with a height of 15–18 ft. (4.5–5.5 m) or more in ten years if given adequate water. The narrowly ovate leaves, some 3–5 in. (8–13 cm) long by 3 in. (8 cm) wide with small teeth, emerge coppery and shiny and age to a dark green. New growth begins to appear in late winter, with flowering in earliest spring. Little fruit is set. Growth is densest and leaf color best with bright light, especially in cooler, damper climes. With age the branch pattern is rather open, and the branches held in layers. Thinning enhances views of the gray bark. Several crosses have been made, all with similar characteristics.

Though drought tolerant, growth is slower and chlorosis can occur in highly alkaline soils. Good light and air circulation are important for plant health, inhibiting mildew.

Photinia serratifolia (Chinese photinia). Native to China and Taiwan. A most attractive large shrub or tree from 15 ft. (4.5 m) to well over 40 ft. (12 m), with oval leaves 5–6 in. (13–15 cm) long, 3–4 in. (8–10 cm) wide, with a delicate saw-toothed and crisped edge. The leaves here also emerge a bronzy color, though less so than *P.* ×*fraseri*, and more quickly attain a deep green, somewhat more matte finish. This large-textured plant, prominent in coastal western North America in the 1950s and 1960s, is now a dominant broadleaved evergreen in many neighborhoods of that era, now forming trees with superb caliper and tall, rounded crowns that can be seen from some distance. Prone to mildew with lack of air circulation or dense shade, but this problem is easily avoided.

The tiny white flowers, often a bit later than *Photinia* ×*fraseri*, appear in early to mid spring in 4 in. (10 cm) or so corymbs; they have

Photinia serratifolia, foliage.
Photo by Michael A. Dirr

Photinia serratifolia. Photo by Michael A. Dirr

a somewhat musty fragrance and are followed by typically rosaceous small red fruit.

Photinia serratifolia has not been commonly planted for some time and is now something of a rarity in newer neighborhoods. It should be considered again as a useful small garden tree. Quite frost tolerant, to about 0°F (–18°C), and able to withstand summer or winter drought even in quite dry, semi-desert locations, though not in overly alkaline soils.

Photinia serratifolia, flowers.
Photo by Michael A. Dirr

| *Pittosporum* | mock orange | Pittosporaceae |

Over 200 species of shrubs and trees from warm, moist areas in Southeast Asia, South Africa, Australia, and New Zealand. Mock orange, the generic name, is also used for *Pittosporum tobira*, commonly used in warm areas for hedging and specimens plants, as well as for the aromatic genera *Philadelphus* and *Choisya*, leading to some confusion in the nursery trade.

The genus is diverse and with a wide range of garden possibilities. For all species, the leaves are simple, and, for many, the flowers are highly scented. Indeed, many of the Asian species have a fragrance reminiscent of citrus flowers, some even leaning toward jasmine (*Jasminum*) or gardenia—though this may be my imagination. In addition, those from Asia often attain picturesque shapes adorned with aromatic, glossy leaves of vibrant green. Along with the somewhat closely related South African species, the Asian species have flowers

Photinia serratifolia, fruit.
Photo by Michael A. Dirr

that are generally creamy yellow or nearly white, while the New Zealand and Australian species produce dark yellow to, often, maroon or nearly black flowers.

Most species enjoy warm, steamy conditions, at least in summer, with the exception of the cool maritime New Zealanders that can collapse with too much heat. All respond well to bright light, though at least half shade is not a problem as some spend their youth as understory plants. As well, all prefer at least occasional summer watering in dry-summer climates, though *Pittosporum tobira* and many other Asian species become quite drought hardy once established. All are capable of growing in lean soils but, as a rule, resent particularly heavy or water-retentive sites.

Propagation varies greatly not only among groups but among individual species. The Asian species are the easiest; all but the newest material roots easily with warmth and mist, though the greatest success is with newly ripened wood in late summer into fall. Seeds, in my experience, have required little stratification. The cool maritime species have been trickier for us. They seem best stuck in late autumn to winter on ripened, recent past season's growth with a little bottom heat but cool air. Some species (*Pittosporum dallii*, for one) have been difficult under any conditions. Seeds from the New Zealanders also seem to appreciate a longer (thirty days or so) cool stratification.

Mixed pittosporums—
choose cultivar carefully!

Outside the rarified atmosphere of specialized public gardens, few Asian species are to be seen other than various forms of *Pittosporum tobira*, most not becoming tree-like. In warm southern hemisphere gardens, the New Zealand species *P. eugenioides* is seemingly ubiquitous, even being listed as a noxious weed in Tasmania. In our garden, *P. tenuifolium*, a New Zealander with infinite variation in leaf size and colors, captured my attention when its deep maroon flowers produced a fragrance like carnations (*Dianthus*). Although relatively few species are able to withstand frosts of any consequence and attain tree size, many plants normally grown as shrubs are easily lifted into standard forms fitting well into small gardens. The following are some that are most easily obtainable or provide the greatest garden potential.

Pittosporum bicolor. Southeastern Australia, Tasmania. Often cultivated as a shrub—though rarely cultivated at all, especially in the northern hemisphere—*P. bicolor* can attain sizes up to 30 ft. (9 m), in its first several years maintaining a narrow columnar shape that fans out with age. The flowers are small, as in most of the genus, a browny yellow, aging to maroon, and occur in mid spring. The leaves are narrow, up to 2½ in. (6 cm) long and under ⅓ in. (1 cm) wide, with slightly recurved margins. The surfaces are leathery and dark green, and the undersides produce a wonderfully contrasting indumentum that ranges from creamy silver to a golden brown, depending on clone and, to some degree, the age of the leaf. On larger specimens, where it's possible to look up into the leaves, the contrast between the dark surfaces and light undersides adds to the ornamental value.

I first encountered this plant at the Chittenden Locks in Seattle, Washington, where, in the distance, planted on the south side of the building among other treasures, it appeared to be a narrow Italian cypress (*Cupressus sempervirens* f. *stricta*) but with a much coarser texture that invited a closer look. Thus discovered, *Pittosporum bicolor* provided a "where have you been all my life?" moment and has been part of our nursery's repertoire ever since. Specimens in our garden have grown quickly the first three or four years to 8–10 ft. (2.5–3 m), then slowed dramatically, creating a wonderful textural contrast in the southern hemisphere section of our garden, with its many low-spreading *Olearia*, *Hebe*, and *Grevillea* species.

This is a perfect plant for cool, coastal climates and even areas that receive some summer heat without excessive humidity. Its greatest downfall might be cold tolerance: temperatures below 13 to 15°F (–10.5 to –9.5°C) can cause leaf damage, and twig dieback occurs with lower temperatures. The Seattle specimen, after experiencing 12°F (–11°C), had a "hammered" look for a year or two, and its recovery, observed on subsequent visits, was slow. When *Pittosporum bicolor* is cultivated in areas where it is marginally frost tolerant, the typical wind protection and even some overhead protection of larger plants would be beneficial. The species is tolerant of light shade though the texture is less dense in lower light. In our garden it has needed fairly consistent moisture, as would be indicated by its cool, wet wild habitat. If the upright narrow form is to be maintained, leaning or straggling branches should be trimmed away.

Propagation has been most successful with late autumn to winter cuttings.

Pittosporum dallii. New Zealand. Growing among some of the archetypal scrub and forest associates, *P. dallii* might be mistaken at first for a juvenile pseudopanax. This small tree, 15–30 ft. (4.5–9 m) in height with a narrow rounded crown, produces leaves of deep green, tinted purple, and young twigs often infused with purple and red. The leaves are shiny with small serrations, especially in the plant's youth, and waxy, almost appearing succulent against silvery bark. Clustered at the ends of the branches, they create a tropical effect. The late spring and summer flowers are small, white, and somewhat honey-scented but are not always abundant.

Growth is slow, but given age and proper pruning, this plant might just be one of those beautiful miniature trees possible for the cool temperate garden. Uncommon in cultivation anywhere except in public gardens in its native New Zealand and the British Isles, it is rarely grown commercially but should be sought. It has withstood temperatures approaching 0°F (−18°C) with only light damage. Not a lover of heat, it might be best out of direct sun in warmer climates.

Possibly the greatest impediment to wider cultivation of *Pittosporum dallii* is its difficulty in rooting. Cuttings often fail to produce calluses, or if calluses are produced these often fail to form roots. And, although the propagules might remain alive for many years, lack of roots certainly causes difficulty in maintaining an upright specimen in the garden. Many of the plants in cultivation in the United Kingdom are quite elderly, and lack of juvenility might be one of the problems associated with the difficulties in rooting. England's Wakehurst Place has at least one specimen worthy of worship. Attempts should be made to propagate and distribute seed and vigorous clones.

Pittosporum dallii. Photo © Global Book Publishing Photo Library

Pittosporum eugenioides (tarata). Another New Zealander, *P. eugenioides* is much more widely planted, not only in cool, maritime climates, but in warmer ones as well. Though not a lover of anything approaching desert, provided adequate irrigation it is able to succeed in the U.S. Southeast and even the Los Angeles area, where

Pittosporum eugenioides. Photo © Global
Book Publishing Photo Library

Pittosporum eugenioides 'Variegatum'

hot and very dry winds provide no barriers. Though often seen as tall hedges—certainly in its native New Zealand and in Australia, as well as warm areas of western Europe and along the West Coast of North America—left untrimmed, *P. eugenioides* will approach 30 ft. (9 m) eventually and can reach 15 ft. (4.5 m) in less than twelve years. Narrow and pyramidal in youth it becomes round-topped with age. The leaves, 2–4 in. (5–10 cm) long and about 1 in. (2.5 cm) wide, can be somewhat undulate. They are shiny and bright spring-green, especially in the new growth, but can become mottled with purple in the winter, a trait some find unattractive. They also have a citrusy scent when crushed or, perhaps, accidentally bruised by a wandering lawn mower. The flowers are small, greenish to dull yellow, in honey-scented clusters.

Tolerant of sun or shade, but in gardens where temperatures below 15°F (–9.5°C) might be expected, especially with wind, *Pittosporum eugenioides* might be treated more as a shrub—or its smaller cultivars, such as *P. eugenioides* 'Platinum' or the slightly more hardy *P. eugenioides* var. *minor*, might be used instead, and in a protected spot.

Specimens in the New Zealand section of the University of Washington Arboretum in Seattle have had only individual damage at temperatures of 12 to 15°F (–11 to –9.5°C), and those made a quick recovery. *Pittosporum eugenioides* 'Variegatum'—a cultivar that does reach tree size, albeit somewhat more slowly—has proven to be a little more cold resistant and has thrived in such places as South Carolina at that low temperature and with high summer heat and humidity.

Pittosporum heterophyllum. Western China. In the early 1990s, J. C. Raulston introduced me to this newly obtained plant, received as a gangly, sparsely branched creature—something like a poor man's *P. tobira*. After spending years in the garden, reacting badly to attempts to keep it shrub-like (too often, after a shearing, it looked like it had had a bad haircut), it was planted where it could reach its greatest size, quickly growing to 8 ft. (2.5 m) and, after six years, to a little over 10 ft. (3 m). With pruning, only to lift the base and accentuate the lower branches, it has become a favorite of passersby. The sharp-tipped leaves, about 2 in. (5 cm) long and ⅓–½ in. (1–1.5 cm) wide, are a dark green and slightly lighter on the underside. On established plants, the flowers are quite conspicuous, light creamy yellow aging to almost egg-yolk, and provide an unusually profuse showing that is intensely fragrant.

The young growth is vigorous and upright, and plants can be easily trained to from one to a few main stems, their grayish color nicely displayed when the lower branches are removed. *Pittosporum heterophyllum* is easily manipulated, making it a good subject for espalier or simply planting against a wall in a narrow space. It is drought tolerant

Pittosporum heterophyllum, flowers. Photo by Michael A. Dirr

Pittosporum heterophyllum. Photo by Michael A. Dirr

(though slower growing under dry conditions) and is at home in both sun and light shade. This species might be among the very hardiest to frost and even freezing winds. It has withstood −2°F (−19°C) with little damage in the U.S. Southeast. *Pittosporum heterophyllum* 'Variegatum' has been introduced into the United States from Japan and has proven vigorous, though it is still not known if it is easily trimmed into a small tree. Several very compact selections are being tested.

Pittosporum illicioides. Southern China. Once quite rare in horticulture, numerous collections have brought this large shrub to small tree into public gardens and, increasingly, into horticulture. Left to its own devices, this denizen of broadleaved evergreen shrub and woodlands would become a multi-trunked mass of shiny green leaves. With a little manipulation, it can easily be maintained as a single stem with its graceful, horizontal side branches dressed in whorls of leaves that are 3 in. (8 cm) by ½ in. (1.5 cm), very pointed and highly reflective. Where many mock oranges hide their flowers with the new growth, *P. illicioides* often flaunts them, dropping them below the emerging new shoots, further enhancing the airy effect. The highly fragrant flowers, occurring in mid spring and occasionally throughout the season, are pale yellow, aging to a buttery color.

A lover of cool, moist situations though willing to accept some drought once established, *Pittosporum illicioides* is happy in full sun but can become dense especially if tip-pruned occasionally, and is most graceful with at least afternoon dappled shade. Although 6 ft. (2 m) in height can be achieved in four years or so, an eventual 10 ft. (3 m) or a bit more might be expected from a standard specimen. Of the numerous clones planted in our garden, all have withstood temperatures in the upper teens (16 to 18°F, −9 to −8°C) without flinching. At least one clone from the JC Raulston Arboretum has had no noticeable damage at −2°F (−19°C)—this under the protection of some taller pines.

Pittosporum illicioides. Photo by Michael A. Dirr

Pittosporum napaulense. A Himalayan species found in Bhutan and Nepal to India, inhabiting the monsoon forests so rich in broadleaved evergreens. Although many of its habitats are quite subtropical, it has been found where relatively hard frosts occur. Though sometimes seen as a large shrub, *P. napaulense* is often used in horticulture as a standard of 20 ft. (6 m) or so, occasionally reaching as high as 30–35 ft. (9–10.5 m), with a broad umbrella-shaped crown. The very shiny leaves, sharp-tipped and somewhat ruffled, can be as long as 5 in. (13 cm) or more and about 1½ in. (4 cm) wide. A specimen planted in a courtyard or as a small-scale street tree can be easily lifted into standard form, so that the rich, spring/summer yellow flower clusters can

Pittosporum undulatum. Photo ©
Global Book Publishing Photo Library

be seen from beneath. However it is sited, the fragrance of the flowers—to me reminiscent of something between Arabian jasmine (*Jasminum sambac*) and egg custard (*Ova custardia . . .*)—can be enjoyed for quite some distance.

Though, like many *Pittosporum* species, somewhat subject to scale insects, it is otherwise sturdy and even able to withstand long periods of summer drought once established. If all this sounds too good to be true, an Achilles' heel should be expected and that is its tenderness to hard frost. Though temperatures, at least briefly, to 18 to 20°F (–8 to –7°C) have caused little visible damage, a prolonged spell at those temperatures or below would cause serious injury or death. However, additional collections are being brought into cultivation with hope that plants from higher-elevation provenances will have greater cold hardiness.

Similar in form is *Pittosporum undulatum* (Victorian box) from eastern Australia. An umbel-shaped tree from 20 ft. (6 m) to over 45 ft. (14 m), it has leaves 3–5 in. (8–13 cm) in length, very sharp-tipped and glossy green. They are somewhat paler beneath and are made even more attractive by their wavy margins. The flowers, ⅓–¾ in. (1–2 cm), are in creamy white clusters through spring and summer, and sporadically at any time of year in the mildest climates. Although just as fragrant as *P. napaulense*, they carry a more pungent scent, as if a bit of *Daphne odora* had been tossed into the mix. *Pittosporum undulatum* 'Variegatum', less common in horticulture, is likely to be slower growing but is worth seeking out. An additional trait shared with *P. napaulense* is tenderness. Though often used in milder areas of Australia and a common sight as a small street tree in southern California, their new growth can be damaged in the low 20s Fahrenheit (–6°C), and twig damage can occur with prolonged periods—more than ten minutes—of temperatures below 18 to 20°F (–8 to –7°C), though inland specimens in the San Francisco Bay area recovered admirably from a December dip to 11 to 14°F (–12 to –10°C). Where temperatures are likely to drop to those levels only occasionally, both *P. napaulense* and *P. undulatum* are worthy of planting in protected courtyards or even as espaliers.

Pittosporum tenuifolium (tawhiwhi, kohuhu). New Zealand. Second only to *P. tobira* in its universal appeal, *P. tenuifolium* has gained great popularity in many cool coastal areas of the world, inhabiting both islands in New Zealand from coast to forest and highly adapted to a range of soils, providing the climate is not intensely summer-hot and soils are not overly fertile. Plants range from diminutive shrubs under 3 ft. (1 m) to handsome, small trees nearly 30 ft. (9 m) tall, though most garden specimens reach 15 ft. (4.5 m) only with age. As the name would imply, the always graceful leaves are delicately attached to narrow stems and, in all except the most compact forms, appear to float amid the branches, an effect that's enhanced when the leaf petioles and young stems are dark enough to completely disappear. Begin with floating leaves, add slender stems and silver bark, and finish with flowers that are single or in clusters of small bells, usually under ⅓ in. (1 cm) and maroon to nearly black—a perfect plant for the Goth garden. The flowers can appear in mid spring or in summer and carry a sweet, spicy cinnamon fragrance that, again, recalls carnations (*Dianthus*).

Dozens of cultivars have been selected over the years, both in the garden and in the wild, and they have been used as garden mainstays in their native New Zealand, the British Isles, and the immediate Pacific Coast of the United States. They are also used in warmer climes of Asia and summer-rainfall areas of the United States, where summer temperatures, again, are not too high. Unfortunately, like *Pittosporum eugenioides*, they are feared as a possible escapee into the wild in southeastern Australia, so wary horticultural eyes are cast upon them. The more upright forms discussed here most often remain narrow in youth, fitting well into small gardens and are easily lifted to make superb small trees. Used as foreground specimens, they are airy enough to see through, especially if planted in dappled shade, and add depth to the space. Many are also good hedge subjects; they take shearing well and with it can become quite dense. All prefer good drainage and, especially in warmer climates, prefer soil on the lean side. Like so many other cool maritime, southern hemisphere plants, too much fertilizer can not only cause rank growth but also increases the possibility of fungal attach and collapse. The following forms are some of the most likely candidates for small garden trees.

Pittosporum tenuifolium 'Purpureum' is a form I first encountered at Western Hills Nursery in northern California. Planted about 1970, at approximately thirty years of age it measured 12–14 ft. (3.5–4 m) in height with nearly 5 ft. (1.5 m) in width. The leaves are perhaps the most striking feature. Measuring a typical 1½–2 in. (4–5 cm) by about ½ in. (1.5 cm) and somewhat ruffled, they emerge as bright yellow-green new growth and remains so for a few weeks, contrasting vividly with the saturated purple-maroon of the older foliage until, by early summer, all foliage has completed the transition. (In the hottest summers, the foliage can lean toward olive in color and remains so until the chill of autumn turns them purple.) The specimen in our garden achieved about 8 ft. (2.5 m) in six years from a cutting. Planted initially in sun, it now resides in the dappled shade of a *Hoheria populnea*. It has been lifted to about 5 ft. (1.5 m), but the branches are in layers on the lower part of the specimen, allowing surrounding plant-

Pittosporum tenuifolium

Pittosporum tenuifolium, flowers.
Photo by Michael A. Dirr

Pittosporum tenuifolium 'Purpureum'.
Photo by Michael A. Dirr

Pittosporum tenuifolium 'Tom Thumb'. Photo by Michael A. Dirr

Pittosporum tenuifolium 'Silver
Sheen'. Photo by Michael A. Dirr

Pittosporum 'Garnettii'

ings to spill through seductively. Nearby, *P. t.* 'Tom Thumb', another deep purple–leaved form to only 3 ft. (1 m), echoes the intensely dark maroon color, and both are set off beautifully by the coppery orange of *Carex testacea*.

Pittosporum tenuifolium 'Purpureum', *P. t.* 'Elizabeth' (an upright though, in our experience, somewhat smaller form with variegated leaves in cream and pink), and *P. t.* 'Irene Patterson', a shrub usually under 6 ft. (2 m) with splashed white variegations, are among the most frost hardy cultivars. Each of these has been reported to survive temperatures of slightly below 0°F (–18°C)—out of wind—with minimal damage.

Though presented to me originally as a diminutive form, a specimen of *Pittosporum tenuifolium* 'Silver Sheen', planted too near a main path in our garden, has grown to 12 ft. (3.5 m) in five years in dappled shade with morning sun and ample garden water. The stems are particularly dark, and the leaves, especially on juvenile growth, appear nearly round and a silvered apple-green. Although we are usually leery of garden lighting, this specimen is one we have chosen to highlight. When grown in sun, the adult leaves tend to become somewhat more ovally shaped and tend toward more green than silver but remain attractive. Slightly less frost hardy than the aforementioned cultivars, temperatures of 16 to 18°F (–9 to –8°C) have caused twig dieback and some bark splitting in vigorously growing specimens. An offspring seedling in our garden retains the black twigs and leaf petioles but has ruffled apple-green leaves, also with a hint of silver, and, after several years of observation, has earned the name *P. t.* 'Silver Ruffles'. At eight years, it was 10 ft. (3 m) in height and 4 ft. (1.2 m) in width.

Pittosporum ralphii, also from New Zealand, is similar to *P. tenuifolium* but with indumentum on the new growth and, to some degree, on the undersides of leaves, which are larger and more rounded. The plant itself can be more spreading, to 10–20 ft. (3–6 m) tall eventually. It has been frost hardy to 12 to 14°F (–11 to –10°C) for short durations with very little damage. Hybrids between *P. tenuifolium* and *P. ralphii* are offered in the nursery trade. One of the most widely available of these, *P.* 'Garnettii', has an upward growth rate with dark twigs and leaf petioles and highly alluring rounded leaves, pink and green infused with silver and white; numerous 10–15 ft. (3–4.5 m) specimens can be seen in old gardens.

Pittosporum tobira (mock orange). Originally from the wilds of Southeast Asia, especially Japan and China, this species has long been in commerce in almost every warm climate of the world where even the most passive horticulture happens. One of the most carefree garden subjects for full sun to dappled shade, it has very dark green,

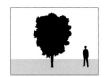

spatulate leaves, 3–4 in. (8–10 cm) long and roughly 1 in. (2.5 cm) wide, clustered at the ends of each branch. The flowers are creamy white to nearly butter-yellow and, indeed, carry the scent of orange blossoms. Held in terminal clusters, they appear in mid to late spring, often occurring throughout the year in favored weather. Though well-developed plants in the wild and certainly old plants in cultivation have been seen to 25 ft. (7.5 m) or even more in height, most forms have been selected for compactness, some remaining under 3 ft. (1 m) high and wide. When choosing *P. tobira* as a small tree, plants should be obtained that are in vigorous growth and preferably not from a nursery where they have been frequently shorn to maintain compactness in a pot, a technique that can lead to tangled stems and difficulty in obtaining an attractive trunk.

One form planted not only in our garden but also included in many of our garden designs was brought to the University of Washington in

Pittosporum tobira, foliage.
Photo by Michael A. Dirr

Pittosporum tobira, fruit.
Photo by Michael A. Dirr

Pittosporum tobira 'Variegatum'

Pittosporum tobira. Photo by Michael A. Dirr

the early 1980s by Arthur Kruckeberg. We began growing this plant because it had survived a near 0°F (−18°C) winter in Seattle; once planted in the relative summer warmth of our Portland, Oregon, garden, 10 ft. (3 m) was achieved in about five years from cuttings. Our plants are now slightly under 15 ft. (4.5 m), with upright stems and gracefully horizontal branches. Unfortunately, the name *Pittosporum tobira* 'University of Washington Hardy' has stuck to this clone, as is so often the case when placeholding names get out. (At least it didn't get a name like *P. tobira* "Repotted 3rd June 72.")

Pittosporum tobira 'Variegatum', also long in horticulture, is only a little slower growing and more compact, though vigorous plants can easily reach 10 ft. (3 m) with ample summer water and fertile soil. We have found with this plant, as well as many others that must be pushed a little to become small trees, that growing them in the early years in a staked upright form under greenhouse conditions can set their course more easily than beginning life as a small plant in the open garden where, having the propensity to be shrubby, they might very well be more interested in covering ground than in claiming airspace.

Polylepis	quiñal, quiñua	Rosaceae

A fascinating genus of fifteen species that collectively create the highest forest associations in the world. Some occur at the upper edges of forests, especially on the east flanks of the Andes, where Atlantic moisture backs up against them; others, on the dry western slopes or in any niches where moisture accumulates. Some stands occur to over 14,000 ft. (4300 m) in the páramo (grassland) from Colombia and Venezuela south to northwestern Argentina. The heights and sizes vary from shrubby at their very frontier, in the highest tundra-like puna country, to over 30 ft. (9 m) downslope and in protected thermal pockets.

The lush appearance of the foliage, at least from a distance, is that of lady's mantle (*Alchemilla*) on a stick, but they are actually more closely related to the genus *Sanguisorba*. Foliage can be three-parted or multi-leafleted with whole leaves ranging from about ¾ in. (2 cm) up to well over 4 in. (10 cm). Some species, such as *Polylepis incana*, have leaves with a silky silver covering, a wonderful adaptation to the high-elevation sun and nightly frost; other species have tiny dark green leaves, another way of dealing with too much sun, by minimizing one's surface area. Plants are slow-growing in habitat but much faster in cultivation and, apparently, quite adaptable to regions warmer than their high elevations, where they are often the only woody species.

Polylepis species. Photo © Global Book Publishing Photo Library

The flowers are small and greenish to whitish with minute petals. The major ornamental feature is the bark, usually deep red, flaking and exfoliating in strips, and looking very much like a paperbark maple (*Acer griseum*).

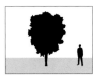

Polylepis australis. Western Argentina and a bit north and west, just into Chile in a few isolated places. This represents the southernmost species, growing as far south as about 23° to 28° S but still above 10,000 ft. (3000 m). *Polylepis australis* is one of only two species I have been fortunate enough to see and collect seed from in the wild; in stands above the ski resort of Tafí del Valle in Argentina's Tucumán Province, above 11,500 ft. (3500 m), it was growing with alpine meadow plants and a few other genera usually thought of as warmer-climate creatures (*Berberis*, *Puya*, *Schinus*), all at their elevational limits.

This species possesses the wonderful, shiny red bark just described along with 3–5 in. (8–13 cm) spring-green leaves of five to nine leaflets, each 1 in. (2.5 cm) in length, narrow and somewhat serrate and arranged in opposites along the petiole ending in a terminal leaf. The largest of these attains roughly 25 ft. (7.5 m) in height in an area often crushed with heavy snows and desiccating winter winds. In summer, warm wet air is pushed in from the Atlantic Ocean to the east, giving them a relatively long frost-free season. Although these are krumholtz (a wonderful German word meaning "twisted wood") trees—that is, at the upper end of their endurance level—it is doubtless true that these are alpine frontier plants solely because of the lack of more temperate species in the region. Several north temperate species growing in Tafí del Valle are happily romping up the mountainsides to well above the current upper limit of *Polylepis australis* and are a potential threat in the damp nooks and crannies they now share.

I have no information on the suitability of *Polylepis australis* for particularly hot, humid summer climates, but in the United Kingdom and western North America, plants have adapted quite well to cultivation along the coast. In the garden at Cistus Nursery on Sauvie Island, Oregon, three-year-old plants from seed were 8 ft. (2.5 m) high and wide, growing vigorously and producing their first flowers. It should be no surprise that a January dip to 21°F (−6.5°C) accompanied by wind caused no leaf drop.

Cuttings have been difficult; lush spring growth melts quickly on the cutting bench, and hardened autumn and winter growth roots at about a twenty percent rate. Techniques still must be worked out. Once a flowering-sized plant is achieved, however, the seeds germinate readily with or without cold stratification, though a forty-five-day rest in a 38°F (3°C) refrigerator increased germination by at least thirty percent.

Prunus   Rosaceae

A genus of over 400 species—plums, cherries, peaches, almonds—of deciduous and evergreen trees and shrubs with flowers most often white to red or pink in short clusters or racemes, the typical fruit being one-seeded and therefore, technically, a drupe. Of those that can be classified as broadleaved evergreen trees, there's a mix from quite common to underused. These can be propagated from just ripened current season's growth through autumn and winter with bottom heat and mist. Seeds vary, but most are not difficult if provided some winter stratification and sown in spring.

Prunus caroliniana (Carolina cherry laurel). This most useful evergreen tree, to 25–30 ft. (7.5–9 m), comes from coastal southeastern North America, where it grows at the edges of water, forest margins, and even in sand, either in sun or as part of the understory. The leaves, 3 in. (8 cm) long, are narrowly oblong and shiny spring-green above,

Prunus caroliniana, foliage.
Photo by Michael A. Dirr

Prunus caroliniana. Photo by Michael A. Dirr

Prunus caroliniana, flowers. Photo by Michael A. Dirr

Prunus caroliniana, fruit. Photo by Michael A. Dirr

gaining a more leathery appearance over time. Flowers are quite small, in a dense raceme, but with fruit up to ½ in. (1.5 cm), usually in clusters of black and shiny ovals that are quite attractive amid the leaves.

Deep-rooted with striking gray bark and a compact upright form, *Prunus caroliniana* has been in common use in the U.S. Southeast for many years and is not uncommon in West Coast gardens of North America where some summer irrigation can be provided. Quite tolerant of heat; in cool climates or coastal areas, some yellowing can occur from lack thereof. Also easily grown in containers for long periods of time. Several compact forms have been introduced, but the nonselected somewhat larger growing varieties make better tree forms.

Most are tolerant at temperatures to 10°F (–12°C), with brief dips to –5 to 0°F (–20 to –18°C) causing only minor foliage loss. Extended periods below 0°F (–18°C) can weaken plants, making them less attractive or sending them into decline.

Prunus ilicifolia (holly leaf cherry). From the Mediterranean chaparral of western North America, mostly California, *P. ilicifolia* might be seen as a West Coast version of Carolina cherry laurel. Somewhat tighter in form, with more divaricating branches and rounded leaves, often spiny-edged but nonetheless quite shiny and appearing bright green, especially considering their dry habitats. A most useful large shrub or small tree for summer-dry gardens, the stature being smaller than *P. caroliniana* with a rounded 15 ft. (4.5 m) to be expected.

The flowers are in small white racemes in early spring, producing (by late summer to early autumn) red to yellow-orange fruit up to ¾ in. (2 cm). Although the "pit" is rather large for the size of the fruit, the flesh is tasty, indeed that of a cherry.

Happiest in winter-rainfall climates in mineral soil. Specimens observed throughout western North America have been frost hardy easily to 10 to 15°F (–12 to –9.5°C), but some are damaged, occasionally permanently, at 0°F (–18°C). Plants of northern provenance could certainly increase frost hardiness.

Prunus ilicifolia

The close relative *Prunus lyonii*, known as the Catalina cherry and endemic to that island, has a taller, more open habit, larger, narrower leaves mostly free of spines, and nearly black fruit. Plants of 20–25 ft. (6–7.5 m) can be found in old West Coast gardens. A little less frost tolerant, it should be grown in gardens that remain above 15°F (–9.5°C) or dip below only briefly. On the plus side, it is more tolerant of summer garden water.

Prunus laurocerasus (cherry laurel). Often referred to as English laurel in North America, though actually native to southeastern Europe and Asia Minor. Evergreen large shrub to tree, to 25 ft. (7.5 m) or more, with leaves to 6–8 in. (15–20 cm) in length and roughly 4 in. (10 cm) in width, oblong but sharp-tipped and a very glossy dark green. The bark is a fine-textured dark green as well. Flowers in narrow racemes, 1 in. (2.5 cm) by 3–4 in. (8–10 cm), are followed by rounded black fruit.

Equally at home in dappled shade to full fun, the species is summer drought tolerant and a very good candidate for dry shade when used as an understory planting, though in extremely arid summers some water should be provided, especially in bright light. Cold tolerance of roughly 5°F (–15°C) can be expected in large forms.

Vastly overused for decades in warmer regions of North America

Prunus laurocerasus, foliage.
Photo by Michael A. Dirr

Prunus laurocerasus, flowers.
Photo by Michael A. Dirr

Prunus laurocerasus 'Camelliifolia'.
Photo by Michael A. Dirr

Prunus laurocerasus 'Marble
Queen'. Photo by Michael A. Dirr

Prunus laurocerasus. Photo by Michael A. Dirr

and often in spaces that cannot accommodate their eventual size, these "monsters" have unfortunately required many willing and unwilling gardeners to devote much of their free time to keeping them under control. Many would question inclusion of this species in a book promoting new plants; an equal number would question its exclusion.

Plants grown as open, more wide-ranging trees rather than as the well-known and useful large-scale hedge, are actually quite graceful, though they can create a dark presence, the large leaves, green on both sides, shutting out light quite easily. Several nonaggressive forms exist, including *Prunus laurocerasus* 'Camelliifolia' with rounded leaves and a very pretty texture, growing to about two-thirds the size of its parent. Both *P. l.* 'Castlewellan' and *P. l.* 'Marble Queen' are much less vigorous, with leaves blotched white, making a light presence in the landscape. There are many others, but they are shrubby forms.

Prunus lusitanica (Portuguese laurel). A native of southwestern Europe, the Iberian Peninsula to the Azores, a tough-as-nails, large shrub or evergreen tree to 30 ft. (9 m), some reaching as high as 50–60 ft. (15–18 m), with silvery bark and densely held, narrow dark green leaves, roughly 1 in. (2.5 cm) by 3 in. (8 cm), sometimes with minute teeth. The late spring flowers in curving racemes of white are followed by a dark purplish black fruit.

Commonly used in gardens where temperatures do not fall below 0°F (–18°C) and a most useful small street tree or background plant,

Prunus lusitanica, flowers

Prunus lusitanica 'Variegata'

Prunus lusitanica, foliage.
Photo by John Grimshaw

Prunus lusitanica 'Variegata', foliage. Photo by Michael A. Dirr

though possibly a bit dark for use as a patio tree. Quite tolerant of summer drought and happy enough in some places, such as western Oregon and California, to cause concerns about invasiveness.

Prunus lusitanica 'Variegata' is a small form, usually remaining under 15 ft. (4.5 m) with a narrow growth habit and crinkled leaves streaked green and white, accentuated by red petioles.

Prunus salicifolia (Mexican bird cherry). Rounded tree to 25–30 ft. (7.5–9 m) from northeastern Mexico south to Peru, often cultivated for its sweet, flavorful fruit. Branches are spreading, with narrow, drooping leaves to 4–5 in. (10–13 cm), quite shiny, with fine teeth along the margins and, in spring, white flowers in loose, narrow racemes.

This deep-rooted species, tolerant of drought in summer or winter, has much to offer the garden. Useful as a patio or street tree (it tends not to lift nearby pavement), though its heavy fruit set in such situations can be a drawback, except perhaps to birds. *Prunus salicifolia* has been frost hardy to several degrees below 0°F (–18°C) with no stem loss but is often pushed into being deciduous with freezes below 15 to 18°F (–9.5 to –8°C).

Quercus	oak	Fagaceae

Over 600 species of both evergreen and deciduous trees and shrubs native throughout temperate to tropical areas, almost entirely in the northern hemisphere, with the great center of diversity in Mexico. My love for oaks began in childhood; although, rather than the forest oaks of the eastern United States, my oaks were the mounding, spreading, deep green individuals of the West's savanna. In both the deciduous and evergreen species, the leaves bake to a deep, dark green, part of the color trio I most often associate with the lowland valleys of California and Oregon in the summer time—the golden grass, blue sky, and the blackened green of the native oaks.

I thought I had a grip on what oaks were about until my first trip into the mountains of Mexico. The diversity of all plant species in that country's rugged mountains is unfathomable; so, too, are the literally dozens of species of oaks to be seen during a single trek into any given mountain range. All that the genus, as I knew it, could express is there, plus a whole new world, from tiny mounding shrubs to towering trees. It is especially thrilling to traverse an oak woodland or mixed forest of temperate-derived plants—indeed, most have proven quite cold hardy to the north—but, instead of the associates being a temperate flora, the woodlands are replete with palms, cycads, splendid orchids, bromeliads of all sorts hanging from the branches, and maybe even a cactus or two quite at home in a pocket of humus in a trunk.

I have experienced the best of oak diversity near the town of Zaragoza on a trip in the Mexican state of Tamaulipas. There, among the many taxa occurring in protected clefts of the mountains, one species in particular stood roughly 50 ft. (15 m) tall and bore rugose, violin-shaped leaves, 10 in. (25 cm) long, underlain with reflective, rich cream indumentum. In the understory grew *Gentiana mexicana*, ferns, and other lush vegetation. Only a dozen miles away, down steep, desert canyons to the west, another oak grew on precipitous gypsum cliffs, associated only with the tiniest of cacti and resurrection plants (*Selaginella*). This little creature stood little over 18 in. (45 cm) in height with leaves under ⅓ in. (1 cm) long. Both oaks had acorns; both have succeeded in the garden here; and both species remain unnamed. The large species has been quite slow; the tiny, desert oak, still bearing tiny leaves, has surpassed 8 ft. (2.5 m).

When most people in temperate climates think of oaks, they think of tall, deciduous trees. In actuality, many species, in fact the majority, are evergreen or nearly so. Though divided taxonomically into three rough groups—black, intermediate, and white—they might be more usefully considered by their eco-types. At the dry end of their

The tricolor look: *Quercus rugosa*, baking in Chihuahua, Mexico

Quercus chrysolepis, urban Portland specimen, planted in the 1920s

range they are often divaricating and thorn-tipped with small, rough, and, often, bluish leaves. Those from Mediterranean climes usually have dark green, glossy leaves with spiny margins, while those from wet, or at least monsoonal places, have, as one would expect, the largest leaves, usually entire with drip tips. With so many species from which to choose, the criteria for inclusion here are availability to the gardening world (or at least the potential of such), ease of cultivation, and ease of propagation—along with personal bias, of course.

In most of North America, if it looks like an oak, it probably is, since, of the related genera, *Lithocarpus* is represented by one, arguably two, species, and only in northern California and southern Oregon, and *Chrysolepis* (also related to the Asian *Castanopsis*) occurs only over the same region and slightly north. In Asia, especially in the south, the genera mix over more widespread areas and in North America, as one moves south and west, the line between oaks and their relatives becomes blurred at first glance, as the leaves diverge from typical oak shape to include all the aforementioned characteristics. So, to distinguish among oaks and oak relatives, it is the "acorns" which must be observed closely.

In oaks, the receptacle, or cup, is scaly and covers from less than one-third to over three-quarters of the acorn, but never the whole. In lithocarps the acorns, following flowers held in upright spikes, have a particularly hard receptacle that is sometimes more heavily scaled or covered by indumentum. *Chrysolepis* seeds are entirely covered by the receptacle and appear to be a knot of spines, showing a clear relationship with *Castanea* (chestnut). *Castanopsis* too has fruit entirely (or nearly so) enclosed in a prickly capsule or covering, exhibiting faint qualities of *Castanea* with maybe a little *Fagus* (beech) thrown in, as they tend to split down both sides.

Despite the overwhelming number of oaks and their relatives—each more beautiful than the last—now in cultivation, the inclination is to want to make more. But propagation is neither obvious nor easy. Because so many of the temperate oaks, and a number of the evergreens from dry or Mediterranean climates, are difficult enough from cuttings to make it impractical for any commercial reproduction, they have had to be done from seed, resulting in variability within crops. In addition, each year seed must be recollected, avoiding parents that could have hybridized with a species nearby; for those selections new to cultivation, this means going back into the wild, an often arduous task fraught with unforeseen adventures, not to mention expenses and paperwork. Though I can think of few tasks more exciting than observing and/or collecting seeds in the wild, collecting commercial quantities is a different activity and one that can exert undue pressure on wild populations of plants, especially those limited in number. Therefore, for those species requiring seed propagation, commercial development is a slow process. Practicality dictates a lapse of time between the first introduction and harvesting the first acorns from plants in confinement.

Still, acorns are a delightful and rewarding way of achieving more oaks than we (or any of our friends) could ever want, and the vigor of the seedling plants is unsurpassed. Once the seed collection problems are resolved, attention to the following few, simple requirements is important. First and most important: acorns have a short viability period. Though dry-climate species have some ability to hang around a bit, allowing them to play hide-and-to-seek with squirrels or wait for eventual rains, those from damp climates hit the ground ready to sprout, adding yet another sense of urgency when timing a collection. The seeds can be stored, often, for at least a few months in a chilled situation with damp sphagnum or any light, moisture-retentive material, but all species should be sown as soon as possible. Those from warmer climates and those from winter-rainfall zones send out radicles that hit the bottom of even a deep pot before much is seen on the surface. If sown in a group container, they can be separated when the root germination is evident, but experience has dictated waiting until the next active growing season in spring or summer and dividing while in active top growth. The bottom of the radicle of all oaks can then be clipped to avoid a spiraling root and promote lateral root formation and the plant placed in an individual container, as deep as possible. In damp-climate species, top growth is usually rapid and a good-sized tree (one that a nursery could present in a standard container) can be produced in a couple of years. A drawback with a number of the dryland and Mediterranean species is the amount of energy put into an extensive root system before top growth of any abundance is seen. As well, a number of dryland species spend many years protecting themselves from browsing animals with a juvenile phase of mounding, sharp-pointed branches that can last several seasons, until, finally, the plant decides it's safe enough to send out a proper leader. This can be hastened in a nursery situation by providing ample moisture and nutrients and trimming to a single leader as soon as practical.

Grafting is increasingly common in oaks, but, as I am not the world's biggest grafting fan, I would suggest avoiding it where possible. Even with same-species grafts, incompatibility often rears its ugly head sooner or later, resulting in excess suckering at the least or even death of the scion. Grafters far better than I will doubtless argue the point.

It is, of course, a great boon to be able to produce a desired clone from cuttings; the results are less variable. As it turns out, several damp-climate species of evergreen oaks are surprisingly easy. Ripened wood from the previous season's growth, cut at a steep angle, with a slightly higher than average level of hormone, has worked on a great number of species. (Too high a hormone level can produce a lot of callus and little rooting, those roots being not well attached.) With a damp, enclosed cutting bench, preferably with light mist or none at all, roots could form as early as a month or two, or as late as a year. Again, as with seed propagation, patience is a must.

That well-adapted species of oaks (and many other trees, for that matter) are so rarely planted in the Mediterranean and (more selfishly) along the U.S. West Coast is very unfortunate. It's true that these species require patience, but the rewards are magnificent and long lasting. Many urban dwellers who have come to expect instant effect from street trees would, undoubtedly, be more patient if they knew the benefits of well-adapted, even native, species as opposed to something unsuitable, planted at 10 ft. (3 m) tall with the best intentions and a realistic life expectancy of only a few years. Here in Portland, Oregon, well-meaning city foresters have planted thousands upon thousands of ill-adapted trees from summer climates much wetter than ours, often placing them in areas where irrigation is impractical. After ten or twenty years, many show signs of decline. A western Oregon native, *Quercus chrysolepis* (canyon live oak), planted in the 1920s at the Autzens' house in Portland's Alameda district, makes one dream about what effect the foresight of planting these and others like them would have had throughout the city. The tree, now 80 ft. (25 m) tall and superbly adapted, is a landmark in the neighborhood, reminiscent of the grand, live oaks of the American South. Educating—indeed, pressuring—those charged with planting one's local, civic canopy to use not only a diverse palette but one that includes regional natives and well-adapted (if a bit slower) species is important and increasingly common, as citizens become more aware of the great number of appropriate species now available.

Quercus acuta (Japanese evergreen oak). Southeast China to Korea and Japan. Among the hardier of the Asian evergreen oaks, this tree sometimes reaches 100 ft. (30 m) in height, but 30–50 ft. (9–15 m) can be expected from a thirty-year-old specimen. Even in youth it forms a graceful umbrella, occasionally wider than tall, with long, oval leaves having gentle serrations and the typical wet-summer area drip tip. The leaves, 3–4 in. (8–10 cm) in length and 1½–2 in. (4–5 cm) wide, are a deep, rich green and quite shiny. The underside, though not hav-

Quercus acuta. Photo by Michael A. Dirr

Quercus acuta, foliage. Photo by Michael A. Dirr

ing indumentum to speak of, contrasts in its very light green to pale yellow color.

The male flowers are attractive, pendulous, golden brown catkins; the female flowers are actually short spikes amid the leaves, producing small clusters of ¾ in. (2 cm) acorns, about one-third enclosed by the cup and noticeably downy, with faint rings.

This is a tree that's best with ample moisture year-round and warm humid summers. In Mediterranean climates, where summer humidity is low, deep and regular watering is preferred. Yellowing of the leaves can be a problem with either summer drought or with long, cool winters but can be easily avoided or corrected by ample care during summer months. One twenty-year-old specimen at Portland's Hoyt Arboretum, planted in an area of summer-dry oak species, was 5 ft. (1.5 m) tall and quite discolored, but, with the addition of regular water, the height doubled in the course of two seasons. To avoid the discomfort of an umbrella-shaped tree under 5 ft. (1.5 m) tall, ample summer water is a must; training to a single stem for the first several years further ensures minimal head-bumping later on. Specimens planted by Bob McCartney at Woodlanders Nursery in Aiken, South Carolina, have reached 25 ft. (7.5 m) and seem their clean, green best in that climate, on the low end of zone 8, with plentiful summer moisture.

Quercus acuta makes a fine garden and street tree with proper early training. Plants in cultivation in North America have endured winter temperatures of 0 to 5°F (–18 to –15°C) with little effect other than temporary leaf bronzing. Where these temperatures occur on a regular basis, planting in a mixed woodland, or at least with wind protection, would be helpful.

Autumn and winter cuttings have been successful with heat and mist (or an otherwise enclosed and damp situation), with medium amount of hormones. Roots will often strike in three to four weeks—pretty good going for an oak.

Quercus alnifolia (golden oak). From Cyprus, growing in dry craggy ravines where, like a true Cypriot, it is able to withstand harsh conditions and yet be gorgeous for the most part. This small oak has rounded, ever so slightly cup-shaped leaves, to 3 in. (8 cm) or so, dark and glossy above and outrageously golden and felty beneath. Though recorded to 30 ft. (9 m) or more with dense rounded crown, garden specimens remain under 20 ft. (6 m) in as many years. Though a lover of limestone rubble, it seems tolerant of all but the most ill-drained garden conditions, provided two-thirds sun or more and winter temperatures remaining above –4°F (–20°C). Little information exists on tolerance of humid summers, so until further notice we're assuming no tolerance. At the very least, with too much moisture, the undersides can become blotched with mildew—rather like the back of one's family pictures—during the summer monsoon season. In North America few specimens exist; one, at the University of Washington Arboretum in Seattle, has regained its stamina in recent years, and small plants in our Cistus garden have taken hold and are thriving. Cuttings have been successful if taken mid November through winter.

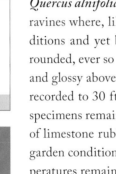

Quercus alnifolia

Quercus alnifolia, foliage

Quercus chrysolepis (canyon live oak, gold cup oak). Southwestern Oregon through the foothills of California south to Baja California, east to Arizona, New Mexico, Texas, and south to Mexico, growing in steep, rugged terrain, sometimes on vertical faces, and occasionally in deep soils, where it reaches its greatest size. One of the few oaks to stretch from the Mediterranean climate of the western United States to that of summer rainfall further east and south. Either way, a dry-country oak, tolerating long periods of drought whether in summer or winter. A medium to large vase-shaped tree when growing in deep soils and/or with woodland competition, reaching up to 80 ft. (25 m) or more. In harsh conditions (such as one would expect from a solid rock cliff), or where it integrates with such species as

Quercus chrysolepis, foliage

Quercus chrysolepis

Quercus chrysolepis, acorn

Q. vaccinifolia, often on serpentine soils in northern California and southern Oregon, *Q. chrysolepis* can be reduced to a shrub less than 6 ft. (2 m) in height. Rafters on Oregon's Rogue River can observe pure stands hanging off the cliffs, showing off their very deep green, lustrous leaves—only 1–2 in. (2.5–5 cm) wide and 3 in. (8 cm) long, rarely to 4 in. (10 cm)—and their eerily dark trunks and branches. In open areas, these dark features contrast sharply with the golden brown of the summer's grass.

With such a wide range one would expect variation, and, indeed, there is. Though uncommon in cultivation, numerous forms have been collected and planted in arboreta and private collections. One feature I have sought is the attribute that triggers one of its common names: the acorn receptacle is covered with a powdery, golden indumentum (as are, sometimes, the undersides of the leaves). Two favorite strains grow naturally in close geographic proximity. Plants in southern Oregon's Illinois Valley and on nearby Oregon Mountain tend to retain juvenile leaves with their spine-tipped lobes and relatively glaucous undersides, remaining under 30 ft. (9 m) in a rather tight, attractive umbrella shape. Others in the Dunsmuir Canyon area (about seventy miles southeast) are large, growing to 60 ft. (18 m) or more, with leaves approaching the maximum 4 in. (10 cm) length, nearly entire and with stunning golden undersides—simply amazing seen from underneath in contrast with the deep green foliage. Acorns collected from both stands have produced plants with consistent characteristics.

Again, *Quercus chrysolepis* is a species superbly adapted for urban planting and droughty landscapes, requiring no summer irrigation in areas receiving a yearly 18 in. (45 cm) or more of rain. Along with its great adaptation to drought, it is also one of the very cold hardiest evergreen oaks. Trees from seed collected at over 6000 ft. (1800 m) in southern Oregon's Siskiyou Mountains have survived (with slower growth) cultivation in the desert community of Christmas Valley, Oregon, withstanding winter temperatures near 0°F (−18°C) and greatly fluctuating weather. Forms with the right provenance can be expected to survive −20°F (−29°C) or even lower with some wind protection, as they have in the garden of Allan Taylor, in Boulder, Colorado.

Deep-rooted and sure-footed in street plantings as, again, would be expected from their rocky habitats, the only impediment to its being more widely planted is the need for patience. As with so many Mediterranean climate species, *Quercus chrysolepis* sulks after the great root disturbance of being transplanted. Young plants should be raised in containers or root sacks with careful transplanting into their designated homes. As well, again like so many dryland species, they are likely to go through a juvenile phase of densely branching shrubbiness, possibly a protection from both browsing and drought. As mentioned earlier, they can be pushed beyond this point by providing luxurious conditions in the nursery, by growing them fairly close together, and by pruning side branches to encourage leader growth. Plants at the North Willamette Experimental Station, grown and planted by fellow plant fanatic Neil Bell, began their upward growth after about the fourth year in the open ground. It is hoped that wise city planners will lean away from planting very large caliper trees with short life expectancies and, instead, interplant this and other species that require more early fussing but will likely be with us for hundreds of years.

Propagation is difficult from cuttings, though success was once had with late summer cuttings taken from the vigorous resprouting of a parent tree that had been burned in a fire. It is not, however, necessary to resort to, nor do we encourage, burning down the landscape to propagate *Quercus chrysolepis*: any juvenile sprouts from the trunk of a healthy tree would be as likely to root . . . about fifty percent. Acorns are a far superior method of propagation, and, if the parent tree is isolated or in a stand of similar forms, the worry of too much variability should not be great.

Quercus glauca (ring-cup oak, Japanese blue oak). Native to East and Southeast Asia to the Himalayas, northern India, Japan, and China. Though sometimes confused in cultivation with *Q. myrsinifolia*, the leaves tend to be more oblong and lighter in color. A medium tree, 30–50 ft. (9–15 m) in height and 25–35 ft. (7.5–10.5 m) in spread, it forms a wide, graceful umbrella with silvery bark and, often, multiple trunks. The leaves are 3–4 in. (8–10 cm) in length, occasionally to 6 in. (15 cm), and 2–3 in. (5–8 cm) wide, obovate to oblong and tapering to a sharp point, usually with prominent shallow toothing near the apex. New growth can be somewhat silky but is most often covered with a fine glaucescence, harmonizing pleasantly with the silvery bark. The lighter colors of bark and leaf together create brightness even in its own shade.

Becoming more common in cultivation, plants originating from more northern locations in China and Japan have been the most successful. Considered a bit more tender than the related *Quercus myrsinifolia*. However, when −9°F (−23°C) cold froze it to the ground at the JC Raulston Arboretum in North Carolina, the trees regrew and are now, a quarter-century on, fine specimens with 8 in. (20 cm) caliper trunks. They appreciate summer warmth and require at least occasional summer watering in droughty places for best color and growth. Also, as with so many other broadleaved evergreens from warm wet-

Quercus glauca. Photo by John Grimshaw

summer regions, slight yellowing can occur in areas lacking summer heat but can be mitigated with a little extra care at the height of summer.

A fine street tree or garden specimen, the scale of the leaves and the size of the tree make it unobtrusive in all but the smallest gardens. A great advantage is the relative ease from cuttings: fifty to eighty percent can be expected from autumn and winter with mist and heat. Acorns are easy as well.

Quercus guyavifolia. I first became acquainted with this lovely tree at the Quarryhill Botanical Garden in Glen Ellen, California. With its 2 in. (5 cm) rounded leaves—shiny above, velvety brown beneath, and ever so slightly cupped—*Q. guyavifolia* grows upwards of 20–25

ft. (6–7.5 m) with silvery bark and a nicely rounded, pyramidal form. It does experience some drought in habitat, but this plant has thus far been deep-rooted and very well behaved in garden situations, watered or not. Though not yet widely available, it is worth the pursuit.

Frost hardy to at least 14°F (–10°C) and likely even tougher. Once established, it grows approximately 3 ft. (1 m) annually for several years, slowing once heavy acorn set begins. It has been trouble-free in the garden, and the specimen at Quarryhill was quite imposing at under twenty years of age.

Another encouraging aspect is that even though acorns have been produced only inconsistently and likely hybridized with others nearby, this is another evergreen oak that roots relatively easily from fall- and winter-ripened, current season's growth.

Quercus guyavifolia

Quercus hypoleucoides (silverleaf oak). Central, southeastern Arizona, southwestern Mexico into northcentral Mexico, often mixed with other oaks, junipers (*Juniperus*), and *Arbutus* in seasonally dry but summer monsoon–fed high country. Even in young plants, the narrow leaves, 1 in. (2.5 cm) wide by 3–4 in. (8–10 cm) long, are entire with an occasional tooth and have shiny, somewhat leathery surfaces contrasted with silver undersides, bright as a freeway reflector. In addition, the new growth emerges pink and entirely covered with wool. Who wouldn't love that?

The two plants given me by plantsmen Boyd Kline and Frank Callahan, who had collected acorns on a botanizing trip into Mexico in the early 1980s, became my street trees; now many years and two houses later, they (or new versions thereof) are again my street trees. I was so taken with the species that in 1990 we made a special excursion to the Chiricahua Mountains in southeastern Arizona to see them in habitat. It was late December, clear and crisp with a thin layer of snow on the ground. Reflecting the snow, the silver undersides of the oak's leaves were as bright as if high-wattage spotlights were shining up into the branches. Though we have little snow in our own part of the world, our trees, now approaching 25 ft. (7.5 m), also reflect—only in this case, it is usually the nearby street light. With the slightest breeze the branches tilt, flashing silver and inspiring bouts of interpretive dance.

When not in dance mode, *Quercus hypoleucoides* occurs in groves or as single plants on the great north-south mountain ranges that were described by geologist Ivo Lucchitta as resembling, when seen from the air, "an army of giant caterpillars marching determinedly north," from Mexico toward Canada through the Great Basin West. Each of these sky islands, as they are often called, surrounded by desert country, harbors both relics and plants in common to areas east, west, north, and south. In far southeastern Arizona, species occur in

Quercus hypoleucoides, foliage

Quercus hypoleucoides

these ranges in their only habitats outside of Mexico, including not only several oaks, pines (*Pinus*), and *Arbutus*, but abundant bird and insect species as well. Though *Q. hypoleucoides* is slow in the wild and rarely over 20–30 ft. (6–9 m) tall, records exist of over 70 ft. (21 m). Strangely, it is successfully planted at low elevations in the American Southwest but does not seem to thrive in higher altitudes. It *has* thriven along the U.S. West Coast, though it is only now gaining popularity. Specimens planted by Carl English in Seattle's Chittenden Locks have reached 50 ft. (15 m) and are noticeably more open than those planted in drier places. Some snow damage has broken branches over the years.

In general, *Quercus hypoleucoides* has grown moderately fast both in the garden and as a street tree, tolerating both summer and winter drought and making a handsome, small tree of 15–20 ft. (4.5–6 m) within five years of planting from a five-gallon container at about 3 ft. (1 m). As a street tree, its deep and sturdy roots hold up well to urban assaults. Summer irrigation speeds its growth.

Cold hardiness can be expected to vary by the location of its collection. All the plants we have grown, save for one specimen, are from either southeastern Arizona or southwestern New Mexico collections and have proven hardy to −4°F (−20°C) or lower. Thriving specimens at the Denver Botanic Garden suggest that this might be one of the few broadleaved evergreens successful below zone 6! Because plants respond to summer rain, it might be best, as with other broadleaved evergreens, to withhold water in the autumn to induce dormancy and ready the plant for frost.

Propagation is generally from acorns, although the seeds produced by our trees seem to be particularly delicious to both blue jays and squirrels, making collection a race. They do germinate quickly. Cuttings have been hit or miss; of a dozen or more tries, only four batches have produced roots, and in those, only a few in each one. Most success has been with newly ripened suckered growth from the base, taken as heel cuttings in autumn.

Quercus ilex (holly oak, holm oak). Native to Mediterranean regions, dry sclerophyllic forests and savanna surrounding the Mediterranean Sea, and east to the Himalayas. Cultivated in western Europe for at least 500 years, the species is common as far north as the southern United Kingdom and Ireland in gardens and is, in some areas, naturalized. The first plants were brought to the U.S. West Coast in the

Quercus ilex, Brookings, Oregon

Quercus ilex in flower. Photo © Global Book Publishing Photo Library

Quercus ilex of great age, Cambridge, England

1850s, and *Q. ilex* is now one of the more common evergreen oaks in the landscape. The size varies from about 30 ft. (9 m), in areas of extreme drought or in particularly cool summer regions, to over 100 ft. (30 m) with great age in ideal conditions. The specimens in Sacramento, California's Capitol Park are a testament to those ideal conditions, with ample summer heat, well-drained soil, and summer irrigation. With ample water early on, the growth rate is fast in warm-summer climates; increases of 4 ft. (1.2 m) or more in a single season can be expected. A spreading tree in habitat, unimpeded the canopy can be nearly as wide as tall, though with careful pruning in the early years it can remain upright and a bit more vase-shaped. With such a long history of cultivation and such a wide natural range, many natural forms and selections exist. Named forms are more common in western Europe; elsewhere, including the western United States, plants tend to be more generic.

The leaves, as the name suggests, are prickly, at least in juvenile foliage, and are about 3 in. (8 cm) by 1–1½ in. (2.5–4 cm); vigorous juveniles can have leaves, briefly, over twice that size. Opinions vary widely as to the merits of this tree. Some find the dark, green leaves oppressive; they are produced in great abundance, and the overall density of the tree casts a rather solid shade. In many forms, however, the leaf undersides have a silver, reflective quality that lightens up their presence. As well, lifting and thinning the canopy can allow significantly more light to penetrate. Some leaf drop occurs either in autumn or early spring as the new growth emerges. It might therefore be best, in a garden situation, to surround a plant with enough shrubs and large-scale ground covers that the leaves can fall harmlessly among them, acting as mulch.

One of the toughest, most adaptable oaks, especially in dry-summer areas, and one of the hardiest of the evergreen oaks. Temperatures of 0 to –10°F (–18 to –23°C) have caused little damage on cultivated specimens. It would be expected that even hardier forms exist. Cold hardiness, as well as growth rate, is affected by summer temperatures. Where little summer heat is accumulated (illustrated sometimes by yellowing or lack of luster in the leaves and certainly by slow growth rate), the cold hardiness rating might be lifted another ten degrees Fahrenheit (approximately six degrees Celsius) or so. As with numerous other plants, ensuring summer vigor via nutrients and additional summer watering can mitigate cooler temperatures.

Acorns, about ½–1 in. (1.5–2.5 cm) by ⅓–½ in. (1–1.5 cm), are single or in small clusters, dropping in early autumn. They are apparently sweet, having long been used as a food source in their native range, and are the best way to propagate the plants which, as with so many of the oaks, is a hindrance to the widespread cultivation of individual clones. Cuttings are possible if taken in autumn following typical oak procedures, including incantations, but the rooting percentage is low. Despite my grafting reservations, this is a good candidate for grafting good clones, as they become available, onto seedling stock.

Quercus ×moreha (oracle oak). A naturally occurring hybrid of *Q. kelloggii* (California black oak) and *Q. wislizeni*. In some areas, even where *Q. wislizeni* no longer occurs, such as in southern Oregon, *Q. ×moreha* has stabilized, making an evergreen or semi-evergreen to 25–30 ft. (7.5–9 m) with large, lobed leaves. Specimens have been cited at high altitudes in the Siskiyou Mountains and should prove to be even more frost hardy than *Q. wislizeni*. Acorns are best for propagation.

Quercus myrsinifolia (Japanese live oak, bamboo oak). From southern China to Laos, to Korea and Japan, growing in high summer rainfall areas, occasionally in single stands, often in mixed evergreen forests. From 15 ft. (4.5 m) to, occasionally, over 100 ft. (30 m) in height, narrow in youth, becoming umbrella-shaped with age, especially in the open. The bark is smooth and silvery and the leaves seem to congregate in clusters at the ends of the branches, indeed appearing similar to some in the genus *Myrsine*. Hanging gracefully downward, the leaves are roughly 1¼–1½ in. (3–4 cm) by 4–6 in. (10–15 cm) with,

Quercus myrsinifolia. Photo by Michael A. Dirr

Quercus myrsinifolia, new growth

Quercus myrsinifolia, foliage.
Photo by Michael A. Dirr

Quercus myrsinifolia, bark. Photo by Michael A. Dirr

Quercus myrsinifolia, acorns.
Photo by Michael A. Dirr

again, a long, narrow taper of a drip tip, typical for the region. The most striking feature is the rather late new growth—in western Oregon not appearing until May—of a deep crimson to maroon. Held against the vibrant, prior season's leaves, it is a great contrast yet does not create a visual "hole" in the landscape, which can happen with a large, specimen tree entirely covered with purple leaves.

Somewhat drought tolerant, they are deeply and sturdily rooted and, even newly established, have survived nearly entirely dry seasons on the U.S. West Coast with no supplemental water. Surprisingly, this and many other species exhibit a correlation between drought tolerance and heat. *Quercus myrsinifolia* appears more tolerant of drought if temperatures are high; it seems more able to successfully metabolize and withstand stress. However, the trees are certainly happier in Mediterranean climates with reasonable summer irrigation.

They are easy to transplant, both from containers and balled and burlapped, making it easier to place a large specimen in the garden or on the street than is the case with many broadleaved evergreens. They were planted along a street at the Portland Classical Chinese Garden as 2 in. (5 cm) caliper specimens and, after about a year of adjusting to their surroundings, began growing vigorously. The glossy green leaves are a striking contrast to the garden's white walls, especially when festooned with maroon new growth. A 130-year-old specimen in the Dunthorpe neighborhood of Portland measures over 70 ft. (21 m) in height, with a 60 ft. (18 m) spread. Another lover of summer heat, plants grown in Vancouver, B.C., have suffered yellowing and slower growth from too little of it. Ensuring good drainage and ample water and nutrients during the growing season helps green them up.

Related to such oaks as *Quercus glauca*, *Q. myrsinifolia* is up to ten degrees Fahrenheit (roughly six degrees Celsius) hardier to frost, with many specimens having endured –10 to 0°F (–23 to –18°C) with no noticeable damage.

Quercus myrsinifolia stands among the group of summer-rainfall oaks that can be rather easily propagated by cuttings. Cuttings taken from the end of summer through mid winter, cut at a steep angle, with above medium but not extremely high hormones, and given bottom heat, root at a relatively high rate and begin growth quickly. Acorns are a given; young trees can begin producing them in as little as five years from seed.

Because it is such an easy grower and its cold hardiness is becoming more widely known, *Quercus myrsinifolia* is readily available from specialty nurseries in the American South and West.

Quercus phillyreoides, called the ubame oak in Japan and often recognized as a Far Eastern subspecies of *Q. ilex*, is a smallish tree, growing to 30 ft. (9 m), presenting a narrow aspect and bearing bright green leaves, often with a bronzy cast in the new growth. Records show some specimens in excess of 50 ft. (15 m). *Quercus phillyreoides* 'Emerald Sentinel', selected by the JC Raulston Arboretum in North Carolina, has proven hardy to at least –10°F (–23°C) and is relatively easy from cuttings.

Quercus phillyreoides, foliage.
Photo by Michael A. Dirr

Quercus phillyreoides. Photo by Michael A. Dirr

Quercus phillyreoides 'Emerald Sentinel'. Photo by Michael A. Dirr

Though, as one might imagine, possibly not a tree for the smallest of gardens—excepting, of course, the two I have in my courtyard—*Quercus phillyreoides* is a superb street and park tree. It is deep-rooted, long-lived, and very drought resistant, presenting sturdy structure with a thick, wear-resistant bark. In urban conditions, they seem to do everything right, except erase graffiti.

Quercus rugosa (netleaf oak). Widespread and variable, a large shrub to medium tree, ranging from west Texas to southeastern Arizona, south through the highlands of Mexico to Guatemala. Found in upland areas just above the deserts to limestone mountains in near rainforests, it often grows in association with other lovely specimens such as *Q. hypoleucoides* and *Q. oblongifolia* (Mexican blue oak). *Arbutus* species, junipers, and dryland pines are also common associates. Further south and with increased moisture, the trees leave the protected ravines and enter mixed forest communities with an astounding abundance of compatriots, including enough other evergreen oaks to make one dizzy. Some forms, especially from damper areas, are medium trees to well over 40 ft. (12 m), whereas those at the highest elevations and in drier habitats can be shrubs.

Foliage is the outstanding characteristic: leaves are deep green with a leathery (rugose), dull surface, almost puckered, and sometimes have minute hairs. They measure 1½ in. (4 cm) by 3–5 in. (8–13 cm) but can be as long as 7–9 in. (18–23 cm), usually depending on the dampness of the surrounds, though plants collected in their extreme

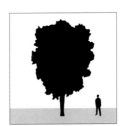

Quercus rugosa, foliage

Quercus rugosa

environs have tended to keep their characteristics. Most exciting to an indumentum fiend are the undersides of the leaves, which are nearly always covered with a woolly indumentum that varies from nearly white to, more commonly, cream to almost gold. The shape of the leaves is a bit violin-like, often with a faint double set of lobes, and they are often somewhat convex, undoubtedly a drought adaptation but also one that allows a good view of the indumentum. In almost all forms, this is a very handsome tree with rounded shape and usually more than one central trunk. The leaves can be held in graceful layers, adding to the pleasing effect of the rounded form.

Personally, even when looking at an oak that keys to *Quercus rugosa*, I always doubt the identification, as the diversity in Mexico is so great. One form that definitely keys out as a form of *Q. rugosa* and reaches only 10–13 ft. (3–4 m) is found near the village of La Siberia, a high-elevation valley with, as the name would imply, quite chilly winters. The leaf is particularly attractive, deep green and fluted, with a very warm, creamy golden indumentum on the underside. Acorns collected with John Fairey of Peckerwood Garden reached a little under 20 ft. (6 m) in seventeen years as Portland, Oregon, street trees. Generous care and a climate with fewer extremes have allowed them, in a few short years, to become much larger than their parents. Some eleven years after planting, we were thrilled that these specimens produced their first crop of acorns (about 500), and they have produced even larger numbers ever since. I think each one has been sown. They have also rooted from cuttings but with more difficulty than the Chinese evergreen oaks.

Though some forms from the south will have less hardiness to frost, *Quercus rugosa* in general has been a tough plant. Temperatures of –10 to –15°F (–23 to –26°C) have not harmed most of those in cultivation. Plants with provenance from the higher mountains in the north might be expected to withstand even colder periods. One factor to keep in mind is that, although they are all subject to summer moisture, they benefit from very good drainage and soils low in organic matter. A little autumn drought, as would be expected when heading into their natural winter dry season, should increase winter frost tolerance.

One of the best places to observe *Quercus rugosa* in the wild is Big Bend National Park, Texas, where outstanding groves occur within easy access and associated with a number of other rare oaks. Though still rare in cultivation, *Q. rugosa* is being offered by more nurseries and, through numerous collections, by Yucca Do Nursery of Waller, Texas. A great diversity of forms and collection locations has been offered to gardeners and arboreta. Acorns and young plants should be found fairly easily by searching at specialty nurseries.

Quercus rysophylla (loquat oak). From rarified mid and high elevations in northeastern Mexico, in protected ravines in semi-arid places to large stands higher in the mountains, where more moisture is received. In the most mesic situations, it is a silver-trunked, more or less single-leadered tree, most often under 35 ft. (10.5 m), though old specimens exceed 80 ft. (25 m). Downslope, they are round-crowned and multi-trunked, growing from between limestone boulders and seeking any moisture they can get. Still exceedingly rare in cultivation, plants first collected by Peckerwood Garden and Yucca Do Nursery in the 1980s are just now reaching any size. One is planted at Portland, Oregon's Hoyt Arboretum; after five years in the ground, it was just approaching 15 ft. (4.5 m), mostly because it spent its first eight years in a pot.

The leaves are stunning, to 10 in. (25 cm) long and 3–5 in. (8–13 cm) wide, and a graceful oval shape, indeed, resembling the leaf of a loquat (*Eriobotrya*). Especially in young trees, some sharp lobing can occur toward the apex of the leaf. They are the brightest of greens and very shiny with an oiled leather texture. Paler beneath, they have only a minute indumentum and that mostly on the veins. These stiff leaves are displayed horizontally toward the ends of the branches and appear to be almost too large for the scale of the twigs. So far, specimens have received only minor leaf bronzing at 12 to 15°F (–11 to –9.5°C) with leaf damage at 10 to 12°F (–12 to –11°C), and have been vigorous, whether in hot or cool summers, provided adequate moisture. It should be noted that with this and other evergreen oaks, damage can occur at higher temperatures with early frost on late season's flushes of new growth.

Always a concern with broadleaved evergreens is their ability to tolerate snow or ice. *Quercus rysophylla* has a branch structure that is quite flexible and, even with the large size and surface area of the leaves, has stood up well to a couple of warm, wet snows at the Hoyt Arboretum. Younger plants at our nursery added 3 ft. (1 m) of growth their first season. Because of its varied habitat, plants have been and should be tolerant of a wide range of garden conditions; both plentiful moisture and periodic drought, even extremes, should prove little trouble. A grand 30 ft. (9 m) specimen planted by Texas plantsman Lynn Lowrey thrives on an unirrigated hillside near San Antonio.

A great advantage to those wishing to grow and propagate *Quercus rysophylla* is its relative ease from cuttings. Though I have experienced a crop failure or two, most batches have come through with seventy or eighty percent rooting, and that fairly quickly in only a month or two with bottom heat and mist. The best time to take cuttings has been November to January. Tissue culture is being attempted on the Hoyt Arboretum plant. While it is always a dilemma whether to discuss plants not easily available, *Q. rysophylla* is such a beautiful creature, it is hoped demand will force supply to increase.

Quercus suber (cork oak). A large rounded tree to over 80 ft. (25 m). Though native to the western Mediterranean, it has been planted around the world in warm temperate climates for centuries. The source of cork for wine bottles and such things as the all-important bulletin boards, the tree's often slightly crooked and very picturesque trunk produces phloem, which can be several inches thick and, carefully harvested, is renewable. The bark is deeply fissured with undulating layers of grays and oranges. The leaves, 1–2 in. (2.5–5 cm) in length and ½–1 in. (1.5–2.5 cm) in width, are oblong to narrowly ovate, sometimes with minute dentations along the margins, often a bit cupped. They are quite shiny above and paler beneath, with, sometimes, a fine indumentum. The darker, often somewhat wider leaves, as well as the cupping, can distinguish young plants from the similar *Q. ilex*. The acorns, borne singly or in pairs, are 1–1¼ in. (2.5–3 cm) long in a deep cup that is loosely fringed.

Quercus suber thrives in places of high summer heat and drought. It is often successful but slower growing and sometimes a bit brittle in areas lacking summer heat. In northern portions of the Pacific

Quercus suber

Quercus suber, bark. Photo by John Grimshaw

Northwest, for example, though hardy to the worst 0 to 10°F (–18 to –12°C) freezes, they remain rather small and are subject to easy snow breakage. They are more successful in the Willamette Valley, where large specimens can be seen in such places as the University of Oregon campus in Eugene; they are even more successful in the heat of the Central Valley of California, where, for example, gorgeous specimens can be seen about the UC Davis campus and in nearby Sacramento. Some of these have exceeded 85 ft. (26.5 m) in height.

This is another sure-footed tree, at home in the well-drained landscape or in harsh urban plantings. It does require more room, however, than some other Mediterranean oaks; a 3 ft. (1 m) tree just won't cut it after a while. One advantage is its ease in container cultivation as a young tree. Large, containerized plants can be found, reducing the vulnerable period of time during which young trees can be injured in public situations. Makes a fine larger companion to smaller textured trees such as olives (*Olea*) and dryland shrubs such as *Ceanothus* and *Cistus* species. In general a little more tender than *Quercus ilex*, sustaining damage, or at least being stunned, where temperatures approach 0°F (–18°C) for any length of time. Tolerant of summer rainfall.

Difficult from cuttings, though they have been done. Acorns are the way to go.

Quercus virginiana (Virginia live oak, southern live oak). Medium to large tree and variable, covering a wide range of habitats from Virginia and Maryland to Florida, and Cuba to Mexico and Texas. The forms in the western part of its range, under drier conditions, have been issued various names but lean toward shrubbiness and smaller leaves. When one thinks of Virginia live oaks, images of *Gone with the Wind* and southern plantations come to mind with large, spreading trees, some 80 ft. (25 m) tall or more, and sometimes much wider, dripping with Spanish moss (*Tillandsia usneoides*). Long-lived and deep-rooted, the plants can be expected to live many hundreds of years. Fast-growing in youth, to 3 ft. (1 m) or more a year, it begins life as a fairly conical plant, beginning to spread into an inverse vase after about thirty years and without too much competition. A lover of heat and summer moisture, plants thrive in the humidity of the South. In the western United States and other dry climates, they are a bit slower growing and tend to be smaller, even with irrigation, and might be less suitable to dry-summer climates than some of the more drought hardy oaks.

The leaves, again, a dark shiny green, and only slightly paler beneath, are 3–5 in. (8–13 cm) long and 1½–2½ in. (4–6 cm) wide. Unlobed as adults and often toothless, leaves on young plants or

Quercus virginiana, leaf and acorn.
Photo by Michael A. Dirr

Quercus virginiana. Photo by Michael A. Dirr

branches undergoing vigorous growth can have undulations and some teeth along the margins. At its best in deep, sandy soil; much smaller in stony or poorly drained conditions.

An essential tree in the American South where, it is hoped, more vigorous planting resumes so future generations can experience the parks and boulevards with majestic canopies meeting even over the widest of spaces. As it is, so many stands are planted with same-age trees, some now reaching senescence, that they are likely, all at once, to be gone with the wind.

Quercus virginiana var. *fusiformis* (syn. *Q. fusiformis*; Texas live oak) grows from Oklahoma through the Edwards Plateau into Mexico. This variety has a slightly more divaricating habit, especially in youth, and the small leaves associated with spring's new growth give the appearance of small whipcords at the top of the plants. This is a rugged subspecies, adapted to dry country and often seen growing in desert canyons at the western end of its range. One of the most adapted oaks for desert southwestern cities, it has even been used as grafting stock for others less tolerant of heat and alkalinity. The plants do remain a bit smaller, depending on provenance, but 25 ft. (7.5 m) or so can be expected for most. Frost hardiness is no more an issue than for the species, many forms having withstood –15°F (–26°C) or a bit colder with little leaf drop. In extreme drought, these trees can go

Quercus virginiana var. *fusiformis*

semi-deciduous in summer, so some supplemental water in drier sites would be appreciated by all.

Cuttings, not as difficult as with other oaks, are best with juvenile branches taken from the base of the tree or close to the trunk. Late autumn and winter cuttings have been best, and percentages of more than half can be expected. Acorns, again, are best.

Quercus wislizeni (interior live oak). Multi-trunked, small tree in dry or rocky situations, to large spreading specimens of 80 ft. (25 m) or more in deep soils, and, along with *Q. agrifolia* (coastal live oak), the classic live oak of California. The range is from northern California south to the foothills, not far from the coast of northern Baja California. Almost unknown in cultivation outside the Pacific Coast of North America. The leaves are deep green and shiny, resembling those of a rather fine, serrated holly (*Ilex*) and only slightly less obnoxious to bare feet in the summertime. Depending on the form, the leaves can be 3–4½ in. (8–12 cm) in length and 1–2 in. (2.5–5 cm) in width; the uniquely shaped acorns are 1½–2 in. (4–5 cm) long but often no more than 6 mm wide.

This species is adaptable to garden situations if planted when young, but many have been lost due to urban encroachment, with its subsequent root disturbance and—worse yet—irrigation over old root systems. Another superb plant for dry-summer regions where temperatures remain above 0 to 10°F (–18 to –12°C), and one that should be planted just beyond the reach of the garden hose. An interesting feature: much like the olives (*Olea*), the shrubby forms of interior live oak can be successfully root pruned and dug as relatively large specimens, up to 20 ft. (6 m) or more, on nursery grounds and successfully transplanted into gardens or onto streets.

Quercus wislizeni. Photo © Global Book Publishing Photo Library

Though cultivation has been successful in the U.S. Southeast, plants appear stunted and seem to resent warm summer evenings and high humidity. They are extremely heat tolerant in dry areas, however. Growth in the United Kingdom, though again successful, has been a bit slow, probably from lack of summer heat. In the U.S. West or other Mediterranean climates, 3–4 ft. (about 1 m) of growth a year can be expected from healthy young specimens. Though leaf drop can be a minor problem, they make fine urban trees. The large forms might be a bit out of scale in small gardens.

Rhamnus	buckthorn	Rhamnaceae

A genus of 160 or so species, mostly of the northern hemisphere with a few as far south as southern Africa and South America, often inhabiting dry places. They range from shrubs in most species to small trees, and from spiny-branched to spineless with, as one would expect, the large-leaved species from friendly climes less inclined to be spiny. The flowers are in small, creamy white clusters with the berries being, often, the most attractive feature, ranging from black to blue or nearly red. With so many drought hardy species, it is a wonder that more are not in common cultivation. Of the evergreen species, few attain tree-like proportions, but several can be only slightly manipulated to provide well-behaved trees for small spaces.

Rhamnus californica (syn. *Frangula californica*; coffeeberry). Wide ranging in the Mediterranean West of North America, exhibits many forms and characteristics suitable for dry-summer gardens, some dwarf, others easily pruned to small trees to 10 ft. (3 m). One form, *R. californica* subsp. *tomentella* (syn. *F. californica* subsp. *tomentella*), sometimes given specific status as *R. tomentella*, often exceeds 10 ft. (3 m) in height and, under garden conditions, does so quickly. The 3–4 in. (8–10 cm) oval leaves, unlike shiny-leaved counterparts, have a pewter velour finish and the texture of velvet. The same woolliness is exhibited on the young stems, which later age to a rough, silver finish. Upright in form when young and umbrella-shaped with age, they can be trimmed to single or few trunks and can achieve 6 ft. (2 m) in fewer than three years.

The berries on all forms of *Rhamnus californica* are a wonderful autumn and winter feature, beginning pea-sized and red, turning, one at a time, blue-black. Another plant for areas receiving little summer water and gardens with lean soil and moderate to full sun. Luckily, most forms of *R. californica* tolerate some summer garden water, and providing it pushes them to a desired size more quickly.

The native haunts of *Rhamnus californica* subsp. *tomentella* regu-

Rhamnus californica. Photo © Global Book Publishing Photo Library

Rhamnus californica subsp.
tomentella, fruit and foliage

Rhamnus californica subsp. tomentella with Cercis orbiculata

Rhamnus alaternus 'Argenteovariegata'.
Photo by Michael A. Dirr

larly dip below 10°F (–12°C) and in some locations below 0°F (–18°C), making 0 to 10°F (–18 to –12°C) a safe bet in the garden.

Propagation is similar to that of other evergreen Mediterraneans: best with mature prior season's growth when the weather cools in autumn and on to early spring. If under mist, the cuttings should, to avoid rot, be removed as soon as possible and placed in a cool damp atmosphere with little water on the leaves. Seeds prefer some cool stratification but are otherwise easy in mineral soil, though for desired clones, one might stick to cuttings.

RHAMNUS ALATERNUS (Italian buckthorn) is a Mediterranean species that remains shrub-like for many years but can reach over 30 ft. (9 m) in height. Its variegated form received an Award of Garden Merit from the Royal Horticultural Society, and *R. alaternus* 'John Edwards', a fast grower to 12–15 ft. (3.5–4.5 m), is suitable as a small, formal garden tree, easily maintained as a single trunk with a pyramidal form and deep green, glossy leaves of about 1 in. (2.5 cm). All are of cold hardiness similar to *R. californica* subsp. *tomentella*.

Rhus   Anacardiaceae

Up to 200 species of trees, shrubs, and vines, both deciduous and evergreen. The family, native to the Old and New Worlds, contains numerous species of trouble-free subjects for the garden. Related to such creatures as *Schinus* and *Pistacia*, many are also exceedingly drought tolerant. The genus *Rhus* itself has both good and bad associations; in North America, *R. typhina*, native in the Northeast and planted throughout the country, and *R. glabra*, native to woodlands of the East and along springs and watercourses in the West, are attractive plants both in the wild and in the garden. *Rhus toxicodendron* and *R. radicans* (poison oak and poison ivy, respectively), now often placed in the genus *Toxicodendron*, have ended many people's enjoyment of the natural world, sometimes with a trip to the hospital for relief of itching and blisters. Blisters aside, a great number of nontoxic evergreen species show great potential for the garden but remain elusive in the trade. A wonderful collection can be seen at the Free State National Botanical Garden, Bloemfontein, South Africa.

Rhus lancea (willow sumac, African sumac). One of several species from South Africa, usually growing away from the coast in arid to semi-arid places with sporadic rainfall in both winter and summer. Found singly or in small, savanna-like groves, sometimes near springs or watercourses. Its habitats vary from sterile, rocky, very dry soil to muddy and poorly drained with abundant moisture.

A tough, fast-growing small tree, usually under 20–25 ft. (6–7.5 m), it was introduced to the United States about 1916 but never widely planted except in more recent years in the Southwest and along the immediate West Coast. The plants are tall and somewhat spindly in youth, then broaden to a graceful flattened crown. Though delicate

Rhus lancea. Photo © Global Book Publishing Photo Library

and pretty in the shade, they are less graceful there in the colder end of their frost tolerance, requiring summer heat to open properly.

The trifoliate leaves, 3–6 in. (8–15 cm) long, are bright spring-green, sometimes infused with oranges and reds, resembling a cluster of shiny willow leaves. The leaf size is largest on young plants and those in moist situations. As its habitat suggests, it is tolerant of many soil types, from poorly drained to rocky and from soggy to droughty (exiled brothers of the Seven Dwarfs).

The greenish winter flowers, borne in clusters, are small, as is the fruit, although in complement with the reddish-hued stems of the tree, the pinkish fruit adds interest in the early summer. Now commonly available, *Rhus lancea* is a top candidate for planting where water restrictions are a problem or where hot or windy weather limits choices. A well-grown plant has the grace of a Japanese maple (*Acer palmatum*) without the need for water and humidity. It makes a better garden tree than a street tree, as its stature might be a bit small for heavily impacted public places.

One drawback of what seems to be an indestructible little tree is its lack of cold hardiness. Temperatures below 15°F (−9.5°C) for any length of time frost back the twigs, and, only a few degrees colder, the top can be entirely lost. If the tree form is not important, and it is to be grown only for the graceful leaves, *Rhus lancea* has proven root hardy through fairly long periods (a few days) of lows below 10°F (−12°C), regaining several feet of new growth the following season. Container culture is also a possibility. As can be personally attested, they can be grown in very small containers, the succulent roots allowing the top to remain attractive for years on end.

Although possible from cuttings, seed is fast and quick to germinate.

Schima   Theaceae

A widespread genus from Southeast Asia in damp broadleaved evergreen forests from tropical to cool temperate regions. Highly variable shrubs to trees, from 25 ft. (7.5 m) or so to over 140 ft. (40 m) in height—though most in cultivation seem to max out at 30 ft. (9 m) in a reasonable amount of time—with shiny leaves to nearly 6 in. (15 cm) in length, almost always a narrow oval and a delightful orangey red when new. The fragrant flowers, 1½–2 in. (4–5 cm) in diameter, emerge from rose-colored buds, opening to cream and white, sometimes with a purple tinge. From twenty-five to dozens of species have been named. Some taxonomists lump the Indonesian species into *Schima wallichii*; others have mistakenly assumed that all species were lumped into the one, single species. Even if the great variability is not recognized taxonomically, the great diversity and horticultural potential is well worth pursuing.

As with all members of the camellia family, the genus *Schima* does not appreciate drought. Though established plants can certainly withstand dry periods, prolonged drought, especially in the subsoil, leads eventually to dead wood, making the plants appear sparse. They are at home in the U.S. Southeast with supplemental watering, and just as at home in the West with an intravenous hose attached. Though not thrilled with freezing winds, plants with at least some overhead protection have received only bronzing—and rather attractive bronzing at that—at temperatures of –5 to –8°F (–20 to –22°C). Provenance, of course, should be studied carefully before obtaining any schima, as, with the wide distribution in the wild, cold hardiness varies greatly.

The following species is the only one at all common in North American horticulture.

Schima wallichii (Chinese guger tree). Exceedingly handsome in all forms and equally useful in the woodland or courtyard garden. The lustrous leaves, 1 in. (2.5 cm) wide by 3–4 in. (8–10 cm) long, and narrow pyramidal form are consistent throughout the year, except that the orange-red new growth is more present during the spring and summer flushes, a talent exhibited by much of the camellia family. Late summer and autumn also have the oldest leaves coloring to reds and oranges and falling, making an attractive display but not diminishing the evergreen quality of the trees. The bark is smooth and somewhat resembles *Stewartia* in age, though lacking some of the patchy, jigsaw-puzzle patterns. The late spring and summer flowers, with a sweet fragrance that can be detected from some distance, indeed appear somewhat like single camellias and stand out handsomely against the dark foliage. Unlike camellias, which can take some time to reach what one might consider tree size, *S. wallichii* is more like a small gordonia (to which it is also related) in form. Happy in sun with adequate water in all but the hottest climates and tolerant of at least light shade.

A form collected in southern China by the Quarryhill Botanical Garden in Glen Ellen, California, reached a broadly pyramidal 20 ft. (6 m) or so in twelve years, with leaves in excess of 5 in. (13 cm) in length, appearing almost avocado-like. It too flowers in earliest spring. Its cold hardiness has only been tested to 16 to 18°F (–9 to –8°C).

Cuttings (which, by the way, are quite easy if taken in late summer or fall) can grow into 8 ft. (2.5 m) specimens in two or three

Schima argentea. Photo by Tony Avent

years with reasonable attention to their needs and can even flower that early. Seed, though infrequently available, prefers a cool moist stratification and then germinates readily if planted in spring.

SCHIMA ARGENTEA, which is making the rounds in the United States of late, quickly achieves 10–15 ft. (3–4.5 m) then slows. It has produced its glistening white flowers, with pleasingly contrasting yellow stamens, in abundance after four years from cuttings.

Tom Ranney of North Carolina State University first crossed the genus *Schima* with its close relative *Franklinia*, resulting in vigorous, fully evergreen intergeneric hybrids with shiny leaves and bronzed winter color. ×*Schimlinia floribunda* has since been created dozens of times, overproducing luxuriant growth and flowers. Adult plants maintain the vigor of the genus *Schima* and lose the disease susceptibility of *Franklinia*. Selections to date only confirm this is a fabulous new addition to horticulture. Expect more good news as these hybrids make their way into cultivation.

Schinus   Anacardiaceae

Thirty, if not more, species of evergreen trees and shrubs native from South America and Central America to China and North Africa. Most inhabit seasonally dry thorn forests or chaparral associations, with only a few reaching tree size. As their arid and semi-arid homes would indicate, most have abbreviated leaves that are either blue-gray or covered with a viscous exudate. Flowers occur in small racemes and are in themselves tiny but produce fruit that can be rosy red to metallic bluish purple or black. The species described is the most widespread and available.

Schinus molle (pepper tree). A majestic tree to 60 ft. (18 m), resembling a fine-grained weeping willow at a distance but with very rough bark. The pendulous branches have finely divided leaves up to 1 ft. (30 cm), and the trees produce a very light shade. The species grows in the chaco from Paraguay to northwestern Argentina and into the Andean foothills even in quite arid areas, at least as far south as Tucumán Province. The largest specimens I have ever seen, over 50 ft. (15 m) with trunks nearly 4 ft. (1.2 m) in diameter, are in and near the town square of Cachi in Argentina's high puna country. Widely planted in warmer areas throughout the world, including the Mediterranean and the U.S. West Coast, they are durable and drought hardy and most at home in bright sunny locations.

Even in habitat, *Schinus molle* can be subject to freezes at least into the low teens (13 to 14°F, –10.5 to –10°C), but, as is typical in these desert places at relatively low latitudes, frosts are short. Plants in cultivation in California suffered greatly at December temperatures between 10 and 15°F (−12 and −9.5°C); even large plants were frozen to the ground in unprotected areas, though most resprouted later.

The flowers are insignificant, except of course to the trees and their pollinators, but the berries are quite attractive to the human eye. Produced in summer and autumn, they hang gracefully amid the leaves in clusters to about 6 in. (15 cm), their rosy red color matching their common name, pimentero. The peppercorns are about 5 mm in diameter and do indeed look and taste like black pepper. Their skin is quite viscous: after harvesting in the wild and becoming coated with the red, papery fruit during bouts of preparation, we found the phrase "overcoming shyness" emerged effortlessly.

Schinus molle var. *areira* (aquarivay), a black-berried form, grows in the eastern Andes, and, although the tree is slightly smaller, to about 25 ft. (8 m), its lofty origins suggest the potential for greater cold hardiness. Several higher-elevation collections are now being tested in our Portland garden, but our recent winters have been easy and the potential remains unconfirmed.

The sticky-seed method of propagation requires little preparation (although some cool stratification seems to enhance germination). Cuttings taken mid to late summer are a little tricky but can be successful with plentiful warmth and careful applications of mist—just enough to keep the atmosphere damp but not the leaf surfaces wet, or cooties will appear.

Schinus molle

Schinus molle var. *areira*. Photo © Global Book Publishing Photo Library

Sophora   Fabaceae

A large and variable genus, consisting of seventy or more trees, shrubs, and perennials native throughout the tropical and warm temperate world. It is still thought by some to be a bit of a catchall genus. One of the most common species is *Sophora japonica*, a tough, drought resistant tree that, beautiful as it is, unfortunately loses its leaves in the winter and cannot be included—or even mentioned—in this volume. Many species are evergreen and obtain tree size; all have pinnate leaves and generous racemes of pea-like flowers.

Sophora microphylla. A smallish, graceful tree from New Zealand, eventually reaching 25–30 ft. (7.5–9 m) but spending plenty of time below 15 ft. (4.5 m). It begins life as a shrubby, divaricating mass, then grows into a loose, angularly branched, spreading adult. The leaves are 3–4 in. (8–10 cm) and divided into leaflets, each roughly 6 mm; they are spring-green, a wonderful complement to the mustard-yellow petioles and branchlets and the bark, which becomes ever more silvery as the tree matures. Casting a very light shade, the tree also has a fine texture created by the tiny leaves held against the small twigs.

The bright, golden-yellow flowers can be over 1 in. (2.5 cm) and hang in small racemes that appear in mid spring to early summer, though in mild climates, flowering can begin in late winter and occur sporadically throughout the year. My first experience with this species was at the Hillier Arboretum, where I happened upon an old specimen of *Sophora microphylla* Sun King (= 'Hilsop'), a smaller selection. Although the plant was only about 8 ft. (2.5 m) tall, its

Sophora microphylla. Photo by Michael A. Dirr

large flowers were stunning, and its earlier flowering time—usually late winter to early spring—also made an impression, as many of the shrubs surrounding its wonderful March display were not yet active. Another more compact form, *S. m.* 'Dragon's Gold', though very slow to reach even the minimum size allowed for the term "tree," is nonetheless beautiful with large flowers of sometimes over 1 in. (2.5 cm) and somewhat more substantial leaves.

As well, *Sophora microphylla* Sun King exhibits somewhat more cold hardiness than is typical. Most collections in cultivation are damaged by temperatures between 10 and 15°F (–12 and –9.5°C), especially with wind and low humidity; but with protection, *S. m.* Sun King has tolerated brief dips under 10°F (–12°C), suffering only a little leaf loss at 0°F (–18°C). At home in coastal or cooler Mediterranean climates, plants can suffer with extreme heat and humidity and should be grown in sand beds and shady conditions if attempted there. Otherwise, they prefer full sun to dappled shade with regular soil and consistent summer water. Not a lover of extremely rich conditions; it might be best to avoid excessive fertilizing or mulching with organic matter.

Propagation is a cinch. Seeds enjoy, but don't always require, thirty days or so of cool stratification, but either way, pouring just-boiled water over them ruptures the endosperm, and germination often occurs within a few days. Early spring sowing when temperatures are cool is best. Cuttings from semi-ripened to ripened wood can be made from late summer through early spring. Mist is not necessary, but it doesn't hurt.

Sophora secundiflora (Texas mountain laurel, fruolito, mescal bean). Evergreen, small tree 25–40 ft. (7.5–12 m), though most forms stay under 20 ft. (6 m) and, in a few cases, remain shrubs, usually as a function of available moisture. Native from north and northeastern Mexico into west Texas and New Mexico in chaparral situations or in ravines that hold a bit of additional moisture. In deep soils (or in the happy land of cultivation), Texas mountain laurel can reach 10–15 ft. (3–4.5 m) in under ten years, developing a narrow, rounded crown with picturesque branches and bark that is rough and silvery, edged charcoal-gray. The deep green, glossy leaves, usually 3–5 in. (8–13 cm) overall, consist of three to five pairs of leaflets, each 1–1½ in. (2.5–4 cm). In several areas of northeastern Mexico, usually drier country yet, forms exist with leaves entirely covered with a silver fur. The small purply blue flowers, ½ in. (1.5 cm), appear in mid spring in 1–3 in. (2.5–8 cm) racemes, carrying the highly fragrant aroma of sweet grapes—think fruity wisteria.

Unlike the New Zealand and Chilean species, this is a plant for

Sophora microphylla Sun King

Sophora secundiflora, flowers.
Photo by George Hull

Sophora secundiflora. Photo by Michael A. Dirr

swamp-cooler climates. They relish the extreme heat of the Gulf Coast of North America, there putting on generous growth of 1 ft. (30 cm) to 3 ft. (1 m) per year, a rate that, while perhaps not so very fast by most standards in the age of insta-gardens, brings them to the size of a small patio tree in only a few years, especially with the encouragement of having the lower branches trimmed. Plants propagated by cuttings flower more quickly, adding to the "instant" effect.

On the other hand, specimens planted in cool-summer climates such as the immediate Pacific Coast of North America or the British Isles can experience imperceptibly slow growth, or even lose ground, especially with improper care. Well-drained soil is a must, as many plants in the wild are growing in what appears to be pure limestone, but rich soil does not seem to be a hindrance and, again, will speed growth. Even in the hottest climes, a south wall can't hurt and will speed growth. Plants are tolerant of dry winter conditions but appreciate deep soaking in summer. In hot desert regions where landscape choices are limited, *Sophora secundiflora* has been a welcome addition to gardens. In Phoenix, Arizona, and other like places, with only a little supplemental summer water, the species appears wonderfully lush and taller-growing than the related *S. arizonica*, a species that, although beautiful, does not attain tree size.

If proper ripening has occurred (i.e., summer heat), temperatures of 10 to 12°F (−12 to −11°C), at least briefly, seem not to have an effect. If plants are being grown from the northern reaches of its distribution, the same can be said for even a touch below 0°F (−18°C). Unfortunately, the beautiful silver-leaved forms of *Sophora secundiflora* from Mexico that we grow seem to resent anything under 12 to 15°F (−11 to −9.5°C).

Propagation is best from seed with a minimal cool stratification and a little bit of boiling water. Cuttings, unfortunately, are difficult but worth the effort for a particularly good clone. Newly ripened wood in late summer or early autumn is best, with moisture, bottom heat, and a strong hormone but short on mist.

Sophora tetraptera (kowhai). Evergreen large shrubs to small trees (though sometimes deciduous in hard frosts). Closely related to *S. microphylla*, but leaflets and leaves and even the structure of the plant are larger and more coarse. In addition this species has a less pronounced, or even nonexistent, period of divaricating shrubbiness. Smaller forms can remain under 12 ft. (3.5 m); larger ones can climb past 30–35 ft. (9–10.5 m) in time, maintaining an arched, flat-topped form throughout. The leaves, 2–4 in. (5–10 cm) long, consist of ten to twenty pairs of oval leaflets, each roughly ¾–1¼ in. (2–3 cm); they are borne on twigs the color of spun gold, a striking feature. The satu-

Sophora tetraptera. Photo by Michael A. Dirr

rated yellow flowers, ½–1¼ in. (1.5–3 cm), are in four- to ten-flowered racemes, appearing in early to mid summer.

Of possibly the most interest is the plant's geographical distribution. Native to both New Zealand and southern Chile, it is one of several Gondwanan species, plants whose distributions are relics of land masses that were once connected or closer together. The genera *Hebe* and *Nothofagus* are, in their distribution, two other woody souvenirs of times long past—at least before 1974.

A plant at its best in cool coastal climates or in climates with summer warmth but generally low humidity. They enjoy consistent moisture, especially in summer, and are quite happy in full sun to dappled shade. The flowering is best in brighter light. Frost hardiness varies, of course, with provenance, but most plants in cultivation have had no quarrel with 12 to 15°F (–11 to –9.5°C), some even withstanding bouts of lower temperatures.

At its best planted as a foreground or patio specimen, so the intricate branches and leaflets, with their color combinations of spring-green and yellow, can be enjoyed. The flowers are best regarded as a bonus; although spectacular en masse, they are not particularly long lasting, but the texture and color of the tree itself is pleasing year-round.

Of the minutely leafleted sophoras, *Sophora tetraptera* is one of the easiest to work with in the nursery world because of its generally straight shot from cuttings or seed into a shapely young tree. Methods of propagation are that of *S. microphylla*—so don't forget the boiling water.

Sycopsis   Hamamelidaceae

Seven species of evergreen trees and shrubs from Southeast Asia, including China and the Himalayas, with flowers in small racemes, indeed, looking like small *Hamamelis* flowers.

Sycopsis sinensis. Common in their native China, they are less widely planted in milder areas of western Europe and southeast and western areas of North America. Shrubby in youth, growing into a narrow, vase-shaped, 30 ft. (9 m) tree with ascending branches clad in an imbricate pattern of oval, very dark green, glossy leaves to about 3½ in. (9 cm). A decorative plant both when young and in its eventual tree form. They are a bit slow-growing if planted in direct sun or without consistent water, but, where nurtured, grow at least 2 ft. (60 cm) per year often with several main trunks, producing fans of branches, one on top of the other.

Even on a small plant the flowers, in January and February, are

Sycopsis sinensis. Photo by Michael A. Dirr

a major attraction. Though individually quite small, the racemes produce several at once, so the roughly ⅓ in. (1 cm) clusters of deep maroon held between the leaves create a pleasant encounter while one waits for the garden to reawaken. The fine-textured silver bark also adds interest, drawing the eye to the beautiful branch structure, allowing it to stand out amid the dark background of the leaves. The flower color contrasts well with the intense green of the leaves and is a particularly rich offering given the predominance of white and cream flowers in the winter garden. It is especially wonderful when associated with other winter performers at their best, especially those with matching or contrasting leaf and flower colors—for example, the deep maroon leaves of *Loropetalum*, also in the witch hazel family— or planted with deep red hellebores (*Helleborus*). And why not? Throw in a red flowering quince (*Chaenomeles*), maybe with a white sarcococca nestled at its base or a good rich red *Camellia sasanqua* for good measure (twinkling lights optional).

A beautiful grove exists in the University of Washington Arboretum in Seattle, with plants dating from 1941 and now up to 37 ft. (11 m) tall still growing vigorously. Rated by most as frost hardy to about 0°F (−18°C), leaf drop occurs at that temperature but recovery is fairly swift, even from temperatures somewhat below. Overhead protection of larger trees is certainly helpful where cold spells threaten.

A hybrid between *Sycopsis sinensis* and the better known and equally attractive *Parrotia persica*—a wonderful, drought hardy, deciduous tree with drop-dead gorgeous bark and autumn color—is ×*Sycoparrotia semidecidua*. (I first memorized the name by thinking of it as a crazy parrotia.) A Swiss introduction in the early 1950s, specimens appeared in North America in the early 1970s. Faster growing, it eventually becomes somewhat taller and wider than *Sycopsis sinensis* and is, indeed, partly deciduous—and on rare occasions, with very cold weather, entirely so. The leaves are larger as well, to 5–6 in. (13–15 cm) by 2½–3 in. (6–8 cm). It has proven hardy to −10°F (−23°C) or below. Two forms appear sporadically in North American horticulture: one with typical green leaves, and ×*Sycoparrotia semidecidua* 'Aureovariegata', presenting leaves streaked and margined bright gold in spring. The combination of the layered branches, aforementioned silvery bark, and now golden patterned leaves is a wonderful happening in the woodland garden. In bright light or with high summer heat, the gold margins darken to a spring-green.

Both *Sycopsis* and its hybrids are amazingly carefree, assuming ample moisture. As with most members of the family Hamamelidaceae the branch structure dictates careful pruning. Avoid heading back; instead, remove unwanted or large branches at their base, so the flowing form is maintained.

Sycopsis sinensis, flowers and foliage. Photo by Michael A. Dirr

×*Sycoparrotia semidecidua*, foliage. Photo by Michael A. Dirr

×*Sycoparrotia semidecidua*, flowers. Photo by Michael A. Dirr

Exbucklandia populnea.
Photo by Tony Avent

Exbucklandia populnea, foliage.
Photo by Tony Avent

Propagation is best with ripened wood of current season's growth from late July through September and, with the fully evergreen *Sycopsis sinensis*, any time of the year, except while in the rush of spring growth. Heat and mist are preferred.

OTHER EXTRAORDINARY hamamelids may be found in the genus *Exbucklandia*. *Exbucklandia populnea* first came to my attention at the University of California Botanical Garden at Berkeley where, planted in the lower Asian garden, there is a 100-year-old specimen, roughly 25 ft. (7.5 m) in height and 15 ft. (4.5 m) or more in width and simply identified as "collected in the Kingdom of Bhutan." The juvenile leaves are sometimes three-lobed, and the adult leaves, entire, and up to 6–8 in. (15–20 cm) in length; all are rounded at the base and pointed at the tip and a rubbery, glossy green, looking for all the world like a giant Algerian ivy (*Hedera canariensis*). In winter the leaves take on copper hues, similar to the genus *Ternstroemia*.

The plant has been exceedingly difficult from cuttings, sometimes taking two or more years to root and then, often, only with callus. After many attempts with cuttings from the Berkeley tree, we now have a few specimens in vigorous growth. Re-establishing "juvenility" has led to somewhat more ease in rooting. Seeds have occasionally been available, and cuttings from truly juvenile plants have still been hit or miss, ensuring that, at least for the time being, *Exbucklandia populnea* won't be appearing in chain garden centers.

December temperatures below 15°F (−9.5°C) in Portland, Oregon, with several days continuing below freezing, did little damage except some bronzing of the leaves; and temperatures of 8°F (−14°C) in Tony Avent's North Carolina garden also produced very little damage except to new growth. If easier methods of propagation can be found, *Exbucklandia populnea* is destined to be a stunning landscape tree in areas where summer water can be provided.

Telopea	waratah	Proteaceae

As the Greek root implies (as seen from a distance), the waratah proteids of the genus *Telopea*, consisting of four evergreen shrubs and small trees allied with the Chilean firebush (*Embothrium*), are all from the cool climes of southeastern Australia including Tasmania. Suitable for the typical, protea-pleasing, cool maritime climates with soils low in phosphates, none are large trees, with most 10–25 ft. (3–7.5 m).

Native to wet forests and shrublands, they love good drainage and low-fertility soils. One cannot go wrong with sand. Species vary in cold hardiness but are united in their dislike of summer heat, especially in areas prone to humidity and high nighttime temperatures. Dappled shade suits all waratahs. Like clematis, they are happiest with sunny faces and shaded feet, especially in warmer zones. Mulches and ground-covering plantings help cool surrounding soil. All have narrow, matte green leaves and flowers in dense clusters or "heads" subtended by brightly colored bracts, sure to elicit comments, if not outright gasps where they can be grown.

Propagation can be from seed—cool stratified, planted in a peaty mix and kept coolish with good air circulation—or cuttings, taken from hardened current season's growth at any time except during spring's flush and kept cool, with possibly some bottom heat.

Telopea mongaensis (monga waratah). Narrow, vase-shaped shrub to small tree, to 10–20 ft. (3–6 m) or a bit more, with silver bark and matte green leaves, 3–4 in. (8–10 cm) long, which are either smooth or with lobes toward the apex. The flowers on this species are rather small, under 3 in. (8 cm) in diameter, and usually a pinkish red, most striking seen from a distance when in full flower. A somewhat tender species, requiring protection below 20°F (–7°C).

Telopea oreades (Victorian waratah). An upright, rather perky shrub, to 8–10 ft. (2.5–3 m) tall and 30 ft. (9 m) in time, showing layered branches and seemingly ever-so-sparse foliage, the advantage being a better view of the silvery bark. The leaves are substantial, up to 6 in. (15 cm), and oval to somewhat flared at the end. Flowers are red

Telopea oreades

Telopea oreades, flowers

to red-orange in compact, flattened clusters of 3–4 in. (8–10 cm), the underlying bracts often a pleasing contrast in pink-going-green.

Telopea oreades is particularly appreciative of sandy soil. Ben Gardner of Pistol River, on Oregon's coast, has several specimens growing on stabilized sand dunes, each topping out at about 20 ft. (6 m) and flowering heavily in spring and early summer and occasionally throughout the year. The species has withstood brief dips to 16 to 18°F (–9 to –8°C) and could probably go a bit lower.

Telopea speciosissima (New South Wales waratah). One of the smaller species, though a bit gawky, has one of the most obvious lignotubers, from which it can continually resprout to a 5–8 ft. (1.5–2.5 m) shrub. The narrow ovate leaves are often toothed, creating a filigreed look. The large red flower heads are rounded and can be 5 in. (13 cm) or more in width, making the species the showiest.

A bit more tender than the others, with 16 to 18°F (–9 to –8°C) certainly the limit. Although the Australian literature suggests harsh pruning after flowering, I've always been reluctant to comply for fear of diminishing the vigor.

Telopea 'Braidwood Brilliant', a cross between this species and *T. mongaensis*, is a large, coarse-leaved shrub to 8–10 ft. (2.5–3 m) with slightly toothed leaves and large 3 in. (8 cm) flowers in early spring, crimson with an almost pink hue. Hardiness has ranged between 16 and 20°F (–9 and –7°C) for brief periods.

Telopea speciosissima

Telopea truncata (Tasmanian waratah). Small tree, with an upright, narrow growth habit, reaching 25–30 ft. (7.5–9 m) eventually. The narrow lanceolate leaves, 1½–3½ in. (4–9 cm), are pleasingly rounded at the ends. The flowers, to 2½–3½ in. (6–9 cm), are most often scarlet-red, but vary to orange, yellow, and nearly white. Certainly among the most frost hardy of the genus, to 10°F (–12°C) or so, with reports of withstanding 0°F (–18°C).

Trochodendron	Trochodendraceae

Telopea truncata

A single species, *Trochodendron aralioides*, from southern Japan and Korea to Taiwan.

Trochodendron aralioides. An exceedingly beautiful broadleaf evergreen from 15 ft. (4.5 m) to nearly 50 ft. (15 m) in height with great age. Records indicate ancient specimens of over 80 ft. (25 m). Most often seen as a delicate, spreading small tree in woodland garden situations. Around 20–25 ft. (6–7.5 m) would be considered a mature garden specimen without having to wait through multiple generations.

A woodland plant, it grows in a spreading vase shape, each smaller branch appearing in layers, with whorls of deep, lustrous green leaves, 3–5 in. (8–13 cm) by ½ in. (1.5 cm), at the branch ends. The bark, though rougher with age, maintains a succulent, shiny green appearance, even mustard-colored in some forms. The flowers are in cymes of about 5 in. (13 cm) across, appearing somewhat carrot-family-like; they occur in late winter to mid spring (later in cooler climates) and are chartreuse in color.

Most plants, at least in western North America, have a tendency to become mottled with maroon blotches in the winter, with or without frost, a happening that is seen both as attractive and the opposite, depending on individual taste. Our selection, *Trochodendron aralioides* 'Curried Gold', grown from seed and now making the rounds, seems to avoid this coloring; the leaves remain glossy and green, contrasting with the succulent golden stems. Lush and tropical in appearance, it looks, when not in flower, like one of the New Zealand schefflera but lacking their tenderness.

The species has proven completely reliable in zone 8 and even 7, showing little or no damage at −10°F (−23°C) or even a little lower. At best in at least dappled shade, although in the Vancouver, B.C., area and in high-humidity southeastern North America, good-looking plants have been seen in nearly full sun. Consistent moisture is a must as plants become yellowed and raggedy with summer drought—but no sitting in water allowed. *Trochodendron aralioides* var. *taiwanensis* is vigorous and larger growing with a very clean look. It seems to have all the cold hardiness of the species but might, in time, make a larger tree. Collections by Dan Hinkley show great promise of its being a wonderful new addition to our gardens.

Another example of Murphy's law—the more excellent the plant, the more difficult they are to obtain or reproduce. Though *Trochodendron aralioides* is occasionally grown from seed, the best clones, of course, are done from cuttings that strike slowly and in a hit-or-miss fashion with heat and mist, winter seeming the most appropriate time. Enough, however, are produced every year that they can be found in specialty nurseries.

Where the climate allows, hardly a better plant can be found to present such a lush appearance year-round. *Trochodendron aralioides* certainly fits within the first tier—along with such important plants as *Fatsia japonica* (Japanese evergreen aralia), *Trachycarpus fortunei* (windmill palm), and a number of bamboos—of plants that offer good tropical-garden bones.

Trochodendron aralioides

Trochodendron aralioides, flowers

| *Ulmus* | elm | Ulmaceae |

Up to forty-five species of shrubs and trees, most deciduous, a few evergreen or semi-evergreen. They occur from central and eastern Asia to temperate North America. As the stately species *Ulmus americana* has been devastated by Dutch elm disease, many of the boulevards, parks, and campuses of Europe and North America and elsewhere have been denuded of these great cathedral-forming plants. Though resistant forms are being planted, many will never attain the same stature. *Ulmus parvifolia*, including the evergreen forms discussed here, is possibly a bit more awkward in youth than more classic elms but has the potential of contributing its own special grace, with its spreading branches, beautifully mottled bark, and small graceful twigs that often weep, while bringing back many of the classical features associated with the great elms so sadly lost to the urban landscape. As well, the evergreen forms, though not hardy in the cold north, are superbly adapted to warmer, drier climates, and elms now are more frequently gracing avenues in areas such as southern California, where the deciduous species have not always thrived.

Ulmus parvifolia (Chinese elm, lacebark elm). A highly variable species from China, Japan, Korea, and Taiwan. The majority of forms in the north are deciduous, with evergreen forms, as one might expect, in the south. The species is grown for the beauty of its bark, a brocade of oranges, tans, and creams, and the airy framework of branches, beautiful in both deciduous and evergreen forms. The root system is deep and stable, and the branch structure, strong. In cultivation for eons, forms (mostly deciduous) have been developed as dwarfs, some with the tiniest of leaves, and for autumn color and bark patterns. Typical plants average up to 80 ft. (25 m) in height with a 35–50 ft. (10.5–15 m) spread. Leaves are 1–2 in. (2.5–5 cm) long and darker and shinier than one might think of as typically elm. They also have minute scallops along the margins, adding to their substance.

Moderately drought tolerant, *Ulmus parvifolia* is deep-rooted and tolerant of bright sun as well as understory conditions. However, the evergreens can be lanky in some forms, especially if not provided with adequate light, creating large, spreading, almost flat-topped trees in age, rather than the upright vases of many other species, so early shaping is important. Fast-growing, the branches can veer in almost any directions, becoming tip heavy and prone to breakage, only to decide later that they alone will be the dominant upright. As well, the quick growth gives the illusion of weeping. Side branches might be headed or cut to a smaller branch growing in the same direction to

Ulmus parvifolia, bark. Photo
by Michael A. Dirr

Ulmus parvifolia. Photo by Michael A. Dirr

Ulmus parvifolia, backlit foliage.
Photo by Michael A. Dirr

slow their growth and encourage upright growth in youth. In street or avenue trees, side branches should begin fairly high on the trunk to ensure that the spreading habit will not impede the passerby. Thinning after some time is also helpful, as the canopy can be rather dense at maturity.

As has been said many times before, even evergreen trees don't keep every leaf they ever produce, and the evergreen forms of *Ulmus parvifolia* usually have at least some leaf drop in mid to late winter, just before the new leaves emerge. If they are being cultivated at the cooler edge of their frost tolerance, a severe bout of cold can also defoliate them, simply resulting in a deciduous tree, for a time, rather than a dead one. In general, most evergreen forms are rated to zone 8, meaning temperatures of 10 to 20°F (–12 to –7°C) are tolerated. *Ulmus parvifolia* 'Drake', one of the more common forms along the U.S. West Coast, was introduced in southern California in the 1950s; and, although almost entirely evergreen, it is subject to dam-

Ulmus parvifolia 'Drake', bark.
Photo by Michael A. Dirr

Ulmus parvifolia 'Drake'. Photo by Michael A. Dirr

age below 15°F (–9.5°C). Similar is *U. p.* 'True Green', a later introduction with spreading, somewhat pendulous branches. Both have a very nice orange-tinted bark. Other forms simply fall under *U. p.* 'Sempervirens'; although the cultivar was a specific introduction, many have been raised from seed, and the identification is often muddled. Plants labeled as *U. p.* 'Sempervirens', though not cold hardy to a zillion degrees or more below 0°F (–18°C) as many of the deciduous species are, have certainly held their own in temperatures below 10°F (–12°C) with only temporary leaf drop. A bigger concern is snow or ice load on the very spreading habit of the trees. All the more important, again, to ensure young trees have good structure.

Though some forms are grafted, and seedlings sometimes happen whether desired or not, the best method of propagation is via summer cuttings of just ripening wood. With a relatively strong hormone and the same old story of mist and a little bottom heat for good measure—along with a gin and tonic at the end of the day—good success is ensured.

| *Umbellularia* | California bay, Oregon myrtle | Lauraceae |

A monotypic genus of western North America, occurring solely in the California Floristic Province, extending from the foothills of the Los Angeles basin north to central western Oregon, the home of so many other delectable broadleaved evergreens. It is the West Coast of North America's only native avocado, a relic of a fossil flora that included many additional species.

Umbellularia californica. Though exceedingly rare in other parts of the mild-climate world, pepperwood (as it is also sometimes commonly known) is often planted along the West Coast, west of the Sierra Nevada/Cascades axis. Here it can be found in old neighborhoods and on farms, visible from some distance, plants from some provenances having grown into hulking, skyline-enhancing adults— a bit of a surprise for those who, upon finding a seedling, thought it would look cute in that special corner. Plants originating from coastal districts have a potential, in fact a probability, of indeed attaining great size and many an old Portland, Oregon, bungalow has been dwarfed by a 50–75 ft. (15–22.5 m) specimen, often with a nearly equal spread, atop a trunk 4–5 ft. (1.2–1.5 m) in diameter.

In the wild, it is one of the most identifiable plants because of its intense fragrance, which, especially in spring's new growth, can become somewhat overwhelming. *Umbellularia californica* sometimes forms pure stands and casts a shade so dense that little grows underneath. In other situations, it can be seen as a gumdrop-shaped savanna tree or, on serpentine soils at high elevations in southwestern Oregon's Siskiyou Mountains, as a dwarf shrub under 3 ft. (1 m). Here it is part of a constituency of voluptuous, broadleaved evergreen shrubs (*Garrya buxifolia* and the many forms of *Rhamnus californica*, *Arctostaphylos*, *Ceanothus*) and a number of dwarf evergreen *Quercus* species that, added to the rest, give one a feeling of Brobdingnagian power, hiking through this evergreen forest that barely reaches knee level.

Umbellularia californica

The geographic region where *Umbellularia californica* probably shows the most variability is the coastal flank of the Siskiyous, again in southwestern Oregon. Stands of plants easily approaching 100 ft. (30 m) can be observed in Alfred A. Loeb State Park within the redwood belt, encouraged by low elevation, deep soil with access to river moisture, and a frost-free climate. Nearby are records to over 175 ft. (53 m), the multi-trunked specimens measuring 20 ft. (6 m) or more at the base. Within fifteen miles and with a 4000–5000 ft. (1200–1500 m) increase in elevation, the dwarf forms are found in a chaparral or a shrub association. One remarkable plant, spotted by plantsman Frank Callahan not far from San Luis Obispo, California, appears from a distance to be a grove nestled in a hillside, but upon inspection is a single plant measuring over 100 ft. (30 m) across and some 40–50 ft. (12–15 m) in height, having spread and layered for eons.

The typically planted form is a narrow pyramid in youth. The larger forms can grow at a rate of 3 ft. (1 m) or more a year, spreading with age, often becoming multi-trunked unless pruned. At its best as a boulevard or park tree, *Umbellularia californica* is suitable only for large gardens, or gardeners with a desire to live in a cave. As the tree grows and spreads, many forms have pendulous branches: thinning the plant accentuates the effect, as well as enhancing the silvery bark and allowing more light through.

The leaves are roughly 4–5 in. (10–13 cm), occasionally 6 in. (15 cm), by 1½ in. (4 cm) or so, smaller in the shrubby forms. They are a deep (yes, again) avocado-green in color but often with a lighter underside and, sometimes, a bluish cast. In some forms, the new growth is a deep maroon color. Flowers occur January to March, depending on site, followed by fruits of over ½ in. (1.5 cm) in late summer and autumn. In Portland gardens, *Umbellularia californica* is one of the most common ambient seedlings.

A truly weeping form—as yet unnamed, though affectionately referred to at our nursery as "the one next to the parking lot"—has been reproduced by the Rancho Santa Ana Botanic Garden in Claremont, California. Dwarf selections are also available at various West Coast specialty nurseries.

Possibly the (evergreen) avocado relative most tolerant of cold, the higher-elevation forms should withstand −10 to −20°F (−23 to −29°C) with protection from prolonged freezing winds. The largest coastal forms have certainly proven tough in temperatures as low as 0 to 10°F (−18 to −12°C), again with some forms undoubtedly tolerating lower temperatures. Tolerant of intense summer heat, they are not, however, fans of summer moisture and should be grown in summer-rainfall areas in very well-drained soil or under the canopy of larger species that shed the water—should there be any. Gardeners with experimental spirit are attempting to grow *Umbellularia* in the U.S. Southeast, and sizeable shrubs (they don't seem to grow beyond shrub size there) can be found in the JC Raulston Arboretum in Raleigh, North Carolina, and southward. Woodlanders Nursery in Aiken, South Carolina, cultivates what appears to be a true hybrid between *Umbellularia* and *Laurus nobilis*. Although these are in cultivation, most others that purport to be hybrids seem to be, in actuality, other species and forms of *Laurus*.

The pungently fragrant leaf—some might call it odoriferous—is occasionally used for cooking (as one would use a leaf of *Laurus nobilis*), though, for me, a mere fragment of a California bay leaf is enough for about 4000 gallons of stew. It is said, not surprisingly, that dried leaves in cupboards can drive bugs away. As to its use against evil sprits, there is no available information known to this author. Its reputation for causing headaches is signaled by another common name, the headache tree, current in the United Kingdom.

Propagation is most often accomplished by seed, with hopes that progeny maintain characteristics similar to the parent (and, most often, they do). Sowing has been successful at all times of the year;

but, to ensure rooting, a special interpretative dance seems to be necessary, though, of course, not the same dance every time, so several should be performed at each sowing. Clonal selections have been more successful though a bit slow. I have collected and propagated a bronze-leaved form from Oregon's Illinois Valley and propagated a golden variegated form collected by Roger Warner from California's Sonoma Valley. Both have been successful and are awaiting further trials.

Vauquelinia	Arizona rosewood	Rosaceae

A most interesting evergreen, rosaceous genus of southwestern North America, ranging from Arizona and New Mexico into Sonora and containing a handful of species, depending on which dissertation is sitting on one's desk.

Vauquelinia californica. To 15–20 ft. (4.5–6 m) with upright form and narrow leaves, under ⅓ in. (1 cm) wide and 4 in. (10 cm) long, each leaf usually bearing minute serrations. The surface is quite shiny and tinted red or purple, especially with exposure to cold or light. Though low branching in nature, the plants are easily trimmed into small trees, exposing an attractive, tight branching pattern and minutely

Vauquelinia californica

Vauquelinia californica, flowers

Vauquelinia californica subsp. *pauciflora*

shredding reddish bark. The flowers are held above the tightly lay-ered branches in flattened corymbs of off-white, with the fruit a rather dried capsule of golden brown that can also add to the texture of the plant. *Vauquelinia californica* subsp. *pauciflora* from northwest-ern Chihuahua, Sonora, and just touching Arizona, with its delight-fully narrow pink- and silver-tinted leaves, can reach 40 ft. (12 m) and shows great garden potential.

Few species native to the dry southwestern mountains maintain such a luxuriant look in dry conditions: plants seem equally happy in narrow desert canyons or amid the grassy open oak woodlands of their native haunts. Indeed, they are most drought tolerant, but regu-lar summer water increases growth, as does placement in the warm-est locations if being attempted in a cooler or maritime climate. Good drainage is a plus.

Most plants in cultivation have easily withstood 0 to 5°F (–18 to –15°C) with some having withstood –10°F (–23°C). In colder zones, it is helpful to withhold water late in the growing season, so the plant is dormant with the onset of cold. Plants appear healthy after several years in the Denver Botanic Garden, having withstood temperatures of –20°F (–29°C) or colder, but plants in such conditions are likely to remain shrubby.

Propagation can be tricky. The fine seeds can be collected in late summer or autumn and stratified for sowing in early spring. Autumn or winter cuttings of current season's growth, using high hormone levels, usually results in success, albeit slowly.

Viburnum	Caprifoliaceae

Widespread throughout the temperate to subtropical areas of the northern hemisphere, with some species extending toward equatorial Asia and into South America. The more than 150 species are characterized by having simple leaves and flowers in corymbs, most resembling the fertile flower of *Hydrangea*. Though widely used in gardens as shrubs, a few of the evergreen species attain tree size or can be pruned into worthy garden or street trees.

Viburnum awabuki. In a group with and resembling *V. japonicum* and *V. odoratissimum* (with which it has, at times, been combined), *V. awabuki* is a fast-growing plant, upright and pyramidal in youth and, with pruning into a single trunk, can reach 10–15 ft. (3–4.5 m) in three to five years. The leaves are oval and pointed and a deep, rich green with a mirror-like finish. Aged leaves, especially in early spring or in full sun, can attain a reddish bronzy tint. Young plants can be mistaken, in horror, for *Prunus laurocerasus*, a plant that has overtaken many a small garden, though such fears are quickly overcome when the habits of this viburnum are understood.

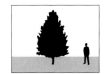

The flowers in mid spring, though lightly fragrant, are a nice contrast to the leaves, held horizontally along the branches. And the orangey fruit, turning black one at a time, seems to appear just in time for Halloween. Though *Viburnum awabuki* makes a fine large shrub, one of its most useful traits is its finite height, seeming to stop in the thinning atmosphere above 15 ft. (4.5 m). The pyramid shape then begins to widen but can be controlled by careful pruning if maintenance of the narrow form is desired. A planting on Portland, Oregon's NE Fremont Street has maintained these proportions for a number of years and is in perfect scale with nearby storefronts, neither imposing on the narrow sidewalk nor obliterating signage.

Tolerant of brief inundation, relatively well-drained soil is preferred to avoid the yellowing and winter leaf drop that can be problems. Regular water in summer or during any period of drought is best for maintaining *Viburnum awabuki*'s clean, green, shiny self. Wind tolerant and hardy to frost of about 10°F (–12°C), though recovers from bouts near 0°F (–18°C) with, apparently, only partial leaf drop. Equally tolerant of sun or shade, though more compact in bright light.

Propagation, as with most evergreen viburnums, is only slightly less easy than tossing cuttings over one's shoulder. Any but the most succulent of new growth will root with warmth, mist, and normal hormone levels. And seed germinates under average seed conditions but is a bit less useful if the known form of its parent is desired.

Viburnum cylindricum. East and Southeast Asia and southern China. Though some forms are smallish shrubs, many others reach tree size to over 50 ft. (15 m), though most garden forms top out at around 25 ft. (7.5 m). Upright when young and, if single or few-stemmed, remains a narrow pyramid, putting on at least 3 ft. (1 m) of growth annually for several years, then broadens with age. The leaves, up to 8 in. (20 cm), are one of the most beautiful features, hanging nearly straight down from the branches, especially in winter. They have a thick cuticle that makes them appear an attractive blue. Still, possi-

Viburnum cylindricum, flowers.
Photo by Michael A. Dirr

Viburnum cylindricum

bly the best treat of all is being able to "write" on the leaves. They turn white wherever they are scratched, making *V. cylindricum* particularly useful as a cheap source of party invitations.

A form brought into cultivation by England's Roy Lancaster is my favorite clone; it is the fastest growing, the bluest leaved, and, in my opinion, the most garden-worthy of the clones we are growing. We are calling it, originally enough, 'Roy Lancaster's Selection'.

Also a lover of consistent moisture, *Viburnum cylindricum* performs well in full sun, though it seems to be just a bit more at ease with a little afternoon shade, at least in our hot summer sun. Possibly just a tad less frost hardy that *V. awabuki*, the species has been subjected to freeze damage in several days of 8 to 10°F (–14 to –12°C) weather in North Carolina but has never been harmed above 14°F (–10°C) in our garden.

Quercus hypoleucoides, foliage

ENVOI
by John Grimshaw

IT IS A GREAT PRIVILEGE to be asked to round up *Trees for All Seasons* with an afterword—or, as Sean would put it, with that humour so evident in the text, a backword. It's very logical when you think about it—forewords, backwords . . .

A botanist, surveying the forests of the world, will notice that the diversity of broadleaved evergreen species increases away from the poles. From a northern European perspective they first become an important, if not major, part of the spectrum in the Mediterranean basin, while in North America they are most abundant in the West Coast Mediterranean climate areas, and in the southeastern states. It is not surprising that broadleaved evergreen trees have become such a passion of Sean's, imbued as his horticulture is in the climate and flora of California and Oregon. As this book has revealed, however, there are similar climates in each continent, all providing trees that can be used wherever garden conditions are congenial.

One of the most active trends in horticulture is the move toward growing plants that are ecologically appropriate for each area, rather than forcing them into inappropriate places by artificial means. Sean Hogan and his Cistus Nursery have been in the forefront of this trend,

311

converting gardeners, and indeed the city of Portland itself, to the joys of the right plants in the right places. It is no good pretending that gardeners in Minneapolis or Berlin will ever grow groves of eucalyptus underplanted with *Magnolia maudiae*, but the diversity presented in *Trees for All Seasons* provides gardeners over a vast area of the world the prospect of an exciting new palette. Further excitement will surely be generated as Sean next turns his attention to broadleaved shrubs; so, having looked backward to one book, we must also look forward to the next.

LISTS OF TREES
with Specific Characteristics and Uses

CHARACTERISTICS

Tolerates Periodic Drought

Acacia spp.

Acer paxii

Acer saccharum var. *skutchii*

Alnus jorullensis

Azara alpina

Azara celastrina

Azara petiolaris

Banksia integrifolia

Brachychiton spp.

Castanopsis cuspidata

Cinnamomum camphora

Cinnamomum japonicum

Cornus capitata

Cornus floccosa

Drimys winteri

Elaeocarpus spp.

Eriobotrya japonica

Euonymus myrianthus

Fraxinus greggii

Fraxinus scheidiana

Fraxinus uhdei and cvs.

Grevillea robusta

Ilex spp. and cvs.

Leptospermum lanigerum

Ligustrum spp. and cvs.

Luma chequen

Magnolia doltsopa

Magnolia moto

Magnolia virginiana var. *australis*

Maytenus boaria

Nothofagus dombeyi

Osmanthus decorus

Phillyrea spp. and cvs.

Photinia serratifolia

Pittosporum heterophyllum

Pittosporum napaulense

Quercus hypoleucoides

Quercus myrsinifolia

Quercus phillyreoides

Quercus rysophylla

Rhus lancea

Sophora secundiflora

Tolerates Mediterranean Summer Drought

Acer sempervirens

Arbutus spp. and cvs.

Arctostaphylos spp. and cvs.

Argyrocytisus battandieri

Azara microphylla

Ceanothus spp.

Chrysolepis chrysophylla

Comarostaphylis diversifolia

Eucalyptus spp. (except *E. pauciflora* and *E. coccifera*)

Gevuina avellana

Heteromeles arbutifolia

Laurus nobilis

Lithocarpus densiflorus

Lyonothamnus floribundus and sspp.

Myrica californica

Olea europaea and cvs.

Prunus ilicifolia

Prunus laurocerasus

Prunus salicifolia

313

Quercus chrysolepis
Quercus virginiana var. *fusiformis*
Quercus wislizeni
Rhamnus californica and sspp.
Schinus molle
Vauquelinia californica

Tolerates Heat and Near-Desert Conditions

Acca sellowiana
Acer sempervirens
Brachychiton spp.
Cercocarpus spp. and cvs.
Eucryphia cordifolia
Euonymus myrianthus
Fraxinus greggii
Quercus chrysolepis
Quercus hypoleucoides
Quercus suber
Quercus virginiana var. *fusiformis*
Quercus wislizeni
Schinus molle

Enjoys Sun and Bright Conditions

Acca sellowiana
Acer sempervirens
Agonis flexuosa and cvs.
Arbutus spp. and cvs.
Arctostaphylos spp.
Argyrocytisus battandieri
Banksia integrifolia
Ceanothus spp.
Comarostaphylis diversifolia
Cornus capitata
Crataegus mexicana
Drimys lanceolata
Eriobotrya japonica
Eucalyptus spp.
Eucryphia spp. and cvs.
Grevillea robusta
Heteromeles arbutifolia and cvs.
Leptospermum grandifolium
Luma chequen
Lyonothamnus floribundus and
    sspp.

Magnolia figo var. *skinneriana*
Myrica californica
Olea europaea cvs.
Pittosporum spp. and cvs.
Prunus caroliniana
Quercus alnifolia
Quercus myrsinifolia
Rhamnus californica and sspp.
Rhus lancea
Umbellularia californica

Accepts Sun or Shade

Acacia baileyana
Acacia dealbata and sspp.
Acer paxii
Acer saccharum var. *skutchii*
Alnus jorullensis
Alnus nitida
Arbutus unedo
Azara dentata
Azara lanceolata
Azara microphylla
Castanopsis cuspidata
Chrysolepis chrysophylla
Cinnamomum spp. and cvs.
Citrus spp. and cvs.
Cornus angustata
Crataegus mexicana
Crinodendron spp.
Dendropanax trifidus
Drimys winteri
Elaeocarpus spp.
Eriobotrya spp. and cvs.
Eucalyptus crenulata
Euonymus myrianthus
Gordonia spp. and cvs.
Hoheria spp. and cvs.
Illicium anisatum
Illicium floridanum
Ligustrum spp. and cvs.
Lithocarpus densiflorus
Litsea japonica
Magnolia ernestii
Mahonia chochoca
Neolitsea sericea
Nothofagus dombeyi

Nothofagus fusca
Olea yunnanensis
Osmanthus spp. and cvs.
Persea americana
Persea borbonia and cvs.
Persea podadenia
Persea yunnanensis
Phillyrea angustifolia
Phoebe chekiangensis
Pittosporum eugenioides
Pittosporum heterophyllum
Pittosporum illicioides
Pittosporum tenuifolium and cvs.
Prunus laurocerasus
Schima wallichii
Sophora microphylla and cvs.
Sophora tetraptera
Ulmus parvifolia
Viburnum awabuki
Viburnum cylindricum

Better with Some Shade

Acer oblongum
Acer paxii
Aristotelia chilensis
Azara dentata
Azara integrifolia
Azara lanceolata
Azara microphylla and cvs.
Cinnamomum chekiangensis
Citrus spp. and cvs.
Cornus angustata
Cornus omeiense
Crinodendron hookerianum
Daphniphyllum macropodum
Elaeocarpus spp.
Fatsia japonica
Ilex spp. and cvs.
Illicium spp. and cvs.
Lithocarpus variolosus
Litsea japonica
Magnolia champaca
Magnolia delavayi
Magnolia grandis
Magnolia ingrata
Magnolia megaphylla

Magnolia moto
Neolitsea sericea
Nothofagus fusca
Osmanthus heterophyllus
  (variegated forms)
Persea thunbergii
Phoebe chekiangensis
Pittosporum dallii
Pittosporum illicioides
Sycopsis sinensis
Telopea spp.
Trochodendron aralioides

Tolerates Cool Coastal Conditions
(low heat accumulation often coupled with winds)
Acca sellowiana and cvs.
Acer oblongum
Acer paxii
Agonis flexuosa and cvs.
Amomyrtus luma
Arbutus menziesii
Argyrocytisus battandieri
Azara integrifolia
Azara microphylla and cvs.
Brachychiton spp.
Ceanothus spp.
Chrysolepis chrysophylla
Citrus spp. and cvs.
Crinodendron spp.
Embothrium cvs.
Eriobotrya deflexa
Eucalyptus neglecta
Eucryphia spp. and cvs.
Gevuina avellana
Hoheria spp. and cvs.
Illicium anisatum
Leptospermum scoparium
Lithocarpus densiflorus
Luma chequen
Lyonothamnus floribundus and
  sspp.
Magnolia champaca
Magnolia figo var. *skinneriana*
Magnolia tamaulipana

Magnolia yunnanensis
Myrica californica
Myrica cerifera
Photinia serratifolia
Pittosporum bicolor
Pittosporum eugenioides
Pittosporum tenuifolium and cvs.
Polylepis australis
Pseudopanax spp.
Quercus hypoleucoides
Sophora microphylla and cvs.
Sophora tetraptera
Telopea spp.

Tolerates Heat and Humidity
Azara uruguayensis
Castanopsis cuspidata
Cornus hongkongensis
Crinodendron tucumanum
Daphniphyllum macropodum
Dendropanax trifidus
Eriobotrya deflexa
Eucalyptus neglecta
Gordonia lasianthus and cvs.
Grevillea robusta
Ilex cassine and cvs.
Ilex latifolia
Ilex opaca and cvs.
Ilex purpurea
Illicium floridanum and cvs.
Lithocarpus edulis
Magnolia grandiflora
Magnolia grandis
Magnolia maudiae
Magnolia moto
Myrica cerifera
Osmanthus americanus
Persea borbonia and cvs.
Pittosporum eugenioides
  'Variegatum'
Prunus caroliniana
Quercus acuta
Quercus glauca
Quercus virginiana
Schima wallichii
Sophora secundiflora

Tolerates Any Soil
Acacia spp.
Acca sellowiana
Acer saccharum var. *skutchii*
Acer sempervirens
Alnus jorullensis
Alnus nitida
Castanopsis cuspidata
Eucalyptus gregsoniana
Eucalyptus urnigera
Ilex cassine and cvs.
Ilex opaca and cvs.
Ilex pedunculosa
Ligustrum lucidum and cvs.
Magnolia maudiae
Magnolia virginiana and cvs.
Maytenus boaria

Enjoys Lean Soils
Acacia baileyana
Acacia pataczekii
Acer paxii
Arbutus spp. and cvs.
Arctostaphylos spp.
Argyrocytisus battandieri
Azara microphylla
Ceanothus spp. and cvs.
Chrysolepis chrysophylla
Crinodendron spp.
Embothrium spp. and cvs.
Eucalyptus spp.
Eucryphia spp.
Heteromeles arbutifolia and cvs.
Lyonothamnus floribundus and
  sspp.
Myrica californica
Phillyrea spp. and cvs.
Pittosporum tenuifolium and cvs.
Prunus ilicifolia
Rhamnus californica and sspp.

Accepts Wet Soils
Acacia dealbata
Acacia pataczekii
Alnus spp.
Amomyrtus luma

Azara petiolaris
Brachychiton acerifolius
Cornus capitata
Cornus floccosa
Cornus 'Porlock'
Eucalyptus coccifera
Eucalyptus crenulata
Myrica cerifera
Nothofagus cunninghamii
Nothofagus fusca
Rhus lancea

Appreciates Fertile Soils

Acacia pravissima
Acer oblongum
Brachychiton spp.
Citrus spp. and cvs.
Cornus angustata
Nothopanax delavayi
Pittosporum tobira and cvs.

Enjoys Consistent Moisture

Acacia pataczekii
Acacia pravissima
Acca sellowiana
Acer buergerianum var. *formosanum*
Acer oblongum
Acer paxii
Alnus nitida
Azara celastrina
Azara dentata
Azara microphylla and cvs.
Brachychiton spp.
Castanopsis cuspidata
Cinnamomum spp. and cvs.
Citrus spp. and cvs.
Cornus spp. and cvs.
Crataegus mexicana
Crinodendron spp.
Daphniphyllum macropodum
Dendropanax trifidus
Drimys spp.
Elaeocarpus spp.
Eriobotrya japonica
Eucalyptus pauciflora subsp.
  niphophila
Eucalyptus vernicosa

Eucryphia spp. and cvs.
Fatsia japonica
Gordonia spp. and cvs.
Hoheria spp. and cvs.
Illicium spp. and cvs.
Leptospermum grandifolium
Lithocarpus variolosus
Litsea japonica
Luma apiculata
Luma chequen
Magnolia spp. and cvs.
Mahonia siamensis
Neolitsea sericea and cvs.
Nothofagus dombeyi
Nothopanax delavayi
Olea yunnanensis
Osmanthus spp. and cvs.
Persea spp. and cvs.
Phillyrea spp. and cvs.
Photinia ×*fraseri*
Pittosporum spp. and cvs.
Prunus caroliniana
Quercus acuta
Quercus glauca
Quercus hypoleucoides
Quercus ilex
Quercus myrsinifolia
Quercus rysophylla
Schima wallichii
Sophora microphylla and cvs.
Sophora secundiflora
Sycopsis sinensis
Telopea spp.
Trochodendron aralioides
Viburnum awabuki

Cold Hardy to Zone 9
(20°F, –7°C)

Acacia baileyana
Agonis flexuosa
Arbutus canariensis
Brachychiton spp.
Cinnamomum camphora
Citrus ×*meyeri*
Cornus hongkongensis
Eriobotrya deflexa
Grevillea robusta

Hoheria populnea and cvs.
Laurus 'Saratoga'
Magnolia doltsopa 'Silver Cloud'
Magnolia megaphylla
Mahonia siamensis
Olea yunnanensis
Osmanthus americanus
Pittosporum napaulense
Pittosporum tenuifolium 'Silver
  Sheen'
Pittosporum undulatum
Pseudopanax arboreus
Schinus molle

Cold Hardy to Zone 8b
(15 to 20°F, –12 to –7°C)

Acacia dealbata
Acacia dealbata subsp. *subalpina*
Acacia pravissima
Acacia riceana
Acca sellowiana
Acer albopurpurascens
Acer paxii
Alnus nepalensis
Alnus nitida
Arbutus andrachne and hybrids
  (coastal forms)
Arbutus 'Marina'
Aristotelia chilensis
Azara dentata
Azara lanceolata
Azara uruguayensis
Banksia integrifolia
Callistemon citrinus
Ceanothus arboreus
Cercocarpus fothergilloides
Crataegus mexicana
Elaeocarpus dentatus
Elaeocarpus japonicus
Eucalyptus crenulata
Eucalyptus glaucescens
Eucryphia cordifolia
Fraxinus uhdei and cvs.
Heteromeles arbutifolia var. *cerina*
  'Davis Gold'
Hoheria 'Glory of Amlwch'
Hoheria sexstylosa

Illicium henryi

Leptospermum scoparium

Luma apiculata

Lyonothamnus floribundus and sspp.

Magnolia doltsopa

Magnolia grandis

Magnolia ingrata

Myrica rubra

Nothofagus cunninghamii

Nothofagus fusca

Nothofagus solanderi

Olea europaea 'Manzanillo'

Osmanthus fragrans (except *O. fragrans* var. *thunbergii*) and cvs.

Pittosporum bicolor

Pittosporum eugenioides

Pittosporum ralphii

Prunus lyonii

Rhus lancea

Sophora microphylla

Telopea 'Braidwood Brilliant'

Telopea mongaensis

Telopea oreades

Telopea speciosissima

Cold Hardy to Zone 8a
(10 to 15°F, −12 to −9.5°C)

Acer buergerianum var. *formosanum*

Acer oblongum

Alnus jorullensis

Amomyrtus luma

Arctostaphylos glauca

Arctostaphylos manzanita and cvs.

Azara alpina

Azara integrifolia

Azara microphylla

Callistemon pallidus

Ceanothus spp. and cvs. (except *C. thyrsiflorus* 'Victoria')

Comarostaphylis diversifolia

Crinodendron spp.

Drimys spp. and cvs.

Elaeocarpus hookerianus

Eriobotrya japonica

Eucalyptus bridgesiana

Eucalyptus globulus subsp. *bicostata*

Eucalyptus nitens

Eucalyptus nova-anglica

Eucalyptus perriniana

Eucalyptus pulverulenta

Eucalyptus subcrenulata

Eucalyptus vernicosa

Eucryphia ×*intermedia*

Eucryphia lucida and cvs.

Eucryphia ×*nymansensis* and cvs.

Exbucklandia populnea

Fatsia japonica

Fraxinus greggii

Gevuina avellana

Gordonia axillaris

Ilex purpurea

Illicium simonsii

Illicium verum

Laurus nobilis

Laurus nobilis 'Aurea'

Leptospermum grandifolium

Leptospermum lanigerum

Leptospermum scoparium 'Washington Park Hardy'

Leptospermum sericeum

Luma chequen

Magnolia delavayi

Magnolia ernestii

Magnolia floribunda

Magnolia tamaulipana

Magnolia yunnanensis

Mahonia chochoca

Mahonia lomariifolia

Nothofagus dombeyi

Osmanthus yunnanensis

Persea borbonia var. *pubescens*

Pittosporum eugenioides 'Variegatum'

Prunus caroliniana

Prunus ilicifolia

Pseudopanax crassifolius

Pseudopanax ferox

Quercus acuta

Quercus rysophylla

Sophora microphylla Sun King

Sophora secundiflora

Sophora tetraptera

Telopea truncata

Ulmus parvifolia and cvs.

Viburnum awabuki

Viburnum cylindricum

Cold Hardy to Zone 7 or Below
(0 to 10°F, −18 to −12°C)

Acacia pataczekii

Acer saccharum var. *skutchii*

Acer sempervirens

Arbutus andrachne and hybrids (mountain forms)

Arbutus arizonica

Arbutus menziesii

Arbutus unedo

Arctostaphylos viscida

Argyrocytisus battandieri

Azara petiolaris

Castanopsis cuspidata

Ceanothus thyrsiflorus 'Victoria'

Cercocarpus ledifolius and cvs.

Cercocarpus montanus and cvs.

Chrysolepis chrysophylla

Cinnamomum chekiangensis

Cinnamomum japonicum

Citrus ichangensis

Cornus angustata

Cornus capitata (cold hardy forms)

Cornus floccosa

Cornus 'Porlock'

Daphniphyllum macropodum and sspp.

Daphniphyllum teijsmannii

Dendropanax trifidus

Elaeocarpus decipiens

Embothrium coccineum and cvs.

Eriobotrya cavaleriei

Eucalyptus archeri (with good provenance)

Eucalyptus cinerea (with good provenance)

Eucalyptus coccifera (with good provenance)

Eucalyptus gregsoniana

Eucalyptus gunnii and cvs. (with good provenance)

Eucalyptus mitchelliana

Eucalyptus neglecta

Eucalyptus parvula
Eucalyptus pauciflora (mountain forms)
Eucalyptus urnigera (with good provenance)
Euonymus myrianthus
Fatsia japonica (with overhead protection)
Gordonia lasianthus and cvs. (with heat)
Heteromeles arbutifolia 'Zenia'
Ilex aquifolium and cvs.
Ilex cassine and cvs.
Ilex latifolia
Ilex opaca
Ilex pedunculosa
Illicium anisatum
Illicium floridanum and cvs.
Laurus nobilis f. *angustifolia*
Ligustrum spp. and cvs.
Lithocarpus spp. and cvs.
Litsea japonica (with overhead protection)
Magnolia compressa
Magnolia figo var. *skinneriana*
Magnolia ×*foggii* 'Jack Fogg'
Magnolia fulva var. *calcicola*
Magnolia grandiflora and cvs.
Magnolia insignis
Magnolia lotungensis
Magnolia maudiae var. *platypetala*
Magnolia moto
Magnolia tamaulipana 'Bronze Sentinel'
Magnolia virginiana and cvs.
Maytenus boaria (mountain forms)
Metapanax davidii
Myrica spp. and cvs. (except *M. rubra*)
Neolitsea sericea
Nothofagus solanderi var. *cliffortioides*
Nothopanax delavayi
Olea europaea 'Arbequina'
Olea europaea 'Mission'
Osmanthus armatus

Osmanthus decorus
Osmanthus fragrans var. *thunbergii*
Osmanthus heterophyllus and cvs.
Osmanthus suavis
Persea americana
Persea borbonia
Persea thunbergii
Persea yunnanensis
Phillyrea spp. and cvs.
Phoebe chekiangensis
Photinia davidiana and cvs.
Photinia serratifolia
Pittosporum dallii
Pittosporum heterophyllum
Pittosporum illicioides
Pittosporum tenuifolium 'Elizabeth'
Pittosporum tenuifolium 'Purpureum'
Pittosporum tobira 'Washington Park Hardy'
Prunus laurocerasus
Prunus lusitanica
Prunus salicifolia (will become deciduous)
Quercus alnifolia
Quercus chrysolepis
Quercus glauca
Quercus ilex
Quercus ×*moreha*
Quercus myrsinifolia
Quercus phillyreoides 'Emerald Sentinel'
Quercus rugosa
Quercus suber
Quercus wislizeni
Rhamnus alaternus and cvs.
Rhamnus californica subsp. *tomentella*
Schefflera delavayi
Schefflera taiwaniana
Schima wallichii
×*Sycoparrotia semidecidua* and cvs.
Sycopsis sinensis
Tetrapanax papyrifer and cvs.
Umbellularia californica
Vauquelinia californica

Very Small Tree (to 15 ft., 4.5 m)
Arctostaphylos glauca
Arctostaphylos manzanita
Arctostaphylos viscida
Argyrocytisus battandieri
Aristotelia chilensis
Azara integrifolia
Callistemon pallidus
Ceanothus thyrsiflorus
Citrus ichangensis
Citrus ×*meyeri*
Comarostaphylis diversifolia
Dendropanax trifidus
Drimys lanceolata
Euonymus myrianthus
Heteromeles arbutifolia
Ilex aquifolium 'Angustifolia'
Ilex cassine 'Pendula'
Ilex pedunculosa
Illicium floridanum
Illicium henryi
Leptospermum grandifolium
Leptospermum lanigerum
Leptospermum scoparium
Ligustrum japonicum
Mahonia lomariifolia
Myrica californica
Osmanthus decorus
Osmanthus suavis
Phillyrea angustifolia
Photinia davidiana
Pittosporum heterophyllum
Pittosporum illicioides
Pittosporum tobira
Polylepis australis
Prunus ilicifolia
Rhamnus californica
Sophora secundiflora
Telopea speciosissima
Viburnum awabuki

Small Tree (15–35 ft., 4.5–10.5 m)
Acacia baileyana
Acacia pataczekii
Acacia pravissima
Acacia riceana

Acca sellowiana
Acer buergerianum var. formosanum
Acer paxii
Acer sempervirens
Arbutus arizonica
Arbutus unedo
Azara dentata
Azara lanceolata
Azara microphylla
Azara petiolaris
Brachychiton populneus
Callistemon citrinus
Ceanothus arboreus
Cercocarpus ledifolius
Chrysolepis chrysophylla
Cornus angustata
Cornus omeiense
Crataegus mexicana
Crinodendron hookerianum
Daphniphyllum macropodum
Elaeocarpus decipiens
Elaeocarpus japonicus
Embothrium coccineum
Eriobotrya deflexa
Eriobotrya japonica
Eucalyptus cinerea
Eucalyptus coccifera
Eucalyptus crenulata
Eucalyptus mitchelliana
Eucalyptus pulverulenta
Eucryphia ×intermedia
Eucryphia lucida
Fraxinus greggii
Gevuina avellana
Gordonia lasianthus
Hoheria populnea
Hoheria sexstylosa
Ilex aquifolium 'Ferox'
Ilex aquifolium 'Integrifolia'
Ilex aquifolium 'Pinto'
Ilex cassine
Ilex cassine 'Lowei'
Ilex cassine var. myrtifolia
Ilex latifolia
Ilex opaca
Ilex opaca 'Canary'

Ilex opaca 'Hampton'
Illicium anisatum
Illicium simonsii
Ligustrum lucidum
Luma apiculata
Luma chequen
Lyonothamnus floribundus
Magnolia compressa
Magnolia figo var. skinneriana
Magnolia floribunda
Magnolia fulva var. calcicola
Magnolia ingrata
Magnolia maudiae
Mahonia chochoca
Mahonia siamensis
Maytenus boaria
Myrica cerifera
Myrica rubra
Neolitsea sericea
Olea europaea
Osmanthus americanus
Osmanthus armatus
Osmanthus fragrans
Osmanthus heterophyllus
Osmanthus yunnanensis
Persea borbonia
Persea thunbergii
Persea yunnanensis
Phillyrea latifolia
Photinia ×fraseri
Photinia serratifolia
Pittosporum bicolor
Pittosporum dallii
Pittosporum eugenioides
Pittosporum napaulense
Pittosporum tenuifolium
Prunus caroliniana
Prunus laurocerasus
Prunus lusitanica
Prunus salicifolia
Quercus alnifolia
Quercus guyavifolia
Quercus ×moreha
Quercus phillyreoides
Quercus rugosa
Rhus lancea

Schima wallichii
Sophora microphylla
Sophora tetraptera
Sycopsis sinensis
Telopea mongaensis
Telopea oreades
Telopea truncata
Trochodendron aralioides
Vauquelinia californica
Viburnum cylindricum

Medium Tree
(35–60 ft., 10.5–18 m)
Acacia dealbata
Acer oblongum
Acer saccharum var. skutchii
Agonis flexuosa
Alnus jorullensis
Alnus nitida
Arbutus andrachne
Banksia integrifolia
Brachychiton acerifolius
Castanopsis cuspidata
Cinnamomum chekiangensis
Cinnamomum japonicum
Cornus capitata
Crinodendron patagua
Drimys winteri
Elaeocarpus dentatus
Eucalyptus archeri
Eucalyptus glaucescens
Eucalyptus neglecta
Eucalyptus nicholii
Eucalyptus parvula
Eucalyptus pauciflora
Eucalyptus perriniana
Eucalyptus subcrenulata
Eucalyptus urnigera
Eucryphia ×nymansensis
Fraxinus uhdei
Gordonia axillaris
Ilex ×altaclerensis
Ilex aquifolium
Ilex aquifolium 'Bacciflava Group'
Ilex aquifolium 'Beacon'
Ilex aquifolium 'Marginata'

Ilex purpurea
Laurus nobilis
Lithocarpus densiflorus
Lithocarpus edulis
Lithocarpus henryi
Lithocarpus variolosus
Magnolia champaca
Magnolia delavayi
Magnolia doltsopa
Magnolia ernestii
Magnolia grandiflora
Magnolia insignis
Magnolia lotungensis
Magnolia maudiae var. *platypetala*
Magnolia megaphylla
Magnolia nitida
Magnolia ovoidea
Magnolia virginiana
Magnolia yunnanensis
Nothofagus fusca
Nothofagus solanderi
Quercus acuta
Quercus glauca
Quercus hypoleucoides
Quercus ilex
Quercus myrsinifolia
Quercus rysophylla
Quercus wislizeni
Schinus molle
Umbellularia californica

Large Tree (over 60 ft., 18 m)

Arbutus menziesii
Cinnamomum camphora
Eucalyptus gunnii
Eucryphia cordifolia
Grevillea robusta
Magnolia grandis
Magnolia moto
Magnolia tamaulipana
Nothofagus cunninghamii
Nothofagus dombeyi
Persea americana
Quercus chrysolepis
Quercus suber
Quercus virginiana
Ulmus parvifolia

USES

Understory Tree

Acer oblongum
Arbutus unedo
Aristotelia chilensis
Azara integrifolia
Azara lanceolata
Azara microphylla and cvs.
Castanopsis cuspidata
Cinnamomum chekiangensis
Cornus angustata
Cornus omeiense
Crinodendron hookerianum
Daphniphyllum macropodum
Elaeocarpus japonicus
Fatsia japonica
Hoheria spp. and cvs.
Illicium anisatum
Lithocarpus henryi
Magnolia megaphylla
Magnolia moto
Neolitsea sericea
Osmanthus americanus
Schima wallichii

Urban Street Tree

Most trees "small" or larger will
work well; these are particularly
useful.

Arbutus 'Marina'
Callistemon citrinus
Castanopsis cuspidata
Cinnamomum camphora
Cinnamomum japonicum
Cornus capitata 'Mountain Moon'
Eucalyptus pauciflora sspp.
Ilex pedunculosa
Magnolia compressa
Magnolia grandiflora and cvs.
Magnolia lotungensis
Magnolia maudiae
Magnolia virginiana var. *australis*
Nothofagus dombeyi
Olea europaea (fruitless forms)
Osmanthus yunnanensis
Pittosporum undulatum

Prunus lusitanica
Quercus chrysolepis
Quercus glauca
Quercus hypoleucoides
Quercus ilex
Quercus myrsinifolia
Quercus phillyreoides
Quercus suber
Quercus virginiana
Rhamnus alaternus
Ulmus parvifolia and cvs.
Umbellularia californica
Viburnum awabuki

Garden Feature

Acacia baileyana and cvs.
Acca sellowiana
Acer paxii
Arbutus spp. and cvs.
Arctostaphylos glauca
Azara microphylla
Ceanothus arboreus and cvs.
Cinnamomum camphora
Eucalyptus spp. and cvs.
Euonymus myrianthus
Gordonia spp. and cvs.
Grevillea robusta
Heteromeles arbutifolia and cvs.
Ilex pedunculosa
Laurus nobilis
Luma apiculata
Lyonothamnus floribundus and sspp.
Magnolia maudiae
Quercus glauca
Rhus lancea
Sophora tetraptera

Background Tree

Acacia baileyana
Acer sempervirens
Azara microphylla and cvs.
Eucalyptus subcrenulata
Hoheria spp. and cvs.
Illicium anisatum
Laurus nobilis
Osmanthus yunnanensis
Prunus lusitanica

Patio/Courtyard Tree
Acer oblongum
Azara microphylla and cvs.
Ceanothus arboreus
Cinnamomum japonicum
Eriobotrya japonica
Eucalyptus gregsoniana
Fatsia japonica
Fraxinus greggii
Ilex latifolia
Illicium anisatum
Leptospermum lanigerum
Magnolia fulva var. *calcicola*
Osmanthus americanus
Phillyrea angustifolia
Pittosporum illicioides
Schima wallichii
Sophora tetraptera

Coppice Plant
Acacia dealbata
Alnus nitida
Argyrocytisus battandieri
Cinnamomum camphora
Eucalyptus cinerea
Eucalyptus glaucescens
Eucalyptus mitchelliana
Eucalyptus parvula
Eucalyptus perriniana
Eucalyptus subcrenulata
Magnolia grandis
Magnolia megaphylla

Container Plant
Acacia baileyana
Agonis flexuosa
Banksia integrifolia
Brachychiton spp.
Callistemon citrinus
Cinnamomum camphora
Citrus spp. and cvs.
Eriobotrya deflexa
Fraxinus greggii
Ilex purpurea
Laurus nobilis
Ligustrum japonicum
Magnolia champaca
Magnolia grandiflora 'Little Gem'
Rhus lancea

GLOSSARY

ACUMINATE narrowing to a point

ALLELOPATHY releasing particular chemicals by which a plant can influence and often suppress the growth of nearby or potentially competing plants

ALTERNATE placed singly along a stem, as leaves that are not opposite or whorled

APICAL DOMINANCE control by the topmost bud on a stem through the release of hormones that inhibit growth in lower stems

APICULATE with a sharp point or apiculus

AXIL the upper angle where a leaf attaches to a stem

AXILLARY in the axil

BASAL BURL an underground, woody mass with many dormant buds that can sprout when a trunk or main stem is injured

BOREAL refers to cool temperature, northern regions lying just below the tundra

CAMPANULATE bell-shaped

CATKIN a cluster of flowers with petals, often in a cylinder and often hanging down, resembling a kitten's tail

CHAPARRAL trees and shrubs of mixed species adapted to hot, dry summers and mild, wet winters

COPPICE to cut a plant nearly to the ground to encourage new growth and maintain a smaller size

CORYMBS a flat-topped flower cluster

322

CRENULATE having small, rounded teeth

CYMES a cluster of branches with flowers at the end of each

DIVARICATION branching at wide angles and subsequent interlacing of branches

DRIP TIP long narrow leaf tip that sheds water easily

DRUPE fleshy fruit that contains one or more encapsulated seeds

ELLIPTIC shaped like an ellipse or elongated circle

EMARGINATE having a notch at the tip

ENTIRE the smooth edges of a leaf

ESPALIER the art of training plants to grow flat against a wall, fence, or wire structure

EXFOLIATION loss of leaves

EXSERTED protruding beyond the surrounding parts

FARINA a powdery covering found on some plant parts

GLAUCESCENCE a waxy covering, often bluish green, on some leaves

INDUMENTUM a hairy or scaly covering of plant parts

INFLORESCENCE a cluster of flowers

KRUMHOLTZ TREES trees at the upper edge of their endurance

LANCEOLATE lance-shaped, tapering toward the point

LEGUMES plants with seedpods such as peas, beans, and peanuts

LIGNOTUBER a woody structure with dormant buds, similar to a basal burl but at ground level rather than underground

MALLEE plants with the ability to resprout from buds at ground level

MESIC intermediately moist, neither very wet nor very dry

NITROGEN FIXING the process by which bacteria in some plants convert nitrogen in the air to usable nitrogen in the soil

OVATE with the outline of an egg

PANICLE a cluster of flowers with many branches

PETIOLE a stalk attaching a leaf to a stem

PHYLLODES a flattened petiole that appears and functions as a leaf

PINNATE feather-like, with leaflets arranged on each side of a stalk

PINNATELY compound a leaf made up of leaflets arranged on either side of a stalk

POLLARD to repeatedly cut back a tree to the trunk or main branches, controlling size and encouraging renewable bushy growth at the cuts

POME a fleshy fruit with a core, such as an apple or pear

PROVENANCE the characteristics of the environment from which a plant or clone was derived

PUBESCENT covered with soft hairs or down

RACEMES an unbranched cluster of flowers on a main stem

RADICLE the first or embryonic root to emerge from a seed

RIPARIAN pertaining to the banks of a stream or watercourse

RUGOSE rough and wrinkly

SAMARA a winged fruit with one seed, such as maples produce

SCLEROPHYLL from the Greek *sclero* ("hard") and *phyllon* ("leaf"), a reference to vegetation with hard, leathery, closely spaced leaves

SPATULATE shaped like a spoon or paddle

STOOLING cutting a plant to the ground to encourage new, bushy growth, as in coppicing

STRATIFICATION treating seeds to conditions such as would be met in the wild to encourage faster germination

SUBTENDING below but close, such as the relationship of a bract to a flower

TRIFOLIATE having three leaves or three leaflets

URCEOLATE urn-shaped, narrowing at the mouth

WHORL a circular arrangement of three or more leaves on a stem

BIBLIOGRAPHY

Bean, W. J., and D. L. Clarke. 1991. *Trees and Shrubs Hardy in the British Isles*. Timber Press, Portland, Ore.

Brooker, M. I. H., and D. A. Kleinig. 1999. *Field Guide to Eucalypts*. Bloomings Books, Melbourne, Australia.

Dirr, Michael A. 2002. *Trees and Shrubs for Warm Climates*. Timber Press, Portland, Ore.

Elliot, W. Rodger, and David L. Jones. 1980–. *Encyclopaedia of Australian Plants Suitable for Cultivation*. Lothian, South Melbourne, Australia.

Felger, Richard Stephen, et al. 2001. *The Trees of Sonora, Mexico*. Oxford University Press.

Hillier, J., and A. Coombes, eds. 2002. *The Hillier Manual of Trees and Shrubs*, 7th ed. David & Charles, Newton Abbot.

Hoffman, Adriana J., et al. 2000. *Enciclopedia de los bosques chilenos*. Defenders of the Chilean Forests.

Jacobson, Arthur Lee. 1996. *North American Landscape Trees*. Ten Speed Press.

Liu, Yu-Hu, ed. 2004. *Magnolias of China*. Beijing Science & Technology Press.

Menitsky, Y. L., and Andrei Aleksandrovich Fedorov. 2005. *Oaks of Asia*. Science Publishers, Enfield, N.H.

Metcalf, Lawrence James. 1987. *The Cultivation of New Zealand Trees and Shrubs*. Reed Methuen.

Munz, Philip Alexander. 1959. *A California Flora*. University of
   California Press for the Rancho Santa Ana Botanic Garden.
Peck, Morton Eaton. 1961. *A Manual of the Higher Plants of Oregon*.
   Binfords & Mort, Portland, Ore.
Ross, Thomas, and Jeffrey Irons. 1997. *Australian Plants: A Guide to Their
   Cultivation in Europe*. Published privately.
Shreve, Forrest, and Ira L. Wiggins. 1964. *Vegetation and Flora of the
   Sonoran Desert*. Stanford University Press, Palo Alto, Calif.

INDEX